REAL

Fifth Edition ESTATE

LAW

ROBERT KRATOVIL
OF THE CHICAGO BAR

PRENTICE-HALL, INC. Englewood Cliffs, New Jersey

PRENTICE-HALL SERIES IN REAL ESTATE

To Ruth and Tony

Current printing (last digit):

10 9 8

PRENTICE-HALL INTERNATIONAL, INC., *London*
PRENTICE-HALL OF AUSTRALIA, PTY. LTD., *Sydney*
PRENTICE-HALL OF CANADA, LTD., *Toronto*
PRENTICE-HALL OF INDIA PRIVATE LTD., *New Delhi*
PRENTICE-HALL OF JAPAN, INC., *Tokyo*

Library of Congress Catalog Card Number: 69-18698

Printed in the United States of America

PREFACE

Like earlier editions of this book, this is an exposition of the basic principles of modern real estate law. Stress is upon the real estate transactions of today. The occupations of many laymen (real estate brokers, architects, builders, title insurance men, abstracters, mortgage men, insurance brokers, land developers, urban planners, housing officials, zoning administrators, surveyors, engineers, and building managers, for example) bring them into daily contact with problems of real estate law. There are also the college students who are preparing themselves to enter one of the real estate professions, each of which demands an increasing degree of expertise and technical competence as land transactions grow in size and complexity. To help all of these toward an understanding of the broad field of real estate law this book has been prepared. With this objective in mind, I have made an effort to employ to the greatest possible extent language that will be understandable to laymen and have included a multitude of examples.

This book has been used by the American Bar Association in a training course for young lawyers. Obviously there is much here that the young lawyer will find helpful, and there is also much that the older lawyer can learn about the new and complex problems his clients must face.

Figuring prominently in this book is a discussion of the sale of real estate, beginning with the broker's listing and concluding with the closing of the deal and the steps to be taken after it has been closed. In the interest of simplicity and clarity, strict chronological sequence has not been preserved. To illustrate: the deed is a much simpler document than the contract of sale. It is therefore discussed in an earlier chapter, and the reader is afforded an opportunity to acquaint himself with some of the terminology and ideas involved before he tackles the complex structure of the contract of sale. In this edition Chapters 1 to 18 inclusive are grouped so as to comprise a logical first semester where this subject is taught as a two-semester course. Chapters 19 to 35 comprise the second semester. This arrangement enables the instructor to treat liens and all the mortgage chapters, which are closely interrelated, in the same semester.

Like so many other things around us, real estate law is changing rapidly these days, posing problems for both authors and instructors. A few illustrations will make the point clear. In the old days, a seller of land had to refrain from deliberate misrepresentation, but he was under no duty to advise the buyer of defects in the building. "Caveat emptor," said the courts. "Let the buyer beware!" Nowadays, as part of the struggle of the law toward better ideals and values, many courts are imposing on the seller an affirmative duty to disclose defects, especially where the seller is a professional builder—so much so that one writer says that we are well on the way toward "caveat vendor." Articles that were formerly treated as chattels are now treated as fixtures, and further changes in this area are inevitable as home buyers come to take it for granted that homes come equipped with stove, refrigerator, clothes washer and dryer, dishwasher, and other articles once considered in the category of chattels. A builder would look at a buyer with surprise if he asked for a bill of sale to the kitchen appliances that had been installed. The builder thinks of them as passing by the deed of the land, and probably sooner or later the courts will agree with him. In the preface to the fourth edition I said that "As the Uniform Commercial Code sweeps across the country it becomes clearer day by day that all the material on chattel mortgages and conditional sales will disappear in the next edition of this book." This has come to pass.

It has always been an objective to keep the book abreast of current developments and even to peer discreetly into the future. Thus, in the last edition, material on the condominium was included, though the idea was then a novelty. Today *condominium* is a household world and its future is secure, as resales demonstrate universal acceptance of the concept. For like reasons this edition expands the popular new chapter on Shopping Centers and introduces a chapter on Planned Unit Developments. The new ideas in zoning are featured here, for zoning is undergoing a major metamorphosis. Euclidean zoning with its rigid system of zones is giving way to elastic zones, which will "float" around the village as needed despite the efforts of traditional courts and lawyers to block the trend.

Mortgage financing dominates the entire building spectrum, from the inexpensive residence to the mammoth shopping center. The United States Government wants 26 million housing units constructed in the decade 1968–1978 (a monster *increase* of over one million units per year) and says that "additional mortgage financing must be generated." The homeowner's "equity," the land developer's "front money," will continue to diminish in size and importance. Hence new chapters appear on mortgage loan closing and construction loans. Sound commercial leases have assumed major significance as a means of obtaining mortgage financing, and their form is therefore dictated by the mortgage lenders. This development is fully reflected in this edition.

Many, many letters have come to me in the past few years suggesting an expansion of the "how-to-do-it" portions of the book. I liked the idea and have added many paragraphs of concrete suggestions to sellers, buyers, mortgage men, land developers, and others.

I cannot thank enough the many instructors who have taken time to offer suggestions for the improvement of this text. My home address is given below to encourage others to yield to this impulse.

ROBERT KRATOVIL
2772 Garrison Avenue
Evanston, Ill. 60201

CONTENTS

Chapter 1   Sources of Real Estate Law   1

Chapter 2   Land and Its Elements   3

Chapter 3   Fixtures   8

Chapter 4   Easements   14

Chapter 5   Land Descriptions   29

Chapter 6   Land Titles and Interests in Land   37

Chapter 7   Deeds   42

Chapter 8   Acknowledgments   58

Chapter 9   Recording and Constructive Notice   61

Chapter 10   Brokers and Managers   67

Chapter 11   Contracts for the Sale of Land   87

Chapter 12   Closing a Cash Real Estate Sale   128

Chapter 13   Escrows   140

Chapter 14   Evidence of Title   147

Chapter 15   Fire Insurance   155

Chapter 16   Co-ownership   164

Chapter 17   Dower, Curtesy, Community Property,
               and Homestead   179

Chapter 18   Wills and Descent   188

Chapter 19   Liens   193

Chapter 20   Mortgages   203

Chapter 21   Construction Loans   237

Chapter 22   Closing Mortgage Loans   247

Chapter 23   Foreclosure and Redemption   251

Chapter 24   FHA Loan Insurance   255

Chapter 25   Subdivisions, Land Development, and
               Dedication   260

Chapter 26   Building Construction   271

Chapter 27   Land Use Controls: Building Restrictions   283

Chapter 28   Land Use Controls: Zoning and
               Building Ordinances   298

Chapter 29   Taxes, Special Assessments, and
               Federal Income Tax   315

Chapter 30   Landlord and Tenant   323

Chapter 31   Shopping Centers   344

Chapter 32   The Co-op and the Condominium   353

Chapter 33   Planned Unit Developments   363

Chapter 34   The Declaration of Restrictions, Easements,
               Liens, and Covenants   369

Chapter 35   Racial Integration in Housing   374

Index   381

Chapter 1

SOURCES OF

REAL ESTATE LAW

§ 1. **Lack of uniformity in laws governing real estate.** In each of the United States, two separate systems of law are in force: federal law and state law. With a few exceptions, federal laws operate uniformly throughout the country. Each state, however, has its own constitution, laws, and court decisions. Because of differences in local conditions, laws relating to real estate vary from state to state, and this variation is a factor that must be kept constantly in mind. However, the basic legal principles governing real estate transactions are much the same throughout the country, and our approach, in consequence, will be to describe these basic principles, mentioning, as space permits, the more important instances wherein the states do not agree.

§ 2. **Sources of real estate law.** The sources of real estate law include the Constitution of the United States, laws passed by Congress, regulations adopted by various federal boards and commissions, the state constitutions, laws passed by state legislatures, regulations adopted by various state and municipal boards, ordinances passed by cities and villages, and court decisions. The last is the most important source of real estate law.

EXPLANATION: Important decisions by lower courts are often appealed to higher courts. The higher courts, in announcing a decision, usually state the reasons for their decision and discuss the legal principles governing the particular case.

1

Such a decision, with its accompanying discussion, is called an *opinion*. The opinions are bound in books called reports and serve as guides in the decision of similar cases in the future.

> **EXAMPLE:** Roots from your adjoining poplar trees penetrate into my land and fill up my sewer and drain pipes. I cut off these roots, taking care to make the cut on my land. Your trees die and you sue me. The lower court holds I acted rightfully and on appeal the supreme court of the state holds likewise, stating that a landowner may in this fashion protect himself against roots of adjoining trees. This is now the law of that state for all such cases that arise in the future. Lawyers will advise their clients accordingly, citing the case, *Michaelson v. Nutting*, 275 Mass. 232, 175 N.E. 490. This case may be found in Volume 275 of the Massachusetts Supreme Court Reports, page 232 and Volume 175 of the Northeastern Reporter, page 490.

Since our American real estate law stems in large part from the real estate law of England, it is not uncommon for courts today to base their decisions on similar cases that arose several hundred years ago in England. However, in dealing with present-day problems, the courts must often evolve new rules of law without much help from the past. Court decisions constitute the chief source of our real estate law.

Since law is manufactured from day to day by the judges, it follows that there will be variations from state to state, and from time to time in the same state, depending on the political, social, and economic views that dominate the court at the time a decision is made.

In textbooks, a statement of a rule of law is often followed by a reference to the case in which that particular point was decided. A well-reasoned case decided in any state often commands respect in other states. For example, the decision in *Michaelson v. Nutting* would be considered a correct statement of the law almost everywhere. This text endeavors to select such cases.

In recent times federal laws have assumed increasing importance in the field of real estate.

> **EXAMPLES:** FHA Loan Insurance (Chapter 24) and the Federal Open Housing Law (Chapter 35).

Also of greatly increasing importance in modern times is the "private law" that lawyers create in the preparation of real estate documentation.

> **EXAMPLE:** Shopping center leases (Chapter 31). In these documents the rights and duties of the parties in various existing and anticipated situations are set forth in some detail. One limitation on the rights of the parties to thus declare the "law" applicable to their situation is found in the tendency of courts today to refuse to enforce contract terms they regard as "unconscionable," meaning grossly unfair.

Chapter 2

LAND AND ITS ELEMENTS

§ 3. **Land defined.**   Land includes not only the ground, or soil, but everything that is attached to the earth, whether by course of nature, as trees and herbage, or by the hand of man, as houses and other buildings. It includes not only the surface of the earth, but everything under it and over it. Thus, in legal theory, a tract of land consists not only of the portion on the surface of the earth, but is an inverted pyramid having its tip, or apex, at the center of the earth, extending outward through the surface of the earth at the boundary lines of the tract, and continuing on upward to the heavens.

§ 4. **Minerals.**   Since land extends to the center of the earth, it is clear that the owner of the land also ordinarily owns the minerals, which are a part of the land, and when the land is sold, the buyer ordinarily acquires such minerals, even though they are not expressly mentioned in his deed. However, a landowner may sell part or all of his land, as he chooses. Consequently, he may sell the minerals only, retaining title to the rest of the land; or he may sell the rest of the land and retain or reserve the minerals to himself.

EXAMPLE: A, a landowner, signs a deed conveying to B all the coal underlying A's land. Now we have two layers of ownership. A continues to own the surface and may farm it or erect buildings on it. B owns the coal. A can sell or mortgage his layer of land, and B can do the same with his. B automatically has the right to sink shafts from the surface and build roads and tracks over the surface for the purpose of

3

mining and transporting the coal. But he must not remove the coal in such a manner that the surface of the land will collapse.

Suppose that A, a farmer, sells and grants the coal under his farm to B Coal Company. The company tunnels beneath A's farm and as it mines the coal uses the tunnels for transporting coal mined from adjoining areas. May the coal company do this? All courts agree that it may, although the explanations vary from state to state. In some states the interesting theory is advanced that a sale of coal and minerals includes not only the coal and minerals, but also the space they occupy, so that when the coal is mined out the coal company remains the owner of the space the coal formerly occupied. *Middleton v. Harlan-Wallins Coal Corp., 252 Ky. 29, 66 S.W.2d 30; 15 A.L.R. 957.*

§ 5. Oil and gas. Contrary to popular opinion, oil does not occur in underground pools or reservoirs, but is tightly held in the tiny pores or openings of porous rocks. Natural gas is held in solution in this oil under great pressure. When a well is drilled into the rock that contains oil and gas, pressure is thereby released, and oil and gas gush forth just as a carbonated drink gushes from a warm pop bottle when the cap is removed. The oil will then flow to the low pressure area, namely, the well bore. Some states (Arkansas, Kansas, Mississippi, Ohio, Pennsylvania, Texas, and West Virginia), impressed with the fact that oil in its natural state and before drilling occurs is immovably trapped in the rocks in which it is found, say that the landowner owns the oil beneath his land in much the same way that he owns coal or other minerals. These states are called *ownership states.* Other courts (California, Louisiana, and Oklahoma), impressed with the fact that oil does move from one underground location to another when wells are drilled, hold that the landowner does not own the oil until he has pumped it and thereby taken possession of it. In all states, if the owner of the oil well pumps the oil and brings it to the surface, it then becomes his personal property.

In ownership states, a landowner may grant ownership of the oil beneath his land to another person. As a result, there will be two vertical layers of ownership, just as when a landowner sells and conveys to another all the coal and minerals beneath his land. Oddly enough, however, all oil states, including the ownership states, follow the rule of *capture,* which holds that if a man drills on his land, he will own all of the oil and gas produced, even though some of the oil or gas has migrated to his well from his neighbor's land. His neighbor, of course, can prevent such a result by drilling his own wells, *offset* wells, on his own land and pumping the oil that would otherwise move away from his land. All oil-producing states now have laws regulating and controlling the drilling of wells and the production of oil.

Landowners lack the skill, experience, capital, and gambling instinct necessary to drill for oil. Therefore, when the presence of oil is suspected, a landowner gives some oil company an oil lease. Many differing views are held as to the technical nature of the interest created by this lease.

But the leases themselves tend to follow a pattern. As a rule, the landowner receives a bonus or cash payment for giving the lease. The lease then provides that if no well is drilled on or before a certain date, the lease shall automatically terminate, *unless* the lessee pays to the landowner a certain sum of money, called a *delay rental*. Such delay rental is a price the oil company pays for the privilege of keeping the lease in force without drilling. Delay rentals will continue to fall due as long as the oil company delays drilling. Because of the provision that the lease will end if no drilling takes place *unless* delay rentals are paid, this is known as an *unless lease*. Once wells are drilled and production begins, the usual lease gives the landowner as his compensation one-eighth of all the oil produced, payable either in oil or in cash, at the current market price, whichever the oil company chooses.

The lease provides that once oil production begins, the lease will continue as long as oil is produced in paying quantities.

> **WARNING:** Oil leases vary considerably in their provisions. There is no such thing as the "usual" form. Many years ago a lease was printed in Oklahoma and the printers christened it the "Producers 88." It was copied extensively, but so many changes have been made in it, that there are now many varying forms bearing that designation. 6 Wyo. L. Rev. 223.

Nomenclature. The word *royalty* originated in England, when it was used to designate the share in production reserved by the king from those to whom the right to work mines and quarries was granted. In oil and gas law it is the term used to designate the rent due for the right or privilege to take oil or gas out of a designated tract of land. It is the compensation provided in the lease to the landowner for the lessee's privilege of drilling and producing oil and gas and consists of a share in the oil and gas produced. It does not include either delay rentals or a bonus.

The *working interest* is the lessee's share of oil, as distinguished from the landowner's interest, or royalty interest.

An *overriding royalty* is an interest carved out of the working interest, often by means of an assignment of the working interest that reserves to the assignor a part of the oil and gas produced by the assignee.

§ 6. **Air rights.** Just as a landowner may sell the minerals lying beneath the surface of the earth, so he may sell the space above the surface of the earth. A railroad company may own a tract of land, needing only so much of the space above the surface of the earth as will provide ample clearance for the tops of its trains. It does not need the space above a height of twenty-three or twenty-four feet from the surface of the earth. Yet this space is valuable for building purposes and may be sold or leased to a building corporation. *Indiana Toll Road Comm. v. Jankovich,* 244 Ind. 574, 193 N.E.2d 237; 1960 *Law Forum* 303; 49 Ill. B. J. 812.

In the case of the Merchandise Mart in Chicago, which was erected over the tracks of the Chicago and Northwestern Railroad, a plat or map was made and recorded, showing a subdivision in three dimensions, as follows:

> 1. An *air lot.* This consists of the space lying above a plane twenty-three feet above the earth's surface.
> 2. Quadrangular prism or *column lots* (for steel columns to support the building). These extend from the surface of the earth up to the air lot and occupy portions of the surface not occupied by railroad tracks.
> 3. Cylindrical or *caisson lots.* These extend from the surface of the earth down to the center of the earth. The bottom of each column lot rests within a caisson lot.

The column lots, which share the level through which the trains move, were made narrower than the caisson lots to eliminate interference with the movement of trains. The railroad thereupon sold the air lot, the column lots, and the caisson lots to the Merchandise Mart, but retained ownership of the remainder of the tract. 23 Ill.L. Rev. 250.

Another conspicuous instance of such utilization of space above the earth's surface is the Park Avenue development in New York, where fabulous sums have been invested in buildings over the New York Central and New Haven tracks.

§ 7. **Trespass.**   If without my permission you enter upon my land, this is a *trespass.* I have a legal right to sue you even though you have caused no damage, and the judge will award me *nominal damages* of $1.00.

> **EXAMPLE:** I have no right to go upon the land of my neighbor for the purpose of putting up screens, or painting, or of effecting repairs on my house. *Taliaferro v. Salyer,* 162 Cal. App.2d 685, 328 P.2d 799.

If instead of trespassing at the surface you do so beneath the surface, this is known as *subsurface trespass* and also gives rise to an action for damages.

> **EXAMPLE:** A and B own adjoining lands. B sinks an oil well near the boundary line. This well is angled so that it crosses the boundary beneath the surface and B is therefore pumping oil from A's land. This is called *crooked-hole drilling.* A can sue B for damages.

Trespass can also take place above the surface in the air space that forms part of the land. The old theory that one's land extends to the sky was adequate when courts were dealing with simple questions.

EXAMPLE: Thrusting one's arm across a boundary fence is a trespass. *Hannabalson v. Sessions,* 116 Ia. 457, 90 N.W. 93. A building owner cannot maintain shutters that swing across adjoining land. *Homewood Realty Corp. v. Safe Deposit & Trust Co.,* 160 Md. 457, 154 Atl. 58.

However, common sense revolts at the notion that the mere flight of aircraft over my land is a trespass. Hence, it has been held that the flight of aircraft at high altitudes, causing no inconvenience to the landowner, is not a violation of the landowner's rights. It is only where the flight is low, as where a plane is taking off or landing causing damage to the landowner, that his rights have been invaded. *U.S. v. Causby,* 328 U.S. 256 (flights at level of eighty-three feet forced landowner to give up chicken farm).

§ 8.   **Real and personal property.**   The distinction between *real* and *personal property* is an important one. An article of personal property, such as an automobile, is called a *chattel*. It is sold by *bill of sale*. In fact, sales of chattels need not even be in writing when the sale price is under a figure fixed by law, usually $500. Ownership of real estate, on the other hand, is transferred by means of a *deed*.

It is a historical fact that rules of law come into existence when and as human beings feel a need for them. In early times when men were nomadic, driving their cattle north for the summer and south for the winter, there was no need for a law relating to real estate. Men did not aspire to the ownership of land. But there was need for a law of personal property to help men decide how cattle could be sold or who would succeed to ownership at the owner's death. And so the first crude rules of property law evolved, relating to cattle. The word *chattel* derives from cattle, the earliest subject of legal ownership. Later, when men learned to cultivate the soil, real estate law evolved to deal with questions regarding the ownership of land. Lawyers are working through their associations to establish more uniformity, but differences still persist as between the law relating to personal property and the law relating to real estate.

§ 9.   **Trees and crops.**   All trees, plants, and other things that grow are divided into classes:

1. Trees, perennial bushes, grasses, etc., which do not require annual cultivation, are called *fructus naturales* and are considered real estate or real property.
2. Annual crops produced by labor, such as wheat, corn, potatoes, beets, are called *fructus industriales* and are considered personal property.

Since growing crops are personal property, they may be sold orally if the sale price is under the figure fixed by law for oral sales of personal property (*Steim v. Crawford,* 133 Md. 579, 105 Atl. 780) or by bill of sale, as are other chattels.

Chapter 3

FIXTURES

§ 10. Fixtures defined.   A *fixture* is an article that was once personal property, but that has been installed in or attached to land or a building thereon in some more or less permanent manner, so that such article is regarded in law as a part of the real estate.

EXAMPLE: A kitchen sink in a plumber's shopwindow is personal property. After it has been installed in a house, it becomes a fixture and is part of the real estate.

§ 11. Tests to determine whether an article is a fixture.   It often becomes important to determine whether or not a particular article is a fixture. If it is a fixture, it goes to the buyer on a sale of the land, even though it is not mentioned in the deed. If it is not a fixture, it does not go with the land and is removable by the seller unless specifically mentioned in the deed or contract of sale.

In determining whether or not an article is a fixture, courts apply the following tests:

1. The manner in which the article is attached to the real estate.

EXPLANATION: If an article is attached to a building in such a permanent fashion that it could not be removed without substantial injury to the building, it is usually held to be a fixture.

8

EXAMPLES: Water pipes, linoleum cemented to the floor.

2. The character of the article and its adaptation to the real estate.

EXPLANATION: If an article was specially constructed or fitted with a view to its location and use in a particular building, or if the article was installed in the building in order to carry out the purpose for which the building was erected, this tends to show that it was intended that the article should become a permanent part of the building. It is usually considered a fixture.

EXAMPLES: Pews in a church; a theater sign constructed for a particular theater; screens and storm windows specially fitted to the house; electronic computing equipment installed on a floor specially constructed for it. 5 A.L.R.3d 497.

3. The intention of the parties.

EXPLANATION: There is a pronounced tendency today to emphasize the factor of intention. Was the article attached, the courts ask, with the intention of making it a permanent part of the building? Tests 1 and 2 are helpful in determining the intention of the parties, but once that intention is determined, it must govern. It is not the secret intention of the person installing the articles that governs. The test is an objective one, and intention is determined from the nature of the article, relation of the parties, adaptation, mode of annexation, and all the surrounding circumstances. Thus the question boils down to this: Would the average person consider this article a permanent fixture?

EXAMPLES: Gas stoves are often installed in apartment buildings for the use of tenants. They are intended to remain there permanently, since they increase the rental value of the apartments. Therefore they are considered fixtures, even though they can be removed from the building with comparative ease. *Leisle v. Welfare B. and L. Assn.,* 232 Wis. 440, 287 N.W. 739. The same is true of electric refrigerators installed in apartment buildings. *Guardian Life Ins. Co. v. Swanson,* 286 Ill. App. 278, 3 N.E.2d 324. Air conditioners are necessities, not luxuries, in a modern apartment and are treated as fixtures when installed by the owner in a more or less permanent fashion. *State Mutual v. Trautwein,* (Ky.) 414 S.W.2d 587. Again, it is important to remember that conservative courts are accustomed to stress Rule 1 above and would not consider a gas stove or refrigerator installed in an apartment building a fixture. *Elliot v. Talmadge,* 207 Ore. 428, 297 P.2d 310. In Oklahoma, Murphy beds fastened to the wall on pivots are considered fixtures, but rollaway beds, which are not fastened to the wall, are not. *Gray v. Prudential Ins. Co. of America,* 182 Okla. 342, 77 P.2d 563. On the other hand, in Wisconsin, rollaway beds are considered fixtures. *Leisle v. Welfare B. and L. Assn.,* 232 Wis. 440, 287 N.W. 739. There is substantial agreement on the point that a gas stove or refrigerator installed in a *private house* is not a fixture, since the owner usually intends to take it with him when he moves. The law of fixtures, however, is constantly developing, expanding, and changing. As customs have changed, articles once considered personal property have become fixtures. Thus if the practice, followed by many builders today, of equipping houses with range, refrigerator, laundry equipment, and the like becomes universal, such articles may move into the category of fixtures, even in single-family dwellings. Since intention is the factor that determines whether or not an article is a fixture, the same type of article may be a fixture in one kind of building and a chattel in another. For example, an old-fashioned gas stove (i.e., one not built into the wall) is a chattel in a private home and would not go automatically to the buyer with a sale of the land. In an apartment building, exactly the same kind of stove would, in many states, be considered a fixture, passing automatically with a sale of the land. Articles of furniture (tables, chairs, etc.), whether in a home, hotel, or furnished apartment, are universally considered chattels. *State v. Feves,* 228 Ore. 273, 365 P.2d 97.

It will help you understand these fixture tests if you understand a little about the history of fixture law. Hundreds of years ago, in agricultural England, where we find the beginnings of this law, buildings tended to be rather simple, and the annexation test worked well enough. In America some problems developed even in early times. A Virginia rail fence rests on the ground but is not attached to it. But the courts thought that, for obvious practical reasons, it ought to go with a sale of the land, and they so decided. Later, when factories began to appear, it became evident that the annexation test was obsolete. If I buy a factory, obviously I am buying a going concern; yet under the old annexation test the seller would be allowed to remove the machinery because this could be done without injury *to the building.* Thus, in response to this need, the courts invented the intention test, which enabled the buyer to claim the machinery. Still later, when landlords began to put gas stoves and electric refrigerators in apartments, the courts faced the same problem, and most of them decided in favor of the intention test, but some did not. Those that did not were bothered by the flimsy connection between the appliance and the building, simply plugging a refrigerator in a wall socket, for example. The current problem takes this development one step further. A professional builder equips his homes with a variety of appliances that are attractive to the housewife, who, many builders will tell you, casts the deciding vote in the purchase of a home. The problem of the "package kitchen" has not, as yet, been litigated. (See § 368.) It is best to ask the builder for a bill of sale as well as a deed, the bill of sale being used to transfer ownership of the appliances. In time, quite possibly, the courts will hold that the appliances pass with the deed as fixtures without the necessity of a bill of sale.

§ 12.   **Articles removable by tenants.**   Special rules are applicable in the landlord and tenant situation. Articles that a tenant is allowed to remove are classified into the following three classes:

1. Trade fixtures.

EXPLANATION: In order to encourage a tenant to equip himself with the tools and implements of his trade, articles installed by a tenant for the purpose of his trade or business are classed as *trade fixtures* and may be removed by the tenant at the expiration of his lease. Intention is significant here also, for it is obvious that the tenant intends to take such articles with him when he moves.

EXAMPLES: Airplane hangars; bowling alleys; greenhouses; booths, bars, and other restaurant equipment; gasoline pumps and tanks in a filling station; barber chairs; soda fountains.

2. Agricultural fixtures.

EXPLANATION: Articles installed by a tenant farmer for the purpose of enabling him to farm the land are called *agricultural fixtures* and may be removed by the tenant when he quits the land.

EXAMPLES: Hen house; tool shed; maple-sugar house.

3. Domestic fixtures.

EXPLANATION: Articles installed in a dwelling by a tenant in order to render it more comfortable and attractive are removable by the tenant.

EXAMPLES: Bookshelves; Venetian blinds.

Of course the tenant is permitted to remove only articles that he has installed. He must not remove articles installed by the landlord. And if the tenant surrenders possession of the land to the landlord, he cannot thereafter return and remove articles installed by him. Also, the lease may expressly prohibit removal of trade fixtures.

The three classes of articles that a tenant is allowed to remove are often referred to collectively as tenant's fixtures. *Fixtures,* as described in preceding sections, are real estate. *Tenant's fixtures* are personal property. Observe, also that *the trade fixtures rule applies only to articles installed by tenants.*

EXAMPLE: Gas pumps installed by a tenant in a rented service station are clearly trade fixtures. Pumps installed by a landowner would be true fixtures and would automatically go with a sale of the land.

§ 13. **Fixtures attached after execution of real estate mortgage.** When only the landowner and the real estate mortgagee are involved, the rule is that fixtures bought, paid for, and installed by the landowner *after* the execution of a mortgage on the land become subject to the lien of the mortgage and cannot thereafter be removed by the landowner. In this situation, in other words, the mortgage lien attaches to *all* fixtures, even trade fixtures, thereafter installed by the mortgagor on the mortgaged premises. Such fixtures must not be removed without the mortgagee's consent. *Bowen v. Wood,* 35 Ind. 268. However, trade fixtures installed by a *tenant,* whether installed before or after the mortgage, are removable by the tenant. *Standard Oil Co. v. La Crosse Super Auto Service,* 217 Wis. 237, 258 N.W. 791.

§ 14. **Conflicting claims of chattel security claimants under the Uniform Commercial Code where purchasers and mortgagees of real estate are involved.** The Uniform Commercial Code has been adopted in nearly all fifty states. Under the Code, a security interest in a chattel, including a chattel that has been or will be installed as a fixture, is created by means of a *security agreement,* which replaces the old *chattel mortgage* and *conditional sale contract.* This document, however, is not recorded. Instead, a brief notice of the existence of the security agreement is filed. This notice is called a *financing statement.* Where an article has become or is to become a fixture, the financing statement must be filed in the recorder's office where mortgages on real estate are filed. When thus filed, it gives notice to all that there exists a security interest in the article. Subsequent purchasers of the real estate and subsequent mortgagees of the land are bound by this filing, and if a default occurs under the security agreement, the articles can be repossessed and removed by the security holder without liability for any incidental damage to the building occasioned by the removal. If the financing statement is not filed as required by law, a subsequent purchaser or mortgagee of the land is protected against removal of the articles and need not pay the unpaid balance due on the articles. Where the article is purchased and installed on the land *after* the recording of a mortgage on real estate, the holder of the chattel security lien may remove the article from the real estate in case of default regardless of the incidental damage to the building. However, he must reimburse the real estate mortgagee for the cost of repairing any immediate physical injury to the building.

§ 15. **Severance.** If the landowner actually removes an article from the land or from the building to which it has been attached, with the intention that the removal shall be *permanent,* such article becomes personal property again and does not pass by a deed of the real estate. Thus if a landowner tears down a fence and piles the material on the land, such material does not pass by a deed of the land. The fixture has again become personal property by *severance.* If the removal is for a *temporary* purpose, as the removal of a piece of machinery for repairs, the article remains a fixture, notwithstanding its removal from the soil, and passes by a deed of the real estate.

§ 16. **Building erected on wrong lot.** A perpetual source of legal controversy concerns the rights of one who through innocent mistakes erects a building on the wrong lot, usually a lot adjoining the one he actually owns. Some states allow compensation to the builder in such cases. *Voss v. Forgue* (Fla.) 84 So.2d 563; *Olin v. Reinecke,* 336 Ill. 530,

168 N.E. 676; *Hardy v. Burroughs,* 251 Mich. 578, 232 N.W. 200; but other states deny any compensation on the ground that if a man builds, it is his duty to see that he builds on the right lot. 5 *De Paul L. Rev.* 321; 104 A.L.R. 577; 76 A.L.R. 304.

Chapter 4

EASEMENTS

§ 17. Easement defined.   An *easement* is a right acquired by the owner of one parcel of land to use the land of another for a special purpose.

> **EXAMPLE:** *A* and *B* own adjoining tracts of land. By a written instrument, signed, sealed, and recorded in the proper office, *B* grants to *A* the right to cross *B's* tract at a particular place for the purpose of ingress to *A's* tract from a certain highway. The right thus created is called an *easement*. *B* remains the owner of the land over which *A* travels. *A* has only a special and particular right in that land.

§ 18. Easement appurtenant runs with the land.   The easement described in the preceding section is an *easement appurtenant*. An easement appurtenant is created for the benefit of another tract of land. Consequently, for such an easement to exist, there must always be two tracts of land owned by different persons, one tract, called the *dominant tenement,* having the benefit of the easement, and another tract, called the *servient tenement,* over which the easement runs. In the example given in the preceding section, *A's* tract was the one enjoying the benefit of the easement. It was therefore the dominant tenement. *B's* tract was the servient tenement since it was the tract subject to the easement.

The dominant tenement need not adjoin the servient tenement. *Allendorf v. Daly,* 6 Ill. 2d 577, 129 N.E.2d 673. However, it usually does.

An easement appurtenant is regarded as being so closely connected to the dominant tenement that, upon a sale and deed of such tenement, the easement will pass to the grantee in the deed, even though the deed does not mention it. Such an easement is therefore said to *run with the land*. In the example, if A should sell his land to C, C would automatically acquire the right to cross B's land. Whoever owns the dominant tenement owns the easement. A separate sale of the easement is not permitted.

§ 19. **Easement and license distinguished.** It is often difficult to distinguish an easement from a *license*. Ordinarily an unauthorized entry on the land of another is called a trespass and makes the trespasser liable to pay damages to the landowner. The owner may, however, grant permission to enter for a particular purpose. This permission is called a license. An example is a theater ticket which authorizes the purchaser thereof to enter the theater for the purpose of viewing the performance.

An easement is usually created by a written instrument; a license is often created verbally. An easement is a more or less permanent right; a license is of temporary character. A license is a purely personal right and cannot be sold; the ownership of an easement changes with the ownership of the land to which it belongs. An easement cannot be revoked; a license is revocable.

EXAMPLE: A and B owned adjoining lots. They entered into a verbal agreement to establish a party driveway on the common boundary line between the lots. B thereafter built concrete walks and steps to the driveway. After this driveway had been in use for some years, A notified B that he intended to construct a driveway entirely upon his own lot and expected B likewise to provide for himself. When A sought to erect a fence along the common boundary, B filed a suit to prevent him from doing so. The court held that A was within his rights. Since the agreement was merely verbal, a license, not an easement, was created, and a license is revocable. *Baird v. Westberg,* 341 Ill. 616, 173 N.E. 820.

Where large sums of money have been expended in reliance upon a verbal license, some courts refuse to sanction a revocation of the license.

EXAMPLE: In accordance with a verbal agreement, A and B, adjoining owners, erected buildings with a party wall and party stairway on the common boundary between their lots. The agreement was held irrevocable. *Binder v. Weinberg,* 94 Miss. 817, 48 So. 1013.

§ 20. **Easement in gross.** An *easement in gross* resembles both a license and an easement appurtenant. It is generally held that an easement in gross running to an *individual* (like a license) cannot be sold and dies with the death of the individual. Right of way easements acquired *by corporations* such as railroads and public utilities (*commercial easements in gross*) usually may be mortgaged and sold. 12 U. of C.L. Rev. 276. Like an easement appurtenant, an easement in gross is irrevocable. The owner of an easement in gross need not, and usually does not, own any land adjoining that over which the easement exists.

EXAMPLES: Right granted to a telephone and telegraph company to maintain poles and wires over grantor's land; right granted to a city to construct, maintain, and operate a canal through granto.'s land; easements for railroads, street railways, pipelines; and power lines.

§ **21.   Creation of easement.**   Easements may be created by *express grant, agreement, express reservation, implied grant, implied reservation, prescription, condemnation,* and *sale of land by reference to a plat.*

§ **22.   Express grant.**   A landowner may create an easement over his land by express grant.

Since an easement is an interest in land, a grant of an easement should contain all the formal requisites of a deed. It should be in writing, should sufficiently describe the easement, the land subject thereto, the character of the easement (easement for ingress and egress, etc.), and should be signed, sealed, witnessed, acknowledged, delivered to the grantee, and recorded in accordance with local rules governing deeds. But no particular words are necessary, and omission of the seal is not a fatal defect.

EXAMPLE: The first example given in this chapter is an illustration of the creation of an easement by grant.

Although an instrument granting an easement is technically known as a *grant,* this is no guarantee that an instrument granting an easement will be so labeled. Very often an instrument in the form of a deed will operate as a grant of an easement by reason of the insertion of language limiting the use of the land to a particular purpose.

EXAMPLE: A, a landowner, signed a warranty deed conveying to B, an adjoining landowner, a strip of land "to be used for road purposes." The quoted phrase appeared immediately following the property description in the deed. It was held that this deed did not make B the owner of the strip, but only gave him an easement thereover for road purposes. *Magnolia Petroleum Co. v. West,* 374 Ill. 516, 30 N.E.2d 24.

A grant of an easement may be incorporated in a deed that conveys land.

EXAMPLE: A owns Lots 1 and 2. He sells and conveys Lot 1 to B. After the property description in this deed, the following clause is inserted: "For the consideration aforesaid, the grantor grants to the grantee, his heirs and assigns, as an easement appurtenant to the premises hereby conveyed an easement for ingress and egress over and across the south ten feet of Lot 2 in the subdivision aforesaid." The deed accomplishes two objects: (1) It transfers ownership of Lot 1 to B. (2) It gives B an easement over the south ten feet of Lot 2.

§ 23. **Express reservation.** A landowner may, in selling and conveying part of his land, reserve in the deed an easement in favor of the tract retained by such landowner.

EXAMPLE: A owns Lots 1 and 2. He sells and conveys Lot 2 to B and, after the property description in the deed, inserts the following clause: "The grantor reserves to himself, his heirs and assigns, as an easement appurtenant to Lot 1 in the subdivision aforesaid, an easement for ingress and egress over and across the south ten feet of the premises hereby conveyed."

As in the case of grants of easements, reservations of easements, not labeled as such, are of frequent occurrence.

EXAMPLE: A, a landowner, sold and conveyed certain land to B by a deed containing the following clause: "Saving and excepting therefrom a strip of land forty feet wide along the bank of the east fork of Austin Creek all the way across said land, for a road to be built at some future time." The court held that, although the deed purported to except from its operation the forty-foot strip in question, nevertheless ownership of the forty-foot strip passed to the grantee in the deed, but the grantor had an easement thereover for road purposes. *Coon v. Sonoma Magnesite Co.,* 182 Cal. 597, 189 Pac. 271.

§ 24. **Creation of easement by agreement.** Easements may be created by contract or agreement, such contract or agreement being, in effect, a grant of an easement. A familiar illustration is the party wall agreement.

§ 25. **Party walls.** Suppose you own Lot 1 and I own adjoining Lot 2. You plan to erect a building on your lot, and I propose to erect an identical building on mine. If we can get together, we can effect an economy by means of a *party wall.* We will erect our buildings in such a way that on the common boundary line where our lots meet only one wall will be built, straddling the line, half on each side of it. Each of us will use that wall as a wall of his house. It will support my floors and roof and yours also. The economies of such an arrangement are obvious. The cost of the wall is shared. Land is conserved. Windows are eliminated, as is the expense of maintenance of one outside wall.

Legally I own the half of the wall that rests on my lot, and you own the half that rests on your lot. I have an easement of support in your half of the wall, and you have an easement of support in my half. Owners planning such an arrangement enter into a party wall agreement. Naturally a written agreement should be used, for an easement is an interest in land, and the law requires that interests in land be created in writing.

Suppose I plan to build at a time when you are not yet ready to go ahead. Here the party wall agreement gives me the right to put half of the wall on your lot and further provides that when you decide to build you will pay me half the cost of the wall.

The duty to repair a party wall falls equally on both owners. If either owner repairs the wall, he is entitled to collect from the other owner half the expenses thus incurred.

Unless the party wall agreement provides otherwise, either owner may increase the height of the wall without the consent of the other owner. However, the entire expense must be borne by the party who heightens the wall, unless the other owner decides to use the added wall.

Additional points on party walls. (1) Each owner has the right to extend the beams of his building into the party wall, but not beyond the centerline of the wall. (2) Use of the wall for flues and fireplaces is legal. (3) If an owner chooses not to erect a building on his side of the party wall, he may use that side of the wall for advertising signs. 2 A.L.R.2d 1138, 69 C.J.S. 154. (4) As a rule, if I wish to demolish my building on my side of the party wall, I may do so, but I must leave the wall intact for the support of your building. *Ceno Theater Co. v. B/G Sandwich Shops,* 24 F.2d 31.

§ **26.   Mortgages.**   When *A* owns Lots 1 and 2 and mortgages Lot 1 to *B*, he may, at *B*'s insistence, include in the mortgage a grant of easement over part of Lot 2. Such a clause may run somewhat as follows:

> And as further security for payment of the debt above described, the mortgagor mortgages and grants to the mortgagee, his heirs and assigns, as an easement appurtenant to Lot 1 aforesaid, an easement for ingress and egress over and across the south ten feet of Lot 2 in the subdivision aforesaid.

When *A* owns Lots 1 and 2 and is mortgaging Lot 1 to *B*, *A* may wish to reserve, for the benefit of Lot 2, an easement over part of Lot 1. In such case, an appropriate clause of reservation may be included in the mortgage.

The foregoing illustrations show how a *mortgage can create an easement.* When such a mortgage is foreclosed, ownership of the dominant and servient tenements passes into separate hands, and the real existence of the easement begins. Suppose, however, that *A* owns a lot that enjoys the benefit of a *previously created* easement. He mortgages the lot, and in the mortgage nothing is said concerning the easement. The mortgage is foreclosed. The purchaser at the foreclosure sale enjoys the benefit of the easement, for *an appurtenant easement runs with the land even though it is not mentioned in the mortgage or in the foreclosure proceedings.* 38 *Cal. L. Rev.* 426.

Also, an easement acquired by a mortgagor subsequent to the giving of a mortgage automatically comes under the lien of the mortgage and passes to the purchaser at any mortgage foreclosure sale. *First Nat. Bank v. Smith*, 284 Mich. 579, 280 N.W. 57, 116 A.L.R. 1078.

Suppose a man mortgages his land in 1954 to A, and the mortgage is duly recorded. In 1955 he gives B, his neighbor, an easement across the same land. Since the easement is given *after* a mortgage has been recorded against the property, it will be extinguished if A forecloses his mortgage. *Kling v. Ghilarducci*, 3 Ill.2d 455, 121 N.E.2d 752. Similarly, if he gives B, his neighbor, an easement over his land, which is properly recorded, and thereafter he mortgages his land to A, foreclosure of A's mortgage will not cut out the easement. 46 A.L.R.2d 1197.

§ 27. **Implied grant or reservation.** Often when the owner of two tracts of land sells or mortgages one of them, there is no mention at all of easements, and yet as a result of the transaction an easement is created. In such cases, the situation of the land is such that the courts feel the parties intended to create an easement even though they did not actually say so. Such easements are called *implied easements*. They are created by *implied grant* and *implied reservation*. Where a landowner uses one part of his land for the benefit of another part, and this use is such that, if the parts were owned by different persons, the right to make such a use would constitute an easement, then upon a sale of either of such parts an implied easement is created.

EXAMPLE: A owned two adjoining lots, on each of which there was a two-story building. The buildings were separated by a partition wall. The stairway to the second floor was located entirely on one lot, and there were doors through the partition wall by which occupants of the second floor on the other lot reached their apartments. A sold and conveyed the lot on which the stairway was located to B. There was an implied reservation of an easement for the use of the stairway, and A could continue to use such stairway even though the deed made no mention whatever of any easement. If A had instead sold B the lot that had no stairway and had retained the lot on which the stairway was located, there would have been an implied grant of an easement to B to use such stairway. *Powers v. Heffernan*, 233 Ill. 597, 84 N.E. 661.

§ 28. **Requirements for creation of implied easement.** The following are the requirements for the creation of an implied easement:

1. The prior use of one part of the land for the benefit of the other part must have been apparent and obvious. That is, the use must have been such that it would have been disclosed on a reasonable inspection of the premises. The theory is that the parties intended to continue the obvious arrangements existing when the sale took place.

EXAMPLE: Suppose a man owns Lots 1 and 2, and sewage from his house on Lot 1 drains through an underground pipe running across Lot 2. There is a catch basin on Lot 2. If A buys Lot 2, the presence of the catch basin with a visible cover on the surface of the ground will give A notice and thereby create an implied easement for drainage over Lot 2. 58 A.L.R. 824.

2. The prior use must have been continuous.

EXAMPLE: A visible and necessary drain is thought to be continuous in its operation. Usually a permanent and clearly defined way is thought of as continuous. Thus where A owned two adjoining lots and constructed a driveway on the common boundary line between the lots and thereafter sold one of the lots to B, an implied easement was created for use of the driveway as a common or party driveway. *Walters v. Gadde*, 390 Ill. 518, 62 N.E.2d 439; *Gorman v. Overmyer*, 199 Okla. 451, 190 P.2d 447. Another example would be a party wall, and still another would be a well on the boundary line serving two adjoining properties. *Frantz v. Collins*, 21 Ill.2d 446, 193 N.E.2d 437.

3. The easement must be necessary. That is, the easement must be highly convenient and beneficial to the property. The test of whether or not an easement is necessary is this: Can a substitute for this easement be obtained without unreasonable expense and trouble? If it cannot, the easement is necessary.

4. The ownership of the two tracts of land must become separated, so that one person owns the benefited tract and someone else owns the burdened tract. This is obvious, for as long as one man owns both tracts there can be no easement. By definition, an easement is a right in *another's* property. The manner in which the separation of ownership takes place is immaterial. Usually it takes place when the original owner sells either the benefited or the burdened tract to another person, but any other manner of separating the ownership will do. For example, if the owner of two such tracts places a mortgage on one of them, and such mortgage is later foreclosed, the ownership of the two tracts passes into different hands and an implied easement is created. *Liberty Bank v. Lux*, 378 Ill. 329, 38 N.E.2d 6. Or if the owner of two such tracts dies, leaving a will by which he gives one tract to A and the other to B, an implied easement will be created. *Hoepker v. Hoepker*, 309 Ill. 407, 141 N.E. 159. Or if a tract of land is divided up by a partition suit (see § 295), an implied easement may be created. *Deisenroth v. Dabe*, 7 Ill.2d 340, 131 N.E.2d 17.

Suppose *A* rents *B* an apartment, office, or store. Naturally *B* will have implied easements to use the stairways, elevators, fire escapes, porches, bathrooms, etc., that are used in common by the tenants. 24 A.L.R.2d 123. It is true that the lease does not create a separation of ownership, but, rather, it puts lawful possession into two or more different persons, and that answers the purpose of the rule.

§ 29. **Easement of necessity.**   When the owner of land sells a part thereof that has no outlet to a highway except over his remaining land or over the land of strangers, a right of way by necessity is created by implied grant over the remaining land of the seller.

§ 30. **Prescription.**   *Prescription* is the acquiring of a right by lapse of time. An easement may be acquired by prescription. Usually the period of time required for the acquisition of an easement by prescription is the same period as that required for the acquisition of ownership of land by adverse possession. (See § **65**.) This period, called the *prescriptive period,* varies from state to state. Periods of ten, fifteen, and twenty years are common.

EXAMPLE: A owned a private alley and an apartment building adjoining thereto. B owned a neighboring apartment building. Without any permission from A, B's tenants constantly used A's private alley in order to enter their apartments from the rear. Whenever A's tenants parked their cars in the alley, B would call the police and have them put out. This continued for more than twenty years. Then A attempted to stop this use of the alley by B's tenants. It was held that he could not do so, since B had acquired an easement by prescription. *Rush v. Collins,* 366 Ill. 307, 8 N.E.2d 659.

EXAMPLE: A owned a house and lot. He constructed a garage in the rear of the lot. Because the space adjoining his house was inadequate for a driveway, he constructed one that ran partly across B's adjoining land. This was done without seeking B's permission. A used this driveway for over twenty years. He has a prescriptive easement to continue to use it. *Nocera v. De Feo,* 340 Mass. 783, 164 N.E. 2d 136.

The following are the requirements for the creation of an easement by prescription:

1. The use must be *adverse.* If it is under permission or consent of the owner, the use is not adverse. There must be such an invasion of the landowner's rights as would entitle him to maintain a suit against the intruder. If the use by me of my neighbor's land is, on its face, permitted by my neighbor as a matter of neighborly accommodation, the use is not adverse or hostile.

EXAMPLE: A had a driveway running to his garage in the rear of his house. B, his neighbor, often used this driveway to get his car into his backyard. He never sought A's permission, although they were good friends. This use will not ripen into a prescriptive easement. It is, on its face, a matter of neighborly accommodation. *Stevenson v. Williams,* 188 Pa. Super. 49, 145 A.2d 734.

2. The use must be *under claim of right,* in that there must be no recognition of the right of the landowner to stop the use.
3. The use must be *visible, open,* and *notorious,* so that the landowner is bound to learn of it if he keeps himself well informed about his property.

EXAMPLE: The secret placing of a drainpipe in a wooded gully would not be considered notorious.

4. The use *must not be merely as a member of the public.* The use by the claimant of the easement must be sufficiently exclusive to give notice of his *individual* claim of right.
5. The use must be *continuous* and *uninterrupted* for the required period of time. That is, the easement must be exercised whenever there is any necessity therefor, and the use must be of such frequency as to apprise the landowner of the right being claimed against him.

EXAMPLE: Occasional entries upon a neighbor's land, for example, to put up screens or storm windows, to paint a wall, to trim a hedge, or to clean gutters, are not such continuous use as will ever ripen into a prescriptive easement. *Romans v. Nadler,* 217 Minn. 174, 14 N.W.2d 482.

It is not necessary that the adverse use be that of one person only.

EXAMPLE: In Illinois the prescriptive period is twenty years. Suppose that A and B are neighbors. A builds a driveway over B's land without B's permission. He uses it for five years. A sells his land to C, who also uses the driveway for five years. C sells to D, who uses the driveway for ten years. Now D has a prescriptive easement. The prescriptive uses that A, C, and D made can be *tacked,* that is, added together to make up the required twenty years. 171 A.L.R. 1279. Also, since the easement was used for the benefit of a tract of land, it is an easement appurtenant and will thereafter run with the land so benefited. 171 A.L.R. 1279.

Party driveways. Suppose you and I own adjoining lots, each with a house on it, and pursuant to a verbal agreement we build a party driveway, straddling the boundary line between our lots and serving our garages in the rear of our lots. Each of us uses this driveway continuously for the required period of time. Most courts hold that a party driveway easement has been created by prescription. 98 A.L.R. 1096. This is quite a legal oddity, for obviously such common use is permissive, not adverse. Yet to prevent injustice courts allow prescriptive easements to be created by such use. 27 A.L.R.2d 332.

§ 31. **Prescription for public highways.** When the public has used a privately owned strip of land for the purpose of passage for the required period of time, courts often hold that an easement for a public highway has been created by prescription.

§ 32. **Creation of easement by condemnation.** Although in some states laws provide that complete ownership of the land may be acquired by condemnation (see § 64), the general rule is that where land is taken by condemnation for a street, highway, railroad right of way, or telephone or electric power line the taker acquires only an easement.

EXAMPLE: The City of X wishes to open a street across A's land, but A is unwilling to sell. The city files a condemnation suit against A, and a judgment is entered fixing the full market value of the strip to be taken for the opening of the street. The city pays this amount into court. Although the city pays the full market value of the strip, it acquires only an easement thereover, and A remains the owner subject to the easement. Thus A may construct subvaults beneath the street without any liability to the city for payment of rent.

As the population continues to explode, concern grows for the preservation of open spaces, especially for scenic treasures that remain in private ownership and offer tempting sites to land developers. Under recent legislation and court decisions the state may condemn or purchase a scenic easement that, in effect, forbids the landowner to build upon his land. The Federal Highway Beautification Act offers incentives to the State to create such easements. *Markham Advertising Co. v. State,* 439 P.2d 248 (Wash.).

EXAMPLE: A owns a stretch of rolling farm land through which a lovely river winds, abutting a highway that commands an excellent view of the scene. The state condemns A's right to build upon his farm and pays him compensation for depriving him of this right. (See §64.) He may continue to occupy and farm the land, but it will never be built upon. This right acquired by the state is called a *scenic easement. Kamrowski v. State,* 31 Wisc.2d 256, 142 N.W.2d 793. In some states such scenic easements are created by laws that do not provide for compensation. *Markham Advertising Co. v. State,* 439 P2d 248 (Wash.).

§ 33.   **Sale by reference to plat.**   Where a landowner subdivides his land into lots, blocks, streets, and alleys and thereafter sells lots in the subdivision, each purchaser of a lot automatically acquires an easement of passage over the streets and alleys shown on the plat or map of the subdivision, even though the deed to the lot makes no mention whatever of such right. Such a private easement becomes important where the subdivider attempts to close up a street or alley before the public has acquired the right to insist that such street or alley remain open. The lot owners are in a position to keep the street open by virtue of their easement rights, even though the street never becomes a public street.

§ 34.   **Row housing.**   In the present building boom, land costs and construction costs have risen sharply, and row houses, now called *town houses,* have penetrated many areas of our country. In former times, row houses were most often erected facing the street, so that in driving by a block of row houses you would see a solid wall of housefronts. Nowadays you are more likely to see the houses erected at right angles to the street line, as in Figure 1.

It is obvious that by laying out the houses at right angles to the street line, many more houses can be erected than would be possible if the houses were erected fronting on the street.

Clearly this arrangement makes extensive use of easements. The walls, of course, are party walls, and easements must exist for this purpose. Also, all houses except those closest to the street need easements of ingress and egress over a central walk, indicated in Figure 1 by the dotted lines. Easements are also needed for common gutters and downspouts, common sewer and water lines, common electric light and telephone wires, and so forth. In many cases, builders of these projects have proceeded with complete indifference to the legal requirements of such a

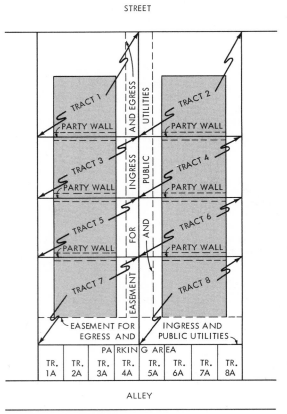

SOLID LINES ARE PROPERTY LINES.
SHADED AREAS DEPICT BUILDINGS.

FIGURE 1

situation and have sold off such units without any mention of the easements required. Probably implied easements exist for all these necessary common uses. *Gilbert v. Chicago T. & T. Co.*, 7 Ill.2d 496, 131 N.E.2d 1. A better way of handling this is by use of a declaration of easements. (*See* Chapter 34.)

§ 35. **Right to profits of the soil.**   An easement does not confer on the owner thereof any right to the profits of the soil, such as oil, hay, coal, or minerals.

EXAMPLE: The County of X acquired a highway over A's land by condemnation. The county has no right to drill oil wells on the land thus acquired, for it has only an easement for road purposes.

It is the landowner whose land is subject to the easement who has the right to oil, minerals, and other profits of the soil, etc.

EXAMPLE: A landowner whose land is subject to an easement for railroad right of way purposes may tunnel under the railroad right of way and mine the coal thereunder.

§ 36. **Use of easement premises.** An easement appurtenant can be used only for the benefit of the dominant tenement. It may not be used for the benefit of any other tract of land. *Land acquired by the owner of the dominant tenement after the creation of the easement has no right to the use of easement.*

EXAMPLE: A owned Lot 1. There was an easement appurtenant in favor of Lot 1 to use a spur or switch track over land adjoining Lot 1 to the west. A thereafter bought Lot 2, which adjoined Lot 1 to the east, and erected a powerhouse on Lot 2. It was held that the switch track could not be used to service the powerhouse since the switch track easement was appurtenant only to Lot 1. *Goodwillie Co. v. Commonwealth Co.*, 241 Ill. 42, 89 N.E. 272.

Particularly in the case of industrial easements it is well to keep in mind at the time easement is created that the dominant owner may later wish to acquire other neighboring land for plant expansion. The easement grant should provide that such subsequently acquired property shall enjoy the benefit of the easement. For example, suppose that the dominant tenement happens to fall in Government Section 34, then let the easement grant provide as follows:

SUGGESTED FORM: Said easement is also appurtenant to any land in said Section 34 that may subsequently come into common ownership with said dominant tenement.

Where an easement of ingress and egress is created by grant, it may be used by the easement owner for all reasonable purposes, and use is not restricted to such purposes as were reasonable at the date of the grant.

EXAMPLE: Use of the easement by automobiles will be permitted even though an easement was created when horse-drawn vehicles were in use. 3 A.L.R.3d 1287.

And with changing conditions more intensive use may be made of the easement than was contemplated at the time the easement was created.

EXAMPLE: At the time an easement of ingress and egress was created, the dominant tenement was occupied by a private dwelling. Later this dwelling was replaced by a hotel. It was held that the hotel could continue to use the easement. *White v. Grand Hotel* (1913) 1 Ch. 113.

However, where an easement is acquired by *prescription*, use of the easement after the prescriptive period has expired must remain pretty much the same as the use that took place during the prescriptive period.

If the width of an easement is fixed at the time of its creation, it will not grow wider even though conditions change.

EXAMPLE: In 1918 A grants B a ten-foot easement for ingress and egress. The fact that today's big trucks cannot use so narrow a way does not increase the size of the easement. *Feldstein v. Segall*, 198 Md. 285, 81 A.2d 610.

If you have a driveway easement over my land, you can park to load and unload but cannot park overnight. 37 A.L.R.2d 944. This does not mean, however, that the owner of an easement for ingress and egress has the *exclusive* right to use the surface of the land for that purpose. The landowner, since he remains the owner of the easement premises subject only to the prescribed rights of the easement owner, has the right to make any use of the easement tract that does not interfere with the easement.

EXAMPLE: In the case of an easement of ingress and egress, the landowner may travel over the easement tract as long as he does not interfere with the easement owner's right of travel. The landowner, indeed, may even erect structures or run power lines above the easement, so long as he leaves space at the surface adequate for travel by the easement owner. *Sakansky v. Wein*, 86 N.H. 337, 169 Atl. 1; *Cleveland Railway Co. v. Public Service Co.*, 380 Ill. 130, 43 N.E. 2d 993. Or a landowner may tunnel and mine minerals beneath an easement for ingress and egress or build over a water pipe easement.

Since an easement is a right to use another's land for a special purpose only, the easement owner must use the easement premises only for that purpose for which the easement exists.

EXAMPLE: A grants B, his neighbor, an easement for ingress and egress over a part of A's land. B has no right to lay gas pipes in the easement premises. 3 A.L.R. 3rd 1278.

§ 37. **Maintenance and repair of easement facilities.** The fact that A gives B an easement over A's property imposes no duty on A to pave the easement tract, keep it in repair, or do anything at all for B's benefit. 169 A.L.R. 1152.

EXAMPLE: A gave B an easement to take water from a well on A's land.

It was held that A was not obliged to operate the pump to furnish B water even though that was the physical situation at the time the easement was created. *Gowing v. Lehmann,* 98 N.H. 414, 101 A.2d 463.

Therefore if the parties agree that the owner of the burdened land is to have some affirmative duties, they must be spelled out in the easement grant.

Of course the easement owner has the right to take all steps necessary to make this easement usable. For example, in an easement of ingress and egress the easement owner would have the right to repair or improve an existing road, to lay down a new road, to build bridges across streams, to trim encroaching trees and shrubs, to blast rocks, and otherwise to remove impediments, and so forth. 169 A.R.L. 1153.

Also, where a private road is used by *both* the landowner and the easement owner, they must divide the cost of repairs in proportion to their use of the road, even though the easement agreement is silent on this score. *Stevens v. Bird Jex Co.,* 81 Utah 355, 18 P.2d 292.

If the easement tract is used only by the easement owner and falls into disrepair as a result of his neglect, he has no right to deviate from the prescribed way and travel over other land belonging to the landowner. *Dudgeon v. Bronson,* 159 Ind. 562, 64 N.E. 910. On the other hand, if the landowner obstructs the easement, the easement owner has the right to travel around the obstruction over other land belonging to the landowner.

§ 38. **Termination of easement.** Easements may be terminated in the following ways:

1. When an easement has been created for a particular purpose, it ceases when the purpose ceases.

EXAMPLE: A party wall agreement ceases when both buildings are destroyed by fire, unless the party wall agreement provides otherwise. An easement for railroad purposes ends when the railroad tears up its tracks and discontinues service. 95 A.L.R.2d 482.

2. When the owner of an easement becomes the owner of the land that is subject to the easement, the easement is extinguished by *merger.*

3. The owner of an easement may release his right to the owner of the land that is subject to the easement.

4. The owner of an easement may terminate it by abandonment. There must be an intention to abandon the easement and acts manifesting such intention.

§ 39. **Suggestions in the preparation of easements:**

1. When possible, avoid the creation of an easement in favor of a *structure.* For example, an easement of ingress and egress is created to and from "the dwelling

house at 123 Spring Road, Chicago, Illinois." There is danger that if the house is demolished, the easement will die, for it services the house, not the land. The easement should have run in favor of the land, not the building.

2. When possible, avoid the creation of an easement over or through a *structure*. For example, an easement of ingress and egress is created through the hallway of a building. There is danger that if the building is destroyed by fire, for example, the easement will die, for it is the building, not the land, that is subject to the easement.

3. It may develop that the owner of the burdened property will at some future time wish to change the location of the easement, as when such owner wishes to change the location of railroad tracks that hamper his plant expansion. The right to do so must be specifically reserved in the easement grant. Otherwise no such right exists.

§ 40. **Easement draftsmanship for the lawyer.**   Detailed suggestions on the preparation of easements will be found in an article in 38 Calif. L. Rev. 426.

Chapter 5

LAND DESCRIPTIONS

§ 41. **Legal descriptions.** Every deed, mortgage, or lease contains a description of the land involved. The purpose of such a description, obviously, is to fix the boundaries of the land intended to be sold, mortgaged, or leased. A street address is adequate for the purpose of guiding guests to your home or for mail delivery. But greater precision is needed to fix the exact point where your land ends and that of your neighbor begins. Hence we have the legal description. Whenever you read a legal description, keep in mind that before the description was written, some person, probably a land surveyor, went out and located on the land the boundaries of the tract of land involved. He then put into words written directions for locating the lines he had traced on the land. These written directions we call a legal description of the land. Various methods have been devised for describing tracts of land.

§42. **Metes and bounds descriptions.** *Metes* are measures of length, such as inches, feet, yards, and rods. *Bounds* are boundaries, both natural and artificial, such as streams or streets. In a *metes and bounds description,* the surveyor takes you by the hand, as it were, and leads you over the land. He starts at a well-marked point of beginning and follows the boundaries of the land until he returns once more to the starting point. Landmarks called *monuments* often mark the several corners of the tract. A monument may be a natural monument, such as a tree or river, or an artificial monument, such as a fence, stake, wall, road, or railroad.

EXAMPLE: A tract of land in Chicago, Cook County, Illinois, is described as follows, to wit: Beginning at a point in the east line of Mason Street one hundred feet north of the north line of Washington Street; running thence east on a line parallel to the north line of Washington Street 125 feet to the west line of an alley; thence north along the west line of said alley, twenty-five feet; thence west on a line parallel to the north line of Washington Street, 125 feet to the east line of Mason Street; thence south along the east line of Mason Street, twenty-five feet to the place of beginning.

The earliest descriptions in history were metes and bounds descriptions. All property in the thirteen original colonies of the United States was originally described by metes and bounds, the descriptions usually running from the mouth of a stream, or from a tree or a stump.

§ 43. The Government Survey.   By the treaty with England at the end of the Revolutionary War, the United States became the owner of the vast Northwest Territory, consisting of the present States of Illinois, Indiana, Ohio, Michigan, and Wisconsin. The end of the war found the United States heavily burdened with debts incurred during the war. It was decided that the new land should be sold and the proceeds used to retire the national debt. However, in selling the land to settlers, metes and bounds descriptions could not be used, for the new land was an untrodden wilderness. Hence some new system of describing land was needed. The system so devised was the rectangular system of land surveys, known as the Government Survey. Under this system, whenever a district, such as part of a state, needs to be made ready for private ownership, the government arranges for a survey of the land to be made. To begin a survey of this character, it is necessary to have some substantial landmark from which a start may be made. A place that can readily be referred to, such as the mouth of a river, is usually selected. From such a point, a line is run due north to the margin of the district to be surveyed. This first north and south line is called a *prime meridian,* or *principal meridian.* Some principal meridians have been numbered, such as the First Principal Meridian, which runs north from the mouth of the Great Miami River on the boundary between Ohio and Indiana and which governs the surveys of public lands in Ohio. Others have been named, as the Tallahassee Meridian, the Mt. Diablo Meridian, the Humboldt Meridian, and the San Bernardino Meridian.

An east and west line is run intersecting the principal meridian at some prominent point. This line is called the *base line.* Both north and south of the base line, additional east and west lines are run at intervals of twenty-four miles.

Since it is the object of the survey to create a huge checkerboard of identical squares covering the entire tract to be surveyed, it is plain that many north and south lines are needed. Owing to the curvature of the earth's surface, however, all true north and south lines converge as they approach the North Pole. This is obvious, since no matter how far apart two north and south lines are at the equator, they must meet at the North Pole. Hence if continuous north and south lines were to be used in the survey, it is clear that because of the convergence of the north and south lines the squares thus formed would grow narrower and narrower as the surveyors worked north. Now this is an imperfection that cannot be altogether eliminated. However, it can be minimized in the following manner: Along the base line, both east and west of the principal meridian, and at intervals of twenty-four miles, lines running due north are run. These are called *guide meridians*. But they are run only as far north as the next *correction line*, i.e., a distance of twenty-four miles. Then new intervals of twenty-four miles are measured off along this correction line, and a new series of guide meridians based on these new intervals is run for another twenty-four miles. This process is repeated until the boundaries of the tract are reached. Similar guide meridians are run based on the correction lines lying south of the base line (Figure 2).

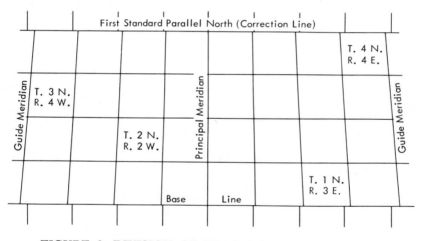

FIGURE 2. DIVISION OF TRACTS INTO TOWNSHIPS.

Thus the district surveyed is divided into tracts approximately twenty-four miles square. These tracts are further divided into parts six miles on each side. These smaller parts are called *townships*.

Each row, or tier, of townships running north and south is called a *range*. The first row east of the principal meridian is referred to as *Range 1 East* of that meridian. Thus the first row of townships east of the Third Principal Meridian is referred to as *Range 1 East of the Third Principal Meridian.* The row of townships next adjoining to the east is called *Range 2 East of the Third Principal Meridian,* and so on. Each row or tier of townships running east and west is identified by the number of townships intervening between it and the base line. Thus a township in the first row north of the base line is called *Township 1 North.* The township next adjoining to the north is called *Township 2 North,* and so on. To identify a township completely, both the range number and the township number must be given, as *Township 40 North, Range 13 East of the Third Principal Meridian.* The township thus identified is in the fortieth row north of the base line and in the thirteenth row east of the Third Principal Meridian. Such a description is often abbreviated, and becomes *T. 40 N., R. 13 E. of the 3rd P.M.*

Each township is divided into thirty-six tracts, each approximately one mile square. These tracts are called *sections.* The sections in a township are numbered from one to thirty-six, always commencing with the section in the northeast corner of the township (Figure 3). Sections are often

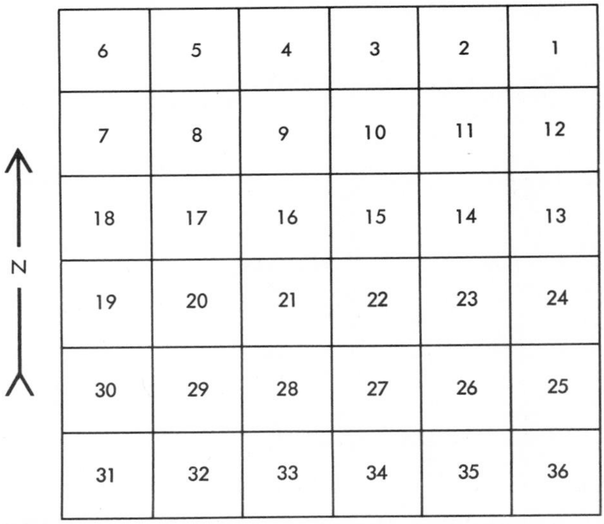

6	5	4	3	2	1
7	8	9	10	11	12
18	17	16	15	14	13
19	20	21	22	23	24
30	29	28	27	26	25
31	32	33	34	35	36

FIGURE 3. DIVISION OF TOWNSHIPS INTO SECTIONS.

divided into quarters, and these quarters are also often divided into quarters.

The government system of rectangular surveys has been employed in surveying the lands of the states of Alabama, Florida, Mississippi, and all of the states north of the Ohio and west of the Mississippi Rivers, except Texas.

Local surveys, which in some respects resemble the Government Survey, will occasionally be encountered in the other states.

§ 44. Plats. Large tracts of land are often subdivided into building lots. Thereafter each building lot is conveyed by its lot number.

> **EXAMPLE:** A, believing that the tract is ripe for subdivision, buys the Northeast Quarter of the Northeast Quarter of Section 7, Township 40 North, Range 13 East of the Third Principal Meridian, in Cook County, Illinois. He hires a surveyor, who divides the tract into *blocks,* separated by streets. Each block is divided into *lots.* The lots and blocks are numbered, and the streets and the subdivision are named. For this particular subdivision, A selects the name "Highwood." The surveyor prepares a map, called a *plat,* showing the lots and blocks, their dimensions and numbers, the widths and names of the streets, the location of the quarter-section lines, and other similar information. After receiving the approval of local officials, the plat is filed or recorded in the office where deeds and mortgages are recorded. A description of a lot in this subdivision will read somewhat as follows: Lot 2 in Block 5 in Highwood, a subdivision of the Northeast Quarter of the Northeast Quarter of Section 7, Township 40 North, Range 13 East of the Third Principal Meridian in Cook County, Illinois.

§ 45. Description by popular name. Descriptions by the popular name of the tract have been held sufficient, as where a deed conveys "The Old Merchant Farm." *Hayes v. O'Brien,* 149 Ill. 403, 37 N.E. 73.

§ 46. General description. A deed sometimes contains no definite description, but merely purports to convey all land owned by the grantor in a certain district, as "all the land owned by the grantor in Cook County, Illinois." Such descriptions are held to be sufficient.

§ 47. Street address. A description by street address alone should never be used in a deed or mortgage. Since the proper legal description is not always available when a contract for the sale of land is being drafted, descriptions by street address will be found in contracts. (See § 165.)

A danger sometimes present in street address descriptions is revealed by the following illustration.

> **EXAMPLE:** R leased to E "certain premises known as 10 East Chicago Avenue, Chicago, Illinois." The building in question bore this address. It was a restaurant. R also owned a vacant lot adjoining, which patrons of the restaurant sometimes used as a parking area, although it was not a regular parking lot. It was held that a lease by street number includes only the lot on which the building is situated. *Killian v. Welfare Engineering Co.,* 328 Ill. App. 375, 66 N.E.2d 305.

§ 48. Area. Land may be described by its area, as the "North one acre of the Southeast Quarter of Section 1, Township 44 North, Range 2 East of the Third Principal Meridian, Lake County, Illinois."

§ 49. Adjoining owners. Lands are also described by reference to adjoining lands.

EXAMPLE: A deed described the land as follows: "Bounded on the east by a fifty-acre tract of land owned by G. B. Turner purchased by him from N. W. Rodden; bounded on the north by the right of way of the Texas and Pacific R. R.; and on the west by a fifty-acre tract owned by the said G. B. Turner and known as the J. F. Neal tract of land; bounded on the south by the Katie Moore Boham tract of land." *Cox v. Campbell*, 135 Tex. 428, 143 S.W.2d 361.

§ **50. Foreign grant.** Portions of this country were once owned by France, Holland, Mexico, and Spain. In fact, the titles to some of the most valuable lands on Manhattan Island are based upon Dutch grants. Hence descriptions employing foreign units of land measure, such as the *vara* and the *arpent*, are often encountered.

§ **51. Indefinite description.** A deed, mortgage, or other document must describe the land conveyed. The land must be so described that it can be located and identified.

EXAMPLE: A deed was made of the "southeast half" of a certain section. This deed was held void for uncertainty in the description. *Pry v. Pry,* 109 Ill. 466.

It is often difficult to determine whether a description is good or bad.

EXAMPLE: A deed was made to "one acre of land in the northwest corner of Block 20" in a certain subdivision. This deed was held good, because a surveyor could go to the northwest corner of the block and measure out a sufficient distance west and south to include one acre of land. *Richey v. Sinclair*, 167 Ill. 184, 47 N.E. 364.

A deed of "my house and lot" is not considered indefinite. Oral evidence can be introduced in court to show what tract of land was intended. *Brenneman v. Dillon*, 296 Ill. 140, 360 N.E. 528.

When a deed description is too indefinite to identify the land, but the grantee, by consent of the grantor, takes possession of premises that are within the general terms of the description and erects permanent improvements on them, the defect in the description is thereby cured.

EXAMPLE: R made a deed to a railroad of "a strip of land one hundred feet in width over the Northeast Quarter of Section 12, Township 14 North, Range 2 East of the Third Principal Meridian." The railroad, with R's consent, actually occupied a strip of land one hundred feet in width and erected railroad tracks thereon. The description, though originally too indefinite, became sufficient by occupation.

The rule that possession cures an indefinite description is also applicable to leases and to contracts of sale.

§**52. Description containing omissions.** A deed, mortgage, or other document is valid, even though part of the description is omitted, if enough remains to identify the land conveyed.

EXAMPLE: A deed to land described as being in Santa Cruz County, California, failed to name the meridian from which the township and range were numbered. This did not invalidate the deed, since all descriptions of land in that county are numbered from the Mt. Diablo Meridian. *Harrington v. Goldsmith,* 136 Cal. 168, 68 Pac. 594.

§ 53. **Correction of deed description by court order.** When an error occurs in the land description in a deed and the seller refuses to give a new deed to correct the error, a court order can usually be obtained correcting the erroneous description. This is known as *reformation* of an instrument. And if in the meantime the grantee has been in possession of the land, probably no great harm will result from the error. If, however, the grantee has not gone into possession, as where the land is vacant, third persons, such as judgment creditors of the grantor, may acquire rights in the land superior to those of the grantee.

§ 54. **Streets or highways as boundaries.** As previously pointed out (see §§ 31–33), a city often does not own the land comprising its roads, streets, or alleys, but only has an easement thereover for street purposes. When a deed or mortgage is made of land abutting on such a road, street, or alley, the land sold or mortgaged generally runs to the center of such road, street, or alley. 49 A.L.R.2d 982.

EXAMPLE: *R* gives *E* a deed selling and conveying that part of a certain section of land "lying south of Dundee Road." By this deed, *E* acquires all land in that particular section lying south of the *center* of Dundee Road.

The reason for this rule is obvious. The seller, having parted with ownership of his land, would have no use for the strip of road adjoining thereto. Hence it is presumed that he intended half of the adjoining road to pass to the buyer with the land sold.

When a street is used as a boundary, keep in mind that legally the street usually includes much more than the paved roadway over which cars travel. It includes the sidewalk, the planted area known as the *parkway* and may even include a narrow strip of land on the house side of the sidewalk. Check the recorded subdivision plat to locate the true street line.

§ 55. **Waters as boundaries.** If *R* owns land through which a stream flows and his ownership includes the stream bed, a deed, mortgage, or lease of land "lying south of Plum Creek" will, under a rule analogous to the highway rule, include the south half of the creek.

§ 56. **Parts of lots.** Care should be exercised in drafting descriptions of parts of lots.

EXAMPLE: A subdivision plat indicates that Lot 2 in Block 3 is eighty feet wide. *R,* the owner, gives *E* a deed to the "east forty feet of Lot 2." When *R* sells the remainder of the lot, his description thereof should be "Lot 2, except the east forty feet thereof," and not "the west forty feet of Lot 2." The reason is obvious. Suppose Lot 2 is actually slightly more than eighty feet in width, as it well may be, for land measurements are not perfectly accurate. Deeds of the east forty feet and the west forty feet of the lot would leave a small strip of land in the middle of the lot still owned by the seller.

When the lot is not a perfect square or rectangle, use of descriptions such as the "east half" or "north half" of the lot should be avoided, since the word "half" usually is considered to mean half by area, and the boundary line will be located with an equal number of square feet on either side thereof. This may result in an unequal division of the frontage of the lot.

A deed of a part of a lot that abuts on a diagonal street should use descriptions like the "northwesterly thirty feet" rather than the "north thirty feet," since, if the diagonal street runs in a true northwesterly or northeasterly direction, it is difficult to determine which side of the lot is the "north" side. Cases will be found where two of the boundary lines may lay equal claim to being the "north" line of the lot.

§ 57. **Buildings.**   Since buildings are usually fixtures and, as such, are part of the land, a deed of the land will automatically give the buyer the buildings thereon. They need not be mentioned in the deed.

§ 58. **Land assemblies.**   It is often necessary to acquire and assemble the lands of several adjoining landowners—for example, for a subdivision, or a factory site. Here the danger is that the descriptions used may leave small gaps between the parcels.

EXAMPLE: A proposes to acquire the Northwest Quarter of Section 10 in a government township. He assumes that it contains exactly 160 acres, which it legally should contain. Actually, of course, owing to inaccuracies in surveying there is no such thing as a perfect quarter section, and it happens that this quarter section contains 161 acres. Suppose, then, that A acquires from B the "east eighty acres" of the quarter section and gets a deed from C to the "west eighty acres" of the quarter section. This leaves a one-acre strip between the two eighty-acre tracts. A thus does not acquire title to this strip. So as to bring such situations to light, it would be prudent to have a survey made of the entire tract before any parcel is purchased.

Often such situations can be cured by the buyer's lawyer, but this is best done before the land is paid for.

§ 59. **Tax bills.**   Tax bills contain abbreviated, vague, and unsatisfactory descriptions of the land. They should never be used in drafting a deed, contract, or lease.

Chapter 6

LAND TITLES AND
INTERESTS IN LAND

§ 60. **Estates in land.** Just as land may be divided into layers by a sale of "air rights" thereover or minerals thereunder, so the ownership of land may be divided into various types of interests. The highest type of interest, of course, is complete ownership.

> **EXAMPLE:** A owns a tract of land. No one else has any interest whatever in the land. He is said to be the owner *in fee simple.* This is merely a technical phrase connoting ownership of the land. When one hears it said that "A has title" to a particular tract of land, it is understood that A is the fee owner, i.e., he owns the land in fee, or in fee simple, or in fee simple absolute. All these are different ways of expressing the idea that A owns the land, that his ownership is of unlimited duration, and that so long as he obeys the law, he may do as he chooses with the land, and, on his death, it will go to his heirs, or, if he leaves a will, to the persons named in his will.

Suppose, however, that A, being the owner in fee simple of a tract of land, executes a ten-year lease thereof to B. Now A has parted with a portion of his rights. He has given up for ten years his right to occupy the land and, in return, has received B's promise to pay rent for those ten years. B has acquired the right to occupy the land in accordance with the provisions of his lease, but has not, of course, become the owner in fee simple. He has merely acquired a *leasehold estate* in the land.

The word *estate* is used to express the degree, quantity, nature, duration, or extent of an interest in land. Complete ownership is an *estate in fee simple,* but there are many other estates, such as *life estates* and *leasehold estates.* Each differs from the others with respect to the rights and duties of the owner of the estate in question.

§ 61. **Life estates.** The owner of a life estate can use and enjoy the land only during his lifetime.

> **EXAMPLE:** A, a landowner, dies leaving a will giving land to his widow, B, for her life, and, at her death, to their children, C and D. B thus acquires a *life estate* in the land and becomes a life tenant. She is entitled to the reasonable and necessary use of the land for her lifetime, but she must not do anything that will in any way injure the permanent value of the property. She may collect and use the rents of the land, but must keep the property in repair and must pay the real estate taxes and the interest on the mortgage. She must not drill any new oil wells or open new mines, but may take oil or minerals from existing wells and mines. On her death, all her rights in the land will cease.

Life estates may be created by will or deed. Often, to save the expense of probating his will after his death, a father while still living will give a deed of his land to his son or daughter, and in the deed will reserve to himself a life estate.

Certain special kinds of life estates are created by law, rather than by will or deed, such as dower, curtesy, and homestead. (See Chapter 17.)

§ 62. **Cemetery lots.** When a cemetery corporation sells a lot, or burial site, the purchaser does not become the absolute owner of the lot. The deed gives him merely an easement right of burial. *Steele v. Rosehill Cemetery Co.,* 370 Ill. 405, 19 N.E.2d 189; 109 *U. of Pa. L. Rev.* 378. He also has the right to enter the cemetery to care for the graves, subject to the reasonable regulations adopted by the cemetery company as to visiting hours, monuments, grave decorations, and so on. Like any other easement, the easement of the burial may be lost by abandonment. *Trustees of First Presbyterian Church v. Alling,* 54 N.J.S. 141, 148 A.2d 510.

§ 63. **Modes of acquiring title to or ownership of land.** While title to or ownership of land is most often acquired by deed, by will, or by descent, there are other modes of acquiring title to land, among them, *condemnation* and *adverse possession.*

§ 64. **Condemnation.** When land is needed for some public use, it can be acquired by the exercise of the power of *eminent domain.* The power of eminent domain is exercised: (1) by the United States, the state in which the land lies, cities, villages, school boards, and other public bodies; (2) by quasi-public corporations, such as railroads and public utility corporations. The power is subject to two conditions: The use to which the property is to be devoted must be a public one, and just compensation must be paid.

Exercise of the power of eminent domain involves a *condemnation* proceeding, which is usually a court proceeding initiated by the city or other public body desiring to acquire title. The just compensation to which the landowner is entitled is the fair, market value of the land at the time of the taking of the land. This value is often determined by a jury.

By condemnation, the condemnor acquires either an easement or fee simple title, although federal legislation now permits the United States to acquire by condemnation the right to occupy the land for a term of years only if that is what is desired. If an easement will serve the purpose for which the land is to be acquired, the condemnor, under many laws, acquires only an easement.

> **EXAMPLE:** As a rule, an easement only is acquired by a railroad condemning for a right of way, a city condemning for a street, a telephone company condemning for a telephone line, or a drainage district condemning for a drainage ditch. In such cases, even though the landowner receives the full market value of the land condemned, he retains the ownership of the land so condemned. The point is of importance, since if an easement for street or right of way purposes acquired by condemnation is later abandoned, the original landowner still retains his ownership free and clear of the easement. *Bell v. Mattoon Water Works Co.,* 245 Ill. 544, 92 N.E. 352.

In many cases, however, it is necessary that fee simple title be acquired, as when land is condemned for a courthouse site. Many states, therefore, Illinois, Kansas, Kentucky, Massachusetts, Michigan, Minnesota, Ohio, Pennsylvania, Texas, Virginia, and Wyoming, for example, permit the condemnor to acquire fee simple title by condemnation.

§ 65. **Adverse possession.** Often the public records will show a complete and perfect succession of perfect deeds from the government down to John Smith. This is known as the *record title* or *paper title.* Yet the true ownership of the land may be outstanding in some one who holds possession of the land without a single document to show his ownership. The ownership here referred to is that acquired by taking possession of the land and staying in possession for a certain number of years fixed by law. At the end of that period, which varies from state to state, the party in possession has ownership to the land. He need not have any deed to the land. He may have entered on the land without any right whatever to do so. He need not place any instrument on the public records showing his title. Yet he owns the land.

The law providing for the acquiring of title to land by going into possession was passed for two reasons: (1) It encourages the use of the land. If persons living in other states or other parts of the state own land in our vicinity and make no attempt to use the land for very long periods of time, it is better for the community to have the title placed in someone who is more interested in using it. (2) Ownership of real estate often depends on transactions that occurred so long ago that the witnesses who were familiar with the transaction are dead or have forgotten the facts. Therefore it is better to discourage any attempt to evict a person who has been in possession for a long period of time, since he might find it very difficult to find the witnesses who could prove that his claim is rightful.

Not every possession of land will ripen into ownership. Possession, in order to ripen into ownership must be adverse possession. For possession to be adverse it must be *hostile, actual, notorious, exclusive, continuous, and under claim of right.*

For possession to be adverse, it must be actual. As the judges put it, the occupant must unfurl his flag on the land and keep it flying so that the owner may see, if he wishes, that an enemy has invaded his domain and planted the standard of conquest. In other words, the occupant must do something that will make the owner notice that a stranger has occupied his land. This does not mean, however, that the occupant must live or reside on the land.

EXAMPLE: A fences and farms some vacant land adjoining his farm in Illinois. This continues for twenty years. He now owns this adjoining land by reason of his adverse possession.

This rule is of importance in boundary disputes, since if a landowner erects a fence on what he claims is the boundary of his land and claims all the land to the fence, his possession will eventually ripen into ownership even though the fence is actually over on his neighbor's land. The same is true when a building encroaches over and upon adjoining land.

Usually possession is not *hostile* when the person in possession occupies a relation of trust and confidence toward the holder of the paper title.

EXAMPLE: A father's possession is not hostile to the child, the possession of a husband is not hostile to the wife, and the possession of an agent is not hostile to his employer.

The requirement that possession be *notorious* merely means that the possession of the occupant must be such that the real owner would be likely to notice it.

Adverse possession, in order to ripen into title, must be continuous. However, seasonal possession is often sufficient, for the possession need only be such as is usual with respect to land of similar character. For example, it is sufficient if farmland is farmed in the farming season, timberland logged in the logging season, and so on.

EXAMPLE: A occupied B's hunting shack each year during the hunting season. Ultimately, A acquired good title by adverse possession. *Kraus v. Mueller,* 12 Wis.2d 430, 107 N.W.2d 467.

For a person to acquire title by adverse possession he must claim that he is the owner of the land, but it is enough if his acts and conduct indicate that he claims to be the owner of the land.

EXAMPLE: A and B owned adjoining lots, A owning Lot 9 and B owning Lot 8. A built a frame cottage on Lot 9, but the same extended two feet over on Lot 8. He thought the house was entirely on his own lot and never made any oral claim to this two-foot strip. He paid the taxes on Lot 9 and B the taxes on Lot 8. After twenty years, a survey was made which disclosed the encroachment. Although A had made no oral claim to the two-foot strip, his acts, namely, erecting a building on this strip, showed that he claimed title to the strip. He therefore had acquired title by adverse possession. *Cassidy v. Lenahan,* 294 Ill. 503, 128 N.E. 544.

Chapter 7

DEEDS

§ 66. Defined. A deed is a written instrument by which a landowner transfers the ownership of his land.

§ 67. Types of deeds. The deeds commonly used in the United States are *quitclaim deeds, warranty deeds,* and *deeds of bargain and sale.*

§ 68. Quitclaim deed. A quitclaim deed purports to convey only the grantor's *present interest in the land,* if any, rather than the land itself. Since such a deed purports to convey whatever interest the grantor has at the time, its use excludes any implication that he has good title, or any title at all. Such a deed in no way obligates the grantor. If he has no interest, none will be conveyed. If he acquires an interest after executing the deed, he retains such interest. If, however, the grantor in such deed has complete ownership at the time of executing the deed, the deed is sufficient to pass such ownership.

A seller who knows that his title is bad or who does not know whether his title is good or bad usually uses a quitclaim deed in conveying.

§ 69. Warranty deed. A warranty deed contains covenants of title. (See § 80.)

§ 70. Deed of bargain and sale. There are deeds that convey the land, and not merely the grantor's *interest* therein. Therefore they are not quitclaim deeds. They do not include warranties of title. Therefore they are not warranty deeds. Such a deed is a deed of *bargain and sale,* or *deed without covenants.*

§ 71.   **Requirements of a valid deed.**   The essential elements of a deed are a competent grantor, a grantee, recital of consideration, words of conveyance, adequate description of the land, signature of grantor and his spouse, and delivery of the completed instrument to the grantee. In addition, a deed may (though it need not) contain warranties of title, recitals showing mortgages and other encumbrances, a date, witnesses, an acknowledgment, and documentary stamps. Delivery is followed by filing or recording of the deed in the proper public office.

§ 72.   **Grantor.**   Every deed must have a grantor. The grantor is he who conveys the property. The fact that the name used by the grantor differs from his true name does not invalidate the deed.

The name of the grantor must appear in the body of the deed.

> **EXAMPLE:**   A, B, and C own certain land. A deed is made, and the names of A and B appear in the body thereof, but all three owners sign the deed. C's interest does not pass under the deed. *Harrison v. Simmons,* 55 Ala. 510.

However, a deed beginning "In consideration of ten dollars, I do hereby convey" is sufficient if signed by the landowner, even though his name does not appear in the body of the deed. *Bowles v. Lowery,* 181 Ala. 603, 62 So. 107. The same is true where the deed begins with the phrase "The undersigned." *Frederick v. Wilcox,* 119 Ala. 355, 24 So. 582.

A mistake in the spelling of the grantor's name or a variance between the spelling of the name in the body of the deed and the spelling in the signature will not invalidate the deed where the identity of the person intended to be designated is obvious.

> **EXAMPLE:**   A deed is good though it names "Emmonds" as grantor, but is signed "Emmens." And a deed is good though it names "Abraham B. Kain" as grantor but is signed "A. Boudoin Kain." *Lyon v. Kain,* 36 Ill. 362.

The grantor and his spouse must be of legal age and of sound mind. In many states, a deed by a person who has been declared insane by a court is void. Even if the grantor has not been declared insane, his deed may later be set aside if, as a matter of fact, he lacked the mental capacity to understand in a reasonable manner the nature of the transaction in which he was engaged and its consequences and effects on his rights and interest.

> **EXAMPLE:**   H, a widower, has three children, A, B, and C. When H becomes too feeble to take care of himself, A, a married but childless daughter, moves into his home with her husband. As time passes H becomes senile and requires constant care. A, feeling she should be rewarded for her care of her father, prepares a deed of the home running to herself as grantee and has H sign it. After H's death B and C learn of the deed. They file a suit to set it aside. If they can show that H was too

senile to understand that he was parting with ownership of his home when he signed the deed, the court will set it aside. Cases of this sort occur by the thousands.

In most states, an individual achieves majority, comes of age, at the age of twenty-one. In some states, females achieve majority at the age of eighteen. Ages of majority, however, vary from state to state. A person who is not of age is an *infant* and, after achieving majority, may sue to set aside any deed executed by him while an infant. If it is necessary that the land of an infant or an insane person be sold for his support or for some other proper purpose, court proceedings may be instituted for that purpose.

A favorable vote of the directors or trustees of a corporation is usually necessary to authorize the sale of corporate real estate. Laws will often be encountered requiring a vote of the holders of two-thirds of the corporate stock to authorize any sale of substantially *all* the corporate assets. A vote of the majority of the members of a church corporation or a non-profit corporation may be necessary for a sale of the property.

§ 73. **Grantor's spouse.**   Whether or not the grantor's spouse must join in the deed depends, of course, upon the local law. Generally speaking, however, it is necessary for the grantor's spouse to join in the deed for one or more of the following reasons:

1. In most states, land occupied by a husband and wife as their home is known as their homestead. Any deed or mortgage of the homestead must be signed by both husband and wife, the theory being that the home should not be disposed of unless a new home satisfactory to both parties has been furnished. (See Chapter 17.)

2. In most states, a wife has certain rights in her husband's land, and her rights in any particular parcel of land are not defeated by any deed made by her husband unless she has joined therein. (See Chapter 17.)

3. Depending on the local law, a husband may have *curtesy, dower,* or other rights in the land owned by his wife, and his signature on his wife's deed is required in order to relinquish these rights. (See Chapter 17.)

4. Some of the western states have the community property system, and in most of these states it is required that deeds of community property be signed by both husband and wife. (See Chapter 17.)

It is obvious from the foregoing that the marital status of the grantor should be clearly stated in the deed, as *bachelor, widow, spinster,* or *divorced and not remarried.*

§ 74. **Grantee.**   Every deed must have a grantee. If it does not, it is void.

EXAMPLE: A makes out a deed to B, who, unknown to A, is dead at the time. The deed is void. A dead grantee is no grantee at all. 148 A.L.R. 252.

The grantee need not be named in the deed if he is sufficiently described therein. Thus a deed to "John Smith and wife" vests good title in John Smith and his wife. *Ballard v. Farley,* 143 Tenn. 161, 226 S.W. 544.

A deed running directly to an unincorporated association is void for want of a grantee.

> **EXAMPLE:** A number of persons attended a particular church that was known as the "First Avenue Baptist Church." The church, however, was not incorporated. One of the members of the congregation made a deed of gift of his real estate to "First Avenue Baptist Church." The deed was void. *Heiligenstein v. Schlotterbeck,* 300 Ill. 206, 133 N.E. 188.

The fact that the name inserted in the deed is not the grantee's true name does not invalidate the deed. In other words, for the purpose of any particular real estate transaction I may assume any name I wish. If I should buy land and direct the seller to insert the name "Robert Cook" as grantee in the deed, intending to hold ownership of the land by that name, the deed is perfectly valid. *Chapman v. Tyson,* 29 Wash. 523, 81 Pac. 1066.

This situation frequently occurs with respect to persons who pass as husband and wife although they are not legally married.

> **EXAMPLE:** A deed designated as grantees Fabrio Casini and Lucy Casini, his wife. Actually, Lucy was not the wife of Fabrio, although they passed as husband and wife. The deed was a valid deed, and the grantees became co-owners of the property. *Casini v. Lupone,* 8 N.J.S. 362, 72 A.2d 907; *Michael v. Lucas,* 152 Md. 512, 137 Atl. 287.

A misspelling of the grantee's name will not invalidate the deed where the identity of the person intended to be designated is obvious. This is also true of deeds to corporations.

> **EXAMPLE:** I attend a church whose proper corporate name is First Avenue Methodist Church, and, intending to convey land to this church, I make out a deed to The Methodist Church of First Avenue. The deed is valid. *Church of Christ v. Christian Church,* 193 Ill. 144, 61 N.E. 1119. This defect is technically termed a *misnomer*. Misnomer does not invalidate a deed.

In a few states, a husband cannot convey directly to his wife, or vice versa, since according to the ancient view, the husband and wife together are but one person, and it takes two persons to make a deed. However, both husband and wife may join in a deed to a third person, who may thereupon convey to the wife.

A deed to a minor or an insane person is valid.

In many states it is required that the deed show the address of the grantee, and a deed will not be accepted for recording unless this appears in the deed. However, failure to show the address does not invalidate the deed.

§ 75. **Deeds in blank.**   The problem of whether a deed is void for want of a grantee often arises in connection with deeds where the name of the grantee is left blank at the time the deed is signed by the grantor. Of course if the blank space for the grantee's name is never filled in, the deed cannot be a good deed, for a deed must convey the land to someone. Where the name of the grantee is inserted by an agent of the grantor after the grantor has signed the deed, the deed is usually valid.

> **EXAMPLE:**   R, a landowner, signs a deed complete in all respects, except that the name of the grantee is left blank. He delivers this deed to a trusted agent, A, with directions to sell the property for not less than a certain sum. A interests E in the purchase of the property. E is willing to pay the stipulated price. A fills in E's name as grantee and delivers the deed to E. E pays the purchase price, not knowing that his name was filled in after the deed was signed. Such a deed is generally held valid, even though A's authority was merely verbal. West v. Witscher, 428 S.W.2d 538; 32 A.L.R. 737; 75 A.L.R. 1108. But a deed delivered with the description left blank is totally void. West v. Witscher, 428 S.W.2d 538.

§ 76. Consideration.   The *consideration* is the price paid for the land. Every deed should contain a recital showing that a consideration was given for the deed. The actual price paid, however, need not be stated. It is customary, in many states, for the deed to recite a consideration of $1.00 or $10, "and other good and valuable consideration."

If the deed recites a consideration, the fact that the deed represents a gift of the land and that actually no money changed hands will not invalidate the deed. An individual may give away his land if he wishes. However, a man must be just before he is generous. If the grantor is indebted at the time of the making of the gift, his creditors may thereafter have the deed set aside as in fraud of their rights. The payment of a nominal consideration, such as $10, will not suffice to sustain the deed in such a case. A valuable consideration is needed to sustain a deed against existing creditors of the grantor.

§ 77. **Support deeds.**   Parents often convey their land to a son or daughter on the understanding that such son or daughter will support the parents for the rest of their lives. Or an elderly person without close relatives may convey his land to a stranger or to a rest home in return for a promise of support. While ordinarily a deed cannot be set aside for *failure of consideration,* that is, for the reason that the grantee failed to receive what he bargained for, support deeds form an exception to the rule. Where the grantee fails to keep his promise to support, the deed can usually be set aside.

EXAMPLE: A father and mother conveyed land to their son. The mother had owned the land, and it had been the home of the parents. The deed recited a consideration of $2500. The actual consideration, however, was the son's agreement to support the parents and give them a home for the rest of their lives. Several years later, the son stopped supporting them and became so abusive that they moved out and went to live with another son. The deed was set aside. *Worrel v. West,* 129 Kan. 467, 296 P.2d 1092. The grantee is not living up to his promise unless he furnishes kindness and attention, as well as physical necessaries. *Zarembski v. Zarembski,* 382 Ill. 622, 48 N.E.2d 394.

§ 78. Words of conveyance.   Every deed must contain words of conveyance. These differ from state to state. In warranty deeds, *convey and warrant* or *grant, bargain, and sell* are often used. In quitclaim deeds the words usually are *convey and quitclaim* or *remise, release, and forever quitclaim.*

§ 79. Description of land.   A deed must describe the land conveyed. (*See* Chapter 5.)

§ 80. Warranties of title.   A warranty deed (sometimes called a *general warranty deed*) contains certain assurances or guarantees by the grantor that the deed conveys a good and unencumbered title. Such guarantees are called *covenants of title*. These covenants differ somewhat in their scope, depending on the local practice, but those usually encountered warrant or guarantee in substance:

1. That the grantor has good title to the land conveyed. This is called the *covenant of seizin*.
2. That there are no encumbrances on the land except as stated in the deed. This is called the *covenant against encumbrances*.
3. That the grantee, or his grantees, will not be evicted or disturbed by a person having a better title or lien. This is called the *covenant for quiet enjoyment*.

If the grantee suffers a loss because the title is not good as covenanted, he may sue the grantor for damages.

If any encumbrances exist that are not mentioned in the deed, the covenant against encumbrances is violated. An encumbrance, within the meaning of this covenant, includes any lien, such as a mortgage, tax lien, or judgment lien; also an easement, a restriction on the use of the land, or an outstanding dower right. The grantor's liability on this covenant is not affected by the fact that the grantee knew of the encumbrance. 64 A.L.R. 1477. If the grantor wishes to escape liability on this covenant, he must insert some qualifying language in the deed, such as *subject to a certain mortgage* (describing the mortgage), or *subject to restrictions of record*. This is called the *subject clause*.

It is still customary in many localities to set out in full in the warranty deed the various covenants of title. However, in many states, laws exist under which the usual covenants of title are implied from the use of certain specified words. When these particular words are used, the deed must be read as though the usual covenants of title were set out in full therein. In Alaska, Illinois, Kansas, Michigan, Minnesota, and Wisconsin, the words *convey and warrant* make a deed a general warranty deed. The same result is achieved in Pennsylvania, Vermont, Virginia, and West Virginia by use of the words *warrant generally,* and in Arkansas, Florida, Idaho, Missouri, and Nevada by the words *grant, bargain, and sell.*

The fact that the seller is willing to give a general warranty deed is little or no assurance that he has good, clear title to the land. Suppose that I were to sit down this instant and write out a warranty deed conveying the Empire State Building to you. Clearly this warranty deed would give you no title to that valuable property for the simple reason that I don't own it. You would, of course, have the right to sue me for breach of my covenants of warranty.

A *special warranty deed* is one in which the grantor covenants only against the lawful claims of all persons claiming by, through, or under him. The grantor is liable in such case if his grantee is disturbed by some claim arising through an act of the grantor himself. For example, if, prior to the execution of the deed, the grantor has himself placed a mortgage on the land that the deed fails to mention, and thereafter the grantee is compelled to pay off the mortgage, the grantor is liable for the damages thus sustained by the grantee. But if the grantor has in no way encumbered the title, but later an outstanding title is asserted by some third person, the grantor is not liable. In some states, Mississippi, Pennsylvania, Vermont, Virginia, and West Virginia, for example, use of the words *warrant specially* is sufficient to create a covenant of special warranty. In California, Idaho, and North Dakota, use of the word *grant* achieves the same purpose.

§ 81. **Waiver of dower and homestead.**   In some states, a deed must contain a clause releasing and relinquishing all homestead, dower, and curtesy rights in the premises.

§ 82. **Date.**   A date is not essential to the validity of a deed, though it is the universal custom to date all deeds.

§ 83. **Signature.**   The signature of the grantor is essential to the validity of the deed. A *forgery* (i.e., a deed to which some unauthorized third person has affixed the grantor's signature) is a nullity and conveys no title whatever.

The fact that the grantor's signature is misspelled will not invalidate the deed.

If the grantor is unable to write, he may sign by mark, in which case the signature line appears as follows:

His

"John × Smith (Seal)"

Mark

Everything but the "×" may be typed. The "×" must be affixed by the grantor.

Occasionally a deed is signed not by the grantor himself, but by an *attorney in fact*. An attorney in fact is simply an agent authorized by the landowner to sell and convey his real estate. In order for such deed to be valid, the following requirements exist:

1. The landowner must first sign and deliver to his attorney in fact a written instrument, called a *power of attorney*, authorizing such attorney to sell and convey the land in question. Such an instrument must be as formal as the deed itself. In states that require a deed to be sealed, the power of attorney must be sealed. In states that require a deed to be witnessed, the power of attorney must be witnessed. All the other requirements relating to deeds should be observed, including acknowledgment and recording.
2. The deed must name the landowner, not the attorney in fact, as the grantor.
3. The name signed to the deed should be that of the landowner. Under the usual method, the attorney signs the grantor's name and then places his name beneath that of the grantor, as follows:

"John Smith (Seal)"

"By Henry Brown, his Attorney in Fact."

4. The grantor must be alive on the date of the delivery of the deed, since death of the grantor automatically terminates the power of attorney. Insanity of the grantor may have the same result.
5. Since the landowner ordinarily has the power to terminate the agency at any time and thus take away the attorney's power to execute deeds on his behalf, it should be established that the agency actually had not been terminated or revoked at the date of the delivery of the deed.

The technical mode of executing the deed of a corporation is for the proper officer to sign the corporate name, adding his own signature and official title beneath the name of the corporation. Usually the corporate bylaws provide that deeds shall be signed by a president or vice-president and a secretary or assistant secretary.

§ 84. **Seal.**   In some states, principally eastern states, a seal is essential to the validity of a deed. In most states, however, a seal is unnecessary, though the custom of using a seal persists. But even in those states where a deed by an individual need not bear a seal, a deed executed by a corporation should have the official corporate seal affixed.

§ 85. **Witnesses.**   In many states a deed must be witnessed, two witnesses being the number commonly required. Most states require witnessing where the deed is signed by mark.

§ 86. **State tax.** State laws imposing a tax on deeds will be encountered in many states. It is usually required that such tax be paid or the land sale be noted on the tax records before recording of the deed will be permitted.

§ 87. **Delivery of deeds.** Delivery is essential to the validity of a deed. The word *delivery* is somewhat misleading, since it would lead one to believe that it is necessary that the deed be actually handed by the grantor to the grantee. This is not the case. Delivery is simply the final act by which the grantor, who has previously signed the deed, signifies his intention that the deed shall take effect. Whether or not a deed has been delivered depends primarily on the *intention* of the grantor. The test is: Did the grantor *do* or *say* anything to show his intention to pass ownership of the land to the grantee? A deed may be delivered by acts without words or by words without acts, though ordinarily there are both words and acts in the making of a delivery.

> **EXAMPLE:** At the closing of a deal, the buyer, B, hands A, the seller, a check. A signs the deed and, without saying a word hands it to B. There is a delivery.

> **EXAMPLE:** At the closing of a deal all the papers, including A's signed deed, are on the closing table. Having received his check A tells B (the grantee) to take his deed. There is a delivery.

> **EXAMPLE:** A signs a deed conveying real estate to B and hands it to B, not with the intention of passing title, but with the understanding that B will check the legal description to see if it is sufficient. There is no delivery.

> **EXAMPLE:** A signs a deed conveying real esate to B but leaves it in his office while he is still thinking over the deal. B steals the deed from A's office and shows it to C, who purchases from B, relying on B's possession of the deed. C acquires no title. There is no delivery of the deed.

§ 88. **Delivery problems where there are several grantors.** Suppose A and B own certain land, and both of them sign a deed running to C as grantee. A hands the deed to B for the sole purpose of having the deed checked by their lawyer. Without A's permission, B hands the deed to C and collects the sale price from him. This is not a good deed so far as A is concerned. He still owns his half interest. One joint grantor who is not authorized by his co-tenant cannot make a valid delivery of the deed that will be binding on the latter. 162 A.L.R. 892.

When land is owned by several persons, all of them named as grantors in one deed, and one of the grantors signs the deed and hands it to the grantee with the statement that his consent to the sale of the land is conditioned on the other grantors also signing the deed, such deed is inoperative unless all grantors sign. *Logue v. Von Almen,* 379 Ill. 208, 40 N.E.2d 73; 14 *Col. L. Rev.* 389.

§ 89. **Delivery during lifetime of the grantor.**   Delivery of a deed must be made in the lifetime of the grantor.

EXAMPLE: On *R's* death, an envelope with *E's* name on it is found in *R's* safety deposit box. The envelope is opened and found to contain a deed from *R* to *E*. The deed is void for want of delivery.

A deed is the proper instrument for transferring ownership of land from one living person to another, and, in general, this means that the deed, to be effective, must operate while both parties are alive.

However, I may legally deliver a deed to you here and now with a clause therein stating that the deed is to take effect only at my death. The deed gives you the right *now* to enjoy the property at my death. 31 A.L.R.2d 535.

§ 90. **Delivery to third persons.**   Where the grantor hands the deed not to the grantee, but to some third person, a wholly new set of rules comes into play. A number of different situations present themselves.

EXAMPLE: A signs a deed running to B as grantee and hands the deed to B's lawyer, C, with the intention of giving B ownership of the land here and now. This is delivery to an *agent of the grantee* and is good delivery.

EXAMPLE: A signs a deed running to B as grantee and hands the deed to his own lawyer to check its form. There is no intention to transfer ownership and no delivery. Here the deed has been handed to the *agent of the grantor.*

EXAMPLE: A enters into a contract to sell land to B and pursuant thereto signs a deed to B. However, he hands the deed to XYZ Bank with directions to deliver the deed to B when certain moneys are paid by B to the bank. This is an *escrow.* (See Chapter 13.)

EXAMPLE: A signs a deed running to his son, B, as grantee, hands the deed to C, and directs C to hand the deed to B after A's death. This brings up the subject of *death escrows.* This is a good delivery as long as it is clear that A intended to part with all control over the land once he handed the deed to C. Oddly enough, the courts allow A, in such cases, to use the land during his lifetime. They do not regard this as inconsistent with the passing of ownership to B. It is as though A had conveyed outright to B, but had reserved a life estate in the property. *Bury v. Young,* 98 Cal. 446, 33 Pac. 338.

§ 91. **Family transactions.**   If a father executes a deed to a minor child, which deed is beneficial to the child, and the father indicates by his words and conduct that he intends the deed to operate at once, actual delivery is unnecessary. Indeed, the courts are most reluctant to upset a deed that is made as a gift by a parent to a child.

§ 92. **Acceptance.**   For a deed to transfer ownership of land, it is necessary that the grantor intend to transfer ownership to the grantee and that the grantee intend to accept ownership of the land. That is to say, delivery by the grantor must be accompanied by acceptance of the deed by the grantee. 74 A.L.R.2d 992. Only rarely will disputes arise regarding acceptance, and the courts are not disposed to be technical about it. Indeed, the courts have gone so far as to hold that if the grantor makes and records a deed without the knowledge of the grantee, ownership will nevertheless pass if the grantee, on being informed of the deed, assents to it, even though this takes place after the death of the grantor. *Mann v. Jummel,* 183 Ill. 523, 56 N.E. 161. Also, if the grantee dies before learning of the deed, his acceptance will be presumed and the deed held good. *Lessee of Mitchell v. Ryan,* 3 Ohio St. 377.

§ 93. **Acknowledgment.**   A deed is usually acknowledged by the grantors before a notary public or some other official. (*See* Chapter 8.)

§ 94. **Recording.**   Virtually all deeds are filed for record in some public office. (*See* Chapter 9.)

§ 95. **Official conveyances.**   Deeds by executors, administrators, guardians of minors, conservators or guardians of insane persons, sheriffs, masters in chancery, receivers, trustees in bankruptcy, and other similar conveyances usually depend for their validity on prior court proceedings. In addition, numerous technical requirements exist that frequently expose such deeds to attack. A discussion of such requirements is not within the scope of this book.

§ 96. **Fraud, coercion and mistake.**   A deed obtained by fraud, misrepresentation, or coercion may be set aside by proper court proceedings. This is particularly true when through old age, mental weakness, ignorance, illness, or some other cause, the grantor was incapable of coping with the grantee, and due to such incapacity of the grantor the grantee has obtained the property for substantially less than its value. Fraud is discussed further in Chapter 11.

Mutual mistake occurs where both parties are under some misapprehension.

EXAMPLE: A owns tracts X and Y. Believing he is buying tract X, B receives and pays for a deed conveying tract Y, while A believes B wishes to buy tract Y. The deed will be set aside and the money refunded to B.

§ 97. **After-acquired title.**   If the grantor in a warranty deed does not have title, or does not have complete title, at the time of executing the deed, but thereafter acquires title, such title will automatically pass to his grantee without any additional conveyance.

EXAMPLE: X, a landowner dies without a will, leaving three sons, A, B, and C, as his only heirs. Each thus becomes an owner of a one-third interest in X's land. A and B, believing C to have died long ago, after a mysterious disappearance, make a warranty deed of the land to D. After that, C who was living in a different town under an assumed name, dies, leaving his brothers A and B as his sole heirs. The title, thus acquired by A and B from C immediately passes to D, giving him complete title to the land.

§ 98. **Title conveyed by deed.**   If the grantor owns the land in fee simple, and the deed contains no qualifying language, the deed gives the grantee good fee simple title to the land. However, deeds often contain qualifying language, which results in the grantee's acquiring something less than the fee simple title.

EXAMPLE: A makes a deed conveying land to B "and the heirs of his body." In some states, B acquires only a life estate by such deed, and his children acquire the remainder. In other states, such a deed will give B the full fee simple title to the land.

EXAMPLE: A conveys land to B by a deed that contains the following clause: "to have and to hold for and during the grantee's life." B acquires only a life estate by this deed.

The law on this subject is so complex and contains so many refinements of reasoning that no one but an experienced attorney should attempt to interpret a deed containing any qualifying language whatever. In particular, words as "heirs," "heirs of the body," "issue," and "death without issue" are danger signals. Indiscriminate use of such language is an invitation to a lawsuit.

§ 99. **Fee or easement.**   It is frequently difficult to determine whether a deed conveys complete ownership (fee simple title) or only an easement. If a deed, even a warranty deed, conveys not the land itself, but a "right of way over the following land," it is universally held that the grantee receives an easement only, not the fee simple title. Suppose the deed conveys certain land and that immediately following the legal description is the phrase, "as a right of way." Here again it seems agreed that the grantee receives only an easement. 136 A.L.R. 379. This is particularly true where the deed runs to a railroad. 6 A.L.R.3rd 973. Suppose, however, the deed conveys the land to E and that following the land description is the phrase, "for a road," or "to be used as a road." In some states, such a deed passes only an easement for road purposes, but in other

states such a deed will convey the fee title, not merely an easement. 23
Am.Jur.2d 243.

§ 100. **Exceptions and reservations.** In conveying land, the
grantor often wishes to retain some part of the land described or to
reserve some right therein. This is accomplished by inserting in the deed
the proper clauses of *exception* and *reservation*. An exception withholds
from the operation of the deed title to a part of the land described in the
deed. Thus a deed of Lot 1 *excepting the north twenty feet thereof* does
not pass ownership of the north twenty feet of the lot. That portion was
excepted from the conveyance. A *reservation* is the creation by the deed
of a new right in favor of the grantor, usually an easement or life estate.
Thus in a deed of Lot 1 *reserving to the grantor an easement for ingress
and egress over and across the north twenty feet of Lot 1,* ownership of
the north twenty feet passes to the grantee, but an easement is reserved
in favor of the grantor. Sometimes the terms *excepting* and *reserving* are
used inaccurately, and the courts will hold that a true reservation was
created by use of the word *excepting* or that a true exception was created
by the use of the word *reserving.*

EXAMPLE: R conveys certain land to E "except the north ten feet for a
right of way." Ownership of the entire tract, including the north ten feet, passes
to E, but the quoted clause reserves an easement for R over the north ten feet. 139
A.L.R. 1348.

It is possible for the grantor in a deed to reserve a life estate in the
property conveyed. Often to save the expense of probating a will after
his death, a father, while still living, will give a deed of his land to his
son or daughter, and in the deed will reserve to himself a life estate. The
grantee becomes the owner of the land, and the grantor retains the use
thereof for his lifetime.

WARNING: Once such a deed is signed, the grantor cannot recall it.
The psychological effect of this change in circumstances often brings about friction
between the parent and child. Hence such transactions should be avoided, if possible.

§ 101. Suggestions.

1. *Form of deed.* If there is a contract for the sale of land, find out if the
contract specifies the form of deed to be given. If the contract specifies that the seller
is to give a warranty deed, then, of course, a warranty deed form must be used. If the
contract does not specify the form of the deed, in most states a quitclaim deed will
suffice. The seller will prefer to use this form, since it subjects him to no personal liability
for defects in title. If there is no written contract for the sale of the land, the seller will
again prefer to give a quitclaim deed.

2. *Grantor.* Check the deed by which the grantor acquired ownership and

see that his name is spelled the same way in the deed by which he is conveying the land. Any difference in spelling may lead to an objection when the title is examined. If a woman acquires title by her maiden name and subsequently marries, the deed should show both names: *Mary Jones, formerly Mary Smith.* Any examiner of the title will thus find a connected chain of title to the land. The grantor's marital status should be given: *bachelor, spinster, widow, widower, divorced and not remarried.* If the grantor is married, his spouse should also be named as grantor, and their marital status given: *John Smith and Mary Smith, his wife.* A married woman or widow should never be described as "Mrs. John Jones." Her legal name is "Mary Jones." Don't describe yourself as "R. John Smith." Legally your middle name or middle initial is no part of your name. Hence you should at least describe yourself as "Robert John Smith," for it is poor practice to use initials only in legal documents. If the state law requires, give the street address of the grantor and grantee. Special forms of deeds are used where the grantor is a corporation, trustee, executor, and so on. Of course all the landowners must convey if the buyer is to get good title, but different landowners may use different deeds. As a rule it is best for a husband and wife to join in the same deed.

3. *Grantee.* Have the proposed grantee write out his name on a slip of paper—first name, middle initial, if any, and last name—and copy the name in this identical form in the proper place in the deed form. His or her marital status may, but need not, be given. State grantee's place of residence. If two or more persons are acquiring title, the names of all must be shown in the deed. If they are taking title as joint tenants, use a joint tenancy form deed. Legal stationers usually print a special form for joint tenancy transactions. Following the names of the grantees in this form is a phrase reading somewhat like this: *as joint tenants with the right of survivorship and not as tenants in common nor as tenants by the entireties.* When husband and wife are taking title, their marital relation should be shown, as *John Smith and Mary Smith, his wife.* If a corporation is taking title, its charter should be checked and the name copied exactly and without the slightest deviation. For example, if the charter describes a corporation as The Elite Hat Shop, Inc., do not omit the *The* and do not spell out the *Inc.* A deed to a trustee should clearly identify the trust. Never draft a deed running simply to *John Smith, as trustee.* Have the deed run to *John Smith, as trustee under Trust Agreement dated June 15, 1946, and known as the Pinecrest Liquidation Trust,* or other proper designation. Have before you the trust instrument creating the trust and describe it accurately in the deed. If the deed to the trustee also creates the trust, it is serving a double purpose. (1) It is operating as a deed of the land and must contain all the necessary elements of a deed. (2) It is creating a trust and must contain all the requisite elements for the creation of a trust. Such a document should be drafted only by one thoroughly conversant with the law of trusts.

The deed should conform to the contract of sale with respect to the grantees. For example, if A contracts to sell to B and C, A should not, even though B requests it, make a deed running to B only. That would violate C's rights and make A liable for damages if C suffers a loss.

If you are creating a corporation that is to acquire real estate, be sure that the corporation's charter has been issued and that all other formalities for corporate existence are complied with *before* the deed to the corporation is made out. In other words, be sure you have an existing, legal grantee to whom to convey.

4. *Consideration.* Let deed recite a monetary consideration, as *in consideration of the sum of $10 and other good and valuable consideration.* In a few states, it is customary or necessary to recite the true sale price of the land. In deeds by corporations, trustees, executors, and so forth, the deed should recite the true sale price.

5. *Words of grant.* Every printed form of deed contains words of grant. It

is not necessary to tamper with these, since the warranty deed form will have words appropriate for a warranty deed, the quitclaim deed form will also have appropriate words.

6. *Description.* Do not attempt to draft a description unless you are sure you know what you are doing. If a title policy, abstract, or Torrens certificate has been previously issued on the land that is being sold, and the land sold is identical with the tract mentioned in the title policy, abstract, or Torrens certificate (that is, there have been no subsequent conveyances of portions of the tract, and so forth), then the description may be copied from title policy, abstract caption, or Torrens certificate, since such documents usually contain accurate descriptions. After the description has been copied into the deed form, have someone read it aloud to you while you follow the description in the title policy, abstract, or Torrens certificate, since even a microscopic error in typing may throw the whole description off.

7. *Subject clause.* If the grantor in a warranty deed wishes to avoid personal liability, he should include in the subject clause all defects in title, such as mortgages, unpaid taxes, existing leases, restrictions, and so forth. However, the contract of sale usually specifies to what objections the title will be subject when conveyed to the buyer; the seller, in preparing the deed, has no right to add items to this list. For example, if the seller agrees, by his contract, to convey the land to the buyer subject only to a certain mortgage, he cannot include in the deed *subject to mortgage recorded as document No. 10356789 and also to restrictions of record.* The buyer has the right to object to the inclusion of the portion relating to the restrictions, since restrictions were not mentioned in the contract. In a quitclaim deed, a subject clause is unnecessary and inappropriate.

8. *Mortgages.* If the land is being sold subject to a mortgage that the grantee is to assume and agree to pay, let the deed so state.

SUGGESTED FORM: "Subject to a mortgage recorded in Book 100, Page 101, as Document No. 999, which the grantee herein assumes and agrees to pay." (See § 393.)

Where the buyer is paying part cash and giving back to the seller either a mortgage or mortgage trust deed for part of the purchase money, it is better that the deed contain a recital somewhat as follows: "As part of the consideration for this transaction, the grantee herein has this day executed to _____, as trustee, a trust deed, of even date herewith, securing a promissory note in the sum of $_____, which represents part of the purchase price for said premises." This is particularly desirable where a mortgage deed of trust is involved, since if A sells and conveys land to B, and B simultaneously executes a mortgage trust deed to C, as trustee, the public records do not clearly show that the trust deed was given as part of the purchase price unless the deed contains the suggested recital. Of course the trust deed or mortgage should also contain a recital that "this trust deed is given to secure payment of part of the purchase price of said premises."

9. *Statement of purpose of deed.* Inexperienced conveyancers tend to put in deeds various legal-sounding phrases without having any clear idea of what purpose such phrases were intended to serve. This is a very dangerous practice. Do not insert a single syllable in a deed unless you are certain what the legal effect of that insertion will be. Remember that if you add in your deed phrases like "to be used for road purposes," the result may be to create a grant of an easement out of what started to be a deed of the land. It is neither necessary nor desirable to state in the deed the purpose for which the land is to be used.

10. *Restrictions and conditions.*   Restrictions and conditions must be drafted with care. Because of the drastic consequences attendant upon the enforcement of a reverter clause, the grantee should view with suspicion any attempt to insert a reverter clause in the deed. (See Chapter 27.) If there is a written contract for the sale of the land, the grantor has no right to insert in the deed any restrictions or conditions not provided for in the contract. If the contract provides for a building restriction, but says nothing about a condition or reverter clause, the grantor has no right to provide in the deed for a reverter of title in the event of a breach of condition. Be sure you understand the words you use in drafting restrictions, as, for example, residence purposes, dwellings purposes, business purposes. Certain words have a well-known technical meaning, and if you use such words in a deed, courts will give them their usual meaning, regardless of what special, individual meaning they may have in your own mind. You will not even be allowed to testify that such a word has a special meaning for you. On the other hand, inexperienced draftsmen often use words that have no meaning at all, such as the provision that "only houses of standard construction shall be erected on said premises." It would be difficult to get two people to agree on the definition of "standard construction." Such a phrase is so devoid of meaning that courts cannot enforce it.

11. *Easements.*   A deed may contain a grant to the grantee of an easement over other lands of the seller. If there is a written contract of sale, and it makes no mention of such an easement, the seller is under no obligation to include it in the deed. A deed may reserve to the grantor an easement over the land conveyed. If there is a written contract of sale, and it makes no mention of such an easement, the grantor has no right to insert such a clause in the deed. For the language of a deed clause granting or reserving an easement, see Chapter 4.

12. *Waiver of dower and homestead.*   Almost without exception, deed forms prepared by your local stationers include the necessary waivers of dower and homestead rights. For this and other reasons, it is dangerous to use a deed form printed in your state in conveying land lying in some other state. Obtain a form printed in the state where the land lies.

13. *Date.*   It is the custom to date all deeds.

14. *Signature.*   Before permitting the grantor to sign, have him write his name on a piece of paper. Check the spelling with the spelling of his name in the body of the deed. Be sure that the two correspond, since even trivial variations are frequently objected to by title examiners. Type the name of the grantor beneath the signature line and direct him to sign exactly as his name is typed.

15. *Seal.*   If a seal is needed on deeds of land in your state, deed forms printed in your state will show a seal on the signature line. If there are more signatures on the deed than there are printed signature lines, be sure the word *Seal* appears after each signature. The corporate seal is always necessary on deeds made by corporations.

16. *Tax stamps.*   The necessary tax stamps should be attached where the state law requires this.

17. *Witnesses.*   Always have two or more witnesses sign the deed if any grantor has signed by mark. If all grantors are able to write, their signatures need not be witnessed unless the state law requires witnesses. Some states require that all deeds be witnessed.

18. *Acknowledgment.*   This subject is discussed in Chapter 8.

19. *Recording.*   File your deed in the proper public office immediately after it has been acknowledged. Delay may prove disastrous. (See Chapter 9.)

ACKNOWLEDGMENTS

§ 102. **Defined.**   An acknowledgment is a formal declaration made before some public officer, usually a notary public, by a person who has signed a deed, mortgage, or other instrument, that the instrument is his voluntary act and deed. This ceremony is the *act of acknowledgment*. *In Re McCauley's Adoption,* 177 Neb. 759, 131 N.W.2d 174.

§ 103. **Certificate of acknowledgment.**   The officer before whom this declaration is made attaches his certificate to the instrument or fills in the printed form of certificate that appears on virtually all deed and mortgage forms. This is known as the *certificate of acknowledgment*. It usually recites that the grantor appeared before the officer and acknowledged that he executed the instrument as his free and voluntary act and deed. However, the form of the certificate of acknowledgment varies considerably from state to state.

An acknowledgment must not be confused with an affidavit. An *affidavit* is a statement made under oath and put in writing. At the conclusion of the affidavit the officer, usually a notary, recites that it was *subscribed and sworn to*. An affidavit is not acceptable as a substitute for an acknowledgment. The two serve different purposes.

§ 104. **Waiver of dower and homestead rights.**   In some states, the certificate of acknowledgment must specifically state that dower and homestead rights were understandingly relinquished.

§ 105. **Necessity of acknowledgment.**   In a few states, Arizona and Ohio, for example, an unacknowledged deed is not valid. In a number of states, certain types of instruments, such as deeds of married women or deeds or mortgages of homestead land, must be acknowledged. Other deeds, however, are legally valid though not acknowledged. This statement is without practical significance, since, as a practical matter, every deed or mortgage should be acknowledged. In the great majority of the states an unacknowledged instrument is not entitled to be recorded (59 A.L.R.2d 1302) and an unrecorded title is a precarious one indeed. Lack of an acknowledgment on a deed may render title unmarketable. Other technical reasons make an acknowledgment a practical necessity.

§ 106. **Who may take an acknowledgment.**　A deed or mortgage may be acknowledged before a notary public or some other officer designated by the local law. Such a person, it is said, *takes* the acknowledgment of the grantor. However, if the officer has any financial interest in the transaction, he is disqualified. For example, a grantee in a deed would be clearly disqualified from taking the grantor's acknowledgment. Other disqualified parties include the grantor in a deed, mortgagor and mortgagee in a mortgage, and the trustee in a trust deed. In some states, a stockholder of a corporation that is a party to the instrument is disqualified from taking the acknowledgment of the corporation. In other states, a stockholder may take the corporation's acknowledgment.

§ 107. **Venue.**　The venue of the certificate of acknowledgment is the caption, which is usually shown as follows:

STATE OF ILLINOIS ⎫
　　　　　　　　　　⎬ SS
COUNTY OF COOK ⎭

The venue shows the place where the acknowledgment took place, that is, the place where the grantor appeared before the notary and made his formal declaration that the deed was his voluntary act.

§ 108. **Effect of invalidity of acknowledgment.**　It is important to keep in mind the fact that invalidity of the *acknowledgment* does not make the *deed* void. However, in most states, a valid acknowledgment is essential for proper recording; that is, if the acknowledgment is void, the deed, though recorded, is treated as an unrecorded deed.

§ 109. **Foreign acknowledgments.**　One who owns land located in a state other than that in which he resides, may sign and acknowledge a deed in the state of his residence. The acknowledgment will be valid if it conforms either to the law of the state of his residence or to the law of the state where the land lies. An acknowledgment taken outside of the state where the land lies is known as a *foreign acknowledgment*. In some states, it is required, either by custom or by law, that every acknowledgment taken outside of the state have attached thereto a certificate by a court clerk to the effect that the officer taking the acknowledgment was authorized by law to do so. This is known as a *certificate of authenticity*, or a *certificate of magistracy*. If the certificate goes on to recite that the acknowledgment is in due form, it is known as a *certificate of authenticity and conformity*, or *certificate of magistracy and conformity*.

§ 110. **Date of certificate of acknowledgment.**   The date of the certificate of acknowledgment is unimportant. Hence omission of the date of the certificate or insertion of an incorrect date will not invalidate the acknowledgment.

§ 111. **Signature of officer taking acknowledgment.**   The certificate of acknowledgment must be signed by the officer taking the acknowledgment. Otherwise it is not valid. The certificate should also show the official character of the person taking the acknowledgment, as Notary Public, Justice of the Peace, and so forth.

§ 112. **Seal.**   An acknowledgment taken by a notary public is usually invalid unless his official seal is placed on the certificate. The requirements as to seals of officers other than notaries vary from state to state.

§ 113. **Date of expiration of commission.**   Failure of the notary public to show the date his commission expires does not invalidate the certificate.

§ 114. **False acknowledgment.**   Both the notary public and the surety on his official bond will be liable for damages caused by the notary's willful misconduct, as where the notary falsely certifies to a forged mortgage and the mortgage is sold to an innocent purchaser. 17 A.L.R.2d 950. The notary and his surety will also be liable when the notary's negligence causes damage, as when the notary acknowledges the signatures on a forged mortgage without knowing the parties who appear before him and without procuring any evidence or information as to their identity. 17 A.L.R.2d 957.

Chapter 9

RECORDING AND
CONSTRUCTIVE NOTICE

§ 115. **Necessity of recording.** Every state has a recording law. These laws provide, in substance, that, until it is recorded, a deed or mortgage is ineffective and void so far as subsequent purchasers or mortgagees of the same land are concerned. The policy behind these laws is that the ownership of real estate should be disclosed by the public records, and that purchasers of land should be able to rely on these records and should be protected against secret, unrecorded deeds and mortgages. Under these laws, although an unrecorded deed or mortgage is good and valid *as between the parties to the instrument,* the grantee or mortgagee is in great danger of losing his rights, because persons who deal with the real estate in ignorance of the unrecorded deed or mortgage will be protected against such unrecorded deed or mortgage.

> **EXAMPLE:** A, the owner of certain vacant land, sells the same to B and gives B a deed, which B fails to record. Later A dies, and his heirs, not knowing that he had previously sold the land, deed the land to C, who records his deed. C purchases in ignorance of the earlier deed to B. C gets good title to the real estate. He is an *innocent purchaser* or *bona fide purchaser.*

§ 116. **Constructive notice from the records.** The recording laws have a double operation or effect. While they protect a purchaser or mortgagee who acts in ignorance of an earlier unrecorded deed or mortgage, they also provide that if a deed or mortgage is, in fact, recorded, it will be taken for granted that all persons who thereafter have occasion to deal with the tract of land do so with full knowledge of such recorded deed or mortgage. The courts will not permit a man to say that he acted in ignorance of a recorded deed or mortgage. Every purchaser or mortgagee of land, it is said, is *charged with notice* of prior recorded deeds and mortgages. The courts say that the public records impart to all subsequent purchasers and mortgagees *constructive notice* of all prior recorded deeds and mortgages.

Constructive notice is a legal substitute for actual knowledge. The law requires that persons intending to purchase real estate or loan money on mortgages thereon examine the public records relating to the tract of land in question. Whether or not such purchaser or mortgagee actually examines the records, the law will assume that he knows everything he would have learned by such examination and will not permit him to say that actually no such examination was made.

EXAMPLE: A conveys land to B, who records his deed. Thereafter A persuades C to buy the same land, telling C that he still owns the land. C fails to examine the public records relating to this tract of land. C acquires nothing. He has constructive notice of the deed to B.

§ 117. **Office where deeds are recorded.** The name of the officer charged with the duty of keeping the public records of deeds and mortgages varies from state to state. He is known variously as a recorder of deeds, county recorder, register of deeds, and registrar of deeds. For convenience, the officer in charge is hereinafter referred to as the *recorder*, and the public office where deeds are filed or recorded is referred to as the *recorder's office*.

§ 118. **What constitutes recording.** A person wishing to record a deed or mortgage simply deposits it with the recorder. Such a deed or mortgage is said to be filed for record. It is thereupon deemed to be recorded, and all the world must take notice of its existence. The recorder copies the document in his record books, indexes it, and returns the original to the person who left it for recording. He does not pass on the validity of the document.

§ 119. **Persons protected by recording laws.** The recording laws are designed primarily to protect subsequent *bona fide purchasers* of the land. A bona fide purchaser is one who has paid the purchase price in good faith and without knowledge of the prior unrecorded deed or mortgage. A mortgagee who loans money in reliance on the public records is also considered a bona fide purchaser and is entitled to the protection of the recording laws.

EXAMPLE: A mortgages his land to B, which mortgage is not recorded.

Thereafter, A puts a mortgage on the same land to C, and C records his mortgage. C does not know of the earlier mortgage to B. C has a first mortgage on the land.

A number of states add the requirement that to be entitled to protection the subsequent purchaser or mortgagee must file his deed or mortgage for record before the recording of the earlier deed or mortgage. Under this rule, for example, it will not suffice that A has purchased a tract of land in good faith and in ignorance of an earlier unrecorded mortgage. He must also record his deed before the prior mortgage is recorded. But if he records his deed in apt time, A is protected even if the mortgagee later discovers his oversight and proceeds to record his mortgage.

In some states, a judgment creditor is also protected against prior unrecorded deeds and mortgages.

EXAMPLE: A makes a mortgage to B on November 15. The mortgage is recorded on November 20. On November 17, C obtains a judgment against A. The judgment enjoys priority of lien over the mortgage, since it was rendered prior to the recording of the mortgage.

A substantial number of states, however, do not extend such protection to judgment creditors.

A person who has acquired land by gift is not protected by the recording laws.

EXAMPLE: A mortgages his land to B. B fails to record the mortgage. A thereafter gives his daughter, C, a deed to the land as a gift, and C records her deed. B can nevertheless enforce the mortgage against her. But if, prior to the recording of the mortgage, C should sell the land to D, D, being a purchaser, would get good title free and clear of the prior, unrecorded mortgage.

A person who acquires title by will or as an heir of the landowner is not protected.

EXAMPLE: A makes a mortgage to B, which B fails to record. Thereafter A dies leaving a will whereby he gives this land to his son, C. B may enforce this mortgage against C.

§ 120. **Instruments entitled to recording.** Deeds, mortgages, release deeds, satisfactions of mortgages, assignments of mortgages, and other instruments affecting the title to land should be recorded. However, it is only the original instrument that is entitled to be recorded. The recording of an unsigned carbon copy of an instrument is without legal effect.

§ 121. **Foreign language.** A deed or mortgage written in a foreign language, though valid as between the parties thereto, does not impart constructive notice and must be treated as an unrecorded document. *Moroz v. Ransom,* 158 Misc. 443, 285 N.Y.S. 846.

§ **122. Prerequisites to valid recording.** In a great majority of the states, an instrument must be properly acknowledged by the grantor or mortgagor in order to be entitled to recording. In a number of states, proper witnessing is accepted as a substitute for an acknowledgment. But if the instrument is neither witnessed nor acknowledged, or the witnessing or acknowledgment is fatally defective, the instrument is not considered as a recorded instrument even though the recorder accepts it and copies it on the public records.

Since a purchaser or mortgagee is under no obligation to examine the records affecting lands other than those that he is buying or upon which he is loaning money, the record of an instrument that was intended to convey or affect the same but which has such an erroneous description that it does not appear to affect the land in question does not bind any subsequent purchaser, mortgagee, or judgment creditor.

EXAMPLE: A owns the West Half of the Northwest Quarter of Section 14, Township 38 North, Range 13 East of the Third Principal Meridian. A executes a mortgage to B that is intended as a mortgage on this same land but which, through inadvertence, describes the land as falling in Section 24 instead of Section 14. The mortgage is recorded. A person searching the records as to A's title has no way of knowing that this mortgage was intended for the particular land in question. Therefore this mortgage does not impart constructive notice, and subsequent purchasers, mortgagees, and judgment creditors will be protected against this mortgage.

§ **123. Chain of title.** Except in a few states a title searcher tracing title by means of the public records employs an official index of names, called the Grantor-Grantee Index. Suppose, for example, that the United States Government records show that the United States sold a particular tract of land to John Jones on March 15, 1840. The title searcher will turn to the Grantor Index, which is arranged alphabetically, and, beginning with the date March 15, 1840, he will look under the letter "J" for any deeds or mortgages made since March 15, 1840, by John Jones. Naturally he would not expect to find any deeds or mortgages of that land made by Jones prior to March 15, 1840, because Jones did not become the owner until that date. Therefore the law does not require him to look for any such deeds or mortgages prior to that date. Suppose he finds that John Jones conveyed the land to Joseph Smith by deed dated September 10, 1860, and recorded November 1, 1860. He will now look under the letter "S" for any deeds or mortgages made by Smith on or after September 10, 1860, the date when Smith acquired title. This process is repeated until he has brought the title down to the present. This process is called *running the chain of title.*

To be considered properly recorded, a deed or mortgage must be in the *chain of title*, that is, it must be dated in the proper chronological order.

EXAMPLES: At a time when his negotiations for the purchase were virtually concluded, Joseph Smith made a mortgage on the land dated September 5, 1860, and recorded September 6, 1860. Both of these dates were prior to the date of the deed by which Smith later acquired ownership, namely, September 10, 1860. A title searcher would not find this mortgage, since he would not look under the name "Smith" for any deed or mortgage prior to September 10, 1860. Such a mortgage is not in the line of title. It is also said that the mortgage is not in the *chain of title*. The *legal result is the same as though the mortgage had not been recorded at all.* A person buying the land not knowing of the existence of this mortgage would get good title free and clear of the mortgage.

In other words, the records show the ownership of land passing from one person to another, and the name of each successive owner as that name appears on the public records must be searched only during the period of his ownership as such period is revealed by the public records to see what recorded deeds and mortgages he has signed.

Because of the *chain of title theory*, it is important that names be spelled correctly in deeds and mortgages.

EXAMPLE: A deed runs to *John O. Malley* and a mortgage is thereafter made by *John O'Malley*. The mortgage is not in the chain of title and is treated as an unrecorded mortgage. The deed is indexed under M, the mortgage under O.

§ **124. Tract indexes.** In a few states (Iowa, Lousiana, Nebraska, North Dakota, Oklahoma, South Dakota, Utah, Wisconsin, and Wyoming, for example), the name index (Grantor-Grantee Index) has been supplemented by a Tract Index. This index allocates a separate page in the index to each piece of property in the county, and if you are interested in a particular piece of property, you simply locate the proper page in the index, where you will find listed all recorded deeds and other documents relating to this piece of property.

§ **125. Record as notice of contents of deed or mortgage.** An instrument duly recorded is notice to subsequent purchasers and mortgagees not only of the instrument itself, but also of all of its contents.

EXAMPLE: A warranty deed contained a covenant that the premises were free and clear of all encumbrances "except a certain mortgage for $900." This mortgage had not been recorded. This was notice to the grantee and to all other persons of the existence of the mortgage.

§ **126. Effect of actual knowledge.** Of course one who actually knows of a prior unrecorded deed or mortgage is not protected against it.

EXAMPLE: A makes a mortgage to B, which B fails to record. Thereafter, A mortgages the land to C, who knows of the existence of the earlier mortgage. C takes subject to the earlier unrecorded mortgage.

§ 127. **Possession as notice.**   The law requires every prospective purchaser or mortgagee to examine into the possession of the real estate and to ascertain what rights are claimed by the parties in possession. Whether or not he actually does make this inspection, such purchaser or mortgagee is deemed to know the facts that such an investigation would have disclosed. In other words, possession imparts constructive notice in much the same way as the recording of a deed.

EXAMPLE: A sells and conveys his home to B. B fails to record the deed but moves into the house. A offers to sell the land to C. C examines the records in the recorder's office and finds title in A, but he fails to examine into the possession of the premises. He takes a deed from A. This deed passes no title. B's possession gave C constructive notice of his deed.

It is obvious that failure to record or a defective recording of a deed is usually less dangerous than the failure to record or the defective recording of a mortgage. This follows since the purchaser usually goes into possession of the land after receiving his deed, and this possession gives all the world notice of his rights, whereas a mortgagee rarely goes into possession before a default has been made and is therefore entirely dependent on the public records to give other persons notice of his rights.

In a few states, South Carolina and Virginia, for example, possession does not impart constructive notice.

§ 128. **Liens that need not be recorded.**   There are certain liens, such as real estate tax liens, inheritance tax liens, and franchise tax liens, that are binding on all persons though not recorded.

Chapter 10

BROKERS AND MANAGERS

§ 129. **Defined.**   A broker is one employed in negotiating the sale, purchase, or exchange of land. Compensation is usually in the form of a commission payable only if a deal is successfully signed up.

§ 130. **License.**   In many states, a person is not authorized to act as a real estate broker unless he first produces a broker's license. Real estate brokerage is a profession requiring knowledge, experience, and honesty, and in order to obtain a license, a candidate must have the qualifications that are specified by the local law. In order for a real estate broker to recover commissions, he must have his license at the time he is hired to perform the services for which he claims a commission. *Schoene v. Hickham,* 397 S.W.2d 596. The rule that unlicensed brokers cannot recover a commission is applied quite strictly. Thus if it can be shown that the broker has agreed to divide his commission with some unlicensed person, the broker will be unable to collect a commission. *Freeman v. Greaves,* 80 Ohio App. 341, 74 N.E.2d 860.

§ 131. **Salesman distinguished.**   A broker often hires salesmen. The broker, because of his superior knowledge and experience, is authorized to deal with the public and collect money from them. A salesman is strictly an employee of the broker and receives his compensation from the broker. He should not actively take charge of the broker's office and cannot collect a commission directly from the broker's customers. *Grand v. Griesinger,* 160 Cal.App.2d 397, 325 P.2d 475.

§ 132. **Necessity for contract of employment.**   A real estate broker acts as an agent. The person who hires him is known as the principal. Usually the broker is hired by the landowner for the purpose of procuring a buyer. In return for finding a buyer willing to buy on the landowner's terms, the broker receives a commission from the landowner. Occasionally the broker is hired by a person wishing to buy real estate. In either case, in order to recover a commission, the broker must be able to show that he was hired by the person from whom he claims a commission. If he claims a commission from the seller, he must show that the seller hired him. And if he was hired by the buyer only, he cannot claim a commission from the seller. Otherwise stated, a broker must show that the person from whom he claims a commission employed him to make the sale. However, an employment contract may be *implied* from the conduct of the parties.

> **EXAMPLE:**   A, a landowner, gave B, a broker, a description of his property and requested that B sell it at a designated price. This is a contract of employment, and B is entitled to a commission if he finds a buyer. The fact that compensation was not discussed is immaterial. A must have understood that B would expect to be paid if he produced a buyer. *Long v. Herr,* 10 Colo. 380, 15 Pac. 802.

> **EXAMPLE:**   A, a real estate broker, without any prior request from B, the landowner, submitted to B an offer of $3000 for the purchase of the land. B declined, stating that his price for the land was $4000. A thereupon procured a buyer who was willing to buy for $4000. B refused to sell. B is not liable for a commission. The mere statement by a landowner that he will take a certain sum for his land is not sufficient to authorize the person to whom the statement is made to act as agent for its sale. B is entitled to assume that A is acting for the buyer and will look to the buyer for his compensation. *O'Donnell v. Carr,* 189 N.C. 77, 126 S.E. 112.

As is evident from the foregoing illustrations, a broker usually tries to collect from the seller. This is due to the obvious fact that it is financially easier to collect money from the seller, who after all is being paid the purchase price of the property, than from the buyer, who may be stretching his finances in order to buy the property. Legally the fact remains that the broker cannot collect from the seller unless he can show that the seller hired him. At the very least the seller must say or do things that make the broker believe he has been hired by the seller. *Reeve v. Shoemaker,* 200 Ia. 983, 205 N.W. 742.

A person other than the property owner may list the property for sale and become liable for a commission.

> **EXAMPLE:**   W owned certain real estate. H, her husband, listed the property for sale with B, a broker, who knew that W owned the property. B found a buyer for the property, but W refused to sell. H was held liable to B for a commission. B was

entitled to assume that at the proper time H would procure W's consent to the sale. *Aler v. Plowman,* 190 Md. 631, 59 A.2d 196; *Rose v. Knoblock,* 194 S.W.2d 943 (Mo.).

EXAMPLE: Property was owned by H and W, husband and wife, in joint tenancy. H alone, without W's permission, listed the property for sale with X, a real estate broker. X found a buyer for the property, but W refused to sign the contract of sale and the deal fell through. H was held liable to X for a commission. 10 A.L.R.3d 665.

§ 133. **Necessity for written contract.** Because of the endless litigation that has arisen concerning the existence of an employment contract, in many states, Arizona, California, Idaho, Indiana, Iowa, Kentucky, Michigan, Montana, Nebraska, New Jersey, Ohio, Oklahoma, Oregon, Utah, Washington, and Wisconsin, for example, the contract of employment must be in writing in order for the broker to be entitled to a commission and must state the amount of commission agreed on. 9 A.L.R.2d 747.

§ 134. **Form of contract.** Often the hiring of a broker is an informal, verbal affair. However, written contracts, called *listing contracts,* are also used. These are usually brief documents, often in the form of printed cards. When such a form is filled in, it contains the following: (1) names of seller and broker; (2) description of property, usually by street address; (3) terms of sale, including sale price, whether sale is for cash or on terms, etc.; (4) duration of broker's employment; (5) commission to be paid; (6) special agreements, such as the provision for an exclusive agency.

§ 135. **Open listing.** There are several different types of listing contracts. The *open listing* contains no provision forbidding the landowner to sell the land himself or to hire other brokers, and ordinarily an owner may hire two or more brokers unless he specifically agrees not to do so. Virtually all informal, verbal listing arrangements are open listings. The disadvantage of this type of contract is that it is likely to produce quarrels over the commission where several brokers produce buyers.

EXAMPLE: A, a landowner, employed a broker to obtain a purchaser. The broker obtained a purchaser on the specified terms, but A refused to pay a commission on the ground that he had already concluded an agreement to sell to a purchaser obtained by another broker. The broker sued A. The court held for A. The primary object to be attained in the employment of agents to sell real estate, the court said, is the production of a single purchaser for such real estate, and that object is attained where one of several agents produces to the owner a purchaser who is ready, able, and willing to buy the real estate on the owner's terms. Where several agents are employed, the sale of the property either by the owner in person, or by any of the brokers, operates at once to terminate the authority of all the brokers, although they had no actual notice of the sale.

When different brokers have the property for sale, and no one of them has the exclusive right to make the sale, the broker who first finds a buyer ready, able, and willing to buy is the procuring cause of the sale and is the one entitled to the commission.

§ 136. **Exclusive agency.**   Unless there is an agreement to the contrary, the landowner may hire two or more brokers to sell the same property and will be liable only to the broker who first finds a buyer. Fear that time and money spent in locating a buyer may be wasted if another broker is working on the deal has led brokers to favor a listing contract which assures the broker that as long as his employment continues no other broker will be hired. Such a listing is called an *exclusive agency*. The giving of an exclusive agency does not bar the landowner from selling the property through his own efforts, without the assistance of other brokers. If the property owner sells the property through his own efforts, the exclusive agency automatically comes to an end, without any liability on the landowner's part for a commission and regardless of the employment period specified in the listing contract. *Martin Realty Co. v. Fletcher*, 103 N.J.L. 294, 136 Atl. 498; *Des Rivieres v. Sullivan*, 247 Mass. 443, 142 N.E. 111.

The mere fact that the listing contract refers to the broker as an *exclusive agent* is enough to create an exclusive agency. *Harris and White v. Stone*, 137 Ark. 23, 207 S.W. 443.

§ 137. **Exclusive right to sell.**   The *exclusive right to sell* goes one step further than the exclusive agency. It not only makes the broker the sole agent of the landowner for the sale of the property, but also provides that the named broker will receive a commission in the event the property is sold by the named broker, by the owner, *or by anyone else*. Thus even if the owner makes a sale through his own efforts, he must pay the broker. *Flynn v. La Salle Nat. Bank*, 9 Ill.2d. 129, 137 N.E.2d 71; 88 A.L.R.2d 941.

A broker who desires an exclusive right to sell should draft his listing contract with great care. Thus it has been held that a listing contract giving the broker the *exclusive sale* of a parcel of land creates an exclusive agency, not an exclusive right to sell. *Roberts v. Harrington*, 168 Wis. 217, 169 N.W. 603. Other courts have held that such language creates an exclusive right to sell. *Harris v. McPherson*, 97 Conn. 164, 115 Atl. 723. Again, it has even been held that a contract that gives the broker the *exclusive right to sell* merely creates an exclusive agency. *Sunnyside Land & Inv. Co. v. Bermier*, 119 Wash. 386, 205 Pac. 1041; *Hedges Co. v. Shanahan*, 195 Ia. 1302, 190 N.W. 957. These courts feel that, to create a true exclusive right to sell, the contract must in unequivocal terms negate the right of the landowner to sell the property himself. 88 A.L.R.2d 948. However, other courts feel that a contract granting the broker an exclusive right to sell means just what it says. *Torrey & Dean, Inc. v.*

Coyle, 138 Ore. 509, 7 P.2d 561; *Piatt & Heath Co. v. Wilmer,* 87 Mont. 382, 288 Pac. 1021. The better reasoning appears to lie with the courts that require unequivocal language. Mere use of the phrase *exclusive right to sell* does not convey to the average person's mind the notion that it involves a surrender by the landowner of the right to make a sale through his own efforts.

§ 138. **Multiple listing.** Multiple listing is simply a means by which brokers in a given area pool their efforts to sell properties listed with any member of the pool. The original, or listing, broker obtains from the property owner an exclusive right to sell. He then furnishes a copy thereof to all members of his pool or this is done through a central office. If any member other than the original broker sells the property, the commission is divided between the original broker and the broker who effects the sale. Only the original broker has the right to sue the property owner for a commission. The property owner has no contract of employment with members of the pool other than the original broker and therefore cannot be sued by them. *Goodwin v. Gleck,* 139 Cal. App.2d. 936, 294 P.2d 192. Nor is he liable for misrepresentations made by them. 58 A.L.R.2d 41. But the members of the pool who work on the sale owe to the landowner the usual duties of a broker, such as loyalty. *Frisell v. Newman,* (Wash.) 429 P.2d. 864. In order to eliminate unethical competition, it is best that the agreement between the members of the pool specifically provide that no member will try to get the listing for himself after the original broker's listing has expired.

§ 139. **Performance required of broker.** A broker earns his commission when he produces a buyer who is ready, able, and willing to buy on the terms specified by the seller in the listing contract. Thus if the broker brings in a buyer, and the seller and buyer negotiate until a contract of sale is signed, the broker has earned his commission. More frequently, a broker who has found a buyer will have the buyer sign a contract to buy the property, and the broker will then tender this contract to the seller. Naturally the seller may reconsider and decline to sign the contract, for at that point he has no liability to the buyer. However, since the broker has done what he was hired to do, namely, to find a buyer, the seller must pay him a commission. Likewise, if seller and buyer reconsider *after* a contract of sale has been signed, so that the deal does not go through, the seller is nevertheless liable to the broker. 74 A.L.R.2d 459. Also, if the buyer, having signed a contract that the seller also has signed, thereafter refuses to go through with the deal, the broker has nevertheless earned his commission. 74 A.L.R.2d 443.

The word *able* in the phrase *ready, able, and willing to buy* means financially able. The buyer must be able to command the necessary funds to close the deal within the time required. *Pellaton v. Brunski,* 69 Cal.

App. 301, 231 Pac. 583. He must actually have the money to meet any cash payment required and be in shape financially to meet any deferred payments. *Raynor v. Mackrill*, 196 Ia. 1298, 164 N.W. 335. Otherwise stated, he must have the present ability to pay. *Boutelle v. Chrislaw*, 34 Wis.2d 665, 150 N.W. 2d 486. Thus a newly organized corporation having limited funds might be considered not *able* to buy. However, it is not necessary to show that the buyer is standing outside the office door with all cash in hand. It is sufficient if the buyer is *able* to command the necessary funds on reasonable notice. *Perper v. Edell*, 160 Fla. 447, 35 So.2d 387. Thus a buyer is *able* to buy if he has already arranged with some mortgage house to loan him the funds necessary to pay for the property. *Schaaf v. Iba*, 73 Ohio L.Abs. 46, 136 N.E.2d 727. To *produce* a willing buyer requires that the broker must reveal his identity to the seller. 2 A.L.R.3d 1128.

A *willing* buyer is one who is willing to enter into an enforceable contract for the purchase of the property.

> **EXAMPLE:** If the buyer needs a large loan in order to complete the sale, he may insist that the sale contract allow him to cancel the contract if within a specified period of time he is unable to procure the required loan. Since such a contract does not impose unqualified liability on the buyer, the broker is entitled to a commission only if the buyer gets the necessary loan. *Cooper v. Liberty Nat. Bank*, 332 Ill. App. 459, 75 N.E.2d 759; *Slonim, Ltd. v. Bankers Mortgage & Realty Co.*, 133 N.J.L. 45, 42 A.2d 396.

But when the broker procures a purchaser ready, willing, and able to purchase on the authorized terms, and through the fault of the *owner* the sale is not consummated, the broker is entitled to a commission. Thus the broker is entitled to a commission:

> 1. When the deal falls through because the owner changes his mind and refuses to sign the deed to the purchaser or a contract to sell. The rule is the same where the land has increased in value and the owner rejects the broker's buyer for this reason. If the seller refuses to sign, giving as his only reason the fact that he has changed his mind, he cannot thereafter shift his ground and claim that the buyer's offer was not in compliance with the listing. *Russell v. Ramm*, 200 Cal. 348, 254 Pac. 532.
> 2. When the deal falls through because the owner's wife refuses to sign the contract or deed. 10 A.L.R.3d 665.
> 3. When the deal falls through because of defects in the owner's title. *Triplett v. Feasal*, 105 Kan. 179, 182 Pac. 551.
> 4. When the deal falls through because of the owner's fraud. *Hathaway v. Smith*, 187 Ill. App. 128.
> 5. When the deal falls through because the owner is unable to deliver possession within a reasonable time.
> 6. When the deal falls through because the seller insists on terms and provisions not mentioned in the listing contract, as where the seller insists on the right to

remain in possession after the deal has been closed. *Brown v. Ogle,* 75 Ind. App. 90, 130 N.E. 147.

    7. When after the contract of sale has been signed the seller and buyer get together and cancel the contract. *Steward v. Brock,* 60 N.M. 216, 290 P.2d 682.

If a binding contract is entered into, the broker is entitled to his commission even though the buyer refuses to pay the purchase price. The owner is not required to accept a buyer produced by a broker without opportunity for investigation as to his ability to comply with the terms of the contract, but where he does accept such purchaser, it is a determination by him of the purchaser's ability to perform the contract, and if the purchaser fails to perform the contract, the owner cannot defeat the broker's commission on the ground that the purchaser was not able to buy the property. 74 A.L.R.2d 454.

    NEW DIRECTIONS: There is some thinking very recently that since the broker is so much better informed as to the buyer's financial ability to consummate the deal, if the deal falls through because the buyer cannot command the necessary financial resources, the seller should not be liable for a commission. *Ellsworth Dobbs Inc. v. Johnson,* 50 N.J. 528, 236A.2d 243.

The broker is entitled to no compensation or reimbursement whatever for unsuccessful efforts to sell unless the listing contract expressly so provides.

Often after a seller has listed property with a broker, and after the broker has found a buyer who is ready, able, and willing to buy at the listed price, the seller changes his mind and looks for some way to turn down the buyer without being liable to the broker for a commission. Such a seller seeks to take refuge behind the rule that if the terms offered by the broker's prospect differ from the terms specified by the seller, the broker is not entitled to a commission. 18 A.L.R.2d 376. This is obvious where the broker's prospect offers less than the seller's listing price, or offers to buy on an installment contract where the seller's listing contemplates a cash deal. But in addition, keep in mind that if the broker's listing contract is silent on other terms of the transaction, the law will read various implications into it. And if the terms of sale as set forth in the contract of sale do not harmonize with the terms of sale set forth *or implied* in the listing contract, the seller may reject the broker's prospect without incurring any liability for commission.

    EXAMPLE: If the broker's listing is silent, the seller is required to convey only the land, building, and articles that are technically fixtures. If the contract of sale tendered by the broker requires the seller to convey furniture or other personal property, the seller may reject the contract without any liability for commission.

§ 140. "No deal, no commission" provision.   While ordinarily
the broker has earned his commission as soon as he has found a buyer
who is ready, able, and willing to buy, the parties may validly contract,
by means of the so-called *no deal, no commission clause* inserted in the
listing contract, that payment of the commission is contingent upon the
closing of the deal and full payment of the purchase price to the seller.
If the listing contract provides that the owner agrees to pay a commission
"out of the sale price" no commission is earned until the transfer is completed. 74 A.L.R.2d 474, 482. Thus if the seller cannot clear his title, or if
the buyer refuses to go through with the deal, the seller need not pay a
commission. 74 A.L.R.2d 437. However, if the seller's refusal to complete
the sale is arbitrary and without reasonable cause or in bad faith, the
broker is entitled to his commission. *Huntley v. Smith,* 153 Minn. 297,
190 N.W. 341; *Goldstein v. Rosenberg,* 331 Ill. App. 374, 73 N.E.2d 171.

§ 141.   Procuring cause of sale.   A broker who has been hired
by the landowner has earned his commission when his efforts were the
primary and procuring cause of the sale. When the owner or several
brokers have been active and a sale is concluded, a broker, to justify his
claim to a commission, must show that he was the efficient cause of the
sale. The following are typical situations in which the problem arises:

1. The broker finds a prospect and introduces him to the owner. Thereupon
the owner and the prospect, without the broker's intervention, negotiate and conclude
a sale. The broker is the procuring cause of the sale and is entitled to a commission.
Ranney v. Rock, 135 Conn. 479, 66 A.2d 111.
2. When several brokers are involved, the rule appears to be substantially this:
If the first broker's efforts result in a disagreement or if negotiations are abandoned,
and thereafter a second broker steps in and brings the parties together, the second
broker is the procuring cause of the sale. 46 A.L.R.2d 865. But if the first broker brings
about a substantial agreement, and the second broker merely works out details of the
transaction, the first broker is the procuring cause of the sale. In other words, the
broker whose efforts predominate in bringing about the sale gets the commission.

There are cases where the broker is entitled to damages or compensation even though he has not been the procuring cause of the sale: (1) For
example, in the case of an exclusive agency, the broker will be entitled
to compensation from his employer if the employer hires another broker,
who succeeds in selling the property, because the employer breached his
contract, which obligated him to refrain from hiring other brokers. (2)
Also, in the case of an exclusive right to sell, the broker may be entitled
to compensation even if his employer sells the building through his own
efforts. Here the employer has breached his contract not to try to sell the
building through his own efforts. *Bell v. Demmerling,* 149 Ohio St. 165,
78 N.E.2d 49. (3) Or the listing contract may provide that the broker
will be entitled to compensation if the property is sold to a person with

whom the broker *has negotiated,* or *whose name has been furnished the seller* by the broker. Here a broker who engages in negotiations with a prospect collects even though the deal is ultimately clinched by the landowner himself or another broker. *Delbon v. Brazil,* 134 Cal. App.2d 461, 285 P.2d 710.

SUGGESTION TO BROKER: Let the listing contract provide that broker will be entitled to a commission if within the specified time the property is sold to a person with whom the broker negotiated.

§ 142. **Effect of seller's ignorance that buyer was procured by broker.** When a seller hires a broker to sell his property, and thereafter sells the property to a buyer procured by the broker, in most states the broker is entitled to a commission despite the fact that the seller is ignorant that the buyer was procured through the broker. *Ranney v. Rock,* 135 Conn. 479, 66 A.2d 111; 142 A.L.R. 275. Having hired a broker, the seller should know that the appearance of a buyer may have been caused by the broker. The seller should check with his *broker* whenever a prospective buyer comes in. Inquiring of the *buyer* is rather pointless, for obviously many buyers, hoping to get a reduced price, will conceal the fact that a broker interested them in the property. Suppose, however, that A, a landowner, hires B, a broker, and B interests C in the purchase of the property. C procures a dummy or strawman, D, to make an offer for the property. A inquires of B if B had interested D in the purchase of the property. Not knowing that D is only a nominee for C, B says no, and A cuts his price by the amount of the commission he would have paid to B. B gets no commission. A has done all he could to protect his broker. *Zetlin v. Scher* (Md.), 217 A.2d 266.

If the seller reduces his price to a prospect in ignorance of the fact that the prospect was procured by the seller's broker, some states, as above stated, allow the broker to collect his commission. The seller is at fault because he failed to check with the broker. Other states refuse the broker a commission. 46 A.L.R.2d 872, 877. These latter states feel that the broker should notify the seller of each prospect he procures.

SUGGESTION TO BROKER: As soon as you find a prospect, send a postcard to the seller notifying him of the name and address of the prospect you have found.

§ 143. **Duration and termination of employment.** Many controversies arise as to the duration and termination of the broker's employment.

When no time limit is specified. If the listing contract specifies no duration, the broker's authority automatically lapses after expiration of a reasonable time. 27 A.L.R.2d 1346, 1390. If after a reasonable time has expired the broker continues to work on the deal without encouragement from the landowner and succeeds in finding a willing buyer, the seller may, without any liability to the broker, refuse to sell. But even before a reasonable time has expired, if no duration is specified, the landowner has the right to revoke the listing at any time before the broker has found a buyer ready, able, and willing to buy—and even while the broker is negotiating with a prospect, so long as the negotiations are not virtually completed. 49 L.R.A.N.S. 985. Such revocation must be in good faith, of course; for example, the landowner has decided in good faith to withdraw the property from sale. The fact that the broker has expended time and money on the deal does not prevent revocation, for the ordinary broker's listing contemplates that such expenditures will be made and that the landowner will nevertheless enjoy freedom of action. 49 L.R.A.N.S. 994. A special rule applies, however, where the listing contemplates extraordinary expenditures by the broker.

> **EXAMPLE:** A landowner listed a large tract of land with a broker under an agreement that the broker was to grade, survey, and subdivide the land, put in streets, etc., at his own expense. His compensation was to come from commission on lot sales. No duration was fixed. After the broker had completed the subdivision, the owner revoked the broker's employment. The owner must pay damages to the broker. *McMillan v. Quincey*, 137 Ga. 63, 72 S.E. 506; 49 L.R.A.N.S. 999.

What is a reasonable time for a broker to sell the property depends on the circumstances. Some properties are harder to sell than others; for example, a one-purpose building, such as a church. A longer period will be allowed in such case than would be true in the case of a quick-selling item, such as a modern single-family dwelling.

Where the listing contract fixes the period of employment. Listing contracts often provide that they are to continue for a specified time. In such case, the broker is not entitled to a commission unless within the time limited he procures a customer who is ready, able, and willing to buy.

> **EXAMPLE:** A, a landowner, gave the broker an exclusive right to sell, with a time limit of six months. During this period the broker showed the property to B. B thought the price too high. The day after the listing expired, A called the broker and asked if he would have to pay the commission if he sold the property to someone who had been shown the house during the period of the listing. The broker said that A would be liable. Nevertheless A advertised the property for sale. B appeared in response to the ad. A contract of sale was entered into at a price of $45,000. The listing price had been $53,000. The court held that the broker was not entitled to a commission. *Brenner & Co. v. Perl*, 72 N.J.S. 160, 178 A.2d 19; 27 A.L.R.2d 1348.

However, in the following cases the broker will recover a commission even if he fails to find a purchaser within the period of the listing.

1. When the expiration of the listing time is attributable to the bad faith of the owner, as when the owner deliberately postpones agreement with the broker's buyer, hoping thereby to defeat the broker's claim for compensation. 27 A.L.R.2d 1346, 1357.

2. If negotiations are begun within the time specified in the listing contract, continue without interruption, and are completed after the time has expired, the broker is entitled to his commission, particularly where the delay is due to the fault of the owner, as where it is occasioned by a defect in title. The seller is considered to have waived or extended the time limit.

3. When the listing contract contains some clause protecting the broker. For example, some listing forms, in large type, purport to run for a fixed period of time, such as thirty days, but following this will be a fine-print provision continuing the listing until a termination notice has been served on the broker. Other listing forms provide that the owner will protect the broker on sales made within ninety days of the expiration of the listing to prospects with whom the broker had *negotiated* or who had been *introduced* to the seller by the broker before expiration of the listing period. 27 A.L.R.2d 1346, 1408.

C A U T I O N : Courts are unfriendly to these provisions for automatic extension of the listing period. Even if the listing contract is an exclusive agency or exclusive right to sell, it will be considered an *open listing during the extended period* if it is at all ambiguous. When a listing stated it was to be "sole and exclusive for three months and thereafter until sixty days written notice had been given," it was exclusive only for the initial three-month period. Thereafter it was only an open listing. *Boggess Realty Co. v. Miller*, 227 Ky. 813, 14 S.W.2d 140, 27 A.L.R.2d 1420; *Wilson v. Franklin*, 282 Pa. 189, 127 Atl. 609.

Revocation where listing fixes a specified time and broker has begun performance. Where the listing contract fixes a period of employment, such as thirty days, the owner may terminate the employment before the agent has expended money or effort, but not afterward. The technical reason for this rule is that the typical listing contract is a *unilateral contract* in which the landowner makes a promise to pay commission when the broker has performed an act, that is, found a buyer ready, able, and willing to buy, and such a contract is revocable by the promisor only up to the time the other party begins performance. *Hutchison v. Dobson-Bainbridge Realty Co.*, 31 Tenn. App. 490, 217 S.W.2d 6; *Patton v. Wilson* (Tex. Civ. App.), 220 S.W.2d 184; 1 Corbin, *Contracts* 154; 37 Ia. *L. Rev.* 370; 12 Am.Jur.2d 796.

In these cases, any revocation after the broker has begun performance is wrongful and makes the owner liable to the broker for damages.

C A U T I O N : A few states still follow the old rule that a listing is revocable at any time before the broker actually finds a willing purchaser even though a fixed

period of employment is specified. In these states, a revocation of the broker's employment is effective even though the broker has begun performance. *Bartlett v. Keith*, 325
Mass. 265, 90 N.E.2d 308. On the other hand, one or two states hold that an exclusive
listing is irrevocable from the date it is signed, even though the broker has not begun
performance. This is on the theory that by accepting employment the broker impliedly
agrees to use reasonable efforts to find a buyer, and this makes the contract *bilateral*
and irrevocable until the specified time has expired. *Hayes v. Clark*, 95 Conn. 510, 111
Atl. 781.

*Revocation where the listing fixes a specified time and requires specific
acts of the broker.* We are beginning to see listing contracts that are
technically *bilateral contracts.* This means that in return for the owner's
promise to pay a specified commission for a buyer, the broker promises to
perform certain specified acts, such as advertising the property in a
specified paper at least once a week. Here the broker has a legal obligation
to do as he has promised. Any revocation by the owner before the listing
period has expired will be wrongful, so long as the broker is keeping his
part of the bargain.

SUGGESTION TO BROKER: Let the listing contract call for
some acts by the broker, for example, provide that "broker agrees to publish an advertisement of the property at least once in a newspaper of general circulation in the
county." The listing should be signed by the broker. This listing is irrevocable from the
date it is signed, assuming, of course, that the broker advertises the property as agreed.

Revocation after broker has performed. Of course the landowner has
no right to revoke the broker's employment after the broker has brought
in a buyer ready, able, and willing to buy.

Revocation in bad faith. In all types of listings the owner will be liable
to the broker for damages if he acts in bad faith in revoking the broker's
employment. 27 A.L.R.2d 1346, 1395. Even when no time of employment
is specified, when the broker is concluding negotiations with a prospective
purchaser the owner cannot revoke the agency *for the purpose of avoiding
payment of commission.* In other words, when the broker has found a
prospect and is concluding negotiations with him, so that the commission
is virtually earned and the broker is approaching success, the owner cannot discharge the broker and thereupon step in and consummate the
transaction, thus defeating the broker's right to his compensation.

EXAMPLE: *A*, a landowner, hired *B*, a broker, to sell his land. While *B*
was negotiating with a prospect, *A* sold the land to his wife and discharged *B*. Thereupon *A* and his wife sold to *B*'s prospect. They were liable for *B*'s commission. *Alexander
v. Smith*, 180 Ala. 541, 61 So. 68; 36 *Boston U. L. Rev.* 302.

Notice of revocation of employment. When a landowner decides to
withdraw his land from sale, he must give the broker notice of the revoca-

tion of his employment before the broker has finished the job. If the broker brings in a buyer ready, able, and willing to buy, obviously no judge will allow the owner to say, "I fired you mentally five days ago." 12 C.J.S. 152; 12 Am.Jur.2d 817.

A different situation is presented when the revocation of employment takes place by virtue of the fact that the land has been sold by someone else. As previously explained, in an open listing the employment of all brokers hired by the owner *automatically ends when a ready, able, and willing buyer is found either by the owner or by one of the brokers;* and in an exclusive agency the broker's employment automatically ends if the owner, through his own efforts, finds a willing buyer. No duty to notify brokers rests on the owner in most states, because all brokers understand that in these situations their employment is subject to such automatic termination. *Des Rivieres v. Sullivan,* 247 Mass. 443, 142 N.E. 111; 12 Am.Jur.2d 817. A few cases hold, however, that after the land has been sold the owner ought, within a reasonable time, to notify all his brokers of the sale. If he fails to do so, and if one of his brokers also finds a willing buyer, the owner may be compelled to pay him a commission. *Lane v. Albright,* 49 Ind. 275; 49 L.R.A.N.S. 1003.

SUGGESTION TO OWNER: Notify all your brokers promptly as soon as the land is sold.

Suppose that in an open listing a broker finds a willing buyer. However, he fails to notify the owner of this fact, and thereafter the owner signs a contract with some other buyer, procured, let us say, through another broker, the owner being still ignorant of the first broker's successful efforts. The first broker loses his commission. It is his duty to notify the owner promptly on finding a buyer. *Wilson v. Franklin,* 282 Pa. 189, 127 Atl. 609.

SUGGESTION TO BROKER: Notify the owner as soon as you have found a willing buyer.

Damages for wrongful revocation of employment. Suppose that under one of the rules discussed in this section the owner's revocation of the broker's employment is legally wrongful. How much should the courts award the broker? Some courts give the broker only the expenses incurred by him for advertising and so forth and a sum that will compensate him for the reasonable value of his services. *Ferguson v. Bovee,* 239 Ia. 775, 32 N.W.2d 924; *Nicholson v. Alderson,* 347 Ill. App. 496, 107 N.E.2d 39; 12 Am.Jur.2d 819. Most courts, however, on one theory or another award the broker a full commission. 37 *Ia. L. Rev.* 367. The broker will have a better chance of collecting a full commission if the listing contract has a clause covering the possibility of the seller's withdrawing the property from sale.

SUGGESTED FORM: Let the listing provide that the broker will receive a full commission "if, within the time above specified, the premises are sold by the broker, owner, or anyone else, or if, within said period, the owner withdraws the property from sale." *Baumgartner v. Meek,* 126 Cal. App.2d 505, 272 Pac. 552.

§ 144. **Sale for less than price fixed.**   Where an agent is employed to sell real estate for the owner, and the owner fixes a sale price, the broker is entitled to a commission if he finds a purchaser and the owner sells to the purchaser for less than the price fixed. The owner has the right to insist on the terms quoted to the broker and may reject a buyer who will not meet his terms. But if he voluntarily reduces his price in order to make the sale to a buyer produced by the broker, the broker is entitled to a commission on the sale price.

§ 145. **Amount of compensation.**   In a case where the broker has found a buyer, he is entitled to the commission agreed upon, and if no commission has been fixed by the parties, he is entitled to the usual and customary commission for such services. He is usually not entitled to extra compensation for incidental services.

The compensation is computed on the gross sale price.

EXAMPLE: A owns land on which there is a $12,000 mortgage. He lists the building with a broker at $15,000, and the broker finds a buyer. Although A will obtain a net of only $3,000 ($15,000 less the $12,000 required to pay the mortgage), he must pay a commission based on a price of $15,000.

§ 146. **Net listings.**   A contract between the seller and broker whereby the broker is to receive as his commission all the purchase price in excess of the price fixed by the seller is valid. *Dowell v. Pumphrey,* 197 Ky. 59, 246 S.W. 157, 30 A.L.R. 822.

EXAMPLE: A seller listed his real estate at $10,000, agreeing that the broker was to receive as his commission everything over that sum. The broker found a buyer willing to pay $13,000. The broker is entitled to $3000 as his commission.

Difficulties arise when a broker inquires of a landowner whether he will accept a certain price for his property and the landowner replies that he will accept a certain figure "net." In the first place, if this is all that is said on the subject, the mere fact that the landowner has given such a reply to an inquiry from an outside broker does not constitute employment of the broker. The seller is entitled to assume that the broker is looking to the buyer for his compensation. *Johnson v. Whalen,* 13 Okla.

320, 74 Pac. 503; *Smith v. Lewis,* 75 Wyo. 29, 291 P.2d 804. If it is clear from the conversation and other circumstances that the seller intended to and did thereby hire the broker to sell the property, the broker may seek to claim as his commission the excess of the sale price over the net price. The courts, however, will not allow this.

> **EXAMPLE:** A, a landowner, hired B, a broker, to sell his property, stating: "I will take $7500 net to me." The broker sold the property for $8000. The court held that the phrase meant that the seller's minimum sale price was a figure that would net the seller $7500 after deducting all expenses. The broker was allowed as commission only 2½ per cent (the going rate) on $8000. He was not allowed the difference between $7500 and $8000. Use of the word "net" means that the property must bring the seller $7500 free of all expenses and deductions, but there is no intention of giving the broker all over that figure. *Turnley v. Michael* (Tex. Civ. App.), 15 S.W. 912. It is still the broker's duty to sell the property for the highest price obtainable. He then receives a compensation not greater than the excess over the net figure, and at the same time not exceeding a reasonable compensation. *Boysen v. Robertson,* 70 Ark. 56, 68 S.W. 243.

§ 147. **Lien for commission.** A broker hired by the seller has no lien on the seller's land for the payment of his commission unless the listing contract so provides. 125 A.L.R. 921. In other words, even though the broker has earned his commission, his only remedy, if the seller fails to pay, is to sue the seller and obtain a judgment against him. The broker cannot do anything to block sale of the land by the seller to the broker's customer or anyone else.

§ 148. **Deposit—payment of purchase price to broker.** Unless the listing contract so provides, the broker has no power to accept a deposit from the buyer on behalf of the seller. *Gold v. Phelan,* 58 Cal. App. 471, 208 Pac. 1001. If despite this lack of authority the broker does accept a down payment from the buyer, then at least until a contract of sale is signed he holds the money as agent for the buyer, and if the broker embezzles the funds, it is the buyer who must bear the loss. *Angell v. Ingram,* 35 Wash.2d 582, 213 P.2d 944; 30 A.L.R.2d 810. And the broker is clearly liable to the seller if he refunds the deposit to the buyer without the seller's consent. *Lake Co. v. Molan,* 269 Minn. 490, 131 N.W.2d 734.

Even when a seller accepts a down payment taken by the broker from the buyer, it does not constitute authority by the seller to the broker to accept the balance of the purchase price. The seller is entitled to assume that the broker was acting as the *buyer's* agent in transmitting the down payment. Suppose that the listing contract authorizes the broker to sign a contract of sale on behalf of the seller. Here the broker necessarily has implied authority to accept the down payment, for a down payment is made when the contract is signed. 30 A.L.R.2d 816. The broker holds the money as agent of the seller, and if the broker embezzles the money, the loss falls on the seller. If the listing contract authorizes the broker to *sell and convey* the property, or if the seller entrusts the deed to the broker for delivery to the buyer, then the broker has implied authority to receive all of the purchase price. This must be so, for the seller's agent, not the seller, will be present at the closing of the deal, and the buyer must pay someone.

§ 149. **Duties of the broker: loyalty and double agency.**   An agent must be loyal to his principal. If, without the knowledge and consent of his principal, he is also acting for the other party to the transaction, the principal may, when he discovers this fact, declare the contract void. This is true even though the transaction is a good one for the principal and the other party acts in good faith and was unaware of the double agency. *Gordon v. Beck*, 196 Cal. 768, 239 Pac. 309. It is to the interest of the seller to obtain the highest possible price and of the buyer to pay the least. Clearly, no one agent can serve both these interests.

> **EXAMPLE:** X employed A, a broker, to sell his property, and Y employed A to buy property of this general character. A negotiated an exchange of the properties, without disclosing his double agency, and charged each a commission. Either one has the right to rescind on discovering the facts. That is, either one is entitled to a return of his former property, but he must in turn convey back the property he received. *C.T.&T. Co. v. Schwartz*, 339 Ill. 184, 171 N.E. 169. Moreover, the broker must return any commission paid to him in such transactions.

Suppose a broker is hired by the buyer to find land or a building in a certain area, the buyer to pay a commission. Suppose that thereafter a property owner lists land of this description for sale with this broker. The broker reveals this fact *to the buyer only*, and a deal is closed between the seller and buyer, without, however, any knowledge on the seller's part that the broker was originally hired by the buyer. The broker collects his commission from the seller and now sues the buyer. To the broker's surprise, the buyer claims that the broker cannot collect any commission whatever in a double agency situation. This is correct. The fact that the buyer knew of the double agency makes no difference. A fraud was perpetrated on the *seller*, and the law will not help a party to the fraud, the broker, to collect from the other party to the fraud, the buyer. *McConnell v. Cowan*, 44 Cal.2d 805, 285 P.2d 261; 80 A.L.R. 1077, 1087. The fact that the broker felt he was acting for the best interests of both parties is immaterial.

A *middleman*, who merely brings the parties together, leaving them to negotiate, may serve both parties. Here the double agency rule does not apply. 14 A.L.R. 472; 58 A.L.R.2d 42, 58. But if the broker assists either party or in some degree influences the parties, he is not a middleman. It is obvious that very few agencies fall in the middleman category.

§ **150.   Duties of the broker: conflict of interest problems.**   An agent must not have any individual interest in the transaction without the knowledge and consent of his principal.

EXAMPLE: X placed his property with A and B, brokers. Negotiations resulted in a sale by X to Y for $3200, the brokers receiving a commission of $160. After the deed was given, X discovered that the real purchaser was B, Y being one of B's employees. X was entitled to have the conveyance set aside. *Johnson v. Bernard*, 323 Ill. 527, 154 N.E. 444.

EXAMPLE: A broker is liable to his seller where he secretly collects a mortgage commission and does not obtain the best possible mortgage terms. *Rushing v. Stephans* (Wash.), 393 P.2d 281.

The rule even precludes a sale by the broker to his wife unless the seller is informed of the relation. If, however, the broker fully discloses the facts to the landowner, he may buy for himself, for a relative, or for himself and others.

§ **151.   Duties of the broker: disclosure and nondisclosure.** The agent must make full disclosure to his principal of all matters that may come to his knowledge pertaining to the subject of the agency. 2 A.L.R.3d 1123.

EXAMPLE: A placed his property with B, a broker. B wrote A, stating that he (B) and several other parties would buy the land at $400 per acre. The contract was signed, and B received a commission. Later A discovered that, prior to making this offer, B had received an offer for this property of $600 per acre. A was entitled to have the contract canceled. *Rieger v. Brandt*, 329 Ill. 21, 160 N.E. 130; 7 A.L.R.3d 693.

EXAMPLE: The broker is liable if he transmits an offer to the principal but conceals a more favorable offer. 7 A.L.R.3d 696.

EXAMPLE: While the property is listed with the broker, it increases in value. The owner is ignorant of this fact, but the broker knows of it. He fails to disclose this circumstance to the owner. He has violated his duty of full disclosure. *Eastburn v. Jos. Espalla, Jr. & Co.*, 215 Ala. 650, 112 So. 232, 53 A.L.R. 134.

EXAMPLE: The buyer procured by the broker has a poor financial status. The broker knows this, but fails to reveal it to the seller. A contract is signed, but the deal fails to go through because the buyer cannot raise the necessary funds. The broker has violated his duty of full disclosure. *McGarry v. McCrone*, 97 Ohio App. 543, 118 N.E.2d 195.

EXAMPLE: The buyer procured by the broker is a distant relative of the broker. He must reveal this fact to the seller. 26 A.L.R.2d 1308. The broker must disclose the true identity of the purchaser. 2 A.L.R.3d 1119.

In other words, the broker's duty is not discharged simply by his handing a contract to the seller for signing. He must notify the seller of all facts that might influence the seller in accepting or rejecting the offer. He must give his opinion as to the price that can be obtained, the likelihood of a higher price being offered in the future, the possibility of making a favorable trade or other use of the property, etc. *Moehling v. O'Neil Construction Co.*, 20 Ill.2d 255, 170 N.E.2d 100.

The converse of the broker's duty of disclosure is his duty not to reveal secret information to prospective buyers. Thus the seller's broker violates his duties if he reveals to a prospective buyer that the seller will take less than the listed price for the property, for obviously no buyer will pay the listed price if he knows that the seller will take less. *Haymes v. Rogers*, 70 Ariz. 257, 219 P.2d 339.

§ 152.   **Duties of the broker: misrepresentations to the buyer.** A broker hired by the seller will be held liable to the buyer in damages if the broker, acting on his own, makes a willful misrepresentation that induces the buyer to enter into the contract of sale. 58 A.L.R.2d 10, 27; 8 A.L.R.3d 553.

> **EXAMPLE:** The broker falsely represented that the house was stucco-covered brick, whereas it was not brick. *Perkins v. Green*, 26 Ariz. 219, 224 P. 620.

§ 153.   **Duties of the broker: skill and care.**   Like other agents, a broker must exercise skill and care in the service of his employer.

> **EXAMPLE:** A broker hired to sell land found a buyer and drew a contract of sale, which the parties signed. Thereafter the buyer refused to go through with the deal. The court held that the contract was so poorly drawn that the buyer was not legally bound. The broker thereby forfeited his commission. *Dingman v. Boyle*, 285 Ill. 144, 120 N.E. 487. Moreover, he is liable to the seller for any damages the seller has suffered. *Mattieliegh v. Poe*, 58 Wash.2d 904, 365 P.2d 328.

> **EXAMPLE:** A broker hired to buy or trade has a duty to determine the value of the real estate he acquires for his employer. If he fails in this respect, and the property turns out to be a poor buy, he is liable and forfeits his commission. *Smith v. Carroll Realty Co.*, 8 Utah2d 356, 335 P.2d 67.

> **EXAMPLE:** A broker employed to find a property for a buyer must exercise skill and care if he undertakes to close the deal for the buyer without an attorney. Thus if the broker fails to procure a clear title for the buyer, he is liable to buyer for damages. *Lester v. Marshall*, 143 Colo. 189, 352 P.2d 786.

§ 154.   **Duties of the broker: liabilities and penalties for breach of duty.**   Where the broker breaches his duties toward his employer, one or more of several penalties may follow.

1. In almost every case the broker will lose his commission. If he has already been paid, he must refund it. 2 A.L.R.3d 1126.

2. If he has made a profit, as where the broker has bought the property from his employer through a nominee and resold it at a profit, he must pay such profit over to his employer.

3. If his employer has suffered any damages as a consequence of the broker's breach of duty, the broker will be liable for such damages.

4. Where the broker's misconduct is deliberate, as where he secretly buys the property from his employer, the court may see fit to punish the broker by compelling him to pay exemplary damages, that is, damages greater than the damage the employer has actually suffered. *Ward v. Taggart*, 51 Cal.2d 736, 336 P.2d 534.

5. For a serious offense, such as secretly buying his employer's property, failing to disclose material facts to his employer, embezzling his employer's funds, etc., the broker may have his license suspended or revoked altogether. 56 A.L.R.2d 573. Fraud in his own land transactions will also result in the loss of his license. *Holland Realty Inv. Co. v. State*, 436 P.2d 422.

As is true with respect to lawyers, doctors, architects, and others, the courts are holding brokers to higher and higher standards of professional ethics and competence. This is a desirable trend and is likely to continue.

In those states that require the broker to post an official bond, the surety on the bond will be liable for the broker's misconduct, as where the broker misappropriates a down payment that has been entrusted to him by the buyer. 17 A.L.R.2d 1021.

§ 155. **Unauthorized practice of law.** The law appears to differ from state to state with respect to the propriety of a broker's filling in a form contract of sale where this is merely incidental to the earning of his commission for procuring a buyer. 53 A.L.R.2d 796. However, if the broker makes a separate charge for filling in a form, he is guilty of unauthorized practice of law. 53 A.L.R.2d 804. Likewise, if a broker prepares a will or deeds to put land in joint tenancy, he is guilty of the unauthorized practice of law. 53 A.L.R.2d 807.

§ 156. **Authority of broker to sign contract.** Ordinarily a broker does not have authority to sign a contract on behalf of his employer. 43 A.L.R.2d 1014.

§ 157. **Managers.** A building manager is the agent of the property owner. An agent owes to his employer the duty of loyalty. This precludes the taking of secret commissions from suppliers with whom the manager deals and also precludes the taking of secret bonuses from tenants. A manager must not enter into any deal to procure a lease through a dummy or nominee unless his interest is revealed to his employer. An agent also is bound to exercise care, diligence, and skill. This means that the manager must procure proper insurance, appropriate to the situation, which may include fidelity bonds, plate glass insurance, elevator liability insurance, workmen's compensation insurance, and other types that a careful manager would be expected to procure. The manager must make periodic inspections, arrange for necessary repairs, re-rent vacant space promptly, see that ordinances are complied with, and do all the other things that a careful owner would do with respect to his property. An agent must keep his employer informed. This means that the manager must promptly forward to his employer all legal notices served by tenants and must notify his employer of any rent delinquency, "lease-jumping" by a tenant, offers of purchase, notices of ordinance violations, and the like. An agent must keep proper records and accounts and must not mingle his funds with those of his employer. A management contract is personal. It is not binding on a purchaser of the property.

Chapter 11

CONTRACTS FOR THE
SALE OF LAND

§ 158.   **Why a contract for sale of land is needed.**   Where *A*, a landowner, agrees to sell his land to *B* for $10,000 in cash, one may ask why it is necessary that a contract be signed. Why does not *A* then and there give a deed to *B*, and *B* pay *A* the agreed price? The chief reason is that at the time the agreement is reached, *B* has no assurance, other than *A*'s statement, that *A* is in fact the owner of the land and that there are no defects in his title. Ordinarily, therefore, *B* will insist that a contract be signed and that it provide for an examination of *A*'s title, such examination to show that *A* has good title, before *B* pays the purchase price. In other words, the prudent purchaser is unwilling to buy a pig in a poke. The cash sale contract defines the type of title the seller will deliver, how, when, and where proof is to be made that title is good, and what is to be done if defects in title are revealed. In the meantime, the parties are bound to their bargain by the contract. The seller cannot sell to someone else who offers a higher price, and the buyer is bound to go through with the deal on the agreed terms set forth in the contract. Also, a land sale involves matters other than the sale of the land itself. There are insurance policies to be transferred, leases to be assigned, mortgages to be paid, and many other matters to be attended to. The rights and duties of seller and buyer with respect to these matters should be set forth in the contract.

The cash sale contract contemplates that the deal will be closed as soon as the seller's title is examined and found to be good. There is also a type of contract called the *installment contract, contract for deed* or *land contract*. An installment contract provides for a down payment, with balance of purchase price payable in monthly installments. The buyer receives his deed when all the installments have been paid or when the unpaid balance of the purchase price has been reduced to a certain agreed figure, whereupon the buyer is to receive a deed and give the seller a purchase money mortgage for the balance of the purchase price. The installment contract in many respects resembles a mortgage transaction. Indeed, in some states when a *default* occurs (i.e., the buyer fails to make his payments), the contract is foreclosed like a mortgage. It also resembles somewhat a purchase on credit of an appliance or automobile, where the seller will repossess the article if the buyer defaults in his payments. This corresponds to the seller's right of forfeiture in an installment contract, hereinafter discussed.

§ 159. **Necessity of written contract.**   As a matter of law it is necessary that a contract for the sale of land be in writing. Verbal contracts for the sale of land are not enforceable. Further, the entire contract must be in writing. It cannot be partly in writing and partly verbal. In any litigation involving the contract, the court will reject oral testimony offered for the purpose of supplying omissions in the written document. *Kris v. Pattison,* 159 Minn. 219, 198 N.W. 541.

§ 160. **Minimum requirements of contract.**   Two questions arise regarding the contents of a contract for the sale of land:

1. What *must* the document include in order to be legally enforceable?
2. What *should* the document include over and above the minimum legal requirements?

So far as the first of these questions is concerned, it is the rule that a contract for the sale of real estate cannot be enforced unless the writing contains the names of seller and buyer, a description of the land sufficient to identify it, the price, and the signature of the party against whom enforcement of the contract is sought. *Stein v. McKinney,* 313 Ill. 84, 144 N.E. 795.

No particular form is required, so that a binding contract may be in the form of one or more letters, escrow instructions, a receipt, a check, a promissory note, and so on.

EXAMPLE: A, the buyer, gave B, the seller, his check payable to B. On the face of this check was written the following: "Deposit for land on Galvin Road, Watertown, price thirty-two cents a foot." This was the only land that A owned. It was held that this was a sufficient contract. *Coushelis v. Alexander,* 315 Mass. 729, 54 N.E.2d 47, 153 A.L.R. 1108.

EXAMPLE: A contract was as follows:

Chicago, January 8, 1904

Received of Anton Ullsperger $100 on said purchase of property No. 1031 Milwaukee Avenue, Chicago, Illinois at a price of $14,000.   C. Meyer.

Meyer refused to perform, and Ullsperger sued him. The court compelled Meyer to give Ullsperger a deed. *Ullsperger v. Meyer,* 217 Ill. 262, 75 N.E. 482.

It will be observed in the last example that Ullsperger, who had *not* signed the contract, was allowed to enforce the contract against Meyer, who *had* signed it. However, Meyer could not have enforced the contract against Ullsperger. This is in accord with the general rule that in a land contract a seller may legally compel performance if he can produce a contract signed by the buyer, and the buyer can demand performance if he can produce a contract signed by the seller. Signature by both parties is not necessary.

Such a contract, although it meets the minimum requirements of the law, is altogether unsatisfactory, as will appear from the subsequent discussion.

Obviously, it is best to have both seller and buyer sign the contract, and this is the usual practice.

Many documents that are legally sufficient as contracts for the sale of land are quite short, as the foregoing discussion reveals. Moreover, such documents are often given misleading names, such as *sales deposit receipt* or *offer to purchase.* People sign such documents without realizing that they have obligated themselves to buy or sell real estate. Sometimes such brief documents state that the parties will later sign a "regular" real estate contract. The court decisions are conflicting as to the effect of the inclusion of this phrase. 32 *Ore. L. Rev.* 267. As long as the main terms of the sale are stated in the document, most courts hold that the failure to sign a formal, detailed contract is unimportant, especially where the parties proceed with the details of the transaction as though a binding contract existed. *Sewel v. Dalby,* 171 Kan. 640, 237 P.2d 366; 122 A.L.R. 1217; 165 A.L.R. 765. Other states feel that the parties did not intend to be bound until a formal, detailed contract was executed, as called for in the short form, and therefore hold that the short document is not binding. *Scott v. Fowler,* 227 Ill. 104, 81 N.E. 34; *Lippman v. Featherston,* 247 Mich. 153, 225 N.W. 489.

§ 161. **The seller.**   Just as a deed must have a grantor, a contract must have a seller.

EXAMPLE: A hotel known as the Glen House, together with its furniture, was sold at auction to Joseph Grafton for $90,000. He refused to go through with the deal. The only document signed by Grafton was the following:

"I, the subscriber, do hereby acknowledge myself to be the purchaser of the estate known as the Glen House, with furniture belonging to it, in Green's Grant, New Hampshire, and sold at auction, Tuesday, May 16, 1871, at 11 o'clock a.m., and for the sum of $90,000, the said property being more particularly described in the advertisement hereunto affixed; and I hereby bind myself, my heirs, and assigns to comply with the terms and conditions of the sale, as declared by the auctioneer at the time and place of sale.   Joseph Grafton."

The court held that this was not an enforceable contract of sale, since the seller was not named therein. *Grafton v. Cummings*, 99 U.S. 100.

The following are the chief requirements as to the seller: (1) If the title is held by co-owners, all should be named as sellers. (2) The seller should be an adult of sound mind. (3) If the seller is a corporation, the sale must be authorized by its directors and sometimes by its stockholders. (See § 72.) (4) Where the seller is a trustee or executor, a check should be made to determine that he had the power to sell the land, since neither an executor nor trustee has power to sell land unless the will or trust instrument expressly gives him that power.

A contract by a shareholder in a corporation to cause the corporation to sell and convey corporate land is valid. *Borg v. Warner*, 16 Ill.2d 234, 156 N.E.2d 513.

§ 162. **Signature of seller's spouse.** In many states, the spouse of a landowner has certain rights, dower, and curtesy in the land, and these rights cannot be extinguished without the spouse's signature. (*See* Chapter 17.) When the seller's spouse, in such a state, has not signed the contract of sale and refuses to sign a deed to the property, courts differ as to the courses open to the buyer. In general, the buyer may decline to go through with the deal and may obtain return of his down payment on the ground that the seller is unable to deliver clear title.

In those community property states that require the wife's consent to a disposition of the community property, the wife's consent is needed for a valid contract to convey community real estate. (*See* Chapter 17.)

Where land is occupied by a family as their home, then regardless of whether the land is owned by the husband or the wife, both must join in any deed of the land. Laws relating to homestead require the double signature. Both must join in the contract to sell. (See § 315.)

In states that have abolished dower and curtesy, and that also permit either spouse to convey his or her own land without the signature of the other spouse, the spouse's signature is not necessary either on the contract of sale or on the deed, unless, of course, the land to be sold is a homestead.

In states that have abolished dower, but have substituted some statutory interest that the wife retains if she fails to sign the husband's deed, the courts show the same conflict of opinion as prevails in the states that still have dower. Some allow a deduction from the purchase price to compensate the buyer when the seller's spouse refuses to sign the deed and some do not. *Williams v. Wessels*, 94 Kan. 71, 145 Pac. 856; *Free v. Little*, 31 Utah 449, 88 Pac. 407.

§ 163. The buyer. Just as a deed must have a grantee, so a contract must have a buyer. The buyer should be named in the contract. If there are two or more buyers and they wish to acquire title as joint tenants (*see* Chapter 16), it is necessary that they be so described in the contract. Otherwise serious difficulties may develop if one of the buyers dies before the deed is executed. The buyer should be an adult of sound mind.

§ 164. Sale price—payment provisions. The contract of sale must state the sale price. A common fault in contracts consists of the failure to state precisely how the purchase price is to be paid. In an installment contract, it is desirable from the buyer's point of view to give the buyer the right to prepay, which can be done by providing for monthly payments of a stated sum *or more*. The buyer has no right to prepay unless the contract so provides. *Burns v. Epstein*, 413 Ill. 476, 109 N.E.2d 774. From the seller's point of view it is desirable that an installment contract authorize the seller to declare the entire purchase price due in case of default. Otherwise a chronically delinquent buyer can drive a seller to distraction by *curing his defaults* each time the seller serves notice on him of the seller's intent to declare a forfeiture.

§ 165. Description of the land sold. The contract must contain a reasonably certain description of the land sold. While the description need not be as formal as that contained in a deed, it must be sufficiently definite to identify the land sold with reasonable certainty. 23 A.L.R.2d 6.

There are two views as to the sufficiency of a contract that contains some description of the property but that requires resort to oral testimony to identify the particular property intended to be sold. In states that take a strict view, such contracts are not enforceable.

EXAMPLE: A contract described the land as "real estate situated in the County of Cook and State of Illinois, to wit: One five-room flat and two six-room flats at 3517 Palmer Street." The city in which the land was located was not mentioned. It was held that this description was too indefinite. *Herous v. Romanowski*, 336 Ill. 297, 168 N.E. 305. Since verbal evidence would be needed to establish the city and state in which the land is located, the contract is not sufficient. This is the rule followed in most states.

On the other hand, liberal courts enforce such contracts.

EXAMPLE: A contract identified the land as "305 S. Negley Ave." Oral testimony was admitted to prove that the seller owned property at this address in Pittsburgh, Pennsylvania. *Sawert v. Lunt,* 360 Pa. 521, 62 A.2d 34.

If the city and state are given, a description by street address is sufficient. 23 A.L.R.2d 39. But it is preferable, of course, to use a correct legal description of the land sold.

The land sold necessarily includes all fixtures comprising part of the land. However, in the case of apartment buildings, hotels, and so on, there may be items of personal property used in connection with the land sold that might not be considered fixtures, such as furniture. If these items are also to go to the buyer, the contract should contain a provision to the effect that such personal property shall be transferred to the buyer at the time of the signing of the deed. In the absence of such provision, the buyer is not entitled to any items that are not fixtures. (*See* Chapter 3.)

The subject of descriptions is discussed in detail in Chapter 5.

§ 166.   Completeness.   In order to be enforceable, a contract must be complete in all its parts. All the terms of the contract must be settled, and none must be left to be determined by future negotiation.

EXAMPLE: A contract called for a sale price of $75,000, $5000 cash, "time of possession and balance of payment to be arranged at a later date." This contract is not enforceable even if the buyer wishes to pay cash. *Murphy v. Koll Grocery Co.,* 311 Ky. 771, 225 S.W.2d 466. Note that if the contract had simply stated a price of $75,000 and had said nothing regarding terms, the contract would have been good. The court would have read into the contract that a cash deal was intended, deal to be closed in a reasonable time. But since the parties intended something other than a cash deal, but left the exact terms unsettled, the contract was incomplete. A similar holding followed where a contract stated that balance of price was payable "by future agreement on or before January 1, 19—." *Bentzen v. H. N. Ranch,* 78 Wyo. 158, 320 P.2d 440, 68 A.L.R.2d 1221. The court held likewise where the contract stated that a price of $85,000 was payable "as per terms agreed on." *Roberts v. Adams,* 164 Cal. App.2d 312, 330 P.2d 900. The same was held where the contract stated "balance in monthly payments." *Cefalu v. Breznik,* 15 Ill.2d 168, 154 N.E.2d 237. The court also held likewise where the contract said that the balance of $50,000 was payable "as lots are released at purchaser's convenience." *Edward H. Snow Co. v. Oxsheer,* 62 N.M. 113, 305 P.2d 727. See also *Wilmot v. Giarraputo,* 5 N.Y.2d 250, 157 N.E.2d 282.

If the contract calls for a purchase money mortgage but fails to specify the due date thereof, it is incomplete and cannot be enforced. *Sweeting v. Campbell,* 8 Ill.2d 54, 132 N.E.2d 507; 60 A.L.R.2d 251. And where a contract provided that the seller would give the buyer a deed that would reserve a vendor's lien for the balance of the purchase price, and the contract further provided that "the rate [of interest] will be agreed upon later," it was too incomplete and indefinite to be enforced. *Hume v. Boyle* (Tex. Civ. App.), 204 S.W. 673.

§ 167. **Certainty.** In addition to being complete, the contract must be definite and certain. If the court cannot tell what the parties agreed upon, it cannot force them to carry out their agreement.

EXAMPLE: A agreed to sell certain land to B for $5000, "one-half cash, balance one to four years, with interest at 7 per cent." This contract is too vague and indefinite to be enforced. No one can be certain what the quoted portion means. *Crawford v. Williford,* 145 Ga. 550, 89 S.E. 488.

§ 168. **Type of deed.** A contract is enforcible even though it does not specify the type of deed to be given. Nevertheless, since there is a vast difference between a quitclaim deed and a warranty deed, the contract should specify the type agreed upon.

If the contract is silent regarding the type of deed to be given, in most states the seller need only give a quitclaim deed. *Morris v. Goldthorp,* 390 Ill. 186, 60 N.E.2d 857; *Boekelheide v. Snyder,* 71 S.D. 470, 26 N.W.2d 74; *Vitra Seal Co. v. Jaycox,* 1 N.J.S. 560, 62 A.2d 431; *Tymon v. Linoki,* 16 N.Y.2d 293, 213 N.E.2d 661. This does not excuse the seller from giving a marketable title. (See § 169.) It simply means that once the title has been shown to be marketable, the seller may deliver a quitclaim deed and be rid of any possibility of future worry regarding presently unknown title defects.

It is best for the buyer to insist on a warranty deed. In a number of states, the mere fact that the buyer is content to take a quitclaim deed is enough to keep him from being a bona fide purchaser, and he will take the land subject to unrecorded deeds, mortgages, liens, and so forth.

§ 169. **Marketable title.** Unless the contract provides otherwise, the seller must convey a marketable title. Such a title is also described as a *merchantable title.* This means that the seller must have a good title, free from liens, encumbrances, or defects other than those specified in the contract. As a general rule, every buyer of land has a right to demand a title that shall put him in all reasonable security against loss or annoyance by litigation. He should have a title that is free from doubt, one that will enable him not only to hold his land, but to hold it in peace and free from the hazard of litigation. If he wishes to sell the land, he should be reasonably sure that no flaw will come up to disturb its market value. *Firebaugh v. Wittenberg,* 309 Ill. 536, 141 N.E. 379.

SUGGESTION: The contract should contain a *subject clause* specifying the *permitted objections.* These are the objections the seller knows are against his title, usually those that were in existence when he bought the land, and usually of a character such that they cannot be removed, like building restrictions, and usually such that the buyer finds unobjectionable. As long as they are listed in the subject clause, they do not render title unmarketable.

*The question of marketability of title must be disposed of before the
deal is closed.* In other words, if the buyer wishes to avail himself of
his right to insist upon a marketable title, he must point out such defects
as he discovers and must do this before he pays his money and receives
his deed. Once the deal is closed, the money paid, and the deed delivered,
the buyer cannot demand his money back if the title proves defective. 57
A.L.R. 1261; 84 A.L.R. 1025, 1027, 1032; 92 C.J.S. 15; 92 C.J.S. 559. However, if the buyer has received a warranty deed from the seller, he may
sue the seller for damages, should the title prove defective.

§ 170. **Marketable title—mortgages and other liens.**   Unless
the contract provides otherwise, the buyer has the right to demand a title
free and clear of all mortgages, tax liens, judgment liens, mechanics'
liens, and all other liens. It is not sufficient for the seller to offer to deduct
the amount of such liens from the purchase price. The buyer may reject
the title unless it is actually cleared of such liens. Suppose, however, that
there is a mortgage or other lien on the property, and the seller can
arrange to have the mortgagee present at the closing of the deal, so that,
at the closing of the deal, the mortgage will be paid in full out of the
purchase money due the seller and the mortgagee will deliver a release
of the mortgage to the buyer. Must the buyer go through with the deal
in this manner if the contract does not require him to do so? In quite a
number of states, the answer is in the affirmative. The seller's title is not
considered unmarketable if he can arrange to have the owner of the
mortgage, judgment, or other lien present at the closing of the deal, ready
to turn over proper releases to the buyer on receiving payment of the
amount due from the buyer. *Gibson v. Brown,* 214 Ill. 330, 73 N.E. 578;
Joslyn v. Irvin Dick Co., 168 Minn. 279, 209 N.W. 889; *Sparks v. Helmer,*
142 Okla. 219, 286 Pac. 306. In other states, a contrary rule is followed.
Any mortgage or other lien not mentioned in the contract must be cleared
before the deal is closed. *Johnson v. Malone,* 252 Ala. 609, 42 So.2d 505;
Carey v. Minor C. Keith Inc., 250 N.Y. 216, 164 N.E. 912.

Many lawyers feel that where the contract requires good title to be
established by title insurance, by inference this requires the seller to produce to the buyer a title company policy or commitment free and clear of
any existing mortgage. Inferentially, the contract obviously contemplates
that the *title company* must, before the deal is closed, be satisfied with
documents produced to discharge the mortgage.

CLAUSE FOR SELLER'S BENEFIT: Title is subject to exist-
ing mortgage which will be paid at closing out of balance of purchase price. Release
of mortgage in proper form and canceled mortgage and note will then be delivered
to purchaser.

§171. **Marketable title—easements.**   Easements render the title unmarketable, unless, of course, the contract requires the buyer to take title subject to easements.

NEW DIRECTIONS: In recent decisions the title is not rendered unmarketable by the existence of a *visible* and *beneficial* easement.

EXAMPLE: The contract is silent regarding easements. A utility company has an easement over the rear five feet of the land for an electric power line, and such a power line is, in fact, located on the rear five feet. The power line services the property in question. In many states, the title would be considered marketable. 57 A.L.R. 1426.

SUGGESTION TO SELLER: Check your title insurance policy or other evidence of title. If it shows your title to be subject to an easement, state in contract that title will be subject "to easement recorded as Document No. 1234567."

SUGGESTION TO BUYER: Do not sign a contract stating that seller will deliver title subject "to easements of record." This would obligate you to take title subject to a recorded easement for a one hundred-foot highway running right through the middle of the house. Insist that the contract specifically describe the easements to which the title is subject and read them over before you sign the contract.

§ 172. **Marketable title—restrictions.** Often the use to which a tract of land may be devoted is restricted by building restrictions contained in recorded deeds or subdivision plats. (*See* Chapter 27.) Unless the contract provides otherwise, the buyer is not required to accept a title encumbered with restrictions as to the character of the buildings that may be erected, the use to which the property may be put, and so on, even though such restrictions actually enhance the value of the property.

EXAMPLE: V contracts to sell P a vacant lot in a high-class residential subdivision. The contract does not mention restrictions. In the recorded plat of the subdivision, there is a restriction providing that only single-family dwellings may be erected in the subdivision. P may reject the title. 57 A.L.R. 1414.

Suppose the contract requires the buyer to accept title subject to "building line and building restrictions," but it appears that the building on the property violates existing restrictions. The buyer may decline to go through with the deal, for a *violation of a restriction* is a defect or encumbrance separate and distinct from the restriction itself.

EXAMPLE: A contract required the buyer to accept title subject to building and use restrictions. There was a building restriction prohibiting the erection of buildings within five feet of any side line. The buildings actually extended into the prohibited area. It was held that the buyer could refuse to go through with the deal. *Herb v. Severson,* 32 Wash.2d 159, 201 P.2d 156; *Lehmeyer v. Bower,* 170 Kan. 442, 227 P.2d 102.

SUGGESTION TO BUYER: Never sign a contract which states that title will be subject to "restrictions of record." This obligates you to take title subject to any restriction, no matter how absurd, even a restriction that the only building permitted on the land is a chicken coop. If the seller's title insurance policy is available, look at it. If it shows a restriction, go to the title company or the recorder's office and read the restriction. If you have no objection to it, let the contract read that title will be "subject to restriction recorded as Document No. 123456." Where the contract must be signed at a time when information as to existing building restrictions is not available, and the land is improved with a building that is the principal subject matter of the sale, you might employ the following clause: "Subject to covenants and restrictions of record, provided same are not violated by the existing improvements and the use thereof." When you are buying *vacant* land you *must* insist on reading the restrictions in full before signing the contract.

§ 173. Marketable title—zoning and building code violations.

Building restrictions imposed by deeds or plats must be distinguished from zoning and building ordinances. Such ordinances, though they may greatly restrict the use that may be made of the land, do not render title unmarketable. Generally the attitude of the courts is that zoning and building ordinances are part of the law of the land, and all persons are supposed to take notice of them. Ignorance of the law excuses no one. Suppose that the premises contain actual, existing *violations* of zoning or building ordinances. Here the rule is different. In all the recent decisions, courts have held that substantial existing violations of *zoning ordinances* render title unmarketable. 5 *De Paul L. Rev.* 270; 5 *American Law of Property* § 11.49; *Lohmeyer v. Bower,* 170 Kan. 442, 227 P.2d 102; *Mayer v. De Vincentis,* 107 Pa. Super. 588, 164 Atl. 111; *Hartman v. Rizzuto,* 123 Cal. App.2d 186, 266 P.2d 539.

EXAMPLE: A building containing three apartments was erected in an area where the ordinance prohibited construction of a building containing more than two apartments. The court held that the buyer could terminate the contract and obtain return of his down payment. *Oates v. Delcuze,* 226 La. 751, 77 So.2d 28.

In many cities, violations of building ordinances (like those forbidding basement apartments, requiring certain minimum sanitary arrangements, requiring separate exits for each apartment, requiring fireproof material, etc.) now entail drastic punishment, for cities have come to recognize that the fight against the slum is a fight for survival. Building ordinance violations, like zoning ordinance violations, are being recognized as flaws in the marketability of title, for they impose on a purchaser the same hazards of litigation that the rule of marketability of title was designed to avoid. *Brunko v. Pharo,* 3 Wis.2d 628, 89 N.W.2d 221, 1958 *Wis. L. Rev.* 641; *Bronen v. Marmer,* 206 N.Y.S.2d 909. *Contra: Stone v. Sexsmith,* 28 Wash.2d 947, 184 P.2d 567; *Ableman v. Slader,* 80 Ill. App.2d 94, 224 N.E.2d 569.

The prudent buyer will insist that the contract of sale provide that the seller will deliver the property "free from all violations of zoning and building ordinances," and a check with city officials for such violations should be made before the deal is closed. The seller will not be allowed to avoid by trickery or subterfuge his responsibility for ordinance violations.

EXAMPLE: The sale involved a house with an illegal basement apartment. The seller could not bring the building into compliance by tearing out the illegal apartment, for what the contract really contemplates is that the seller will get a permit from the city legalizing the condition as it was when the contract was signed. As it stands, the title is unmarketable. *Hammer v. Michael*, 243 N.Y. 445, 154 N.E. 305.

Advertising for sale a building that contains ordinance violations may constitute a fraud upon the buyer. (See § 208.)

§ 174. **Marketable title—leases and tenancies.**   Unless the contract so provides, the buyer need not accept a title subject to existing leases, or even to existing tenancies without leases. *Haiss v. Schmukler*, 201 N.Y.S. 332. If such leases or tenancies exist, the contract should provide that the title is subject to such leases or tenancies.

SUGGESTION TO BUYER: Do not sign a contract to accept title subject to *existing leases and tenancies*. The existing leases may be very favorable to the tenant and disadvantageous to the property owner. The seller should therefore be required to include a schedule, either in the contract or in a separate document, listing the expiration date, tenants, and rentals on all existing leases and tenancies, together with a statement as to whether the leases include an option to renew or to purchase the property.

§ 175. **Marketable title—encroachments.**   Encroachments are of three kinds: (1) The building on the land sold encroaches on neighboring land. (2) The building on the land sold encroaches on adjoining streets or alleys. (3) Buildings on adjoining land encroach upon the land sold. 47 A.L.R.2d 331.

When the seller's buildings extend over and upon neighboring land, the factor that renders title unmarketable is the danger that the neighbor may obtain a court order directing removal of the offending portion of the structure, a task that may involve great expense; or the neighbor may institute litigation in an effort to obtain such an order, and the buyer will be put to the expense of defending the litigation. This is in harmony with the principle that a title is not marketable if there is an appreciable risk of litigation. *Very slight* encroachments will not render the title unmarketable, as where a wall of the building on the premises sold extends three-fourths of an inch on neighboring land. *Traxler v. McLeran*, 116 Cal. App. 226, 2 P.2d 553. The reason such property remains marketable is that, when (a) the encroachment of my building on your land is slight, (b) the cost of removal is great, and (c) the benefit to you from removal of the building is slight, courts will not compel removal of the encroachment. *Nitterauer v. Pulley*, 401 Ill. 494, 82 N.E.2d 643. Also, when the building that encroaches on neighboring land is old or dilapidated, or a temporary structure of small value, or a structure that is removable at only slight effort or expense, the title is deemed marketable. 27 *Chicago-Kent L. Rev.* 118. With respect to permanent structures, it is hard to draw the line between objectionable and unobjectionable encroachments. The encroachment of a house one and one-half inches on neighboring land has been held to render title unmarketable. *Stokes v. Johnson*, 57 N.Y. 673.

When buildings on neighboring land encroach on the premises being sold, courts are more liberal. At the worst, the buyer will be deprived of some portion of the land that the seller has agreed to sell. If the area occupied by the encroaching building is insignificant when compared with the total area of the land being sold, the title is marketable. *Merges v. Ringler*, 54 N.Y.S. 280.

When buildings on the land sold extend over adjoining streets or alleys, as in the case of buildings extending over and upon neighboring privately owned land, there is danger that a suit will be instituted to compel removal of the encroachment. Title is unmarketable. Still, if the encroachment is trivial, so that action by the city authorities is highly improbable and it is unlikely that a court would order the encroachment removed, the title is marketable.

EXAMPLE: A building encroached two inches on an adjoining street. The title was held to be marketable. *Mertens v. Berendsen*, 213 Cal. 111, 1 P.2d 440.

Suppose the contract provides that the seller agrees to deliver a title "subject to questions of survey" or "subject to such a state of facts as an accurate survey would show." Such clauses are inserted to relieve the seller of all responsibility with respect to encroachments. If the existence of encroachments is revealed, the buyer must nevertheless go through with the deal. *McCarter v. Crawford*, 245 N.Y. 43, 156 N.E. 90.

Suppose the contract requires the seller to deliver title "free from all encumbrances and encroachments." Here the existence of trivial encroachments, such as would ordinarily not render title unmarketable, will nevertheless justify the buyer's rejection of the title. 27 *Chicago-Kent L. Rev.* 120.

§ 176. **Marketable title—miscellaneous defects.**   There are many other defects or encumbrances that may render a title unmarketable. For example, a deed signed by some prior landowner may be defective in that the property is not properly described therein, or a signature may be lacking, or the grantor's wife may have failed to sign the deed. Court proceedings on which the title depends, such as mortgage foreclosures, sales by guardians, and the like, may have been defectively conducted. Estates of deceased landowners may have been improperly probated. It is impossible to enumerate within the allotted space the many defects that may render a title unmarketable. Marketability of title plays an important part in those situations where the buyer, after having signed a contract to purchase the land, regrets his bargain and wishes to get out of the deal. His attorney will then subject the title to a minute scrutiny, hoping to find some defect that renders the title unmarketable, so that his client may declare the contract at an end and obtain a return of his down payment.

§ 177. **Marketable title laws.** With each passing year it has grown increasingly difficult to prove that any given title to land is marketable. Year by year the chain of deeds, mortgages, wills, and other recorded matter relating to the title, beginning with the original grant from the government, grows longer and more complex. In consequence, abstracts of title and title searches grow longer, more difficult, and more complex. Many more opportunities present themselves for technical errors that impair the marketability of title. For these difficulties a solution had to be found. It has, indeed, been found in a number of states. In these states (Illinois, Indiana, Iowa, Massachusetts, Michigan, Minnesota, Nebraska, North Dakota, Ohio, South Dakota, and Wisconsin, for example) new laws have been passed to promote the marketability of title. In general, laws such as this select a particular period of time. In Illinois, for example, the period is forty years. If an examination of the public records shows that for the last forty years title to a particular tract of land has passed from one person to another in a connected fashion, that this connected chain of title culminates in a deed to X, and that X is in peaceable possession of the land in question, X will be deemed to have good and marketable title to that tract of land free and clear from any adverse claims to the title that antedate the forty-year period. This does not mean that all claims that are forty years old or more are automatically wiped out. Each of these marketability laws provides a period of time during which a person claiming an interest that is more than forty years old (or whatever the statutory period may be) may record an affidavit or other claim stating the nature of his interest in a particular piece of land. In this fashion, any claim to the title of land must appear on the records within the last forty years or it is automatically outlawed. Consequently, a person searching the title to the land need only search the title during the past forty years, and if he finds a connected chain, he need not concern himself with recorded matters that antedate the forty-year period.

Each of these marketability laws lists certain interests that are not affected or outlawed by the legislation.

EXAMPLE: A common provision is to the effect that a person claiming an easement need not record his claim of easement if the existence of such an easement is revealed by a physical examination of the land itself. Thus if a neighbor claims party wall rights or an easement for a driveway extending over the premises, it is fairly clear that a mere glance at the property will reveal the existence of such easement claims. Therefore they need not be re-recorded.

Another common exception relates to claims of the United States Government. No state has the power or right to pass laws that extinguish the rights of the United States Government. But whatever the claim may be, if it does not fall within the list of claims not affected by the legislation, it is outlawed unless a document in proper form showing the existence of such claim is recorded within the forty-year period. As to these laws see 47 *Ia. L. Rev.* 261; 71 A.L.R.2d 846.

§ 178. **Time of existence of good title.** Ordinarily the seller need not have good title on the date of the contract. It is sufficient if he has good title at the time fixed for delivery of the deed, or even later, for example, at the time the court, in a specific performance suit, orders the contract to be enforced. *Gibson v. Brown,* 214 Ill. 330, 73 N.E. 578.

If the contract provides that *time is of the essence* and also provides that the seller will furnish the buyer an abstract of title or other evidence of title within a specified period of time, the seller must meet this deadline, or the buyer will have the right to declare the contract at an end.

It is likewise sufficient in installment contracts if the seller has good title on the date fixed for the delivery of the deed. Thus if the buyer contracts to pay the purchase price in installments, the seller is entitled to the entire life of the contract in which to clear up his title. The buyer may thus find himself making payment after payment to a seller whose title later proves defective. 109 A.L.R. 242. This danger is aggravated where the seller is a corporation having little or no financial responsibility. If, however, during the life of the contract it develops that the defects in the seller's title are *hopelessly incurable,* the buyer may declare the contract at an end even though the time for conveyance has not yet arrived. 109 A.L.R. 242.

EXAMPLE: While the purchaser was paying on an installment contract, he learned that a recorded public utility easement ran through the middle of the property. He may declare the contract at an end.

§ 179. **Evidence of title.** It is important to distinguish between the seller's duty to deliver *good title* and his duty to furnish *evi-*

dence that his title is good. As above stated, unless the contract provides otherwise, the seller must furnish the buyer a *marketable title*. But if the contract does not require him to do so, the seller is under no obligation to furnish the buyer *any evidence that the title is good*. The buyer makes his own title search unless the contract specifies otherwise. Usually the buyer will insist that the contract require the seller to furnish evidence that his title is good. (*See* Chapter 14.)

§ 180.   **Time for furnishing evidence of title and curing defects in title.**   If the contract requires the seller to furnish evidence of title, but does not fix a time limit for the furnishing and examination of the abstract or other evidence of title, it is assumed that a reasonable time was intended. In such case:

1. The seller has a reasonable time to furnish the buyer the abstract.
2. The buyer has a reasonable time to examine the abstract and point out defects in title.
3. The seller has a reasonable time to eliminate or cure defects in title disclosed by the abstract.

To eliminate uncertainties and speculation by either party on the rise or fall of the value of the property before choosing to perform his part of the contract, the contract should:

1. Fix the time allowed the seller to furnish the buyer evidence of title.

EXPLANATION: When the contract requires the seller to furnish evidence of title by a day named and provides that time is of the essence, and the title evidence is not furnished by the day named, the buyer may rescind, i.e., declare the contract terminated, and may recover his deposit. Most forms of contracts fix a specific time for furnishing the evidence of title and provide that time is of the essence.

2. Fix the time allowed the buyer to examine the abstract and require him to point out any defects in title within the time limited, failure to do so to constitute an acceptance of the title as good.
3. Fix the time allowed the seller to cure defects in title.
4. Fix a time within which the buyer must choose to accept or reject a defective title that the seller cannot cure within the time allowed him.

§ 181.   **Earnest money.**   Earnest money is a deposit, or down payment, made by the buyer as a guaranty that the contract will be performed on his part. If he does perform, it applies as a part payment of the purchase price, but if he defaults, it is retained by the seller. The contract usually specifically permits the seller to retain the earnest money where the buyer defaults, but even in the absence of such provision a buyer who is in default cannot recover his earnest money from the seller.

Glenn v. Price, 337 Ill. App. 637, 86 N.E.2d 542; 31 A.L.R.2d 8. Courts have allowed the seller to retain rather substantial down payments; for example, $300,000 on a sale price of $3,900,000, and $35,000 on a sale price of $140,000. 40 *Yale L. J.* 103.

SUGGESTION TO SELLER: The seller should, for his protection, require a deposit large enough to cover the broker's commission, expense of the title search, and compensation to the seller for the loss of his bargain should the buyer default.

SUGGESTION TO BUYER: Provide that the earnest money shall be held *in escrow* by some third person pending the closing of the deal, so that the buyer will experience no difficulty in obtaining a return of his deposit should it prove impossible for the seller to deliver clear title. *Gauss v. Kirk* (D.C.), 77 A.2d 323.

§ 182. **Contingent contracts.** Often a clause will be inserted in a contract making it subject to some contingency, so that if the specified event does not occur the deal is off and the buyer gets back his down payment. Usually such clauses are inserted at the buyer's request. One example would be a clause making the contract contingent on the buyer's ability to procure a mortgage loan of a specified sum. (See § 183.) Or the contract may be contingent on the buyer's ability to procure a transfer to himself of the seller's liquor license. Or the contract may be contingent on the rezoning of the premises within a specified time. For example, if a buyer needs the property for an industrial plant, but it is presently zoned for residential purposes, he will insist that the contract provide that the contract will become void unless rezoning is obtained within a certain number of days.

At times these contingency clauses tend to be rather vague. Nevertheless the courts will enforce them.

EXAMPLE: A contract of sale provided that the contract was contingent upon the buyer's ability to get leases satisfactory to the buyer. This is a good contract. The courts will hold that the buyer must exercise an honest judgment in good faith, but the contract is valid. *Mattei v. Hopper*, 51 Cal.2d 119, 330 P.2d 625. And where the contract called for a soil compaction report satisfactory to the buyer, the court held that this meant a report satisfactory to a reasonable person. *Collins v. Vickter Manor*, 47 Cal.2d 875, 306 P.2d 783.

Any contingency clause inserted for the buyer's benefit is one that he may waive or dispense with. *Funke v. Paist*, 356 Pa. 594, 52 A.2d 655. If the buyer decides that he wants the property even though he cannot get the specified mortgage loan, or liquor license, or rezoning, as the case may be, he has the right to insist that the deal go through.

If the contract is subject to a contingency that requires action on the part of the buyer—for example, procuring approval by the village of a proposed plat of a subdivision—and the buyer makes no effort to do what is required, that clause drops out and the buyer is bound, even though the necessary approval is not secured.

§ 183. **Mortgages and financing in real estate sales.** In the financing of real estate sales several possibilities are present:

1. The land may have no mortgage on it, and the buyer may be ready to pay cash. No mortgage figures in the sale of the land.

2. The land may have no mortgage on it, but the seller may be willing to accept part cash and to take back a purchase money mortgage for the balance of the purchase price. For example, an insurance company owns a building that it has acquired by foreclosure of a mortgage. It will wish to sell the land, since it is not in the real estate business, but since it also wishes to keep its money in good investments, a purchase money mortgage may be the ideal solution for both seller and buyer.

3. The land is clear of mortgages, but the buyer will need to mortgage the property in order to raise the full purchase price.

4. The land is subject to an existing mortgage, and the buyer is willing to buy the property subject to such existing mortgage.

5. The land is subject to an existing mortgage, but it is too small, or the payments are not convenient for the buyer, so that it will be necessary for the buyer to put a new mortgage on the property for an amount and payable on such terms as will meet his needs. This means that the sale involves paying the existing mortgage and simultaneously placing a new mortgage on the property.

6. The sale may be by an installment contract with clause reserving right to seller to mortgage the land, buyer to take title subject to the mortgage.

7. The sale may be by an installment contract with provision that buyer will receive deed when specified amount is paid in, buyer then to give seller mortgage for balance of purchase price.

8. The sale may be by an installment contract with no mortgage provisions.

Special laws. In Maryland, a law provides that when the purchaser in an installment contract has paid 40 per cent of the purchase price he is entitled to demand a deed upon executing a purchase money mortgage to the seller for the balance. 13 Rutgers L. Rev. 625.

Unless the contract provides otherwise, the buyer need not accept title subject to a mortgage. If there is a mortgage on the land and the buyer is to accept the land with the mortgage remaining unpaid, the contract should specify: (1) that the land is being sold subject to such mortgage; (2) the amount remaining unpaid thereon; (3) whether or not the buyer *assumes and agrees* to pay the mortgage, since if he does, he becomes personally liable to the mortgagee for the mortgage debt. If he does not *assume and agree* to pay the mortgage, he may lose the land by foreclosure should he default in his mortgage payments, but no personal judgment can be rendered against him. If the contract calls for the buyer to take the land subject to a mortgage but misdescribes the mortgage, the buyer can back out of the deed. *Crooke v. Nelson,* 195 Ia. 681, 191 N.W. 122.

If a purchase money mortgage is to be given by the buyer as part payment, the contract should state the amount thereof, the rate of interest, how principal and interest shall be payable, whether or not monthly deposits are to be made to cover taxes, any other special provisions to be inserted in the mortgage, and the form of mortgage to be employed. Great care should be exercised in drafting the purchase money mortgage provision, since it is on this particular point that many contracts have been held too vague and uncertain to be enforced. Once again it must be emphasized that courts cannot enforce a contract unless the parties have clearly set forth therein the terms of their agreement. If the contract calls for a purchase money mortgage, but fails to specify a due date thereof, the contract is incomplete and cannot be enforced. The contract should also specify who is to pay for the recording of the purchase money mortgage and the cost of bringing down the abstract or title policy thereon. The buyer usually pays this expense.

If there is already a first mortgage on the land to which the purchase money mortgage will be subject, it is customary to provide that the purchase money mortgage will be subject to any extension or replacement of the existing first mortgage. This is done to make it possible for the buyer to obtain a new mortgage to pay off the existing first mortgage when it falls due.

Where the contract buyer directs the seller to name as grantee in the deed some nominee or strawman for the buyer, and such nominee signs a mortgage on the land, the buyer, since he has not signed either the mortgage or mortgage note, has no personal liability thereon. *Barkhausen v. Continental Illinois Bank*, 3 Ill.2d 254, 120 N.E.2d 649; *Naas v. Peters*, 388 Ill. 505, 58 N.E.2d 530.

Suppose a landowner is willing to sell his land for $15,000 cash. The buyer has $4,000 cash but is not certain that he can obtain a mortgage loan of $11,000, which is the amount needed to complete the deal. He may insist that the contract expressly permit him to terminate the contract and demand return of his earnest money if he cannot obtain a loan in the required amount within a certain specified time. If the buyer produces the full purchase price in *cash* within the allotted time, the seller must accept it. *Nyder v. Champlin*, 401 Ill. 317, 81 N.E.2d 923; *Gottlaub v. Cohen*, 139 N.J.Eq. 323, 51 A.2d 254.

SUGGESTION TO SELLER: There is danger to the seller that the buyer may make only half-hearted efforts to procure the loan if he decides that he does not really want to go through with the deal. It is therefore desirable from the seller's viewpoint that the clause give the buyer a specified time in which to procure the loan, and in case of his failure so to do, the seller is given a further period of time in which to procure the loan for the buyer.

If the contract is contingent upon the buyer's procuring a mortgage of a specified amount, and he makes no effort to procure one (as is likely to occur when the buyer has changed his mind about buying the property), the clause is waived, and the seller is entitled to forfeit the buyer's earnest money. *Huckleberry v. Wilson* (Tex. Civ. App.), 284 S.W.2d 205.

One common fault with *contingent clauses* is that they often fail to give details of the mortgage, such as interest rate, time of payment, and so forth. A seller may procure a mortgage loan of the desired amount for the buyer and the buyer rejects it in horror because the interest rate is too high. Obviously, all such details should be covered in the clause. If, however, the details are omitted, courts are likely to insist that the terms of the offered mortgage be "reasonable"; otherwise the buyer is not required to accept it. *Lach v. Cahill*, 138 Conn. 418, 85 A.2d 481. Minds differ so much as to what is reasonable that controversy and litigation easily develop in such a situation.

> **SUGGESTION TO SELLER:** Tie the contingent clause into the printed clause of the contract form. The contract may give the buyer *thirty* days in which to procure a mortgage of a specified amount. Yet the printed portion of the contract may state that seller must deliver the buyer evidence of seller's good title within *twenty* days of the date of the contract. Why should seller have his title examined when he does not even know that he has a deal with the buyer?

§ 184. **Possession and rents.** The general rule of law is that the right to possession of land follows the legal title. Since the purchaser does not acquire the legal title to the land until he receives his deed, as a rule he is not entitled to possession until that time. 56 A.L.R.2d 1272. The contract, however, may expressly authorize the buyer to take possession before he receives his deed, and such a provision should normally be included in an installment contract, for a purchaser in such a contract usually expects to take possession long before he is ready to receive his deed. Also, the contract may by implication confer the right of possession on the buyer, as where it contains a provision requiring the buyer to keep the buildings in repair or to give up possession in case of default.

The party who is entitled to possession is entitled to the rents of the land. Ordinarily, therefore, rents falling due before the seller gives the buyer a deed belong to the seller, and rents due after the delivery of the deed are payable to the buyer.

§ 185. **Taxes.** Unless the contract provides otherwise, the seller must give the buyer good title free and clear of taxes that were a lien at the time the contract was made. In fact, if the seller remains in possession after the contract is made, and taxes become a lien while the seller is in possession, the seller must pay these taxes. However, if the buyer goes into possession and taxes thereafter become a lien, the buyer must pay these taxes. To eliminate questions, the contract usually specifies the taxes to which the land will be subject when the deed is made.

§ 186. **Insurance and risk of loss.** It sometimes happens that before the deal is closed the building is destroyed or damaged by fire or other casualty. In most states, the loss so caused falls on the buyer. In other words, the buyer must go through with the deal and pay the full contract price, even though the building has been destroyed. 27 A.L.R.2d 446. But in an increasing number of states, including California, Connecticut, Illinois, Kentucky, Maine, Massachusetts, Michigan, New Hampshire, New York, Oregon, Rhode Island, South Carolina, South Dakota, and Wisconsin, laws or court decisions put the risk of loss on the seller, so that if a substantial loss by fire or other casualty occurs before the buyer has been given a deed to the property, the buyer may cancel the deal and obtain return of his down payment. However, an important factor in some of these states is the fact of possession. The one in possession is in a better position to prevent fires. Hence in these states, if the buyer is put in possession before the deal is closed, you will find the courts or the laws assigning this as a reason for putting the risk of loss back on the buyer.

In all states the risk of loss falls on the seller where: (1) The contract specifically provides that risk of loss pending closing of the deal rests on the seller. (2) The seller does not have good marketable title at the time of the loss, the reason being that it is unfair to put the risk of loss on a buyer when the seller is in no position to perform his obligations under the contract. *Eppstein v. Kuhn*, 225 Ill. 115, 80 N.E. 80. (3) The seller is at fault in causing the delay in closing the deal, and during this delayed period a loss occurs. (4) The loss is due to the carelessness of the seller, as when he leaves the house during a cold spell without draining the heating system and all the radiators are cracked by ice formation. 33 *Ia. L. Rev.* 171; 3 Corbin, *Contracts* 661.

§ 187. **Prorating or apportionment.** Provision is frequently made for prorating, adjustment, or apportionment of rents, taxes, insurance, premiums, water taxes, interest accrued on mortgage indebtedness, personal property taxes on personal property transferred to the buyer, gas and electric bills, janitor's salary, management fees on current rent collections, and charges on service contracts, such as exterminator or scavenger service. It is also customary to provide that fuel on hand shall be purchased by the buyer at current prices as of the proration date. Although it is usual to prorate certain items not mentioned in the contract, it must be remembered that, in the event of controversy, the party contending that an item should be prorated will be unable legally to compel proration in the absence of provision in the contract therefor. *Lathers* *v. Keogh,* 109 N.Y. 583, 17 N.E. 131. A special prorating clause is needed where there are percentage leases, since the actual rental will not be known until after the deal is closed.

§ **188.   Date.**   The contract need not be, but usually is, dated.

§ **189.   Signature.**   As heretofore pointed out, the contract must be signed by the party against whom enforcement of the contract is sought. Of course in practice the contract is almost invariably signed by both seller and buyer.

Suppose land is owned jointly by A and B. C negotiates with A for the purchase of the property and agrees with A that the land will be sold for the sum of $10,000. A contract is prepared, designating A and B as sellers and C as buyer. A and C sign the contract; B refuses to sign. Is the contract binding on A? No, for the contract shows on its face that a sale was intended only if both landowners agreed. *Madia v. Collins,* 408 Ill. 358, 97 N.E.2d 313; 154 A.L.R. 778; 92 C.J.S. 547.

§ **190.   Contracts signed by agents.**   A person may authorize an agent to enter into contracts on his behalf for the purchase or sale of real estate. In many states, this authorization must be in writing, and in all states it is customary to employ a written authorization. Such an agent is called an *attorney in fact,* and the document granting this authority is called a *power of attorney.*

§ **191.   Seal.**   A seal is not necessary to the validity of a contract.

§ **192.   Delivery.**   Suppose you list your land with a broker for sale and he finds a buyer interested in its purchase but who does not wish to pay the price you are asking. The buyer prepares and signs a contract of sale stipulating a lower price. This is an *offer.* He hands the contract to the broker, who hands it to you. You sign the contract and return it to the buyer. This is an *acceptance.* The contract is now in force. Suppose, however, that you simply hold on to the contract, hoping that a higher offer will appear, and refuse to answer the buyer's telephone calls. This last situation poses the questions: (1) Must the buyer be *notified* that his offer has been accepted? In other words, can he legally withdraw his offer at any time before he is *notified* that the offer has been accepted? (2) Is delivery necessary to the validity of a contract? The buyer, you will notice, is in an awkward spot. He cannot risk signing a contract to buy some other house, for if he does, he may find himself obligated to buy two houses. Some courts protect the buyer and allow him to revoke his offer in this last situation, stating either that the acceptance is ineffective until the buyer is notified thereof or that delivery is necessary for a written contract to be binding. *Hollingshead v. Morris,* 172 Mich. 126, 137 N.W. 527. However, there are also contrary decisions. 1 Corbin, *Contracts* 93, 208.

SUGGESTION TO BUYER: Let the contract be prepared in duplicate. The buyer signs both duplicates. Each duplicate contains a provision that the buyer's liability, if any, is terminated and his down payment returned, unless a duplicate signed by the seller is delivered to the buyer within three days after the date of the contract. The buyer hands both duplicates to the seller but retains a carbon copy, so that he can always prove his nonliability if he fails to receive a signed duplicate within the specified time.

§ 193. **Acknowledgments.** An acknowledgment is not necessary, although it is desirable since it simplifies proof of the contract in any suit brought thereon. If the contract is to be recorded, acknowledgment is necessary in nearly all states.

§ 194. **Witnesses.** If the contract is not acknowledged, it should, as a practical matter, be witnessed, although this is not necessary as a matter of law. The fact that the signatures are witnessed simplifies use of the contract in any litigation that may develop.

§ 195. **Effect of contract.** The signing of a contract for the sale of land does not give the buyer legal title to the land. Ownership can be transferred to the buyer only by a deed. However, the buyer does acquire an interest in the land. This interest is known as *equitable title*. If the parties decide not to go through with the deal, the buyer should give the seller a quitclaim deed.

§ 196. **Effect of deed.** When the deal is closed and the seller's deed delivered to the buyer, the deal is regarded as consummated. The contract of sale has served its purpose. It is *merged* in the deed. 38 A.L.R.2d 1310. The contract no longer exists. For this reason, if matters remain to be attended to after closing of the deal, it is best that they be set forth in the deed. This is particularly important as to title matters, for the buyer waives his right to cancel the contract because of defects in title if he accepts and pays for a deed while the title is defective or encumbered. (See § 169.) However, there are some exceptions to the merger rule. In particular, when the contract calls for something to be done after the deal is closed, delivery of the deed does not extinguish that aspect of the contract.

EXAMPLE: The contract required the seller to lay water mains and sewers after closing of the deal. The deal was closed, and the deed delivered to buyer. Thereafter, the seller failed to lay the water mains and sewers. The buyer filed a damage suit against the seller, and the seller was held liable. *McMillan v. American Suburban Corp.,* 136 Tenn. 53, 188 S.W. 615. The same would be true where the contract requires the seller to build a house on the land sold. 84 A.L.R. 1023. If the contract warrants that the building is in sound condition, this warranty survives the closing of the deal, for that obviously was what the parties intended. *Levin v. Cook,* 186 Md. 535, 47 A.2d 505. Contract provisions as to the date on which possession will be turned over to the buyer are not merged in the deed. In all these cases the buyer's only remedy, if the seller fails to perform, is to sue the seller for damages. He cannot sue to get his money back. *De Bisschop v. Crump,* 24 F.2d 807.

§ 197. **Assignment of the contract.** The buyer may assign his interest in the contract. By virtue of the contract, the buyer has the right to demand a deed to the property on performing his part of the contract. He may sell and transfer this right to a third party, which is accomplished by means of a brief instrument called an *assignment.* Such third party is called the *assignee.* The assignee has the right to make the payments required by the contract and to demand a deed from the seller. In other words, the assignee steps into the shoes of the buyer and may compel the seller to perform his part of the contract.

However, the assignee does not become personally liable to the seller for payment of the purchase price, unless the assignment provides that the assignee *assumes and agrees to pay* the purchase price. *Lisenby v. Newton,* 120 Cal. 571, 52 Pac. 813.

Of course the buyer cannot escape personal liability for payment of the purchase price by assigning the contract. He remains liable to the seller notwithstanding the assignment. If the rule were otherwise, a buyer could always rid himself of a burdensome contract by assigning it to a pauper.

§ 198. **Deed by seller to stranger.** When the seller, after entering into the contract, sells and conveys the land to some third party, the question arises as to whether the buyer under the contract can compel such third party to give him a deed to the land on payment of the contract price. The buyer can compel such third party to give him a deed on payment of the contract price in the following cases:

1. When the contract was recorded prior to the making of the deed to the third party.
2. When, though the contract was not recorded, the buyer took possession of the land prior to the making of the deed to the third party.
3. When, even though the contract was not recorded and the buyer did not take possession of the land, the third party actually knew of the earlier contract at the time he received his deed.

If the case does not fall within these three rules, the buyer cannot compel the third party to give him a deed. In other words, he has lost all his rights in the land. However, the buyer may then sue his seller and recover from him any amounts paid on the purchase price.

If the contract requires the seller to give a warranty deed, the buyer need not accept a warranty deed signed only by the seller's grantee. The seller must also join in the deed. *Crabtree v. Levings,* 53 Ill. 526.

§ 199. **Time for performance.** The contract should specify the date on which the deal is to be closed. If the contract does not specifically fix the time when it is to be performed, it will be implied that it is to be performed within a reasonable time, and the purchase price must be paid at that time. Most contracts fix a specific time for the performance of all acts thereunder. If the contract provides that *time is of the essence,* each act required by the contract must be done promptly at the time specified. In a cash sale, where time is of the essence, if either party fails to perform promptly he will be unable to obtain specific performance.

> **EXAMPLE:** Contract called for earnest money down payment, balance to be paid within five days after seller's title was shown to be good, and time to be of the essence. Seller delivered evidence of good title on August 5. Buyer did nothing. On August 19, seller served notice on buyer to close deal within five days. Buyer again did nothing. On September 10, buyer tendered balance of purchase price. Seller refused to accept. Buyer now filed suit for specific performance and the court refused to grant it. Buyer was in default and time was of the essence. *Johnson v. Riedler,* 395 Ill. 412, 70 N.E.2d 570.

§ 200.   Remedies of the seller—forfeiture by seller.

When the buyer defaults in his payments under the contract, the seller faces several problems: (1) He must terminate the buyer's rights under the contract so that he can proceed to sell the property to others. (2) He must accomplish this termination in such a way that the buyer will not be entitled to a return of such payments as he has made. (3) He must evict the buyer if the latter has taken possession. (4) If the buyer has recorded the contract, steps must be taken to remove the cloud thus created.

So far as *cash sales* are concerned, the problem is usually relatively simple. The seller must, within the time allowed by the contract, do the things he is required to do. For example, if the contract requires the seller to furnish the buyer, within thirty days of the date of the contract, an abstract showing good title in the seller, this must be done. Then, at the time and place fixed for closing, the seller should be present and should offer or tender his deed to the buyer and demand payment for the balance of the purchase price. *Frink v. Thomas,* 20 Ore. 265, 25 Pac. 717. If the buyer fails to pay the balance of the purchase price, the seller may declare the contract terminated and retain the earnest money, and the buyer's rights are at an end. *Boston v. Clifford,* 68 Ill. 67. The seller need not make a formal tender where the buyer clearly has shown an intention not to perform, so that tender would be a useless act. *Citizens' Nat. Bank v. Davisson,* 229 U.S. 212. Since in a cash sale the buyer is rarely permitted to take possession before the deal is closed, possession offers no problem. As long as the seller has done the things that the contract requires of him (e.g., furnishing evidence of marketable title within the time allowed by the contract) the seller will have the right to declare a forfeiture of the buyer's earnest money and contract rights *even though the contract does not spell this out.* 31 A.L.R.2d 96. After all, earnest money is given to prove that the buyer is earnest. If he is not, he deserves to lose his deposit. However, it is better to have a clause in the contract spelling out this right of forfeiture, although it is not necessary. 31 A.L.R.2d 20, 34, 36. A seller who has done all that the contract requires of him need not give the buyer notice and warning of his intention to forfeit the earnest money. He may simply send the buyer a notice declaring the contract forfeited when the buyer defaults.

We now turn our attention to forfeitures of *installment contracts.* Almost every installment contract you encounter will contain a clause stating that, if the buyer defaults, the seller may declare his rights under the contract forfeited and retain all payments that the buyer has made. The situation differs from the cash sale situation in several respects. First, the buyer has usually occupied the property and thinks of it as his home, his store, or the like. Second, the buyer usually has been making payments over a period of years, and when he stops making payments it is often because he has suffered some personal disaster, such as illness or loss of employment. For these reasons the courts are far more sympathetic toward the buyer than in the case of cash sales.

As against this is the fact that, in installment contracts, the buyer's down payment is usually small. If I want to buy a house for $15,000 and have saved $3000 for a down payment, I can get a mortgage for $12,000. If I default in my payments, I will have all the protection of redemption laws, public auction sale laws, and the other protective measures that the law accords a mortgagor. But if I am buying an old, single-family dwelling for $10,000 and can make a down payment of only $500, no one in his right mind is going to give me a mortgage. I must buy this house on an installment contract. To ask the seller to go through the expense of a costly foreclosure suit, with redemption rights in many states, is unrealistic. The only sensible solution is to allow the seller to declare a forfeiture if I should default and to evict me in the same way a landlord evicts a tenant who does not pay his rent.

In order to create an enforcible right of forfeiture, *it is indispensable that an installment contract contain a provision giving the seller the right to declare a forfeiture in the event of the buyer's default.* This is what distinguishes *forfeiture* from *rescission.* If there is no provision in the contract regarding forfeiture, then in the event the buyer defaults, the seller has the right to terminate the contract. But such termination is called *rescission.* The seller who rescinds must refund to the buyer the payments he has made, less a fair rent for the time the buyer has been in possession. *Hillman v. Busselle,* 66 Ariz. 139, 185 P.2d 311. *Forfeiture* is a right expressly given in the contract itself. *Realty Securities Corp. v. Johnson,* 93 Fla. 46, 111 So. 532. By declaring a forfeiture the seller terminates the

contract and *retains all payments previously made by the buyer.* 55 Am.
Jur. 929.

Just as we so often find that tenants do not pay their monthly rent exactly on the day it is due, so we often find that purchasers under installment contracts do not pay their payments exactly on the day they are
due, or they may from time to time make payments of less than the
amount due. The overwhelming majority of installment sellers go along
with the buyer, hoping that he will ultimately be able to straighten out
his finances. Ultimately the seller may decide that he can no longer be
indulgent. Then he faces a problem that his own indulgence has created.

> **EXAMPLE:** An installment contract provided that time was of the essence,
> but the seller often accepted payments after the dates fixed for payment. This consti-
> tuted a waiver of the provision that time was of the essence. The reason is that the
> seller, by accepting payments after the dates fixed, had led the buyer to believe that
> he would not insist on the provision that payments must be made strictly on the speci-
> fied dates. It would therefore be highly unjust to permit the seller suddenly to declare
> a forfeiture of the contract for the buyer's failure to pay one of the installments
> promptly. *Fox v. Grange,* 261 Ill. 116, 103 N.E. 576; 31 A.L.R.2d 55, 85.

The seller may *revive* the provision that time is of the essence. He may
serve a *warning notice* on the buyer that in the future he will insist on
strict performance of the contract according to its terms, and thereafter
the buyer must make his payments promptly or the seller may declare a
forfeiture. This warning notice must be followed by a declaration of forfeiture if the buyer fails to cure his defaults within the allotted time. Such
a warning notice must not be a mere dun. It must state unequivocally that
the contract will be forfeited if the defaults are not cured within the
specified time. *Monson v. Bragdon,* 159 Ill. 61, 42 N.E. 383. Many printed
contract forms contain a provision that acceptance of late payments shall
not constitute a waiver of the provision that time is of the essence. Some
courts refuse to give this provision effect. *Morrey v. Bartlett,* 288 Ill. App.
620; *Scott v. Cal. Farming Co.,* 4 Cal. App.2d 232, 40 P.2d 850. In many
states, a warning notice must always be given before an installment contract is forfeited. *County of Lincoln v. Fischer,* 216 Ore. 421, 339 P.2d
1084; 31 A.L.R.2d 14.

Even where a forfeiture has been declared, it is possible that the
buyer's rights may be revived. This occurs where the seller waives the forfeiture by conduct indicating that he considers the contract still in force,
as by negotiating with the buyer concerning the title of the property, possible repurchase by the seller, extension of time of payment, and the like.
107 A.L.R. 345.

Where a recorded contract has been properly forfeited, the seller can
obtain a court decree declaring the buyer's rights terminated.

Where the buyer is in military service, the contract cannot be forfeited without a court order. The court may either postpone the forfeiture or order the repayment of prior installments before permitting forfeiture of the contract.

Special laws. In California, Georgia, Montana, South Dakota, Wisconsin, and Utah, a purchaser whose contract has been forfeited is allowed to get back the amount he has paid, less a reasonable compensation to the seller for the use of his land. Iowa and Minnesota allow the purchaser to cure his defaults within a specified grace period and thus preserve his contract. Arizona also provides a grace period within which the purchaser can cure his defaults, and the grace period increases in proportion to the amount paid on the contract. 13 *Rutgers L. Rev.* 624; 24 *Mo. L. Rev.* 244. In Florida and Maryland, the contract must be foreclosed like a mortgage. *Mid State Inv. Corp. v. O'Steen* (Fla.), 133 S.2d 455. However, in most states, the forfeiture provisions in the contract will be enforced. *Coe v. Bennett,* 46 Ida. 62, 266 Pac. 413; 31 A.L.R.2d 38, 71.

Perhaps the most important clause in an installment contract, from the seller's point of view, is the forfeiture clause.

§ 201. **Remedies of the seller—remedies other than forfeiture.** If the buyer fails or refuses to perform, the seller, in lieu of declaring a forfeiture, may pursue one of the following courses:

1. He may *rescind* the contract. *Rescission* is not the same as *forfeiture. Coe v. Bennett,* 46 Ida. 62, 266 Pac. 413. By rescinding, the seller declares the contract at an end and surrenders all rights thereunder. Both seller and buyer must be restored, as far as possible, to the situation existing before the contract was made. The seller, on rescinding, must give back to the buyer the payments he has made, less a fair rent for the time the buyer has been in possession. *Hillman v. Busselle,* 66 Ariz. 139, 185 P.2d 311. The right to rescind does not depend upon any provision in the contract. However, most contracts give the seller the right to declare the contract *forfeited* if the buyer defaults. *Forfeiture is a right expressly reserved in the contract itself. Realty Securities Corp. v. Johnson,* 93 Fla. 46, 111 So. 532. By declaring a forfeiture, the seller terminates the contract *but retains all payments previously made by the buyer,* since this right is expressly conferred by the contract. The seller may thereupon file a suit to clear his title of the cloud created by the forfeited contract. *Ibid.*

2. In some states, he may tender a deed to the buyer and then sue the buyer for the purchase price.

3. He may sue the buyer for damages.

4. He may sue the buyer for *specific performance* of the contract.

5. He may file a suit for foreclosure of his *vendor's lien.* In such a suit, the court usually enters an order giving the buyer a specified time, anywhere from sixty days to six months, to pay up the contract, and if he fails to pay up, the buyer's rights are extinguished. 51 A.L.R.2d 672. At times a foreclosure sale is held. In some states foreclosure is mandatory where an installment contract is involved.

§ 202. **Remedies of the buyer.** In case of the seller's refusal or failure to perform, the buyer may pursue one of the following courses:

1. He may rescind, that is, declare the contract terminated, and recover his deposit. To rescind is the buyer's normal remedy when the land has decreased in value. One difficulty here is that the seller usually is reluctant to give back the buyer's deposit. The buyer, of course, has the right to file a suit against the seller and obtain a judgment, which can be enforced in the usual ways, by levy on property, by garnishment, and so forth. However, while the suit is pending, the seller may very well decide to sell the particular land to someone else and then spend or secrete the money.

2. The buyer has a lien on the land as security for repayment of purchase money paid in and may enforce such lien if the seller is unable or unwilling to convey good title. A buyer who wishes to obtain return of his down payment from a defaulting seller would be well advised to file a suit to enforce his purchaser's lien, for this ties up the seller's property and prevents him from selling the land to others. This is not true if the buyer merely sues the seller for a money judgment.

3. The buyer may sue the seller to compel *specific performance* of the contract, that is, to compel the seller to give him a deed on receiving payment of the purchase price. The buyer will resort to this remedy when he wants the land for some particular purpose, for example, to keep out a competitor, or when he anticipates that the land will appreciate in value. In general, specific performance is a more effective remedy than a suit for money damages, since damages are always hard to prove and judgments for money are hard to collect.

4. The seller, of course, cannot compel the buyer to accept a bad title. But sometimes the buyer wants to go through with the contract and the seller refuses. The seller's title may be clouded with some unpaid tax, unpaid mortgage, or easement. To make things more difficult for the buyer, the seller refuses to make any effort to eliminate these defects. Here the buyer may wish to file a suit for specific performance and ask the court to make deductions from the purchase price because of the defects in title.

EXAMPLE: The contract price is $10,000. An examination of title reveals the existence of $1000 in unpaid taxes. The court will order specific performance on the buyer's depositing $9000 in court for the seller if the seller refuses to pay the taxes. This remedy of the buyer is called *specific performance with an abatement from the purchase price.*

5. Where the seller will not or cannot go through with the deal, the buyer may sue the seller for *damages.* In such an action, the buyer ultimately will receive a judgment for money damages. In the meantime, however, while the suit is pending, the seller is at liberty to sell the land to others, and any buyer who gets a deed before the buyer obtains his judgment takes the land free of the buyer's claims.

§ 203.   **Remedies of the seller and buyer—exclusiveness of the remedies spelled out in contract—choice of inconsistent remedies.**   In the case of a cash sale, even though the contract is silent on the point, the seller may, in the event of default by the buyer, retain the buyer's earnest money deposit. This is a form of forfeiture that is universally permitted. Often the contract specifically provides that in the case of the buyer's default the seller may declare the contract ended and keep the earnest money. This is not an *exclusive remedy.* 81 C.J.S. 531; 32 A.L.R. 584, 98 A.L.R. 887. In other words, the seller, *in lieu of retaining the earnest* *money, has the right to sue the buyer for specific performance or for damages.*

But, the contract often provides that, in the event the seller's title proves defective, the buyer must either take the title *as is* or be content with a return of his earnest money deposit. This is then the buyer's exclusive remedy if the seller is *in good faith unable* to clear his title. *Old Colony Trust Co. v. Chauncey*, 214 Mass. 271, 101 N.E. 423; *Nostdal v. Morehart*, 132 Minn. 351, 157 N.W. 584; Corbin, *Contracts*, 107.4. If the buyer wishes to accept title *as is*, he must notify the seller of his decision within the time allowed by the contract. *Miller v. Shea*, 300 Ill. 180, 133 N.E. 183. However, if the seller's title examination reveals defects that the seller could easily clear, but he refuses to do so because of his reluctance to go through with the transaction or if the seller knew his title was defective when he signed the contract of sale, then the clause is not deemed to provide an exclusive remedy, and the buyer may file for specific performance with an abatement from the purchase price or for damages. *Mokar Properties Corp. v. Hall*, 179 N.Y.S.2d 814. This clause protects the seller only where he is truly unable to deliver a clear title.

If a seller has a right to declare a forfeiture of the contract because of the buyer's default, and he does so, he cannot thereafter sue the buyer for damages or for the balance due on the purchase price. *Morey v.Huston*, 85 Ill.App.2d 195; 92 C.J.S. 311. He must choose to forfeit *or* sue for damages or recovery of the purchase price. And if the seller files a suit to foreclose the contract, this automatically sets aside any forfeiture that the seller has previously declared because of the buyer's defaults. *Zumstein v. Stockton*, 199 Ore. 633, 264 P.2d 455.

§ 204. Abandonment. Through abandonment, either buyer or seller may lose his rights under the contract. If either party clearly shows by his acts that he does not intend to go through with the contract, the other party may assume that he has abandoned the contract.

EXAMPLE: The buyer, under an installment contract, took possession of the premises. Later he fell far behind in his payments and eventually accepted a lease from the seller. When oil was discovered, he attempted to enforce the contract. The court held that his rights had been lost by abandonment. *Dundas v. Foster*, 281 Mich. 117, 274 N.W. 731.

§ 205. Warranties of the building. In the sale of a completed building, whether the sale is by one who has constructed the building or by some later owner, it is possible for the seller to give the buyer a written warranty that the building is structurally sound, and, if this proves false, the buyer may sue the seller for damages or may even rescind the contract and get his money back. Indeed, where a builder sells an FHA-insured home, the FHA regulations require that a written warranty be given. 14 *Vanderbilt L. Rev.* 553. It is good for one year.

But if there is no written warranty and the sale is of a *completed* building, the courts will not read into the contract any implied warranty that the building is sound. 78 A.L.R.2d 440; 8 A.L.R2d 221; 14 *Ala. L. Rev.* 245. However, where the house is partly completed or has not yet been begun when the contract of sale is entered into, the situation is governed by the rules of builder liability. (See § 434.) And if the seller *knows* of a serious defect that cannot be discovered by the buyer on an ordinary inspection, then even in the case of the sale of a completed building the situation is governed by the rules relating to fraud and nondisclosure. (See § 213.)

Where there is an express warranty in a *contract of sale,* it is wise to include a like warranty in the *deed of conveyance.* However, failure to do so does not invalidate a warranty. The warranty continues in full force and effect.

EXAMPLE: A contract contained the following clause: "The vendors hereby state and represent heating plant and oil burner to be in efficient and good condition." This clause was not inserted in the deed. Nevertheless the buyer was able to sue the seller for breach of this warranty. *Levin v. Cook,* 186 Md. 535, 47 A.2d 505.

§ **206. Fairness and inadequacy of consideration.** A contract for the sale of land will be enforced, regardless of whether the price is too high or too low. Although a person has made a very bad bargain, the courts will force him to carry out his contract.

EXAMPLE: The holder of a tax title to a tract of land went to the owner of the land and told him that his, the owner's, title was worthless, since the land had been sold for taxes. However, the tax title holder said he was willing to give the owner $125 for a deed to the land. The owner accepted the $125 and gave the tax title holder a deed. The land was worth about $3200, and the tax title was really worthless. It was held that the deed would not be set aside. *Grant v. Fellows,* 58 Ill. 242.

However, if the price is far below the real value of the land, and the parties are not on equal terms, as when the buyer is an experienced businessman and the seller is ignorant, mentally feeble, or inexperienced, the court will refuse to compel the seller to give a deed.

EXAMPLE: Shortly after the Chicago Fire, the owner of certain lots in Chicago, a weak-minded man who was ignorant of the value of the land and of business generally and who was unable to understand English well, was persuaded by a shrewd man to sell the lots for $21,000. The lots were worth much more, and their value was rapidly rising. Owners of adjoining lots had just made arrangements to build on these adjoining lots. These facts were known to the buyer but not to the seller. The court refused to compel the seller to give a deed. *Fish v. Leser,* 69 Ill. 394.

§ 207. **Mistake.** The very word *contract* implies that there must be a meeting of the minds. Occasionally both parties to the contract are mistaken as to some material matter. This is called a *mutual mistake*. When there is a mutual mistake, either party may cancel or rescind the contract.

> **EXAMPLE:** The owner of certain land verbally offered to sell the land for $6000. The buyer misunderstood the price to be $3000 and agreed. Under such misunderstanding the deed was executed and delivered. There was no meeting of the minds here, and the owner was entitled to a reconveyance. *Neel v. Lang*, 236 Mass. 61, 127 N.E. 512.

§ 208. **Misrepresentation and fraud.** So many statements are made by each party in the course of a sale of land that almost always some untrue statement called a *misrepresentation* is made. If the misrepresentation is of some unimportant or trivial matter, generally speaking it will not affect the contract. Such a misrepresentation is said to be immaterial. Suppose, however, that a misrepresentation is made as to some important matter. It is clear, first of all, that such a misrepresentation does not make the contract null and void. After the misrepresentation has been discovered, the party who was deceived may nevertheless wish to enforce the contract. He may do so. If the contract has not yet been performed, that is, the seller has not yet given a deed and the buyer has not yet paid the purchase price, and the fraud is discovered, and the party who was guilty of the fraud files a suit to enforce the contract, the other party may use the fraud as a defense to such a suit. He will bring to the court's attention the fact that the party who is bringing the suit made a misrepresentation as to an important matter, and the court will refuse to enforce the contract. If the contract *has* been performed, that is, the seller has given the deed and the buyer paid the purchase price, and one party then discovers that an important misrepresentation has been made, he may file a suit to get his land back, if he was the seller, or to get his money, if he was the buyer.

Some matters with respect to which misrepresentation are common follow:

1. Rents, profits, volume of business, or income of the property.
2. Location of boundaries of the property.
3. Area or frontage of the property.
4. Age of buildings on the property.
5. Drainage conditions.
6. Buildings erected on filled ground.
7. True identity of purchaser.
8. Existence or nonexistence of encumbrances, such as tax liens, mortgages.

§ 209.   **Misrepresentation—opinion, value, and puffing.**   Misrepresentations of matters of *opinion* will not justify cancellation of the contract.

It is often difficult to distinguish an expression of opinion from a representation of a fact. For example, a misrepresentation by the seller's broker that *he now has a commitment from a mortgage house to make a loan of a certain sum on the property* allows the buyer to cancel the deal, but a statement by the broker that a loan of a certain amount *can be obtained* is simply his opinion and does not allow the buyer to back out if such a loan cannot be obtained. *Owen v. Schwartz*, 177 F.2d 641, 14 A.L.R.2d 1337.

A representation made by a *builder* will sometimes be held to be a representation of fact even though such a representation made by someone else would be a matter of opinion.

> **EXAMPLE:** A builder who owned the house he had constructed stated to a buyer that it was "well constructed in a good and substantial manner." This was untrue. The builder was liable for fraud. *Tate v. Jackson*, 22 Ill. App.2d 471, 161 N.E.2d 156. Likewise where the builder said "there will be no water in the cellar," he was liable for fraud. *Pietrazak v. McDermott*, 341 Mass. 107, 167 N.E.2d 166.

Value is usually a matter of opinion. Representations as to the value of the property, though greatly exaggerated, do not ordinarily justify a cancellation of the contract when the other party had an opportunity to learn the truth or falsity of the representations. If the buyer has an opportunity to examine the land, it is his duty to make use of this opportunity. He can then form an opinion as correct as the seller's as to the worth of the land.

Puffing is praise of the property by the seller couched in more or less general terms. Generally the law requires the buyer to be wary of such puffing talk. Unwarranted praise that does not include concrete misrepresentations of specific facts does not entitle the buyer to back out of the deal.

> **EXAMPLE:** The seller told the buyer that he "could not go wrong" in buying the house and that he "would never regret" the purchase. This is mere puffing. *Fegeas v. Sherrill*, 218 Md. 472, 147 A.2d 223.

§ 210.   **Misrepresentation as to zoning or building ordinances.** When a seller makes a misrepresentation as to zoning or building ordinances affecting the property, for example, when the seller states that the land is in a district zoned for manufacturing, whereas it is in fact in a district zoned for stores, the buyer, upon discovering the facts, may rescind and cancel the contract. *Bobak v. Mackey,* 107 Cal. App.2d 55, 236 P.2d 626; 175 A.L.R. 1055.

In an effort to give greater protection to buyers against imposition, courts have evolved the idea of *tacit misrepresentation.* Under this doctrine, it is not necessary that the seller be guilty of a direct falsehood for a misrepresentation to exist. What he says and does may amount to a misrepresentation.

> **EXAMPLE:** The seller showed the property to the buyer as a multiple-family dwelling and commented on the rents he collected. This was a *tacit representation* that the premises were legally usable as an apartment building, which was false, for such use violated the city ordinances. It was held that the buyer could declare the contract void on discovering the imposition. *Gamble v. Beahm,* 198 Ore. 537, 257 P.2d 882.

This would be true also if there is any statement in the contract or advertisement for sale that can be construed as representing that the existing use of the building is a *legal one,* as when the contract describes the building as a "store and dwelling" but such use is actually illegal. 27 *Rocky Mt. L. Rev.* 258; 1958 *Wis. L. Rev.* 641. The presence of zoning or building ordinance violations may render title unmarketable. (See §§ 173, 434.) Or it may give the buyer a right to sue the seller for damages. (See § 202.)

§ 211. **Right to rely upon a representation.** Even a misrepresentation of a material fact will not always entitle the other party to cancel the contract. For example, some courts say that a buyer has no right to rely on a representation when the sources of information are equally available to both parties.

> **EXAMPLE:** Seller represented to buyer that the tax assessor had valued the property at a certain figure. Actually, the assessor's figure was a good deal lower. The court held that the buyer was not entitled to rely on this information since the tax assessor's valuation was a public record equally available to both parties. *Morel v. Masalski,* 333 Ill. 41, 164 N.E. 205.

Again, some courts say that the buyer is not entitled to rely on the seller's representation as to matters that would be disclosed by the buyer's inspection of the property.

> **EXAMPLE:** The seller made a false representation as to the volume of water and the daily flow in the well on the property. It was held that the buyer had no right to rely on this representation, for it was a matter that an inspection would reveal. *Hays v. McGinness,* 208 Ga. 547, 67 S.E.2d 720.

Along the same lines is the rule that the buyer cannot rely on the seller's representations as to the condition of the building when the buyer has actually made a careful inspection of the building, for in such case he is relying on his own observation, not on the seller's representation. 70 A.L.R. 942. But if the buyer makes only a cursory or casual inspection, the rule does not apply, for in such case he is really relying on the seller's representations. *Baylies v. Vanden Boom,* 40 Wyo. 441, 278 Pac. 551; 70 A.L.R. 924. For example, where a buyer inspects the land but makes no attempt to check the seller's representations as to area, the buyer may rescind the contract if there is a misrepresentation in this respect. 54 A.L.R.2d 690. But a buyer who learns of a defect, such as decay or crumbling of the foundation, has no right to make a merely casual inspection. He must make a careful inspection. *Carpenter v. Hamilton,* 18 Cal. App.2d 69, 62 P.2d 1397.

> **NEW DIRECTIONS:** The rule forbidding a buyer to rely on certain representations made by the seller is a bad one. In effect, it legalizes fraud in many situations. Many courts have discarded this barbarous rule, and no doubt it will disappear in time. *Yorke v. Taylor,* 332 Mass. 368, 124 N.E.2d 912. No rogue should enjoy his ill-gotten plunder for the simple reason that his victim is by chance a fool.

When the parties are not dealing on equal terms, the party to whom a representation is made is usually justified in relying thereon.

> **EXAMPLE:** The seller was a real estate dealer, familiar with the locality, and the buyer was a laborer from the city, unacquainted with farming. The seller misrepresented the number and condition of fruit trees on the land. The buyer was entitled to cancel the contract, even though he had inspected the land. The seller had superior means of knowledge. *Mitchell v. Coleman,* 127 Ark. 373, 192 S.W. 231.

> **EXAMPLE:** A farm broker misrepresented to the buyer, who was a city rooming house operator, the amount of acreage in the farm. It was held that the buyer could rescind. *Owen v. Schwartz,* 177 F.2d 641.

§ 212. **Misrepresentation—buyer's fraud.**   Fraud and misrepresentation on the buyer's part are uncommon. When they occur, the result is the same as where the seller is the guilty party. When the buyer has been guilty of fraud, the seller may either rescind the contract or sue the buyer for damages.

> **EXAMPLE:** Where the parties were negotiating for the sale of timber land, the buyer sent in a timber cruiser, who determined that there were in excess of 2,300,000 feet of timber in the tract. The buyer represented to the seller that the cruise disclosed the presence of 1,537,500 feet of timber. Later the seller discovered the misrepresentation. He may sue the buyer for fraud. *Heise v. Pilot Rock Lumber Co.,* 222 Ore. 78, 352 P.2d 1072.

§ 213. **Nondisclosure.**   The old law was *caveat emptor,* "let the buyer beware." The buyer had to investigate before buying. If he failed to discover defects in the building, that was his bad luck. Nowadays the courts are getting away from this primitive rule. Many modern courts say that *when the seller knows certain material facts relating to defects in the property being sold, and knows them not to be within the reach of reasonable inspection by the buyer, the seller is bound to disclose such facts to the buyer. Jenkins v. McCormick,* 184 Kan. 842, 339 P.2d 8. Under the modern view, nondisclosure is often regarded as *misrepresentation by silence.* 80 A.L.R.2d 1453.

EXAMPLES: The seller knew that the house being sold was inadequately based on filled earth. When the buyer discovered this, he was entitled to a return of his money on deeding the property back to the seller. *Rothstein v. Janss Inv. Corp.,* 45 Cal. App.2d 64, 113 P.2d 465; *Wolford v. Freeman,* 150 Neb. 537, 35 N.W.2d 98; 32 Tex. L. Rev. 1. The seller knew that the driveway of the premises was partly on adjoining property and failed to disclose this fact. Again, on discovering this, the buyer was entitled to a return of his money. *Dugan v. Bosco* (Del.), 108 A.2d 586. Seller failed to disclose that the adjoining owner claimed two feet of the sixty-foot lot being sold. Buyer could rescind. *Hall v. Carter* (Ky.), 324 S.W.2d 410.

OTHER EXAMPLES: Seller failed to disclose the following defects and the court held it was fraud: (1) The house was built over a ditch covered with decayed timber. (2) A drain-tile ran beneath the house and caused water to accumulate. (3) The basement was subject to flooding. (4) Rents charged were in excess of those allowed by law. (5) The house was in a slide area, dangerous to life. (6) There was a defective sewer installation potentially dangerous to health. *8 Western Reserve L. Rev.* 5; *Kaze v. Compton* (Ky.), 283 S.W.2d 204.

Some courts still cling to the old, primitive notions.

EXAMPLE: The buyer, after purchasing, found the house was infested with termites, a matter not readily disclosed by inspection. The court held that the seller had no duty to disclose this fact to the buyer. *Swinton v. Whitinsville Savings Bank,* 311 Mass. 677, 42 N.E.2d 808. Most courts today would allow the buyer to get his money back in these circumstances. *Obde v. Schlemeyer,* 56 Wash.2d 449, 353 P.2d 672.

Naturally the seller is guilty of fraud if he deliberately hides a defect.

§ 214. **Nondisclosure—violations of zoning and building ordinances.** When a seller knows that the building sold violates a zoning or building ordinance, it is his duty, according to recent court decisions, to disclose that fact to the buyer, and if he fails to do so, he is liable to the buyer for damages. *Barder v. McClurg,* 93 Cal.App.2d 476, 252 P.2d 378.

EXAMPLE: A builder violated the building code in that the wall studs of the building were spaced too far apart and plaster had been applied on an unauthorized base. The builder was under a duty to disclose these ordinance violations to the buyer, and, where he failed to do so, the buyer had the right to revoke the deal and obtain a return of his down payment. The fact that the buyer inspected the property was immaterial, for these are matters that no ordinary inspection is likely to reveal. Moreover, the seller has superior means of knowledge. *Milmoe v. Dixon,* 101 Cal. App.2d 257, 225 P.2d 273.

NEW DIRECTIONS: The modern view is that concealment is tantamount to actual fraud when the seller knows of facts that materially affect the desirability of the property and that he knows are unknown to the buyer.

Again, you will find more conservative courts following the old "let the buyer beware" line.

EXAMPLE: Seller failed to disclose that a septic tank did not comply with the building code. He was held not liable. *Egan v. Hudson Nut Products Inc.,* 142 Conn. 344, 114 A.2d 213.

§ 215. **Nondisclosure—half-truths.**   To tell part of the truth is often the same as telling a lie. If a man states a fact that by itself is true, he must tell all the other facts that qualify or modify the fact stated.

EXAMPLE: The seller told the buyer that he personally constructed the building and that it was well built. He now has a duty to go on and state, if that is the case, that he built it without a building permit, for even a well-built structure may violate an ordinance, and costly alterations may be needed to bring the building into compliance with the law. *Milmoe v. Dixon,* 101 Cal. App.2d 257, 225 P.2d 273.

EXAMPLE: The seller stated that the buyer could use all the water he wanted at a flat rate of $2 per month. It was held that the buyer could set the deal aside when he discovered that the water was never supplied by the water company between 7 P.M. and 7 A.M., *Simmons v. Evans,* 185 Tenn. 282, 206 S.W.2d 295.

EXAMPLE: The seller of a hotel disclosed the amount of its income accurately but failed to reveal that the source of the income was largely through the operation of a brothel. The seller is liable for fraud. *Ikeda v. Curtia,* 43 Wash. 449, 261 P.2d 684.

EXAMPLE: The seller had two engineers make a report on the property but disclosed only the favorable report to the buyer. Seller is guilty of fraud. *Gilbert v. Corlett,* 171 Cal. App.2d 116, 339 P.2d 960.

§ 216. **Returning benefits received under the contract.**   If a party wishes to cancel a contract for fraud, he must offer to return whatever he has received under the contract.

EXAMPLE: The buyer went into possession of the farm he had purchased and, after discovering a fraud, sold all the livestock on the farm. He could not rescind, since he could not return what he had received under the contract.

§ 217. Ratification. If a misrepresentation is made, and the other party, after discovering the fraud, fails to take prompt action to call the deal off, he is said to ratify or approve the contract and thereafter cannot have it set aside.

EXAMPLE: The seller of a saloon property told the buyer that the tenant in possession of the property was making money, when in fact the tenant was losing money and had lost over $4000 in the business in the last four years. The seller also said that there was sufficient stock on hand in the saloon to run for thirty to sixty days, when the supply was in fact good for only three or four days. The buyer paid the purchase price and went into possession. He discovered the misrepresentation almost immediately, but remained in possession over seven months, trying to make the business pay. It was held that this constituted a ratification of the contract, and the buyer was not entitled to get his money back.

§ 218. Options. A valid contract of sale is binding on both seller and buyer. Each can be compelled to do the things he has promised to do. Each is liable in damages if he fails to do the things he has promised to do. An option differs from a contract of sale in these respects: An option is simply a contract by which a landowner gives to another person, called the optionee, the right to buy the land at a fixed price within a specified time. The owner does not then sell his land or any interest in it. The optionee gets, not lands or an interest therein or an agreement that he shall have lands, but the right to call for and receive lands if he so chooses. *Keogh v. Peck*, 316 Ill. 318, 147 N.E. 266. If, within the time specified in the option, the optionee gives the owner notice that he elects to exercise the option, the option then ripens into a contract of sale. If the optionee lets the specified time go by without taking any action, he has no further rights in the land, nor can he recover from the landowner the money paid for the option.

§ 219. Suggestions on contract draftsmanship.

Preliminary observations. The goal to be achieved in drafting a contract of sale is twofold: (1) to draft a contract that the courts will enforce, since many contracts are so poorly drafted that courts cannot and will not enforce them; (2) after the seller and buyer have explored all aspects of the deal and reached an agreement as to all their rights and duties, to specify all the terms that the parties have agreed on, and to state them so clearly that there can be no controversy as to their meaning.

Parties. In general the suggestions made regarding parties to deeds are applicable to contracts to parties. (See §§ 72-74.)

Purchase price. State the purchase price and terms of payment, including prepayment privilege, if any, and acceleration clause, in complete detail and with utmost clarity. If sellers are joint tenants, state that price is payable to them "as joint tenants with right of survivorship and not as tenants in common or by the entireties." (See § 292.)

Earnest money. For the seller's protection, the deposit should be adequate.

Insist on a certified or cashier's check. Buyer should insist that money be held in escrow by a bank or trust company.

Purpose for which buyer is purchasing the property.   Careful thought must be given to the purpose for which the buyer is purchasing the property. For example, it may be that the buyer intends to use the property for a purpose forbidden by the zoning ordinance. If so, the contract must contain a clause for the buyer's protection requiring an amendment to the zoning ordinance to be procured within a limited time, and in default thereof, the buyer to be entitled to cancel the contract and obtain a return of his money. If the contract is prepared and signed at a time when information concerning the provisions of recorded building restrictions or applicable zoning and building ordinances is unavailable, but the seller feels that neither restrictions nor ordinances will prevent use for the buyer's intended purpose, a clause may be added giving the buyer the right to terminate the contract within a specified time if it shall appear from recorded covenants, conditions, or restrictions or from zoning or building ordinances, official maps or plans, or applicable statutes that the premises cannot legally be used for the intended purpose.

Description of the land.   In considering the adequacy of the land description of the contract, the parties should consult Chapter 5, also the specific suggestions hereinafter set forth.

Buying assembled land—survey to protect against outstanding strips.   Often a seller has acquired different pieces of property at different times and will offer the buyer a contract that contains all the various descriptions in the various deeds running to the seller. This raises the question in the buyer's mind as to whether there may be some gap between the various parcels of property. This is important to the buyer, for normally he will be planning to erect some structure that crosses the boundary lines of the various parcels. In such case the buyer will certainly want a clause in the contract requiring the seller to give a survey and allowing the buyer to back out of the deal if the survey reveals gaps between the parcels.

Streets and alleys.   The seller will usually have some right, title, or interest in and to the streets or alleys adjoining the premises sold, and it is desirable that the contract of sale call for the seller to convey, without warranty, all such right, title, and interest.

Items to be conveyed to buyer or retained by seller.   A contract for the sale of land obligates the seller to deliver title to the land and all fixtures, including the building, for it, of course, is a fixture, and fixtures are part of the land. *Chattels*, however, such as furniture, are not included, unless the contract expressly so provides. Any items that are clearly personal property or might give rise to controversy—air conditioning equipment, awnings, bookcases, cabinets, carpets (particularly stair carpets), chandeliers and lighting fixtures, crops, curtains, curtain rods, draperies and other interior decorations, driers, electric fans, electrical equipment, fireplace grates and andirons, fuel, furniture, garbage cans, garbage disposal, gas logs, ironing boards, kitchen cabinets, lamps, lawn mowers and garden equipment, linoleum, mirrors, refrigerators, rugs, screen doors, shelves, sprinkling equipment, storm doors and windows, stoves and heaters, supplies, tools and equipment (particularly janitor's tools), trade fixtures, venetian blinds, ventilators, wash tubs, washers and driers, water heaters, water meter, window shades, and window screens—should be specifically dealt with in the contract. Does the buyer need an easement over adjoining land to provide access to the land purchased? If he does, let the contract provide for execution of an easement grant, and since the buyer will want an abstract or title insurance policy to evidence the seller's good title to the land sold, consider whether a similar precaution is not advisable as to the land over which the easement passes. Only the man who really owns the land can grant an easement over it. As a minimum, the contract should require the seller to warrant his title to the easement premises. (See Chapter 4.) Are there leases to tenants or fire insurance policies? Let the contract call for the assignment and delivery thereof to the purchaser. The contract should also require seller to assign to buyer any other items that buyer wishes to receive, e.g., service contracts (contracts with exterminators, scavengers, and so on) roof guarantees, or tenant's deposits.

What does the seller expect to retain after the deal is closed? Once the contract is signed, the seller is obligated to deliver to the buyer all fixtures, for they are legally part of the land. If the seller expects to retain attached machinery or other items that might be considered fixtures, provision to this effect should be included in the contract. If the seller needs to reserve an easement over the land sold, a provision to that effect should be included in the contract.

Encumbrances to which the title is to be subject and to which the buyer agrees. The seller should see that he has listed in the contract all the encumbrances or other defects in title that he does not propose to clear before the deal is closed. Most contract forms contain a printed list of common encumbrances, such as leases or building restrictions, but it is intended that the seller will add to this list as necessary. Suppose, for example, that the seller's title is subject to an easement. Is it mentioned in the contract? If not, and the buyer changes his mind and decides to back out of the deal, he may be able to do so because the title, as finally examined before the deal is closed, must reveal no encumbrances other than those listed either in general or in specific language in the contract.

The buyer should carefully analyze every encumbrance listed by the seller. For example, if in the contract he agrees to take subject to "existing leases," he must accept the property subject to any lease, no matter how ridiculously low the rent may be. If the contract says that the buyer will accept title subject to "building and other restrictions of record," "easements of record," and "mineral rights," as many printed forms provide, will any of these restrictions, easements, or mineral rights interfere with his building program, assuming that he is buying land to build on? Moreover, will some easement document to which the land is subject obligate the buyer in some way as owner of this land? For example, an easement for road purposes may obligate me to keep my neighbor's road in repair. Similar personal liability provisions may be contained in restriction documents. If the contract says that the buyer will accept title subject to restrictions against Negroes or other non-Caucasians, were any such restrictions recorded after February 15, 1950? If they were, the property will not be eligible for FHA or VA financing.

Mortgage provisions. These should be detailed and complete. For example, if the contract calls for a purchase money mortgage, are the amount, interest rate, maturity date, and form of mortgage clearly set forth? (See § 166.) Similar details should be included in a clause giving the buyer the right to cancel if he cannot procure a mortgage of a specified amount, and in this clause also specify the time allowed to procure the mortgage. (See § 183.) If land is being sold subject to a mortgage, specify the amount and whether or not the buyer assumes personal liability. (See § 183.) If the seller has a mortgage on his land that must be released, the contract should provide that the seller will have the right to pay it off at the closing of the deal, using the buyer's sale price for this purpose, the seller to have the mortgagee present prepared to release the mortgage and surrender the canceled papers. (See § 170.) Occasionally a seller in an installment contract wants to reserve the right to mortgage the land. In these cases the contract should: (1) give details of the loan, maximum amount, maximum interest rate, and so forth; (2) specify that the mortgage will be prior and superior to the rights of the contract buyer; (3) give the buyer the right to make the mortgage payments if the seller fails to do so and to deduct payments so made from his contract payments.

Evidence of title. The contract should provide: (1) What type of title evidence is to be furnished, title insurance, abstract, and so forth. (2) Who is to furnish and pay for same. (3) Time allowed: (a) for furnishing evidence of title, (b) for buyer to point out defects in title not permitted by the contract, (c) for seller's clearance of objections, and (d) for buyer to decide whether to accept title *as is* if objections cannot be cured. (4) If abstract of title is specified, for the seller's protection a clause should be included giving the seller the right to cure any of the buyer's objections to the title by delivery of a clear policy of title insurance. This may save the seller the time and expense of a quiet title suit when the buyer's attorney raises numerous unimportant objections to the title. (5) The seller should not sign a form of contract that calls for title insurance if his land is registered under the Torrens system, for this will subject him to a double expense if the buyer insists on his contract rights.

Clearing title by escrow deposits. For the protection of the seller, the contract should contain a provision allowing the seller to leave money in escrow with some bank or title company if his title is not clear on the day that he must deliver clear title. Otherwise a deal may fall through simply because a seller is not in a position to remove some trivial defect, such as a small mechanic's lien, within the time allowed for clearing title.

Chattel lien search. Specify if the seller is to furnish search for financing statements or other liens on personal property being sold, and if so, time allowed for same.

Building ordinance violations. If the seller is to furnish a formal, official report as to building code violations, cover this, including time allowed for this purpose. The buyer should endeavor to have the contract provide that the seller "warrants the building on said premises is now and at the date of closing will be free and clear of all violations of laws and ordinances, and for breach of this warranty buyer may rescind this contract, before or after closing, or, at his election, may sue for damages."

Survey. If the seller is to furnish a survey, specify the time allowed for this and that it is to be satisfactory to the buyer's attorney. The time allowed for the buyer to raise objections based on the survey should tie into the time allowed the buyer for raising objections to the title. If the seller objects to paying for a survey, the buyer may decide to get one at his own expense. Is a survey necessary? Business judgment should be used in answering this question. For example, if A is buying a forty-year-old dwelling where the fences have also been up for that length of time, it is unlikely that any encroachment trouble will develop. Age has set the matter at rest. If, on the other hand, A is buying a recently erected commercial building that apparently extends to the property lines, a survey is definitely advisable, for the building may actually extend over property lines. Again, how can the buyer be sure that the legal description in the contract covers the property that the buyer has inspected and wants to buy? The only really satisfactory proof of this is a land survey. A survey is always advisable if new construction is contemplated, so that the building is set within the lot lines and within lines established by ordinances and private restrictions.

Building and other restrictions. If the seller wishes to place building restrictions on the land sold, he must make provision for this in the contract.

Risk of loss. Suppose the building is destroyed or damaged by fire or other casualty before the deal is closed. The right of the buyer to cancel the deal, his right to insurance money if he does not back out, both should be covered.

Warranties of building. The buyer should try to get a clause in the contract stating that basement does not flood, building is free of termite infestation, roof does not leak, and heating plant and electrical system are now and at closing will be in good working order.

Miscellaneous documents to be furnished to the buyer. If a new building requires a certificate of occupancy or an approval by fire underwriters of electrical installations, or if it is customary to obtain similar certificates with respect to plumbing and the like, the contract should provide that the seller will deliver these at the closing. In case of a new building, guarantees by the subcontractors are customary. There is usually a roof guaranty and a guaranty of the plumbing and heating equipment and electrical installations. The contract should provide that the seller will transfer and deliver these to the purchaser at the closing.

Installment contracts. The forfeiture clause is of the greatest importance here. Also cover the buyer's duty to pay taxes, carry insurance, and keep buildings in repair and free of mechanic's liens, restrictions on assignment of contract, and so forth. The seller should be given the right to declare the entire purchase price due if the buyer defaults. For the seller's protection provide that the buyer shall not assign the contract without the seller's consent. Also provide that the buyer is to pay taxes and furnish insurance with seller named in the policy. Buyer should agree to keep the premises in repair and in compliance with ordinances and laws, not to remodel without the seller's consent, and to keep the premises free from mechanic's liens.

Possession. Cover the date on which possession is to be given.

Leases. Provide for assignment to buyer of all seller's leases, including leases for advertising signs.

Concessionaire contracts. Provide for assignment of all such contracts.

Tenant's security deposits. Assignment of tenant's security deposits to buyer must be covered specifically.

Advance payments of rent. The contract should allow the buyer a credit against the purchase price where a tenant has already paid the seller the rent for the last several months of the term.

Prorated items. These should be covered in great detail to avoid arguments at closing over who pays for janitor's vacation pay, water bills, and so forth.

Income tax. The seller should consider whether an income tax savings will result if the property is sold under an installment contract rather than for cash.

Building construction. If the contract calls for construction of a building, many additional matters must be considered. (See Chapter 26.)

Documents. All miscellaneous documents that the buyer will need, for example, all documents listed in Chapter 12, should be provided for in the contract. The seller is under no legal obligation to furnish any document that the contract does not call for.

Signatures, acknowledgment, witnessing. All the parties must sign, being careful to sign as their names appear on the contract. Witnessing and acknowledgment are desirable, so that the buyer may record the contract, for without witnessing or acknowledgment, the contract is not recordable in many states.

Chapter 12

CLOSING A CASH
REAL ESTATE DEAL

§ 220. **Questions the parties should ask.**   Before listing his property with a broker for sale, the *seller* should ask himself:

1. Do I really want to sell?

COMMENT: If I list my property and the broker finds a buyer ready, able, and willing to buy at my price, I must pay a commission even if I then decide that I really don't want to sell.

2. Does my wife want to sell?

COMMENT: If the broker finds a buyer and I am willing to sign the contract of sale, but my wife refuses to do so, in most states the buyer will refuse to go through with the deal because, unless she signs the contract, she is not legally obligated to sign the deed, and this will leave her dower or other legal rights outstanding. The deal fails, but the broker gets his commission. (See §§ 141, 142.)

3. Am I really in a position to sell?

COMMENT: Suppose my broker finds a willing buyer, but it develops that my title is defective, or I cannot pay off the existing mortgage, or my new house will not be ready for occupancy for a long time. Again the deal falls through, but I must nevertheless pay a commission.

Before signing a contract of sale the *buyer* should ask himself these questions and attend to the following matters:

1. If I am buying vacant land, are there any zoning ordinances that forbid or hamper the use I wish to make of the land?

COMMENT: Suppose I sign a contract to buy a vacant lot and intend to erect a filling station thereon, and thereafter I discover that the lot is zoned for residences only. I must nevertheless go through with the deal. (See § 173.) Suppose my *building* complies with the ordinance. Do my plans provide adequate off-street parking to comply with the ordinance?

2. Under local ordinances, how far from the front, side, and real lines must buildings be erected and does this leave room for the type of building that I have in mind?

3. If I plan to use septic tank construction, is the lot big enough to qualify for septic tank construction under local ordinances?

4. If there is an airport in the vicinity, are there any regulations prohibiting the erection of electric poles or other structures that might prove a hazard to aircraft?

5. If there is a building on the land but I expect to remodel it, are there any ordinances that prohibit such remodeling?

6. Does the building on the property violate existing zoning or building ordinances?

COMMENT: If it does, I may be compelled to remodel the building to conform to the ordinances, or even to tear it down. (See Chapter 28.)

7. Is the building a nonconforming use?

COMMENT: If it is, I cannot enlarge or alter it or rebuild it if it is substantially damaged by fire. If it was legally abandoned, the city can forbid its use. (See Chapter 28.)

8. Especially if the building is new, has a certificate of occupancy been issued? (*See* Chapter 28.)

9. Does the seller have a permit for any structure that requires a city permit, such as a swimming pool, a water tank on a roof, or a sign that extends over a sidewalk? Where a cocktail lounge is involved, am I, as the buyer, certain that I can procure an assignment of the liquor license?

10. If the contract of sale states that title will be subject to building restrictions, easements, mineral rights, and so on, how will these affect my building plans?

11. Are there sewers and water pipes in adjoining streets and if there are, will I have the legal right to connect my proposed building to them? (See § 425.)

12. Are there any utility lines, including underground lines, drainage

ditches, drain-tiles, and so on, that will interfere with my building program?

13. Are existing streets, walks, sewers, or water pipes fully paid for and if not, will they be paid for by the seller, buyer, or by future special assessments? What does the contract say regarding this matter?

14. Will my building program interfere with my neighbor's drainage?

15. Keeping in mind that the law often says, "let the buyer beware," are there any defects in the building, for example, termites, defective heating plant, basement that floods, inadequate well or septic tank?

16. Is the soil adequate for my building program and should soil tests be made?

17. Is the building I'm buying so close to adjoining vacant land that, if my neighbor excavates, there is danger that my building will fall into the excavation?

18. Is my neighbor's building so close to the boundary line that, if I build on the vacant land I'm buying, my excavation will involve possible collapse of his building and possible litigation?

19. Keeping in mind that I will become personally liable for personal injuries as soon as the deal is closed, are the elevators, boilers, gas, water, and sewer in the building in safe condition?

20. Since risk of loss in many states falls on the buyer as soon as the contract is signed (see § 186), is the existing insurance policy for an adequate amount? Suppose, for example, that the building burns to the ground before the deal is closed.

21. Is the property being used for a purpose that invalidates existing insurance policies?

> **SUGGESTION:** Have the insurance policies checked by a reliable insurance broker. Have a rider (*contract of sale clause*) attached immediately to the policies so that you, as well as the seller, are covered. Only the seller is covered until this is done.

22. Are any public projects scheduled for this area that may result in the taking of this property by the public?

> **COMMENT:** It is discouraging for a businessman to build up neighborhood good-will over a period of time and then find his property taken for a superhighway.

23. Are any zoning or building code changes likely to take place that will interfere with my building program?

24. Are there any judgments against me?

> **COMMENT:** Once I sign a contract to buy land, the seller will be obligated to deed the land to me, and then my creditors may take it away from me.

25. Where the contract calls for the buyer to accept the property subject to "existing leases," what do the leases provide?

COMMENT: If the leases contain clauses that are very burdensome to the landlord, the buyer may wish to reconsider the desirability of entering into the deal.

26. If the contract requires the buyer to accept the property subject to the existing mortgage, the contract should require the seller to furnish, at closing, a statement signed by the mortgagee showing the balance due on the mortgage. The buyer should check the mortgage to make sure it does not give the mortgagee the right to declare the mortgage debt due in case the mortgagor sells the property without the mortgagee's permission.

Questions the *seller* should ask before signing the contract.

1. Is my title to the property a good, clear title?

COMMENT: If not, I may be liable for damages if I cannot clear the title.

2. What problems will I have with my existing mortgage in the property?

COMMENT: If I, as seller, must get my existing mortgage released, I should check to see that it has a prepayment clause, and, if not, determine that the mortgagee is willing to accept prepayment. (See § 378.) I should also get the mortgagee to agree either to accept payment at the closing of the deal or to deposit his mortgage papers and release or satisfaction thereof in escrow since I will have no funds to pay the mortgage debt before then.

3. Can I accept the buyer's word that I will not have to pay my broker a commission?

COMMENT: The buyer may be seeking a reduction in the seller's asking price on the ground that no broker's commission is involved. Check with the *broker* as to the truth of the buyer's claim that the broker was not instrumental in interesting this buyer in the property.

§ 221. **Matters to be considered before closing.** *Evidence of title.* If the contract requires the seller to furnish an abstract or other evidence of title, he should do so *within the time allowed by the contract,* for if he fails to do so, a reluctant buyer may seize the opportunity to cancel the deal. The buyer, in turn, should, *within the time allowed by the contract,* draw attention to any defects in title not permitted by the contract. Otherwise he will be regarded as waiving such defects. The seller should then, *within the permitted time,* cure any defects pointed out by the buyer. When the contract specifies that the seller shall furnish an abstract of title showing clear title, the buyer has a right to insist that

quitclaim deeds needed to clear the buyer's title objections be recorded
in the recorder's office and included in the abstract of title. *Kincaid v.
Dobrinsky,* 225 Ill. App. 85. When the contract calls for a title insurance
policy showing clear title in the seller, the buyer has the right to insist
that all unauthorized objections be cleared from the title policy by the
seller.

Since closings are apt to be fairly hectic, it is a good idea for the parties
to submit to each other, in advance of closing, all the documents that will
then be exchanged, such as the deed, mortgage, mortgage note, survey,
leases, assignments. After one has checked these in the quietude of one's
office, penciling initials in a corner of the document to show that it has
been checked enables one to omit further scrutiny of the form at the time
of closing, though a check of signatures will still be needed at that time.

Checking the survey. Check the date on the survey. A survey made
ten years ago, for example, obviously will not cover buildings erected
since then. Does the survey locate the property with reference to known
monuments, such as government section corners? Does it show the location of all our buildings? All neighboring buildings? Our walks, drives,
fences, and those of our neighbors? Are all buildings, walks, and so on
well within the lines of the lot on which they belong? Do any structures
extend over the setback lines established by city ordinances or building
restrictions? Does the survey show whether upper portions of the building (bay windows or eaves) extend over the lot lines? Are there possible
subsurface encroachments, such as footings on the building, extending
into adjoining land?

Chattel lien search. If valuable chattels are included in the sale, a
search of the Uniform Commercial Code records should be made for
financing statements affecting such chattels. This search requires care.
Code filings relating to fixtures, crops, and consumer goods (stoves, refrigerators, and other appliances found in the ordinary home) are found
in some local office, often the recorder's office, but in a department separate from the department where ordinary deeds are filed. Filings covering
furniture and other chattels in a hotel or furnished apartment, or raw
materials in an industrial plant, are likely to be found in some central
office, usually that of the Secretary of State in the state capitol.

Ordinance violations search. If in the particular community it is possible to procure a title company or other search of city records as to building ordinance violations, this should be done. In lieu thereof, an architect
or engineer should check the building carefully for violations.

Inspection of the property by the buyer. Before closing the deal the
buyer should make a careful physical check of the property. Possession
imparts constructive notice. (See § 127.) The buyer will take subject to
the rights of the grantee in an unrecorded contract, or to other rights dis-

closed by occupancy. Tenants' leases should be checked for options to renew or to purchase. If the premises are occupied by tenants, their occupancy is notice of their rights. The buyer must not accept the seller's assurance that tenants are month-to-month tenants. He should check with the tenants. This check with the tenants will also determine what furniture, appliances, etc., the tenants claim belong to them.

EXAMPLE: A is selling a furnished apartment building to B. The entire building is under lease to C. The lease has only one month to run, and B plans to operate the building himself. B inquires of C and finds that C owns all the furniture. B must plan to acquire new furniture or plan to buy the old furniture from C.

As the buyer, during the inspection, check for the existence of unrecorded easements that inspection would reveal, for the buyer takes subject to unrecorded easements if their existence would be revealed by an inspection of the premises. Check to see whether this particular sale will result in the creation of any implied easements. (See §§ 27, 28.) Check to see whether rear or side exits run over adjoining property, thus making an easement necessary, and whether shutters open over adjoining premises. Check to see if heat is furnished by an adjoining building, thus making a written agreement necessary. Check for vaults, marquees, and so forth extending into public streets, which would make permits necessary. If you defer inspection until after the abstract or other evidence of title has been furnished, you can check to see whether the building violates any recorded building restrictions. It should be remembered that, even if the contract requires the buyer to take subject to "building restrictions," he is not required to take subject to violations of restrictions. Such violations constitute a separate and distinct defect in title. (See § 172.) Check also for violations of zoning or building ordinances and for recent repairs or construction that might ripen into a mechanic's lien. If valuable chattels are included in the sale, inquire of the tenants whether they claim ownership of such chattels.

§ 222. **Bulk sales affidavits and notices.** A sale of real estate may incidentally involve the sale of the entire stock of goods, wares, or merchandise of some retail establishment operated by the seller on the premises. It is necessary that such a sale comply with the local Bulk Sales Act, which usually involves giving notice of the pending sale to the creditors of the business so that they can protect their rights. 37 C.J.S. 1325.

§ 223. **Closing date.** The contract of sale should fix a closing date, the time the deed is to be delivered and the balance of the purchase price paid. If no closing date is fixed in the contract, it is presumed that the deal is to be closed within a reasonable time, and either buyer or seller may select a reasonable date and notify the other that he will be prepared to close at such time. Often one of the parties is not prepared to close on the date specified in the contract and requests an adjournment of closing. In such case, the other party, in granting the request for adjournment, specifies that the prorating or apportionment will be computed as of the original date or the adjourned date, whichever is more favorable to him. For example, if the adjournment is made at the request of the seller and the income of the building is greater than the carrying charges, the buyer will insist that the apportionment or prorating be computed as of the original date. The buyer will receive the rents from the date originally fixed for closing, and the seller will be entitled to interest on the unpaid balance of the purchase price and the purchase money mortgage from the original closing date. Of course if the contract fixes a closing date and provides that time is of the essence, the party who is ready to close on the date fixed need not grant a request for an adjournment.

Some contracts fix a date that is to govern the prorating of apportionment, regardless of the date of the delivery of the deed. Other contracts provide that prorating or apportionment shall be computed as of the date of the delivery of the deed.

The buyer should not rely on any extension of time granted by the sellers's lawyer or broker. Normally, neither of them has the power to grant extensions.

§ 224. **Matters to be attended to at closing.** *Title.* The buyer should make a final check to see that the title is clear and subject only to the encumbrances permitted by the contract of sale. If the deal is not closed in escrow, an informal check should be made of the records to cover the period between the date of the abstract or title search and the date of the closing of the deal. Judgments or other liens may attach during this interval, and will, of course, be good against the buyer. The buyer should at least insist that the seller's attorney give him a written statement that he will not turn the buyer's check over to the seller until after the deed to the buyer has been recorded and the title searched to cover that date. Of course if the deal is closed in escrow, all danger from this source is obviated. If, by agreement, the seller is to clear certain objections after closing, the buyer should retain part of the purchase price, usually double the amount of the lien involved, to insure performance on the part of the seller.

Form and contents of documents involved. The documents should all be checked to see if they are in proper form and comply with the contract. For example, if the deed to be given is a warranty deed, the subject clause of the deed should be checked (see § 80) to make certain that it does not include any items that were not included in the subject clause of the contract (see § 169). The deed should also be checked to see if the recorder of deeds will accept it for recording. For example, in many states, laws forbid "metes and bounds" subdivisions, that is, the division of a tract of land into plots for sale without the formality of recording a subdivision plat. The recorder will often reject such a deed, and the buyer is left with a deed that he has paid for but cannot record.

If, as is so often the case, the major portion of the purchase price is being furnished by the buyer's mortgage lender, the attorneys will make a final check of the mortgage and note to see that the principal amount, interest rate, and monthly payments are in accordance with the loan commitment. If this has not previously been attended to, a similar check should be made of the other loan documents, such as the assignment of rents or waiver of defenses.

Water and other utility bills. The buyer should call for the production of paid water and other utility bills. If these bills have not been paid, service to the building may be cut off.

Insurance premiums. The buyer should see that the seller's insurance premiums have been paid, since the seller will receive credit for insurance in the prorating.

Production of seller's deed. The buyer should require the seller to produce the deed by which he acquired title. This affords some measure of protection against forgery and impersonation.

Prorations or adjustments. Prorations or adjustments should be computed and a closing statement prepared.

Payment of purchase price and delivery of documents. The balance due according to the closing statement should be paid and the documents to which each party is entitled delivered to him.

§ 225. **Apportionment or prorating—the closing statement.** The contract of sale usually provides that various items shall be adjusted or prorated. Items not mentioned in the contract are nevertheless often prorated because of the prevailing local custom. This prorating, or adjustment, results in credits and debits against each party. These are usually shown on a closing statement, which is also called a settlement sheet. Forms of closing statements vary. A form commonly used lists in one column all credits due the seller and in a separate column all credits due the buyer. The completed statement is approved by buyer and seller.

Prorations can be computed by reference to a prorating table.

§ 226. **Credits due seller.** The following are the usual credits due the seller:

1. Full purchase price
2. Unearned insurance premiums
3. Fuel on hand
4. Any items paid by seller in advance, as water tax (if same has been so paid), prepayments on exterminator or other service contracts, prepayments on taxes

and insurance made by seller to mortgagee under the terms of the mortgage, when such mortgage is to be assumed by buyer

§ 227. **Credits due buyer.** The following are some of the credits due the buyer:

1. Earnest money
2. Existing mortgages if the sale is for part cash and balance by assumption of existing mortgages
3. Interest accrued and unpaid on existing mortgages that are to be assumed by the buyer
4. Amount of purchase money mortgage if seller has agreed to receive such mortgage as part of the purchase price
5. Unearned rents that have already been collected, since rents are usually collected on the first of the month. If the deal is closed after the first of the month, the buyer is, under most contracts, entitled to his proportionate part of the current month's rent collections. This includes unearned rent on leases of advertising space or advertising signs
6. Deposits by tenants made as security for payment of rent for the last month of the lease
7. Taxes. Since the seller has had possession or the rents of the property for prior years and for part of the current year, it is only fair that he pay all taxes for prior years and his proportionate part of the taxes for the current year, if these have not already been paid, and contracts usually so provide. In some localities, however, it is not customary to apportion current taxes.
8. Items based on meter readings, such as water tax, electricity, and gas, if same are not paid in advance.
9. Wages and other charges accrued and unpaid, such as janitor's salary or scavenger service.
10. Release fee and recording charge, when buyer will record or obtain release of mortgage that seller should have removed from his title.

§ 228. **Other items.** The buyer pays for recording of the deed, unless the contract provides otherwise. Since the seller would otherwise bear this expense, the contract usually requires the buyer to pay for the recording of any purchase money mortgage and for the abstract or other evidence of title to cover the said mortgage. The escrow agreement specifies who pays for the escrow. These items may or may not be included in the closing statement.

§ 229. **Documents to be obtained by buyer.** The following are some of the items and documents to be obtained by the buyer at closing:

1. Deed.
2. Abstract, title policy, or other evidence of title.
3. Bill of sale of personal property.
4. Receipt for purchase price paid.
5. Survey.
6. All paid notes on existing mortgages, which buyer assumes, since these notes will be needed in obtaining a release deed; also any mortgage and mortgage

PRO-RATING TABLE FOR RENTS, TAXES AND INSURANCE

Number of years, months and days	RENTS One Month		TAXES & INS. One Year		INSURANCE						Number of years, months and days
	Days to Month		One Year		Three Years			Five Years			
	30	31	Months	Days	Years	Months	Days	Years	Months	Days	
1	.0333	.0323	.0833	.0028	.3333	.0278	.0009	.2000	.0167	.0006	1
2	.0667	.0645	.1667	.0056	.6667	.0556	.0019	.4000	.0333	.0011	2
3	.1000	.0968	.2500	.0083	1.0000	.0833	.0028	.6000	.0500	.0017	3
4	.1333	.1290	.3333	.0111		.1111	.0037	.8000	.0667	.0022	4
5	.1667	.1613	.4167	.0139		.1389	.0046	1.0000	.0833	.0028	5
6	.2000	.1935	.5000	.0167		.1667	.0056		.1000	.0033	6
7	.2333	.2258	.5833	.0194		.1944	.0065		.1167	.0039	7
8	.2667	.2581	.6667	.0222		.2222	.0074		.1333	.0044	8
9	.3000	.2903	.7500	.0250		.2500	.0083		.1500	.0050	9
10	.3333	.3226	.8333	.0278		.2778	.0093		.1667	.0056	10
11	.3667	.3548	.9167	.0306		.3056	.0102		.1833	.0061	11
12	.4000	.3871	1.0000	.0333		.3333	.0111		.2000	.0067	12
13	.4333	.4194		.0361			.0120			.0072	13
14	.4667	.4516		.0389			.0130			.0078	14
15	.5000	.4839		.0417			.0139			.0083	15
16	.5333	.5161		.0444			.0148			.0089	16
17	.5667	.5484		.0472			.0157			.0094	17
18	.6000	.5806		.0500			.0167			.0100	18
19	.6333	.6129		.0528			.0176			.0106	19
20	.6667	.6452		.0556			.0185			.0111	20
21	.7000	.6774		.0583			.0194			.0117	21
22	.7333	.7097		.0611			.0204			.0122	22
23	.7667	.7419		.0639			.0213			.0128	23
24	.8000	.7742		.0667			.0222			.0133	24
25	.8333	.8065		.0694			.0231			.0139	25
26	.8667	.8387		.0722			.0241			.0144	26
27	.9000	.8710		.0750			.0250			.0150	27
28	.9333	.9032		.0778			.0259			.0156	28
29	.9667	.9355		.0806			.0269			.0161	29
30	1.0000	.9677		.0833			.0278			.0167	30
31		1.0000									31

Example:

Rent $135.00 per mo.
To find value of 23
days of a 31 day mo.
From Table:—
23 days = .7419
.7419 × 135.00 =
$100.16

Example:

Taxes = 1215.12.
To find value of 7
mos. and 19 days
From Table:—
7 mos. = .5833
19 days = .0528
7 mos. 19
days = .6361
.6361 × 1215.12
= 772.95

Example:

3 Year Policy Premium
= 58.75
To find the value of 1
yr. 3 mos. 11 days
From Table:—
1 yr. = .3333
3 mos. = .0833
11 days = .0102
1 yr. 3 mo. 11
days = .4268
.4268 × 58.75
= 25.07

Example:

5 Yr. Policy Premium
312.82
To find value of 3
yrs. 4 mos. 13 days
From Table:—
3 yrs. = .6000
4 mos. = .0667
13 days = .0072
3 yrs. 4 mos. 13
days = .6739
.6739 × 312.82
= 210.81

notes that have been paid in full and the release or satisfaction of the mortgage, if such release has not yet been recorded.

7. Statement by mortgagee showing amount due on existing mortgage, so that mortgagee cannot thereafter assert that any greater amount remains due. This applies only where buyer is taking land subject to an existing mortgage.

8. Insurance policies and assignments thereof.

9. Leases and assignments thereof, including leases of advertising space or advertising signs.

10. Letter by seller to tenants advising them to pay future rent to buyer.

11. Letter by seller to seller's building manager or rental agent advising him of sale of building and of termination of his authority.

12. Statement by seller as to names of tenants, rents paid and unpaid, and due date of rents, and that no rents have been paid in advance except for current month.

13. Rent control registration.

14. Service contracts (for example, elevator maintenance contract, scavenger service contract, exterminator contract), roof guarantees, and so forth, if they are to be assigned to buyer, with assignment thereof.

15. Last receipts for taxes, special assessments, gas, electricity, and water.

16. Seller's affidavit of title, which states, among other things, that there are no judgments, bankruptcies, or divorces against him, no unrecorded deeds or contracts, no repairs or improvements that have not been paid for, that the seller knows of no defects in his title, and that he has been in undisputed possession of the premises. The affidavit of title has several functions: (1) In many cases, the abstract or title search covers only the date of the contract, and the deal is closed at some later date. The affidavit covers the period between the date of title search and the date of closing. (2) Some defects in title are not revealed by a title search, for example, a divorce obtained in some other state. Indeed, the only way in which one can be assured of the seller's marital status is by procuring an affidavit relative thereto. Other defects, such as mechanics' liens for work or material furnished in the building, may also not be revealed by the title examination. (3) The warranty deed gives the buyer the right to sue *for damages* if a defect in title is later revealed. But the affidavit may give the buyer the right to have the seller prosecuted *criminally* for obtaining money through false pretenses. The threat of a criminal prosecution is often more effective than the threat of a suit for damages.

17. Securities deposited by tenants as security for payment of rent and money deposits by tenants made as security for payment of rent for last month of lease. But if lease does not provide that on any sale of property the deposit shall go to buyer, tenants' consent should be obtained to a transfer of the deposit.

18. If the property being sold has employees, seller should furnish employment records, social security data, Fair Wages and Hours Law records, income tax withholding records, union agreements, if any, and agreements with janitor.

19. Affidavit by seller that: (1) all chattels included in the sale are fully paid for; (2) seller knows of no building or zoning ordinance violations affecting the property; (3) rents are being collected according to the leases, that is, no rents have been collected in advance and no concessions have been granted tenants, such as one month's free rent each year; (4) seller has no knowledge of any contemplated acquisition of the property for public purposes.

20. If the seller is selling only part of his land, he should sign and deliver to the buyer all documents necessary to have future real estate taxes apportioned as between the land sold and the land retained by the buyer.

21. The keys to the building.

§ 230. **Documents to be obtained by seller.**   At closing, the seller should obtain the balance of the purchase price. If a purchase money mortgage is given, the seller should receive the purchase money mortgage and notes, chattel mortgage on personal property sold, fire insurance policies and abstract of title.

§ 231. **Matters to attend to after closing.**   After closing, the buyer should immediately record his deed and any release of mortgage obtained at the closing and have his evidence of title brought down to cover the same. The seller should do likewise with any purchase money mortgage. The buyer's title insurance policy and the title policy covering the mortgage the buyer put on at closing should be issued as soon as possible. If this has not already been attended to, the seller should notify the janitor, building manager, scavenger, exterminator, and so forth of the termination of their employment and that he will no longer be responsible for their compensation. The buyer should: (1) have water, gas, and electric bills, and real estate tax books changed to his name; (2) arrange for janitor, scavenger, building manager, and other services; (3) obtain consent of insurance company to assignment of policy; (4) have mortgage loss clause attached to existing insurance policies if mortgage has been executed; (5) obtain workmen's compensation and employer's liability insurance, if necessary.

Chapter 13

ESCROWS

§ 232. **Nature of escrow.** A deed is delivered *in escrow* when it is deposited with a third person with directions to deliver the deed to the grantee only upon the performance of some condition set forth in the escrow instructions but not in the deed. The third person, to whom the deed is delivered, is called the *escrow holder, escrow agent,* or *escrowee.* The instructions defining the conditions to be performed prior to delivery of the deed to the grantee are called the *escrow agreement* or *escrow instructions.*

§ 233. **Operation and purpose of escrows.** A contract for the sale of land usually requires the seller to furnish an abstract or other evidence of title showing the condition of his title *on the date of the contract.* Suppose that on May 10, R agrees to sell certain land to E for $5000. The contract is not recorded, and the seller remains in possession of the land. R orders an abstract or other evidence of title. This abstract is received by R on May 20. It does not, however, show the condition of the title on May 20, but on some earlier date, probably May 10. E's lawyer completes his examination of the abstract on May 25 and finds title clear in R as of May 10. On May 26 E pays the money to R, and receives his deed. Then it develops that on May 11 the United States had filed an income tax lien of $1,000 against R. This is a lien on the land, like a mortgage. Other objections to the title may also arise during this interval between the date of the contract and the recording of the deed, such as judgment liens or suits attacking the title. The seller might even mortgage the land in the interval. Or he might die during the interval, leaving minor heirs, who obviously would be incapable of signing any deed.

In order to avoid these and other similar risks, sales may be closed in escrow. Escrows usually operate somewhat as follows: Both the deed and the purchase price are delivered to some disinterested third party, often a title insurance company, with written instructions to record the deed, to order an examination of title, and, if the title shows clear *in the buyer,* to pay over the purchase price to the seller. The escrow agreement also provides that, if it shall appear that the seller's title is defective and the defects are not cured within a certain specified time, the buyer shall be entitled to the return of his money upon reconveying the title to the seller. In those cases where the seller has not had his title examined as of some recent date in the past, the procedure is often divided into two steps. First, before the deed is recorded, the escrow holder is instructed to cause the seller's title to be examined down to the date of the contract. This first step may even be taken before the escrow agreement is signed. Then if title shows clear in the seller, the instructions provide that the deed be recorded and the examination of title brought down to cover the recording of the deed.

When the transaction follows the procedure above outlined, it is common for the grantee to deposit with the escrowee a quitclaim deed conveying the land back to the grantor. Then if the title proves defective, the quitclaim deed can be recorded by the escrowee so that the records will once more show title in the grantor.

In counties where it is possible to examine titles very quickly, the procedure may follow these lines: The seller will have his title examined down to the date of the contract of sale. If title shows clear, the seller deposits his deed with a title company as escrowee. The escrowee orders a second examination of title to cover the period intervening between the date of the last examination and the close of recording hours on the day the deed is deposited. This examination can be made quickly, for it covers a period of only a few days. If title shows clear, the seller's deed is recorded the next morning the moment the recorder's office opens.

Under either system, the buyer's money is not paid to the seller until the buyer is assured of receiving clear title.

Escrow practices differ quite a bit from state to state. In many communities, escrows are virtually unknown. This is particularly true of small communities where seller and buyer know and trust each other. The danger here that the seller will make a deed or mortgage to some third person in order to get out of the deal is not so great as in larger communities, where relationships are apt to be more impersonal. When a deal is closed without benefit of escrow, the buyer often requires the seller, at the time the deal is closed, to give an affidavit that he has not signed any deeds, mortgages, or contracts since the date of the contract of sale, and that since that date no judgments have been rendered against him. (See § 227.)

Another benefit of the escrow is that if objections to the title that can be removed by use of the purchase money appear, such as judgments against the seller or unpaid taxes, the buyer may with absolute safety, after title is recorded in his name, allow the escrow holder to use part of the purchase money for the purpose of removing such objections. An escrow also protects the buyer against the seller's changing his mind and conveying the property to some third person in order to escape performance of the agreement. On the other hand, it assures the seller that the purchase price will be paid to him if the title is clear and enables a seller who has liens against his title to use the buyer's money to pay off such liens.

§ 234.   **Requirements of valid escrow.**   The following are the requirements for a valid escrow for the sale of land:

1. There must be a valid and enforceable contract for the sale of the land. *Johnson v. Walden,* 342 Ill. 201, 173 N.E. 790. The escrow agreement may in itself contain all the essential requirements of a contract of sale. *Wood Bldg. Corp. v. Griffiths,* 164 Cal. App.2d 559, 330 P.2d 847. The existence of a valid contract of sale, either in the escrow instructions or in a separate instrument, is, however, indispensable for a binding escrow. If this were not true, it would be possible to have what is in effect a contract for the sale of land without the written agreement that the law requires for land sales. *Campbell v. Thomas,* 42 Wis. 437.

EXAMPLE: Two landowners executed deeds to each other pursuant to an oral exchange agreement and delivered such deeds to an attorney with verbal directions to deliver each deed to the grantee named therein when each landowner had presented a receipt showing payment of back interest on existing mortgages. Before these receipts were delivered, one of the landowners demanded return of his deed. The court held that he was entitled to return of his deed. The contract of exchange was only oral and therefore unenforceable. *Jozefowicz v. Leickem,* 174 Wis. 475, 182 N.W. 729.

2. The escrow agreement must contain a *condition,* something that must be done before the buyer's money is paid to the seller. The usual condition, of course, is the showing of clear title of record in the buyer, subject only to those objections listed in the contract of sale and escrow instructions.
3. The deed must be a good and valid deed.
4. The escrow holder must be some third person. Neither buyer nor seller may act as escrow holder.

§ 235.   **Contents of escrow agreement.**   The escrow agreement usually covers the following matters:

1. Names and signatures of buyer and seller and name of escrow holder.

2. Documents to be deposited by seller, such as deed, insurance policies, separate assignments of insurance policies, leases, assignments of leases, abstracts or other evidence of title, tax bills, canceled mortgage notes, notice to tenants to pay rent to buyer, and service contracts.

3. Deposits to be made by buyer, such as purchase price and purchase money mortgage, if any.

4. When deed is to be recorded, whether immediately, after buyer's check clears, or after seller furnishes evidence of good title at date of contract.

5. Objections to which buyer agrees to take subject.

6. Type of evidence of title to be furnished.

7. Time allowed seller to clear defects in title.

8. How and when purchase price is to be disbursed, with directions as to what items are to be prorated or apportioned if escrow holder is to do the prorating.

9. Directions to deliver deeds, leases, insurance policies, assignments of policy, and service contracts to buyer when title shows clear.

10. Return of deposits to the respective parties where title cannot be cleared.

11. Reconveyance by buyer to seller if deed to buyer has been recorded immediately on signing of escrow agreement and examination of title thereafter discloses seller's title was defective and cannot be cured.

12. Payment of escrow, title and recording charges, broker's commission, and attorney's fees.

While an escrow often takes the form of *instructions* by the buyer and seller to the escrowee, the legal fact remains that it is an agreement or contract, and is so referred to herein.

§ 236. **Escrow is irrevocable.** When a valid escrow agreement has been executed and the instruments therein provided for are delivered to the escrow holder, neither party can revoke the escrow and obtain return of his deposit.

§ 237. **Conflict between contract of sale and escrow agreement.** Since the escrow is a means of carrying out the terms of the contract of sale, there should be no conflict between the two agreements. In the event of conflict, however, disposition of the deed and money deposited in escrow must be governed by the escrow instructions. *Widess v. Doane*, 112 Cal. App. 343, 296 Pac. 899.

§ 238. **When title passes.** Prior to the performance of the condition specified in the escrow, title to the land remains in the seller even though his deed to the buyer is recorded. Even an innocent purchaser or mortgagee from the grantee is not protected in such cases. *Osby v. Reynolds*, 260 Ill. 576, 103 N.E. 556; *Clevenger v. Moore*, 126 Okla. 246, 259 Pac. 219.

EXAMPLE: An escrow agreement required the buyer to deposit the purchase price in escrow. Before this was done, the buyer persuaded the escrow holder to give him the deed, which the buyer thereupon recorded. He thereafter placed a mortgage on the property. When the seller discovered this mortgage, he filed suit, and the court canceled the mortgage as a cloud on his title, even though the mortgagee had acted in entire good faith. *Blakeney v. Home Owners' Loan Corp.,* 192 Okla. 158, 135 P.2d 339.

However, if the grantor allows his deed to be recorded, an innocent purchaser from the grantee will usually be protected if the grantor has also allowed the grantee to take possession of the land, for in such case *both the records and the possession show the grantee as the apparent owner,* and an innocent purchaser from such grantee should be protected, for there is nothing to apprise him of the grantor's rights. *Mays v. Shields,* 117 Ga. 814, 45 S.E. 68.

Immediately upon the performance of the conditions specified in the escrow agreement, ownership of the land passes to the buyer and ownership of the purchase price passes to the seller. Thereupon the escrow holder becomes the agent of the buyer as to the deed and of the seller as to the money. *Shreeves v. Pearson,* 194 Cal. 699, 230 Pac. 448. Since at that moment the escrow holder holds the deed for the grantee, this is as though the grantee himself held the deed. Thus delivery of the deed has been completed, and actual manual delivery of the deed by the escrow holder to the grantee adds nothing to the grantee's title. *Shirley v. Ayers,* 14 Ohio 307. However, it is the practice to provide for a delivery of the deed by the escrow holder to the grantee. This is the so-called *second delivery.*

§ 239. **Relation back.**   Where the grantor delivers a deed in escrow, then dies, and thereafter the condition of the escrow is performed, the deed is considered as passing title as of the date of the delivery of the deed to the escrow holder. It is said that the title *relates back* to such time.

> **EXAMPLE:** R enters into a written contract to sell land to E. R signs a deed to E and delivers this deed to X as escrowee. E also deposits the purchase price with X. X records the deed under escrow instructions, which provide that the purchase price is to be paid to R when an examination of title shows the title clear of all objections. Before the examination is completed, R dies, leaving minor children as his heirs. Thereafter the title examination is completed and shows clear title in E. The deed is good, since the transfer of title to E relates back to the time when R was alive.

The same is true when the seller marries or becomes insane after delivering a deed in escrow.

If the *grantee* dies after the deed has been delivered in escrow, and the condition of the escrow is thereafter performed, the deed will be treated as relating back to the delivery in escrow and may be delivered to the grantee's heirs. *Prewitt v. Ashford,* 90 Ala. 294, 7 So. 831.

The rule that title relates back to the time of the original delivery of the deed to the escrowee is confined to the examples given above. In all other situations, *transfer of ownership of the land takes place as of the time when the terms and conditions of the escrow are performed,* illustrated by the defalcation cases. For example, if the escrowee absconds with the buyer's purchase money before the terms and conditions of the escrow have been performed, the loss must fall on the buyer, because *at the time of the defalcation the purchase money still belongs to the buyer. Hildebrand v. Beck,* 196 Cal. 141, 236 Pac. 301, 39 A.L.R. 1080. On the other hand, if the terms of the escrow have been performed and thereafter the escrowee absconds with the money, the loss falls on the seller, because *after the escrow terms have been met and performed, the money on deposit belongs to the seller. Lechner v. Halling,* 35 Wash.2d 903, 216 P.2d 179.

Thus if a lender is a party to an escrow and the escrowee embezzles the mortgage money before the title has been cleared as required by the escrow instructions, the mortgage funds still belong to the mortgagee, and therefore he must suffer the loss of his funds and cannot collect from the mortgagor even though he holds the mortgagor's promissory note. *Ward, Cook, Inc. v. Davenport,* (Ore.) 413 P.2d 387.

§ 240. **Mortgages.** Since a mortgage does not become a lien until a debt which the mortgage secures exists, mere recording of a mortgage does not create a lien. Liens attaching to the land *prior to the time that the mortgage money is disbursed to the mortgagor* may obtain *priority of lien* over the mortgage. But if the mortgagee deposits his mortgage money in escrow, with directions to pay the money over to the mortgagor if an examination of title shows the mortgage as a first lien on the date of its recording, then immediately upon the recording of the mortgage its position as a first lien is established. Payment into escrow is treated as payment by the mortgagee to or for the benefit of the mortgagor. Thus there are mortgage escrows as well as sale escrows.

Again, there are cases where a buyer is borrowing money to complete his purchase. The mortgagee does not want his money paid out until title shows clear in the buyer, who is the mortgagor. The seller will not want to give a deed until and unless he is assured of receiving the purchase price. This difficult situation is easily taken care of through an escrow. The deed, mortgage, and mortgage money are deposited with an escrowee under written instructions to record the deed and mortgage and pay the mortgage money to the seller if the title examination shows the mortgage as a first lien. The interests of all parties are protected.

§ 241. **Long-term escrows.** In the West and Southwest, the long-term escrow is used in the financing of real estate. This operates somewhat as follows: A, a landowner, enters into a contract to sell the land to B. B is unable to pay the full price at once. A desires to retain control of the land so as to insure the payment of the price in full or the restoration of the land to him. *A* therefore executes a deed of the land to *B* and places the deed in the hands of *C*, as escrowee, to be delivered to *B* on full payment of the price by *B* to *C*. If *B* makes timely payment of the price to *C*, the latter will hand the deed to *B*. *C* will also pay the money to *A*. If *B* fails to make such payment, *C* will be under a duty to return the deed to *A*. 21 *Ill. L. Rev.* 655. The disadvantages of this arrangement are as follows:

1. Until completion of the payments, the public records show title in *A*, and this gives *A* the opportunity to defraud *B* by making a deed or mortgage to some third person who is unaware of the contract's existence. *Waldock v. Frisco Lumber Co.,* 71 Okla. 200, 176 Pac. 218. This would not be true if the contract were recorded or if the buyer went into possession of the land.

2. The depositary may deliver the deed to the buyer notwithstanding the fact that he has not completed his payments, and recording of this deed will cloud the seller's title.

3. Default on the buyer's part after he has made substantial payments may result in a lawsuit against the depositary. *Phoenix Title & Trust Co. v. Horworth,* 41 Ariz. 417, 19 P.2d 82.

4. In some states a buyer in an escrow deal takes subject to judgments rendered against the seller while the deal is in escrow but before the purchase price is fully paid and the deed recorded. *May v. Emerson,* 52 Ore. 262, 96 Pac. 454; 117 A.L.R. 69, 85-88. The danger from this risk is increased when the escrow extends over a long period of time. In addition to the danger of judgments, there is the danger that, while the escrow is running, federal income tax liens may be filed against the seller or the seller may go into bankruptcy. These matters would cloud the buyer's title.

Chapter 14

EVIDENCE OF TITLE

§ 242. **In general.** Every prudent purchaser insists upon production of satisfactory evidence that the seller has good title to the land in question. The fact that the seller is willing to sign a deed to a tract of land is by no means satisfactory proof that he has good title to the land. He may have title to all, part, or none of the land. And if he has title, it may be a good title or it may be so heavily encumbered as to be worthless. And since a lender demands a mortgage precisely because he is unwilling to rely on the mortgagor's unsecured promise, it is clear that proof of good title is as important to a mortgagee as it is to a purchaser.

There are four kinds of evidence of title: *abstract and opinion, certificate of title, title insurance, and Torrens certificate.* The certificate of title is used extensively in the Eastern states and in some Southern states. In urban centers in a great many sections of the country, title insurance occupies a dominant position in real estate transactions. In farm areas the abstract and opinion method is common. To a great extent, the acceptability of a particular kind of evidence of title depends on the local custom.

§ 243. **Abstract.** An abstract is a history of the title to a particular tract of land. It consists of a summary of the material parts of every recorded instrument affecting the title. It begins with a description of the land covered by the abstract, which description is called the *caption,* or *head,* of the abstract, and then proceeds to show, usually in chronological order, the original governmental grant and all subsequent deeds, mortgages, release deeds, wills, judgments, mechanics' liens, foreclosure proceedings, tax sales, and other matters affecting the title.

Of course all these items are shown in a highly abbreviated form. In fact, usually a bare outline of the deed, mortgage, or other instrument is shown. "Fine print" provisions are omitted altogether or summarized in a few words. The manner in which the instrument was signed is not shown unless there is some irregularity in this respect. If the acknowledgment is in due form, the abstracter merely indicates that the instrument was acknowledged. A purchaser or mortgagee may rely on the abstracter to draw attention to these irregularities, since where an abstract purports to state the substance of a deed, mortgage, or other instrument, and there is nothing on the face of the abstract to indicate an error, the customer is justified in assuming that no irregularity exists in those portions of the document that the abstracter has omitted from his abstract. *Equitable B. & L. Assn. v. Bank of Commerce,* 118 Tenn. 678, 102 S.W. 901.

The abstract concludes with the *abstracter's certificate.* This discloses what records the abstracter has examined and, what is more important, what records he has *not examined.* For example, some abstracters will not examine records located outside of the county seat, and their certificates reflect that fact. In such case, it is necessary to supplement the abstract by obtaining the necessary searches. If an abstracter certifies that he has made no search of federal court proceedings affecting the property, it will be necessary to write to the clerk of the district court, who will supply the search for a small charge. The certificate also shows the date covered by the abstracter's search of the records. Because of the unavoidable delay intervening between the filing in the recorder's office of a particular day's deeds and mortgages and the entry of the same on the abstracter's books, the abstracter is not in a position to certify on any particular day as to the status of the record title on that day. His certificate will certify today as to the status of the record title on some previous day.

§ 244. **The abstracter.**   Abstracts are prepared by public officials, lawyers, and abstract companies. In some states, an abstracter is required to post bond to protect all those who rely on his abstracts against any loss resulting from a lack of care or skill on his part. Many abstracters keep their own books. They take great pride in their "abstract plant," and, in many communities, the abstracter's records are infinitely more accurate than the public records. Other abstracters prepare their abstracts from the public records.

A prudent purchaser or mortgagee will rely only on abstracts furnished by abstracters possessing the requisite skill, care, and experience, since abstracting is a profession requiring much legal knowledge and careful

research. The financial responsibility of the abstracter is likewise important, since if an error is made in preparing the abstract of the title to a
valuable tract of land, there should be no doubt as to the ability of the
abstracter to respond in damages.

§ 245. **Abstracter's liability.**   The abstracter is in no sense
a guarantor of title. He merely undertakes to exercise due care in the
preparation of his abstract. He renders no opinion as to the title. If he
includes in his abstract all recorded instruments affecting the title, and,
as a consequence, the abstract discloses a fatally defective title, the abstracter has fully discharged his responsibilities. But if an intending
purchaser orders an abstract prepared and the abstracter negligently
omits therefrom a mortgage, judgment, or other lien that the purchaser is
thereafter compelled to pay, the purchaser can obtain reimbursement
from the abstracter. 28 A.L.R.2d 891.

§ 246. **Examination of title.**   The mere fact that a purchaser
or mortgagee has received an abstract of title affords him no protection.
In fact, examination of the abstract may disclose that the title is hopelessly
clouded. Hence after an abstract has been prepared by a reliable abstracter and certified so that the buyer or mortgagee can rely thereon, it
should be delivered to a competent attorney for examination. This attorney will thereupon examine the abstract and prepare his *opinion* as to
the title, which will show the name of the titleholder and all defects and
encumbrances disclosed by the abstract.

§ 247. **Certificate of title.**   In some localities the making of
an abstract is dispensed with. The attorney merely examines the public
records and issues his certificate, which is his opinion of title based on the
public records that he has examined. Like an abstracter, such an attorney
is liable only for damages occasioned by his negligence. The same is true
when a certificate of title is issued by a title company. *Lattin v. Gillette,*
95 Cal. 317, 30 Pac. 545; *Bridgeport Airport v. Title Guaranty & Trust Co.,*
111 Conn. 537, 150 Atl. 509.

§ 248. **Risks involved in relying on record title.**   There are
certain defects in title that even a perfect abstract or certificate of title
will not disclose because these hidden defects cannot be discovered by
an examination of the public records. Among these defects are:

1. *Forgery.*   A deed in the chain of title may seem entirely regular but may
nevertheless be a forgery. Such a deed is totally void and a purchaser or mortgagee
of such title is not protected. Likewise, a forged release of mortgage does not discharge
the mortgage lien.

EXAMPLE: Suppose that you own some land and someone forges your
signature on a deed purporting to deed the land to him or even to some innocent
person to whom the forger represents that he is the real owner of the land. Obviously,

you would expect the law to protect you, even as against an innocent purchaser. It does. Or suppose that you owned a mortgage of $100,000 on an apartment building, and the apartment owner signed your name to a release purporting to discharge this mortgage. Even if the land were sold to an innocent purchaser, you would expect the law to permit you to foreclose your mortgage. It does.

2. *Insanity and minority.* A deed or release of mortgage executed by a minor or insane person may be subject to cancellation by subsequent court proceedings.

3. *Marital status incorrectly given.* A deed or mortgage may recite that the grantor or mortgagor is single, whereas in fact he may be married. This may later result in a dower or other claim by his spouse.

EXAMPLE: *H* owns an apartment building and is married to *W*, but is separated from her. *H* has an opportunity to sell the building to you at a good price, and does so. *H* signs *W*'s name to the deed. Her dower remains outstanding, and if *W* survives *H*, she will be able to force a sale of the building and her dower rights will be paid her out of the sale price. (See Chapter 17.)

4. *Defective deeds.* A recorded deed may never have been properly delivered. For example, it may have been found by the grantee among the grantor's effects after the grantor's death and then placed on record. Such deeds, of course, pass no title.

EXAMPLE: *A* owns an apartment building. He is a bachelor. He shares a safety deposit box with his nephew, *X. A* dies. *X* opens the box and finds a deed from *A* to *X* of the apartment building, with a note pinned to it, stating that *A* wants *X* to have the building. *X* records the deed. The deed is void. The mere fact that the deed was recorded after *A*'s death discloses that there is something wrong with the deed.

There are many other defects in title that the public records do not disclose.

There are also certain other risks not of a legal character that are encountered when a deal is closed in reliance on a certificate of title or abstract and opinion. One of these risks is the risk of unwarranted litigation attacking the title. A landowner's title may be good as a matter of law, but if some other person entertains the notion that he has some title to, or interest in, the land, he may institute litigation asserting his supposed rights, and such litigation, even though successfully defended, may prove costly. Again, a competent attorney examining an abstract for a purchaser may reach an entirely correct opinion that the title is good. But when the purchaser, in turn, is selling or mortgaging the land, the attorney for the subsequent buyer or mortgagee may arrive at a different conclusion. This may necessitate the institution of litigation to clear the title. It is this fear of objections to the title by some subsequent examiner that prompts attorneys to scrutinize abstracts closely and raise every technical objection apparent therefrom. This practice is known as *flyspecking.*

§ 249. **Nature of title insurance.** It is the function of title insurance to shift or transfer to a responsible insurer risks such as those mentioned in the preceding section. Title insurance is a contract to make good a loss arising through defects in title to real estate or liens or encumbrances thereon. *Beaullieu v. Atlanta Title & Trust Co.,* 60 Ga. App. 400, 4 S.E.2d 78. As a rule, a title company will not insure a bad title any more than a fire insurance company would issue a policy on a burning building. However, title companies disregard many of the technical objections that would be raised by an attorney examining an abstract. If an examination of the title discloses that good title is vested in a particular person, the company will issue its policy whereby it agrees, subject to the terms of its policy, to indemnify such person against any loss he may sustain by reason of any defects in title not enumerated in the policy and to defend at its own expense any lawsuit attacking the title where such lawsuit is based on a defect in title against which the policy insured.

§ 250.   **The title insurance policy.**   Title companies issue both *owner's policies* and *mortgage policies,* the latter being known also as *loan policies.* The owner's policy is usually issued to the landowner himself. Mortgage policies, of course, are issued to mortgagees. Unlike other types of insurance policies, which insure for limited periods of time and are kept in force by periodic payment of renewal premiums, an owner's title insurance policy is bought and paid for only once, and then continues in force without any further payment until a sale of the property is made. At that time, the title is examined to cover the period of time since the issuance of the policy, and a new policy is issued to the purchaser. A charge is usually then made for the issuance of this new policy. The mortgage policy terminates when the mortgage debt is paid. However, if the mortgage is foreclosed, then the protection of the mortgage policy continues in force, protecting against any defects of title that existed on, or prior to, the date of the policy. In both policies, the company usually undertakes, subject to the terms of its policy, to defend at its own expense any lawsuit attacking the title where such lawsuit is based on a defect in title against which the policy insures. This is one of the attractive features of title insurance to property owners, since "nuisance" litigation affecting real estate is quite common and is expensive to defend, even though not well founded. A policy of title insurance usually shows the name of the party insured and the character of his title, which is usually fee simple title, although title policies are also issued on other interests, such as leaseholds or easements. It also contains a description of the land and, if the policy is a mortgage policy, a description of the mortgage. The policy lists those matters which affect that particular tract of land, such as any mortgage, easement, lien, or restriction thereon. Like other insurance policies, it contains printed conditions and stipulations.

Common printed exceptions found in owner's policies relate to the rights of parties in possession and questions of survey. Often real property is in the possession of those whose rights are not disclosed by the records. Common instances are tenancies under oral or unrecorded leases and rights of those in possession under unrecorded contracts of purchase. When no survey has been furnished the company, it has no means of knowing what encroachments exist, if any. The policy will therefore be subject to encroachments and other matters that a survey would reveal, also the rights of persons in possession claiming under some unrecorded document.

Title insurance policies are largely standardized throughout the country in that the American Land Title Association policy forms have become far and away the most popular.

§ 251. **Leasehold policies.**   Suppose a tenant is about to take a lease on a store, theater, restaurant, or other commercial location in which he plans to make a substantial investment for remodeling. Just as a buyer of land needs to know that his seller has a good, clear title, this tenant needs to know that his landlord has a good, clear title to the leased premises and that the tenant will not be dispossessed in the middle of his lease by foreclosures of mortgages or other liens on the landlord's title. Contracts for such leases are drawn along the lines of a contract for the sale of land. They require the landlord to have his title examined and to furnish the tenant a *leasehold policy* issued by a title company insuring the validity of the tenant's lease free from mortgages or other encumbrances.

§ 252. **Easement policies.**   Suppose you are selling me a tract of industrial property that has access to a railroad by means of an easement for a spur track over adjoining land. The validity of the easement is just as important to me as the fact that you have good title to the land I am buying. I will therefore insist that the title policy you furnish me insures the validity of the easement.

§ 253. **Special coverage.**   When there are building lines or building restrictions affecting the land, a mortgagee often requests that the title insurance company insure that the building conforms to such building lines and restrictions. The title company issues an *endorsement* furnishing this coverage. If the building violates existing building restrictions, the company may, in its discretion, issue special insurance against any loss that may occur by reason of such violation. If the title search discloses an encroachment, the company will, in some cases, insure against any loss due to such encroachment. A landowner or mortgagee may want other special protection created by the circumstances of the particular title. The flexibility of the title insurance business makes it possible to supply the needed protection in almost all cases.

§ 254. **Title commitments.**   Suppose that A had purchased some land in 1940 and had received a title policy at that time. He is now selling this same land to B. Naturally, B would not want to rely on such an outdated document. Therefore the contract of sale will call upon A to have the title company bring its title search down to the present date, which they will do. Thereupon the title company will issue a *commitment* obligating the company to issue its policy to B subject only to the matters shown in the commitment. If any defects appear on the commitment that the seller must clear up, unpaid back taxes, for example, the seller pays off the item, receives paid tax bills or other documents and exhibits them to the title company, which thereupon stamps the item "waived." When the title is clear, the land is conveyed by the seller to the buyer, the deed recorded, and a title policy issued in the name of the buyer.

§ 255. **The Torrens system.** In a few counties in the United States, there is, in addition to the system of transferring title under the Recording Acts, a system known as the *Torrens system.* Under the Recording Acts, when a deed is made conveying land, the grantee in the deed usually takes it to the recorder's office and leaves it there for recording. The recorder makes a copy of the deed, places this copy in record books, which are available to the public, and returns the original deed to the grantee. The recorder does not pass upon the validity of the deed. If the grantee wishes to satisfy himself that he has received a good title, he may obtain title insurance, an abstract and opinion of title, or a title certificate.

The Torrens system operates quite differently. A landowner who wishes to register his land under the Torrens system first obtains a complete abstract of title to the land. He then files in the proper public office an application for the registration of title. This application lists the names of all persons who appear to have any interest in the land. These names are obtained from the abstract and from an investigation of the possession of the premises. The application constitutes the filing of a lawsuit against all persons named therein, and any person wishing to contest the applicant's claim of title may do so on receiving notice of the filing of the application. If the applicant is successful in proving that he is the owner of the land, the court enters an order so finding and also stating the mortgages, liens, restrictions, and so on to which said title is subject. The court also orders an official known as the *Registrar of Titles* to *register* such title. The registrar then makes out a *certificate* of title showing the title as found by the court. These certificates are bound up in books and are public records. At the same time that the registrar makes out the original certificate, he makes out a *duplicate certificate of title,* which he delivers to the owner.

When a tract of land has been registered under the Torrens system, no subsequent transaction binds the land until such transaction has also been registered. When the land is sold, the deed itself does not pass ownership of the land. The deed must be taken to the registrar's office, and if the registrar is satisfied that the deed is valid, he cancels the old certificate of title and issues a new one to the grantee. It is this *registration* that puts ownership in the grantee. The deed is not returned to the grantee but remains in the registrar's office. In other words, the registrar of titles, unlike the recorder of deeds, investigates to determine the validity of the transfer, and only after he is satisfied that the transfer of title is valid will he issue a new certificate in the grantee's name. Thus, as to Torrens land it is said that "title passes by registration, not by deed." Likewise, a mortgage is not effective against the property until the registrar has checked it as to form and signature and entered it on the certificate of title. However, the registrar does not check on or guarantee the essential validity of the mortgage, for example, to see whether or not the mortgage money has been paid out or whether the interest is usurious. No judgment or other lien is valid against Torrens property until a copy has been filed in the registrar's office and the lien noted on the certificate of title.

Use of the Torrens system is largely confined to a few metropolitan areas, Boston, Chicago, Duluth, Minneapolis-St. Paul, and New York City.

The Torrens certificate purports to be conclusive proof that the title is as therein stated. As in the case of other evidences of title, there are exceptions and objections that the Torrens certificate does not cover. These vary somewhat from state to state. Unlike a policy of title insurance, the Torrens certificate does not require the registrar to assume the defense of litigation attacking the title of the registered owner. The property owner must defend the litigation at his own expense, and if he is successful, he cannot obtain reimbursement from the registrar for the expenses of the litigation.

Chapter 15

FIRE INSURANCE

§ **256. Defined.** Fire insurance is a contract to indemnify the insured against loss by fire.

§ **257. Development of standard policy.** The need for fire insurance first became apparent after the Great Fire of London in 1666. However, the policies that came into use in England following that catastrophe contained numerous and varied fine-print exceptions that led to much litigation and disappointment on the part of the policyholder. These conditions also prevailed in America, and, in 1873, agitation for a standard policy led to the adoption of a standard policy form in Massachusetts. In 1886, New York adopted a standard policy form, which was revised by a law effective in 1918. This policy still strongly favored the insurer, and in 1943 New York adopted a revised form more favorable to the insured. This form has been widely adopted in this country and the discussion in this chapter is largely keyed to this form of policy.

§ **258. Hazards covered—fire loss.** The policy covers direct loss and damage *caused by fire*. Loss and damage caused by hazards *other than fire* must be covered by riders attached to the policy, for which an additional premium is charged, or by separate insurance. Among the hazards *not* covered are:

1. Explosion damage. If an explosion not caused by fire occurs on the premises and no fire results, none of the damage is covered. If a fire starts *first* and

155

the fire causes an explosion, all loss is covered whether due to fire or explosion, for the fire is the cause of the loss. 82 A.L.R.2d 1128. If an explosion occurs first and fire results, the policy covers the damage caused by the fire but not the damage caused by the explosion.

2. Water damage not resulting from a fire, as damage from water seepage in a basement or from a leaking sprinkler system.
3. Windstorm damage. As in the case of explosions, if a fire results from windstorm damage, the fire loss is covered by the policy.
4. Loss from hail, riot, civil commotion, aircraft, and many other hazards.

Breakage, water damage, and damage from chemicals caused through efforts to extinguish the fire are considered to be caused by fire and are therefore covered by the policy.

§ 259. **Extended coverage endorsement.** A rider attached to the fire policy on payment of an extra premium is known as an *extended coverage endorsement.* Its content varies according to locality, but it often covers loss from windstorm, hail, explosion, riot, civil commotion, aircraft, vehicles, and smoke from friendly fires, except those in fireplaces. The windstorm damage coverage of the extended coverage endorsement does not cover rain, snow, or other water damage as such, except where caused by or resulting from windstorm or another peril specified in the extended coverage endorsement.

EXAMPLE: In a heavy rain, the sewer backs up and floods the basement of your house. The damage is not covered by the extended coverage endorsement.

EXAMPLE: A tornado tears off a roof and the debris breaks water pipes. The water rushes out of the pipes, causing damage. All the damage is covered by the insurance, for the basic cause of the entire loss is the windstorm.

EXAMPLE: A hailstorm breaks windows, and the rain and wind sweep in, causing damage. All the damage is covered, because the original cause is a hailstorm, which is a peril specified in the extended coverage endorsement.

Damage caused by explosion of a steam boiler on the premises is not covered. Damage caused by vehicles driven *by the landowner* is not covered, but if, for example, a delivery truck entering a side drive runs into the house, this damage is covered.

§ 260. **Comprehensive coverage.** New policies are now available that in one package cover damage to the home, such as damage caused by fire, wind, hail, blasting, dust, tenants, earthquake, waves, surface waters, industrial smoke, freezing of plumbing, vandalism; also damage to contents, such as furniture. They also provide insurance protecting against liability for personal injuries. They are called *homeowner's policies* and vary as to coverage.

§ **261.   Hazards covered—hostile and friendly fires.**   The fire policy does not cover damage caused by smoke from a fire that is confined to the place where it is intended to be. Such a fire is called a *friendly fire*. Damage caused by smoke and soot issuing from a defective furnace is not covered. Damage caused by steam escaping from heat pipes is not fire damage, since the fire is a friendly one. But if the fire, though originally kindled in a stove, furnace, or fireplace, escapes therefrom, it becomes a hostile fire, and loss caused is covered by the policy. Nor is it necessary that the hostile fire be on the premises covered by the policy. For example, if my neighbor's house catches fire and the heat destroys the paint on the wall of my house facing the fire, this is fire damage, covered by my policy, even though my building does not catch fire. Damage from smoke or soot is covered if it is caused by a hostile fire.

§ **262.   Hazards covered—rent loss and business interruption.** Since the policy covers fire damage to the *building*, it does not cover loss of rents when a rental building is rendered untenantable by fire, nor does it cover loss of *profits* when operation of a business is interrupted by fire. Both items can be covered by riders attached to the policy or by separate insurance such as rent insurance and business interruption insurance.

§ **263.   When protection attaches.**   It often takes some time for a formal policy of insurance to be prepared and forwarded to the insurer. Hence oral coverage is perfectly valid pending the issuance of the policy. 44 C.J.S. 951.

§ **264.   Description of the property insured.**   The property insured should be accurately described in the policy, and all policies applying to the same property should contain identical descriptions.

The street address of the property is often used in insurance policies. There has been a tendency in recent times, however, to insist on the insertion of a full legal description so that there will be no dispute as to the property covered. This is particularly true with respect to houses recently constructed which often do not have a street address at the time the policy is written.

§ **265.   Insurable interest.**   The insured must have some insurable interest in the property. Otherwise the policy is void. Persons having an insurable interest include both buyer and seller in a contract for the sale of land, mortgagor, mortgagee, part owner, trustee, receiver, and life tenant.

§ **266.   Interest covered by policy.**   The present form of policy is an *interest policy. It protects only the party insured and covers only the financial loss suffered by the insured, which can never be more than the value of his interest in the property and which may be less than the actual damage to the building.*

This aspect of the policy is of importance in co-ownership situations.

Suppose, for example, that H and W (husband and wife) own property in joint tenancy, but the policy is issued in the name of H only. If a fire loss occurs while both are alive, it is doubtful that the company is legally liable to H for the full amount of the loss, for he is the owner of only a one-half interest in the property, although, of course, companies often make voluntary payment of the full amount of the loss in such cases. Suppose further that a loss occurs after H's death. Here his entire interest in the property has passed to W (*see* Chapter 16), but W has no insurance whatever, for the insurance does not pass with the property. It insures the *person*, not the *property*.

This aspect of insurance is frequently overlooked. Suppose A owns property, takes out insurance, and thereafter has title to the property placed in joint tenancy or tenancy by the entireties. Often the parties neglect to change the fire insurance to cover the new situation. Where land is owned by co-owners, insurance taken out by one does not benefit the other.

EXAMPLE: H and W, husband and wife, owned their home in joint tenancy. They became estranged. H took out a policy in his name only for the full value of the property. Then he died. W has no right to collect on this insurance. *Russell v. Williams*, 24 Cal. Reptr. 859, 374 P.2d 827.

It is obvious that when property is owned by several people and the insurance is intended to cover all of them, the names of all co-owners should appear in the policy.

Since insurance does not cover the building, but only the interest of the insured in the building, and persons other than the insured cannot collect on the policy, persons having liens on insured property are not covered by the insurance.

EXAMPLE: A city has no right to have insurance money applied to payment of delinquent real estate taxes, which are a lien on the insured property. *Shelton v. Providence Washington Ins. Co.* (Tex. Civ. App.), 131 S.W.2d 330. Nor can a mechanic's lien claimant become entitled to fire insurance proceeds. 9 A.L.R.2d 307.

Insurance taken out by a tenant does not benefit the landlord, nor does the landlord's insurance benefit the tenant. Insurance taken out by a builder does not benefit the landowner. *Russell v. Williams*, 24 Cal. Reptr. 859, 374 P.2d 827.

§ 267. **Amount recoverable.**   The company is not liable for damage in excess of the face amount of the policy, and any insurance paid reduces the amount of coverage. For example, if I take out a policy for $5000 and the company pays me $1000 for a loss, its maximum liability thereafter is $4000. Some policies have riders containing an automatic reinstatement clause under which small losses do not reduce the amount of insurance.

If only *part* of the building is destroyed, but rebuilding the structure is prohibited by law (as where the building is a nonconforming use under the zoning ordinance), the loss is treated as *total* and the insured is allowed to collect the full face amount of the policy up to, but not exceeding, the full value of the building before the fire loss occurred. *Feinbloom v. Camden,* 54 N.J.S. 541, 149 A.2d 616. However, it is customary to add a rider extending the policy to cover such loss.

Replacement cost insurance can be procured by adding a rider to the policy. Instead of getting paid the actual cash value of the destroyed building, the insured is paid the actual cost of replacing or restoring the building. This eliminates the guesswork and argument involved in agreeing on the value of a destroyed building, but it does have disadvantages. For example, you recover the cost of replacing an identical building, but this will create problems when the building destroyed was old and of a type that one would not build today. If the insured spends more in replacing the building than was actually necessary, he will probably not recover the full amount spent. The new building may be on a different site, if the insured prefers. He also has the option of settling on the old "actual cash value" basis.

§ 268. **Acts of the assured.**   Naturally, where the party insured causes the loss, as where he sets the building on fire in order to collect the insurance, the insurance company is not liable.

§ 269. **Unoccupancy clause.**   The policy provides that the insurer shall not be liable while the building is vacant or unoccupied beyond a period of sixty consecutive days. The words *vacant* and *unoccupied* are not synonymous. *Vacant* means without inanimate objects; *unoccupied* means without animate occupants. A dwelling is unoccupied when it has ceased to be a customary place of habitation or abode and no one is living in it. Thus if furniture remains in the building, it is not vacant, but if the owner has left the dwelling with the intention of permanently residing elsewhere, the building is unoccupied, and the insurance may become void. *Vandalism coverage* usually ceases if the building is unoccupied for thirty days.

§ 270. **Increase of hazard.**   The policy provides that the company shall not be liable for any loss occurring while the hazard is increased by any means within the control or knowledge of the insured. The operation of this clause is restricted to physical changes in the building or in the use or occupancy of the premises. Any alteration or change in the building or in the use of the property that will increase the risk violates this clause if it is of a more or less permanent nature. 28 A.L.R.2d 762.

EXAMPLE: The following operations increase the hazard and invalidate the insurance: (1) Tenant began operating a still. (2) Owner turned off a sprinkler system. (3) Owner brought fireworks on the premises. (4) Owner began use of a room as a tinshop.

But doing something that involves risk, but that is a more or less normal and expected routine operation, is not considered an increase of hazard that invalidates the policy, for example, using a torch to burn off old paint preparatory to repainting. 28 A.L.R.2d 771.

§ 271. **Double insurance.** The policy provides only that other insurance may be prohibited by endorsement attached to the policy. Unless such endorsement is attached, the insured may procure additional insurance. However, the liability of each company is limited to the proportion of the loss that its insurance bears to the whole insurance covering the property. Thus if the same property is insured in two companies through two policies of $5000 each, and if a loss of $2000 occurs, the maximum liability of each company would be $1000.

The insured should check to see that all portions of all policies covering the same property read exactly alike.

§ 272. **Co-insurance clause.** Very few fires cause a total destruction of the property. Property owners are aware of this fact. If it were not for the co-insurance clause, many property owners would save themselves premiums by taking out insurance for half the value of the property, or even less. To prevent this, the policy generally requires the property owner to take out insurance equal to at least 80 per cent of the value of the property. When he does so, the property owner collects the *full amount* of any loss. But if he insures for less than 80 per cent of value, a co-insurance clause is added. Suppose a building is worth $10,000. The company requires insurance up to 80 per cent of value, or $8000. The insured takes out only a policy of $4000. Under the co-insurance clause, the company will pay only $4000/$8000, or one-half of the loss.

Customary use of this 80 per cent in co-insurance clauses stems from the fact that generally only 80 per cent of the building's value is destructible by fire. A certain portion of the masonry and concrete work will remain standing.

§ 273. **Mortgage interests.** Both the mortgagor and the mortgagee have an insurable interest. Both interests may be, and usually are, covered in one policy. But each may take out a separate policy. This right is of value to the mortgagee when the mortgagor has defaulted in his mortgage payments and declines to take out insurance since he feels that he will lose the property anyway. If the mortgagee obtains his own insurance with his own money and a loss occurs, the mortgagor is not entitled to the insurance money. If the insurer pays off the mortgage in such case, he is entitled to an assignment thereof and may foreclose. Of course the mortgagee's recovery is limited to the balance due on the debt, for that is the measure of his interest in the property.

On the other hand, in the absence of any clause in the mortgage requiring the mortgagor to insure for the mortgagee's benefit, the mortgagee is not entitled to insurance money paid under a policy obtained by the mortgagor in his own name and at his own expense. 9 A.L.R.2d 299. However, most mortgage forms require the mortgagor to keep the buildings insured for the benefit of the mortgagee, and if a loss occurs in such case, the mortgagee is entitled to have the insurance money applied in reduction or payment of the mortgage debt.

§ 274.   **The mortgage clause.**   Formerly it was customary for the mortgagor to take out insurance in his own name and, with the insurer's consent, to assign the policy to the mortgagee. This did not adequately protect the mortgagee. He simply stood in the mortgagor's shoes, and if the mortgagor violated the conditions of the policy so that it became void, the mortgagee was unable to collect the insurance. For example, if the mortgagor committed arson, the policy became void. The same result followed where the *open mortgage clause* was used. This clause simply stated that loss, if any, was payable to the mortgagee *as his interest shall appear,* which still left the mortgagee's insurance subject to be destroyed by the ignorance, carelessness, or fraud of the mortgagor. Hence the *mortgagee loss clause,* also known as the *New York, standard,* or *union loss clause,* was developed. *Syndicate Ins. Co. v. Bohn,* 65 Fed. 165. This clause, now in very general use, provides that the insurance shall not be invalidated by acts of the mortgagor. Under this clause, if the mortgagor does any act that would ordinarily make the policy void, for example, committing arson or bringing dynamite on the premises, *such act merely makes the policy void as to the mortgagor, but the insurance remains in force for the benefit of the mortgagee.* When such a clause is used, there are really two separate contracts, one between the insurer and the mortgagor and the other between the insurer and the mortgagee, and most matters that would invalidate the first of these contracts leave the second intact and in full force.

Under the standard mortgage clause, the following are some matters that will not render the mortgagee's insurance void:

1. Misrepresentation or concealment by mortgagor.
2. Increase of hazard of which the mortgagee remains ignorant.
3. Any act or neglect of mortgagor, including arson by the mortgagor.
4. Foreclosure of the mortgage. *Northwestern Ins. Co. v. Mildenberger* (Mo.), 359 S.W.2d 380. However, if the mortgagee is the purchaser at the foreclosure sale, the mortgage debt is regarded as paid and satisfied by the amount of the foreclosure sale price, so that the insurance company is liable to the mortgagee only for any balance over and above such sale

price up to the amount of the mortgage debt. If the fire loss exceeds the amount of the mortgage debt, then any balance over and above that amount goes to the mortgagor.

5. Deed by mortgagor to mortgagee given in satisfaction of the mortgage debt and in lieu of foreclosure of mortgage. *Union Central Fire Ins. Co. v. Franklin County Farmers Mutual Ins. Assn.*, 222 Ia. 964, 270 N.W. 398.

§ 275.   **Contracts for the sale of land.**   When a landowner takes out insurance and thereafter contracts to sell the land to a purchaser, the sensible course is to have the insurance endorsed to cover both parties as their interests may appear. Then in case of serious loss the company will pay the seller the balance due on the contract and the balance will be paid to the buyer.

When the buyer takes out the insurance in his own name, with a loss payable clause for the benefit of the seller, and the fire is caused by the buyer, the company is not liable to either seller or buyer. *Langhorne v. Capitol Fire Ins. Co.*, 44 Fed. Sup. 739.

When a policy taken out by the buyer is payable to the seller, and a fire occurs and the company pays the unpaid balance of the purchase price to the seller in satisfaction of the insurance claim, all rights of the seller in the property are extinguished, and the company is not entitled to any assignment of the contract. *Fields v. Western Millers Mutual Fire Ins. Co.*, 265 App. Div. 891, 37 N.Y.S.2d 757. The buyer is entitled to the balance of the insurance money in such case. He is also entitled to a deed to the land since the insurance money has paid the purchase price. *Dysart v. Colonial, etc., Co.*, 142 Wash. 601, 254 Pac. 240.

When the buyer takes out a policy with loss payable to the buyer and seller as their interests may appear, and thereafter the seller declares the contract forfeited because of the buyer's default in his payments, the seller is still covered by such insurance. *Aetna Ins. Co. v. Robinson*, 213 Ind. 44, 10 N.E.2d 601. And mere default in his payments does not terminate the buyer's insurance. He remains covered until the seller declares a forfeiture of the contract.

Suppose the contract of sale (as is customary in installment contracts) requires the buyer to take out insurance for the benefit of seller and buyer but the buyer takes out insurance in his own name only. If a loss occurs, the courts will require the buyer to carry out his contract by forcing him to apply his insurance money in payment of the contract price due to the seller. *American Equitable Assurance Co. v. Newman*, 132 Mont. 63, 313 P.2d 1023; 64 A.L.R.2d 1416.

It now seems clear that where a landowner has entered into a contract of sale and a fire occurs after the buyer has substantially reduced the balance due, the seller may nevertheless collect for the full amount of the loss.

EXAMPLE: A took out a fire insurance policy and thereafter contracted to sell the land to B. When the contract had been paid down to $16,000, a fire loss occurred. A was allowed to collect $46,750 in fire insurance. *First National Bank v. Boston Ins. Co.,* 17 Ill.2d 147, 160 N.E.2d 802; *Edlin v. Security Ins. Co.,* 269 F.2d 159.

§ 276. **Assignment.** Assignment of the policy does not render the policy void, but the assignment itself is not valid except with the written consent of the company. However, the policy is usually assigned in connection with a sale and deed by the seller of all his title to the property. In such case, the seller could not collect on the policy for a subsequent loss since after sale he has no insurable interest in the property. Nor could the buyer collect if the assignment had not been consented to by the company. *Homeowners' policies* are not assignable.

Chapter 16

CO-OWNERSHIP

§ 277. **In general.** A person can be the sole owner of a tract of land. However, a tract of land may also be owned by two or more persons. Such co-owners are known as *co-tenants.* There are different kinds of co-ownerships, or co-tenancies, as they are called. Persons may own the land as *joint tenants,* as *tenants by the entireties,* or as *tenants in common.*

§ 278. **Joint tenancy and tenancy in common distinguished.** When a deed is made to two or more persons who are not husband and wife and nothing is said in the deed concerning the character of the tenancy created by the deed, the grantees acquire title as tenants in common. That is, on the death of either party, his interest in the real estate will go to his heirs, if he dies without leaving a will, or, if he leaves a will, to the persons named therein.

EXAMPLE: *X* conveys land to *A* and *B,* who are brothers. They are *tenants in common,* since the deed is not a joint tenancy form. *A,* a widower, dies without a will, leaving *C* and *D* as his only children. *B, C,* and *D* own the land as tenants in common, *B* owning a half and *C* and *D* each a fourth.

If, however, the deed runs to two or more persons as joint tenants, a different rule applies. While both joint tenants are alive, they are co-owners of the land, but as soon as one dies, his title passes automatically to the surviving joint tenant.

EXAMPLE: X makes a deed of his land to A and B as joint tenants. A dies. Without the need of any will or probate, B succeeds to A's interest and becomes the sole owner of the property. This is the chief advantage of a joint tenancy. It renders probate of an estate unnecessary.

Any number of persons may hold real estate in joint tenancy.

EXAMPLE: X makes a deed to A, B, C, and D, as joint tenants. D dies. A, B, and C now own the land as joint tenants. A dies. B and C own the land as joint tenants. B dies. C is now the sole owner.

§ 279. Creation of joint tenancy. To create a joint tenancy, a deed must state that the grantees are acquiring title as joint tenants. The actual language used varies somewhat from state to state. 156 A.L.R. 566, 569. It is best to use comprehensive language in creating a joint tenancy.

SUGGESTED FORM: To A and B as joint tenants with the right of survivorship, and not as tenants in common nor as tenants by the entirety, nor as community property.

A deed to persons who are husband and wife poses special problems. It may create a tenancy by the entireties. (See § 284.) It may create community property. (*See* Chapter 17.) But if it does neither of these things and is not a joint tenancy deed, the husband and wife are tenants in common.

EXCEPTION: In Wisconsin, a deed to husband and wife creates a joint tenancy unless the deed states otherwise.

A joint tenancy may also be created when the parties have ineffectively attempted to create a tenancy by the entireties. (See § 286.)

Rather frequently today we find a husband and wife helping a newly married son or daughter to procure housing. Often the two couples buy a two-apartment dwelling for their joint occupancy, each couple acquiring a one-half interest in the property. The old couple wants their half interest held in joint tenancy, but does not want the young couple to have any interest in the old couple's half. The young people feel the same about their half. Each couple wants its half to be in joint tenancy, so that when one dies the surviving wife or husband will own the entire half interest, but they want a tenancy in common as between the two half interests.

SUGGESTION: John and Mary Smith, his wife, wish to buy a two-flat with William, their son, and his wife, Helen. Use two separate joint tenancy form deeds, one going to the John Smiths, the other to the William Smiths. Before the land description in each deed, insert: "An undivided one-half interest in." Thus each couple will have its own deed.

EXAMPLE: In the **SUGGESTION** above, if one of the Smiths dies, his or her spouse will own their half interest as surviving joint tenant. The others continue to own their half as joint tenants. The two halves are as separate for this purpose as if they were separate tracts of land.

§ 280. **Abolition of survivorship.** Some states, Alabama, Arizona, Florida, Georgia, Kansas, Kentucky, Maine, North Carolina, Ohio, Oregon, Pennsylvania, South Carolina, Tennessee, Texas, Virginia, Washington, West Virginia, and perhaps others, have laws that purport to abolish the joint tenant's right of survivorship, so that on the death of a joint tenant, his share goes to his heirs or to the persons named in his will, just as if a tenancy in common had been created. However, in these states, if the deed expressly states that the property shall go to the surviving grantee, the right of survivorship is thereby created. *Chandler v. Kountze* (Tex. Civ. App.), 130 S.W.2d 327.

§ 281. **The four unities.** Not every deed that describes the grantees as joint tenants is sufficient to create a joint tenancy. In the creation of a joint tenancy, there must be present the four unities of time, title, interest, and possession. That is, the joint tenants must have one and the same interest, acquired by one and the same deed, commencing at one and the same time; and they must hold by one and the same undivided possession.

EXAMPLE: A owned a tract of land. Thereafter, he married and executed a deed to himself and his wife "as joint tenants." No joint tenancy was created by this deed. A and his wife did not acquire title at the same time or by the same conveyance, since A had owned the land long prior to the making of the deed. The unities of time and title were not present. The deed actually created a tenancy in common. A and his wife should have conveyed title to a third person, and this third person should have thereupon reconveyed the title to A and his wife as joint tenants. *Deslauriers v. Senesac,* 331 Ill. 437, 163 N.E. 327.

Pointless technicalities like these are going out of fashion. Hence in a majority of the states today, Alabama, Arizona, California, Colorado, Illinois, Iowa, Kansas, Kentucky, Maryland, Maine, Massachusetts, Michigan, Missouri, Nebraska, Nevada, New Hampshire, New Jersey, New Mexico, New York, North Dakota, Ohio, Oklahoma, Pennsylvania, Rhode Island, Tennessee, Virginia, Wisconsin, and perhaps others, laws have been passed under which a deed by a landowner to himself and another in joint tenancy creates a good joint tenancy. For reasons relating to community property, dower, and homestead, the landowner's spouse should join in the deed. One often sees a landowner and his wife conveying to themselves as joint tenants, and the whole thing, though odd, is quite legal in most states. 44 A.L.R.2d 605.

When a deed reveals an intention to create a joint tenancy, but fails to for some technical reason, some modern courts tend to show little patience with the old technicalities and give the property to the survivor, even though a true joint tenancy has not been created.

> **EXAMPLE:** A husband who owned some land in his own individual name signed a deed conveying a half interest in this land to his wife, the deed stating that they were to hold the land as joint tenants. Obviously this is no way to create a joint tenancy, for the four unities are lacking. Nevertheless, on the death of the husband the court awarded the entire property to the surviving wife. *Runions v. Runions,* 186 Tenn. 25, 207 S.W.2d 1016, 1 A.L.R.2d 242. There can be a right of survivorship even though the land is not owned in joint tenancy, which is something of a subtle distinction but has the happy result of achieving what the parties wanted.

It is impossible to make a deed to *A* of a one-fourth interest in the land and to *B* of a three-fourths interest to hold as joint tenants. A deed creating joint tenancies must give the joint tenants equal shares as to the property conveyed in joint tenancy. This does not prevent a joint tenant from owning a different and distinct interest in the land.

> **EXAMPLE:** X conveys a half interest to A and a half interest to A and B as joint tenants. This is perfectly valid. *In re Galletto's Estate,* 75 Cal. App.2d 580, 171 P.2d 152.

§ 282. **Severance of joint tenancy.** There is nothing sacred about a joint tenancy. Either joint tenant has the right to break the joint tenancy as he wishes, and certain things will break the joint tenancy and convert it into a tenancy in common even against the wishes of the parties. However, there are other things that do not break the joint tenancy, such as:

1. A will by the deceased joint tenants.

> **EXAMPLE:** A and B own land as joint tenants. A makes a will giving all his property to C. A dies. B takes all the joint tenancy property, and C gets no part of it. A will does not break a joint tenancy. *Eckhardt v. Osborne,* 338 Ill. 611, 170 N.E. 774.

2. A lien created against one of the joint tenants.

> **EXAMPLE:** A and B own land as joint tenants. A judgment lien, internal revenue lien, or other lien is filed against A only. A dies before he has lost his title through enforcement of the lien. B takes the entire title free and clear of the lien. In other words, if A is a joint tenant, a lien against him attaches not to the land *but to A's interest in the land,* which is an interest that will be totally extinguished if A dies

before B does, so long as the parties are joint tenants when A dies. One who has a lien on A's interest ordinarily can have no greater rights than A has, and if A's rights will be extinguished by his death, so will the lien.

3. An easement created by one joint tenant only.

EXAMPLE: A and B own land as joint tenants. A alone signs an easement grant to C, and A dies before B does. B then owns the entire title free and clear of the easement.

4. Dower and curtesy of a spouse of a deceased joint tenant.

EXAMPLE: If A and B, both married men, own land as joint tenants, and A dies first, his wife has no dower in the land because at A's death all his title to the land is extinguished, leaving nothing to which dower can attach. (See §300.)

5. Divorce. State laws differ on this subject. In some states, a divorce does not break a joint tenancy. Where no specific law exists, if H and W own land as joint tenants and are divorced, and if nothing is said in the divorce decree about the property, the joint tenancy is unbroken. Suppose that H thereafter marries another person, X. H dies before W does. W, the former wife of H, takes the entire property, and X takes nothing. H could have prevented this by breaking the joint tenancy by deed. On the other hand, in some states the entry of a divorce decree automatically converts the joint tenancy into a tenancy in common. This is by virtue of special laws.

6. The making of a lease by one of two joint tenants does not sever the joint tenancy. *Tindall v. Yeats*, 392 Ill. 502, 64 N.E.2d 503. *Hammond v. McArthur*, 30 Cal.2d 512, 183 P.2d 1.

7. One joint tenant files a partition suit against the other, but one of them dies before a partition decree is entered. The survivor takes all as surviving joint tenant. 129 A.L.R. 813.

Certain events, however, will break or sever the joint tenancy, thereby converting it into a tenancy in common:

1. A conveyance by a joint tenant destroys the joint tenancy.

EXAMPLE: A conveys to B and C in joint tenancy. C conveys his half of title to D. D thereafter conveys this interest back to C. C dies. His title passes to his heirs, not to B. The conveyance from C to D severed, that is, terminated, the joint tenancy, and the joint tenancy was not revived by the reconveyance. At C's death, B and C were holding title as tenants in common. *Szymczak v. Szymczak*, 306 Ill. 541, 138 N.E. 218. It is not necessary that B be informed of the fact that C is breaking the joint tenancy. *Burke v. Stevens.* 70 Cal. Reptr. 87.

Suppose, however, that *A*, *B*, and *C* own land as joint tenants. *C* conveys his one third to *X*. *A* and *B* continue to hold their two thirds as joint tenants. *Morgan v. Catherwood*, 95 Ind. App. 266, 167 N.E. 619; *Hammond v. McArthur*, 30 Cal.2d 512, 183 P.2d 1. Or suppose that *A*, *B*, and *C* own land in joint tenancy. *A* conveys to *B* by quitclaim deed. *B* and *C* continue to own a two-thirds interest in the land in joint tenancy, and *B* owns a one-third interest as tenant in common. *Shelton v. Vance*, 106 Cal. App.2d 194, 234 P.2d 1012; *Jackson v. O'Connell*, 23 Ill.2d 52, 177 N.E.2d 194. Or suppose that *A*, *B*, and *C* own land in joint tenancy. *C* conveys ½₀th of his interest to *X*. *A* and *B* continue to own their two-thirds in joint tenancy. *C* and *X* are tenants in common. *Giles v. Sheridan*, 137 N.W.2d 828 (Neb. 1968).

2. An involuntary transfer of title will sever a joint tenancy.

> **EXAMPLE:** *A* and *B* hold title as joint tenants. *A* goes into bankruptcy. Under the Bankruptcy Act, title to all of *A*'s property is automatically transferred to his trustee in bankruptcy. This transfer severs the joint tenancy.

> **EXAMPLE:** *A* and *B* hold title as joint tenants. *C* obtains a judgment against *A*, and a sheriff's sale is held to obtain money to pay the judgment. *D* purchases the property at the sheriff's sale and obtains a sheriff's deed. This severs the joint tenancy. *D* and *B* now hold as tenants in common. However, the rendition of a judgment against one joint tenant and the making of a levy on his interest will not sever a joint tenancy. *Van Antwerp v. Horan*, 390 Ill. 449, 61 N.E.2d 358; *Hammond v. McArthur*, 30 Cal.2d 512, 183 P.2d 1. It has even been held that a sheriff's sale under such a judgment does not sever the joint tenancy and that the joint tenancy is not severed until a sheriff's deed issues. If the joint tenant against whom the judgment was rendered dies before the sheriff's deed issues, the other joint tenant takes all the property free and clear of the judgment creditor's rights. *Jackson v. Lacey*, 408 Ill. 530, 97 N.E.2d 839.

3. In title and intermediate states (see § 356), a mortgage executed by one of the joint tenants severs the joint tenancy notwithstanding the fact that the mortgage is subsequently paid and released by the mortgagee. 129 A.L.R. 813.

> **EXAMPLE:** *A* and *B* hold title as joint tenants. *A* executes a mortgage on his half of the title and thereafter pays off the mortgage, which is released. Thereafter, *B* dies. *B*'s half of the title passes to his heirs, not to *A*. *A*'s mortgage severed the joint tenancy.

But a mortgage executed by both joint tenants does not sever the joint tenancy.

> **EXAMPLE:** *A* and *B* hold title as joint tenants. They both join in a mortgage. Thereafter, *A* dies. *B* takes title as the surviving joint tenant.

The cases do not agree as to the effect of a mortgage by one joint tenant in a lien state. *People v. Nogarr*, 164 Cal. App.2d 591, 330 P.2d 858.

4. A contract by one joint tenant to sell or convey his interest in the land to a third person will operate as a severance of the joint tenancy. *Naiburg v. Hendriksen*, 370 Ill. 502, 19 N.E.2d 348.

5. One joint tenant files a partition suit against the other and a partition decree is entered. The joint tenancy is now severed. *Schuck v. Schuck*, 413 Ill. 390, 108 N.E.2d 905; *Hammond v. McArthur*, 30 Cal.2d 512, 183 P.2d 1.

6. A husband and wife own land in joint tenancy. One files a divorce suit against the other. A divorce decree is entered. It orders the land sold and the proceeds of sale divided between them. The joint tenancy is now severed. *Beade v. Ratner*, 187 Kan. 741, 359 P.2d 877. Indeed, if a husband and wife own land in joint tenancy and they enter into a separation agreement providing that the land will be sold when the divorce decree is entered and the proceeds of sale divided between them, this agreement will sever the joint tenancy. *Carson v. Ellis*, 186 Kan. 112, 348 P.2d 807.

§ 283. **Disadvantages of a joint tenancy.**   Rather frequently when title is held in joint tenancy by a husband and wife and one of them dies, the survivor, impressed with the simplicity of transfer of ownership on the death of a joint tenant, ponders the advisability of creating a new joint tenancy in which the surviving spouse will be joint tenant with one of the spouse's children. This has certain disadvantages. Once such a deed is made it cannot be unmade without the consent of both parties. Suppose that the surviving spouse and the child named as joint tenant quarrel, which is not uncommon. Indeed, the mere fact that the parties share ownership of the real estate seems to trigger quarrels. The child may file a partition suit and put the property up for sale. Thus the surviving spouse may find himself or herself without a place to live. Perhaps judgments may be rendered against the child, and creditors will force the property to a sale. Many lawyers counsel the surviving joint tenant to avoid setting up a joint tenancy such as this. Where a will is made, it can always be changed. It gives no one any right in the property until the landowner dies. Perhaps this may strike a cynical note, but the fact remains that when there is a will rather than a deed, there is much less likelihood of family quarrels.

§ 284. **Tenancy by the entireties—in general.**   In Arkansas, Delaware, District of Columbia, Florida, Indiana, Kentucky, Maryland, Massachusetts, Michigan, Mississippi, Missouri, New Jersey, New York, North Carolina, Oklahoma, Oregon, Pennsylvania, Rhode Island, Tennessee, Utah, Vermont, Virginia, and Wyoming, a form of joint tenancy, known as tenancy by the entireties, exists. This is a tenancy that exists only where the co-owners are husband and wife. Unlike a joint tenancy, no words are necessary to create such a tenancy.

EXAMPLE: In a tenancy by the entireties state, X makes a deed to H and W, husband and wife. Nothing is said as to the character of their co-ownership. They are tenants by the entireties.

EXCEPTION: In Kansas, Kentucky, Massachusetts, Mississippi, Montana, Oklahoma, Rhode Island, Utah, and Virginia, laws have been passed stating that the deed must expressly show an intention to create a tenancy by the entireties. *52 Mich. L. Rev. 804.*

Tenancy by the entireties is a form of joint tenancy. It resembles joint tenancy in that upon the death of either husband or wife the survivor automatically acquires title to the share of the deceased spouse. Like a joint tenancy, also, it is necessary for the creation of a tenancy by the entireties that the husband and wife acquire title by the same deed or will.

EXAMPLE: X, a landowner, conveys a one-half interest in the land to A and later, by another deed, conveys the remaining one-half interest to B, who is A's wife. The husband and wife hold title as tenants in common and not as tenants by the entireties.

Tenancy by the entireties differs from joint tenancy in that neither spouse has the power to defeat or sever the tenancy by any deed or mortgage to a stranger made without the signature of the other spouse. *Hoffman v. Newell,* 249 Ky. 270, 60 S.W.2d 607.

EXAMPLE: A deed is made to a husband and wife, nothing being said as to the character of their tenancy. Thereafter, the husband makes a deed that purports to convey his interest in the land to X. The wife does not join in this deed. Thereafter, the husband dies. The wife now has full title to all the land. X has nothing.

However, a deed by both husband and wife will, of course, give the grantee good title.

In community property states, tenancy by the entireties is not recognized.

§ 285. **Creation of tenancy by the entireties.** In the states where tenancies by the entireties are recognized, there is much difference of opinion as to the legal effect of a deed to a husband and wife that describes the grantees as joint tenants. In some states, Indiana, Maryland, New Jersey, New York, and Wyoming, for example, such a deed creates a joint tenancy rather than a tenancy by the entireties. *Witzel v. Witzel* (Wyo.), 386 P.2d 103. But in most of the states that recognize tenancies by the entireties, such deeds are held to create a tenancy by the entireties. *Hoag v. Hoag*, 213 Mass. 50, 99 N.E. 521; 161 A.L.R. 470. The deed should always state that the grantees are joint tenants *and not tenants in common or by the entireties*. In this way, litigation can be avoided.

However, when a deed to a husband and wife describes them as tenants in common, such a deed is almost universally regarded as creating a good tenancy in common rather than a tenancy by the entireties.

For the creation of a tenancy by the entireties it is necessary that the grantees be husband and wife. If they are not husband and wife, even express language in the deed declaring an intention to create a tenancy by the entireties will not create such a tenancy.

§ 286. **Defective tenancy by entireties as creating a joint tenancy.** Tenancy by the entireties exists only as between husband and wife. A deed to parties who are not husband and wife creates some other kind of tenancy even though a tenancy by the entireties is specified.

EXAMPLE: A deed to A and B, who claimed to be, but were not, husband and wife, recited that it was made to them as tenants by the entireties and not as tenants in common. Since this revealed a general intention to create survivorship rights, but could not create a tenancy by the entireties, the parties not being husband and wife, the court held that a joint tenancy was created. *Morris v. McCarty*, 158 Mass. 11, 32 N.E. 938; *Coleman v. Jackson*, 286 F.2d 98; 52 Mich. L. Rev. 970; 6 Rutgers L. Rev. 550.

In New Hampshire and Wisconsin, which do not recognize tenancy by the entireties, a deed to husband and wife *as tenants by the entireties* creates a joint tenancy. *In re Ray's Will*, 188 Wis. 180, 205 N.W. 917; 1 A.L.R.2d 247. And a deed to two sisters *as tenants by the entireties* has been held to create a joint tenancy. *In re Richardson's Estate*, 229 Wis. 426, 282 N.W. 585.

When the deed describes the grantees as husband and wife even though both parties know that they are not lawfully married, and no specific mention is made of tenancy by the entireties, the grantees are tenants in common. *Pierce v. Hall*, 223 Ore. 563, 355 P.2d 259.

§ 287. **Tenancy by the entireties—deeds between spouses.** Suppose a husband or wife owns land in his or her own name or they own land as tenants in common. They wish to put the land in their names as tenants by the entireties. The traditional way of accomplishing this is to have the husband and wife join in a deed to a dummy, or nominee, and such nominee then deeds the land back to the husband and wife as tenants by the entireties. Just as in the case of joint tenancies, the old rule is: in order to have a good tenancy by the entireties, the husband and wife must acquire title by the same deed, and the dummy conveyance satisfies this requirement.

Just as in the case of joint tenancies, recent laws and court decisions allow a husband or wife to create a tenancy by the entireties without deeding out to a dummy. In these states, among which are Arkansas, Florida, Massachusetts, Missouri, New Jersey, New York, Oklahoma, Oregon, Pennsylvania, Rhode Island, Tennessee, and Utah, if the husband owns land and wishes to create a tenancy by the entireties with his wife, he makes out a deed running to himself and his wife "as tenants by the entireties, and not as joint tenants or as tenants in common." 25 *Temple L.Q.* 43; 44 A.L.R.2d 598. For reasons relating to dower and homestead, the wife should join in this deed as co-grantor.

However, in a number of other states, including Oregon, it has been held that it is still necessary, if a good tenancy by the entireties is to be created, that the husband landowner and his wife join in a deed to a third person, who thereupon conveys to the husband and wife. This practice should be followed unless it is clear that your state has abolished the need for a third party conveyance.

When land is held in tenancy by the entireties, a deed by the husband to the wife gives her good title even though she does not join in the deed to herself. The same is true of a deed by the wife to the husband. 8 A.L.R.2d 634.

§ 288. **Tenancy by the entireties—deeds, mortgages, leases, rents, and brokers' listings.**   As a rule, a deed or mortgage of property owned in tenancy by the entireties must be signed by both husband and wife.

In most states, when a tenancy by the entirety exists, a deed to a stranger signed by the husband or wife alone is void. 25 *Temple L.Q.* 46. In a few states, the deed is given some effect, but the effect varies from state to state. It may grant a share of the rents or may be operative if the grantor survives the other spouse. In any event, *in all states the deed becomes void if the spouse who did not join in the deed survives the spouse who conveyed.*

In a few states, Massachusetts, Michigan, and North Carolina, a tenancy by the entireties gives the husband the exclusive right during his lifetime to the possession and all rents of the property. Therefore he can make a valid lease of the property without his wife's signature. *In re Perry's Estate,* 256 N.C. 65, 123 S.E.2d 99; 52 *Mich. L. Rev.* 781. But on the husband's death, the lease comes to an end if the wife survives. Hence both parties should sign any lease. In the other tenancy by the entirety states, husband and wife have equal rights to rents and possession, and any lease must be signed by both. 25 *Temple L.Q.* 46; 141 A.L.R. 202.

If the husband alone lists property with a real estate broker for sale, he will be liable for a commission if the broker finds a buyer. It is no defense that the wife failed to sign. *Taub v. Shampanier,* 95 N.J.L. 349. 112 Atl. 322.

§ 289.   **Tenancy by the entireties—creditor's rights.**   In most tenancy by the entireties states, a judgment creditor of either husband or wife alone can acquire no rights by a sheriff's sale of the land. Since neither husband nor wife alone can make a voluntary sale of his or her interest in the land, an involuntary or forced sale of the interest of either husband or wife alone cannot be valid. 75 A.L.R.2d 1175. In a few states, Arkansas, New Jersey, New York, and Oregon, for example, a husband's interest can be sold by the sheriff under a judgment against the husband alone, but the sheriff's deed will automatically become void if the wife survives the husband. The wife then remains the sole owner, free of the judgment. 25 *Temple L.Q.* 39; 75 A.L.R.2d 1183.

Of course if the judgment is against both husband and wife, the land may be sold by the sheriff, provided it is not their homestead.

As above stated, in nearly all the tenancy by entirety states, the rents of the land belong to the husband and wife jointly. Therefore a creditor of either the husband or wife alone cannot reach the rents, income, or crops of the land.

EXCEPTIONS: In Arkansas, New Jersey, New York, and Oregon, creditors of either the husband or wife are allowed to reach the debtor's share of the rents, income, or crops of the land. 52 *Mich. L. Rev.* 795. In Massachusetts and North Carolina, creditors of the husband, but not those of the wife, may reach all the income of the land held in tenancy by the entireties while the tenancy continues. 25 *Temple L.Q.* 39.

§ 290.   **Tenancy by the entireties—divorce.**   A divorce converts a tenancy by the entireties into a tenancy in common.

§ 291.   **Joint tenancies and tenancies by the entireties—murder.** When one joint tenant or tenant by the entireties murders his co-tenant and later is convicted of such murder in a court trial, one of three results is possible.

1. The murderer will, despite his crime, take the entire property by virtue of his right of survivorship. This is a bad rule that is certainly doomed to disappear in time, but meanwhile it is still followed in some states. *In re Foster's Estate,* 182 Kan. 315, 320 P.2d 855.
2. The murderer, because of his crime, loses all his interest in the property, and the heirs of the murdered co-owner take the entire property, which rule is followed in Minnesota and Wisconsin. *Vesey v. Vesey,* 237 Minn. 295, 54 N.W.2d 385; *In re King's Estate,* 261 Wis. 266, 52 N.W.2d 885.
3. The murder is regarded, in legal effect, as converting the tenancy into a tenancy in common, so that the murderer retains his half interest, and the heirs of the murdered co-tenant take the other half. This rule is followed in most states. *Abbey v. Lord,* 168 Cal. App.2d 666, 336 P.2d 226; *Bradley v. Fox,* 7 Ill.2d 106, 129 N.E.2d 699; 5 *De Paul L. Rev.* 316.

Of course if in the murder trial the killer is acquitted, on the ground of self-defense, for example, the killing is not murder but justifiable homicide, and the survivor will take the entire property even though he caused the death of his co-tenant.

§ 292. **Joint tenancies and tenancies by the entireties—contracts of sale.** A contract to sell property owned in tenancy by the entireties obviously should be signed by both husband and wife. If it is not, the buyer will be unable to obtain specific performance, though the seller who signed might be liable for damages.

In tenancy by the entireties states, when a landowner signs a contract to sell his land to a husband and wife, the buyers hold the contract interest as tenants by the entireties, so that if either dies before the deal is closed, the seller's deed should be made to the survivor. *Comfort v. Robinson,* 155 Mich. 143, 118 N.W. 943.

If the state does not recognize tenancy by the entireties or community property, a contract to sell land to *H* and *W*, who are husband and wife, creates a tenancy in common in the contract interest. If *H* dies, his contract interest passes to his heirs or devisees, and the seller must not make the deed to *W* alone. Obviously when an installment contract is involved, it may take years to pay up, and the death of one of the buyers is a distinct possibility.

SUGGESTED FORM: To avoid the endless complications of tenancy in common or necessity of probate, suggest to the buyers that they agree to buy the land "as joint tenants with the right of survivorship, and not as tenants in common nor by the entireties nor as community property."

Of course if land is owned in joint tenancy, all owners must join as sellers in any contract to sell the land.

Where a husband and wife enter into an installment contract to sell their land, and one of them dies before the purchase price is fully paid, questions arise as to who gets the balance of the purchase price, the surviving spouse or the estate of the decedent. Where the sellers held the land in joint tenancy or tenancy by the entireties some courts hold that the right to the money goes to the survivor just as though there were a joint tenancy in the contract price. *Watson v. Watson,* 5 Ill.2d 526, 126 N.E.2d 220 (1955); *Hewitt v. Biege,* 183 Kan. 352, 329 P.2d 872 (1958); *DeYoung v. Mesler,* 373 Mich. 499, 130 N.W.2d 38, 41 (1964). *In re Maguire's Estate,* 296 N.Y.S. 528.

EXAMPLE: H and W, joint tenants, enter into a contract to sell their land to X. After a few payments are made on the contract, H dies leaving a will giving all his property to children by a former marriage. W will get the entire remainder of the purchase price.

Some states hold, however, that where joint tenants sell land the contract price is held in tenancy in common. *Register of Wills v. Madine,* 242 Md. 437, 219 A.2d 245 (1966). In Arizona the court held that although the sellers were joint tenants the sale price became community property. *Smith v. Tang,* 100 Ariz. 196, 412 P.2d 697 (1966).

SUGGESTION: Let the contract read that the price is payable to the sellers *as joint tenants with the right of survivorship and not as tenants in common nor as tenants by the entireties nor as community property.*

Of course once the money has been paid by the buyer to the sellers, the cash money, even if held intact by the sellers in a joint safety deposit box, is owned by them in tenancy in common. *Ill. Public Aid Commission v. Stille,* 14 Ill.2d 344, 153 N.E.2d 59.

Suppose that the sellers are tenants by the entireties. They give a deed to the buyer and take back a purchase money mortgage. Some states hold that the mortgage is owned as tenants by the entireties. *Ciconte v. Barba,* 19 Del. Ch. 6, 161 Atl. 925. Others hold that the mortgage is owned in tenancy in common. *Webb v. Woodcock,* 134 Ore. 319, 290 Pac. 751; 64 A.L.R.2d 8. The same problem arises in joint tenancies. Obviously the note and mortgage should specifically provide as in the last suggestion given above.

In community property states, these problems are settled by different rules altogether. (*See* Chapter 17.)

§ 293. **Joint tenancy and tenancy by the entireties—inheritance and estate tax.** The automatic transfer of title to a surviving joint tenant or tenant by the entireties when his co-owner dies is subject to state inheritance tax and federal estate tax if the deceased owner's estate is in excess of the exemptions allowed by law. It follows that the lien of such tax attaches to the land of the survivor.

§ 294. **Tenancy in common—in general.** Co-owners who are not joint tenants, tenants by the entireties, or owners of community property are tenants in common. Their shares need not be equal. For example, one co-owner may have an undivided one-tenth interest and the other the remaining undivided nine-tenths interest. They need not have acquired their titles at the same time or by the same instrument.

Tenancies in common often occur when title is acquired by descent or will.

EXAMPLE: *X* dies without a will, leaving his children, *A, B,* and *C,* as his only heirs. The children own *X*'s real estate as tenants in common.

EXAMPLE: *X* dies leaving a will, by which he gives his land to his children, *A* and *B,* in equal shares. They own the land as tenants in common.

Tenants in common are entitled to share the possession and rents of the property according to their shares in the property. Except for their sharing of possession and rents, however, the situation is almost as if each tenant in common owned a separate piece of real estate. Each tenant in common may convey or mortgage his share, and the share of each tenant in common is subject to the lien of judgments against him.

§ 295. **Partition.** If tenants in common, or joint tenants, for that matter, wish to terminate their joint possession of the land, any of the co-tenants may file a suit to partition the real estate. The court will appoint commissioners to divide the land into separate tracts according to the shares of the co-tenants, so that each will become the sole owner of the tract set aside for him. If the land cannot be divided in this manner, the court will order the land sold and will divide the proceeds of the sale among the co-tenants according to their respective interest.

EXAMPLE: A dies owning a tract of land improved with a single family dwelling and leaving no widow and no will, but leaving as his heirs a son, B, and two grandchildren, C and D, who are children of a deceased son, E. B owns one half of the title, and C and D own one fourth each. B files a partition suit against C and D. The courts finds, as it obviously must, that the land cannot be divided among the three tenants in common. It orders the land sold at public auction, whereupon the same is sold to F, the highest bidder, for $6000. B receives $3000 from the proceeds of the sale, and C and D each receive $1500.

Partition can, of course, be accomplished by the voluntary action of all co-owners without the necessity of court proceedings. Frequently this action is impossible, since many co-ownerships involve minor heirs, who cannot participate in voluntary partition.

As a rule, community property and land held in tenancy by the entireties are not subject to partition during the continuance of the marriage. *Stanley v. Mueller*, 220 Ore. 194, 350 P.2d 880; *Lawrence v. Lawrence* (N.J.), 190 A.2d 206.

§ 296. **Rights and obligations of co-owners.** Co-owners must, as a rule, contribute ratably toward payment of taxes, special assessments, mortgages, and repairs of the property. If one co-owner, through refusal of the other co-owners to contribute, is compelled to pay more than his share of the necessary expenses, he thereby acquires a lien analogous to a mortgage lien on the shares of the other co-owners, and he may foreclose such lien if they persist in their refusal to contribute. *Calcagni v. Cirino*, 65 R.I. 408, 14 A.2d 803. But one co-owner cannot purchase the property at a mortgage foreclosure sale or tax sale of the land and thus acquire a title that would enable him to oust the other co-owners. The title thus acquired is acquired for the benefit of all co-owners if they seasonably contribute their respective proportions of the expense incurred by the tenant who purchased the outstanding title.

If one of the co-owners is in exclusive possession of the premises, he alone must bear the burden of taxes, repairs, and mortgage interest payments. *Clute v. Clute*, 197 N.Y. 439, 90 N.E. 988.

If one co-owner collects all the rents but does not himself occupy the land, he must account to the other co-owners for their share of the rents. *Thompson v. Flynn*, 102 Mont. 446, 58 P.2d 769. A few states have laws making a co-owner liable to the other co-owners for rent where he alone occupies the land, collecting no rent therefrom. *Hazard v. Albro*, 17 R.I. 181, 20 Atl. 834. But in many states, a co-owner who personally occupies the premises and does not rent them out is not liable to the other co-owners for the rental value of the premises unless he has agreed to pay them rent or has forcibly kept them out of possession. *Burk v. Burk*, 247 Ala. 91, 22 So.2d 609.

Obviously a mortgage signed by only one of the co-owners does not bind the others. It creates a lien only on the interest of the one who signs. *Rostan v. Huggins*, 216 N.C. 386, 5 S.E.2d 162. Likewise, a judgment, federal lien, or other lien against one of the co-owners creates no lien on the shares of the others.

Chapter 17

DOWER, CURTESY, COMMUNITY PROPERTY, AND HOMESTEAD

§ 297. **Dower—in general.** Dower is the interest in the real estate of the husband which in many states the law gives to his widow to provide her with a means of support after her husband's death. It is a life estate in one third of the lands that the husband owned during the continuance of the marriage relation. The requirements for dower are: (1) a valid marriage, (2) that the husband own the land during the continuance of the marriage relation, and (3) that the husband die prior to the death of the wife.

The right of dower originated in early times when a man's wealth consisted largely of real estate. Nowadays it is necessary for the widow's protection to give her rights in her husband's stocks, bonds, and other personal property as well, and many states have passed laws giving the widow a portion of the personal property left by her husband.

The widow's dower rights are seldom the same in any two states.

Some form of dower exists in the following states: Alabama, Alaska, Arkansas, Delaware, District of Columbia, Florida, Georgia, Hawaii, Illinois, Kansas, Kentucky, Maryland, Massachusetts, Michigan, Montana, New Hampshire, New Jersey, North Carolina, Ohio, Oregon, Rhode Island, South Carolina, Tennessee, Vermont, Virginia, West Virginia, and Wisconsin.

§ 298. **Inchoate and consummate dower.** During her husband's lifetime, the wife's rights consist merely of the possibility that she may become entitled to her dower. Until his death, the wife's dower is said to be *inchoate*. It is not such an interest that the wife can convey to a stranger, nor can it be sold at a forced sale to pay the wife's debts. It can be released to a purchaser by joining in her husband's deed. Should she predecease her husband, even this incipient right is automatically extinguished. Thus if her husband has previously conveyed his land without obtaining her signature on the deed, the grantee's title thereupon becomes perfect. It is as though her dower had never existed.

On the husband's death, her dower becomes *consummate*. It has ripened into something that she is certain to enjoy.

§ 299. **Assignment of dower.** On the husband's death, one third of the land that the husband owned during the marriage and in which the wife did not release her dower (which includes the land owned by him at the time of his death and also the land that he conveyed during the marriage without obtaining her signature) is set apart for the widow, usually by court order. This is called *assignment of dower*. In this third, the widow has an ordinary life estate. She may occupy the land herself or rent it to a tenant. On her death, all her rights therein are terminated.

If the land cannot be divided, the widow may be given one third of the rents for her lifetime as her dower. Or, in many states, the land will be sold and a portion of the proceeds allotted to her.

In any case, if the husband is indebted at the time of his death, the widow's dower rights are superior to any claims of his creditors in and to the land. This is one of the important characteristics of dower.

§ 300. **Joint tenancy and dower.** Although a widow has dower in lands owned by her husband in tenancy in common with others, there is no dower in a joint tenancy.

EXAMPLE: Two men, A and B, hold title in joint tenancy. A is married to C, and B is married to D. A conveys to X. A's wife, C, does not join in the deed. Ordinarily when a wife does not join in her husband's deed, her dower remains outstanding, but here no dower remains outstanding in C because A held title as a joint tenant. However, B and X now hold title as tenants in common, and their wives have dower in the real estate. *Johnston v. Muntz*, 364 Ill. 482, 4 N.E.2d 826.

EXAMPLE: H and W, husband and wife, own land in joint tenancy. H conveys his half interest to X. X takes this interest free of any dower rights of W, because when H signed the deed, he was a joint tenant and there is no dower in a joint tenancy. *Laterza v. Murray*, 2 Ill.2d 219, 117 N.E.2d 779. However, H now has dower in W's half interest.

§ 301. **Mortgages and other liens.** When a wife fails to join with her husband in the execution of a mortgage on the husband's land, any title acquired through foreclosure of such mortgage will be subject to the wife's dower in states where dower is recognized. *Thomas v.*

Thomas, 245 Ala. 607, 18 S.2d 544. The same result follows in states that have substituted some ownership share for dower but require the wife to join in any deed in order to release her ownership share. And the same result follows in many states where the husband has curtesy, dower, or an ownership share in the wife's real estate and fails to join in her mortgage. Obviously where land is owned by either husband or wife, it will usually be necessary for the spouse to join in any mortgage on the land.

Dower is subject to any liens or encumbrances to which the land was subject at the time of the marriage or at the time the husband acquired title.

EXAMPLE: A buys a tract of land on which there is a mortgage. On foreclosure of this mortgage, the dower of A's wife will be extinguished.

EXAMPLE: A places a mortgage on his land and thereafter marries B. B's rights again are subject to those of the mortgagee, and foreclosure will extinguish her rights.

EXAMPLE: X obtains a judgment against A, a landowner. Thereafter, A marries. His wife's dower is subject to the lien of X's judgment. But if a judgment is rendered against a married man, as a rule any sheriff's sale under such a judgment will be subject to the wife's dower. *Seibert v. Todd*, 31 S.C. 206, 98 S.E. 822.

§ 302. **Leaseholds.** The leasehold interest of a tenant under his lease is personal property, and since dower is a right that attaches to real estate only, a tenant's wife has no dower in the leasehold. Ordinarily a tenant may assign his leasehold without the wife's signature when no homestead rights are involved.

In Ohio, a wife has dower in a perpetual leasehold.

§ 303. **Contract for sale of land.** If I sign a contract for the sale of my land, but my wife does not join, she cannot be compelled to give a deed to the buyer. If she does not join in a deed to the buyer, her dower remains outstanding. Obviously any prudent buyer will insist that the wife sign. Dower acquired by a landowner's spouse after he has signed a contract of sale, however, does not affect the rights of the contract purchaser.

EXAMPLE: A, a bachelor, signs a contract to sell land to B. Thereafter, A marries W. When the last of the purchase price is paid, W refuses to sign the deed to B. Nevertheless, A's deed to B gives B good title to the land, free of the wife's dower. Her dower was subject to the contract. *Newberry Co. v. Shannon*, 268 Mass. 116, 167 N.E. 292; 63 A.L.R. 136.

§ 304. **Release of dower.** The widow is entitled to have dower assigned out of any land conveyed, mortgaged, or leased by her husband during the marriage without her signature. Hence it is important that the landowner's wife release her dower by joining with him in any deed, mortgage, or lease of his land.

Even if a grantor or mortgagor describes himself in the deed or mortgage as a bachelor or widower, and the grantee or mortgagee honestly believes that the grantor's marital status is as he describes it to be, the wife, should the grantor or mortgagor actually have one, is entitled to dower in the land if she survives the grantor or mortgagor. However, in a number of states, Georgia, Tennessee, and Vermont, for example, the widow's dower is limited to the land owned by the husband *at the time of his death,* so that any deed made by him in his lifetime defeats her dower even though she did not sign the deed. And in some states, Michigan, Montana, Oregon, and Wisconsin, for example, a woman who is residing outside of the state at the time her husband makes a deed to land within the state has no right of dower even though she does not sign the deed.

§ 305. **Dower—election.**   Many states where dower exists give the widow, at her husband's death, a right to elect between her dower or some ownership (fee simple) share of the land.

§ 306. **Dower—fee title given in lieu of dower.**   In a number of states, a widow is given a share in fee simple of her deceased husband's land in lieu of dower. Instead of acquiring merely a life estate, she may become the owner of one third, or some other fraction, outright of her husband's land on his death. Remember that dower is only a life estate. (See § 61.)

In some of these states, Colorado, Connecticut, Mississippi, New York, North Dakota, Oklahoma, South Dakota, Vermont, and Wyoming, for example, the widow's share is limited to land that the husband *owned at his death,* which means that the widow has no claim whatever upon land conveyed by the husband in his lifetime without her signature.

In other states that give the widow an ownership share in lieu of dower, the widow is entitled to her ownership share in any land conveyed by the husband in his lifetime without her signature. These states include Florida, Indiana, Iowa, Kansas, Maine, Minnesota, Nebraska, Pennsylvania, and Utah. Obviously in these states, the wife's signature is necessary on any deed, mortgage, or contract of sale given by the husband. Kansas, Nebraska, and Utah belong in this group but dispense with the wife's signature on a deed if she is a nonresident.

§ 307. **Curtesy.**   In some states—Alabama, Delaware, Hawaii, Massachusetts, New Hampshire, New Jersey, Rhode Island, Tennessee, Vermont, and Virginia—a widower has a life estate, known as curtesy, in the lands owned by his wife during their marriage. It is somewhat analogous to the widow's dower, but there are these points of difference:

1. A child must be born to the couple for this interest in land to arise. This requirement has been abolished in Alabama, Arkansas, Delaware, New Jersey, Oregon, Virginia, and perhaps other states.
2. The widower's curtesy, according to the old English law, was a life estate in *all* the land owned by the wife during the marriage, as contrasted with the one third allowed the widow as her dower. In most of the curtesy states, however, the husband's share has been reduced by modern laws to some fraction, such as one third.

In a number of states—Arkansas, Illinois, Kansas, Kentucky, Maryland, Ohio, and Pennsylvania—the husband is given dower instead of curtesy.

Whenever a husband has dower or curtesy, obviously he should join in the wife's deed, mortgage, or contract of sale of her property. However, in Arkansas, District of Columbia, Hawaii, Tennessee, and perhaps other states, a deed given by the wife conveying her own land bars the husband's curtesy even if he does not join in the deed.

In a number of states, a surviving husband is given a share in fee simple of the wife's lands in lieu of curtesy. In some of these states, Colorado, Connecticut, Georgia, Michigan, Mississippi, Montana, North Dakota, Oklahoma, South Carolina, South Dakota, Utah, Vermont, Wisconsin, and Wyoming, for example, the widower's share is limited to the land that the wife owned at her death. He has no claim whatever upon land conveyed by her in her lifetime without his signature.

In other states that give the widower an ownership share in lieu of curtesy, the widower is entitled to his ownership share in any land conveyed by the wife in her lifetime without his signature. These states include Florida, Iowa, Kansas, Maine, Minnesota, Nebraska, and Pennsylvania.

Many states that give a widower curtesy or dower allow him, at the wife's death, to choose an ownership share instead.

§ 308. **Divorce.**   Divorce terminates dower, curtesy, and their statutory substitutes. In Illinois, Massachusetts, Oregon, Rhode Island, and West Virginia, a divorce bars only the dower or curtesy of the spouse for whose fault the divorce was obtained.

§ 309. **Community property—in general.**   The community property system is of Spanish origin and obtains in states that were subject to Spanish influence, namely, Arizona, California, Idaho, Louisiana, Nevada, New Mexico, Texas, and Washington. The law of these states recognizes two kinds of property that may belong to the spouses in case of marriage—the *separate property* and the *community property*. The separate property of either husband or wife is what he or she owned at the time of marriage and what he or she acquired during marriage by inheritance, will, or gift. The separate property of each spouse is wholly free from all interest or claim on the part of the other and is entirely under the management and control, whether by deed, mortgage, will, or otherwise, of the spouse to whom it belongs. All other property is community property.

§ 310. **Theory of community property.** It is the theory in these states that the husband and wife should share equally property acquired by their joint efforts during marriage. Thus the husband is as much entitled to share equally in acquisitions by the wife through her industry as she is entitled to share equally in acquisitions by the husband, and each spouse owns one half of all that is earned or gained, even though one earned or gained more than the other or actually earned or gained nothing.

§ 311. **Property acquired during the marriage.** As a general rule, all property owned by either husband or wife before marriage and all property acquired by either spouse during the marriage by *gift*, by *will*, or *inheritance* is separate property.

Property *purchased* with separate funds is the separate property of the purchaser, whereas property purchased with community funds is community property.

Property acquired by *purchase* during the marriage is ordinarily presumed to vest in the husband and wife as community property, regardless of whether the deed is made to the husband, wife, or both. Under the community property system, the ownership of property does not depend upon the question of who happens to be named as grantee in the deed.

In California and New Mexico, it is provided that real estate conveyed to a married woman in her own separate name is presumed to be her separate property. So far as the husband and wife are concerned, this presumption can be destroyed by proof that the property was purchased with community funds and that the placing of title in the wife's name was not made with the intention of making a gift to her. Such property is community property. But the presumption that the property is the separate property of the wife and can be sold or mortgaged without the husband's signature is conclusive in favor of purchasers and mortgagees dealing with the wife in good faith and for a valuable consideration. *Fulkerson v. Stiles*, 156 Cal. 703, 105 Pac. 966.

Except possibly in Louisiana and Texas, a husband and wife may by agreement change the status of property from separate to community property or from community to separate property. Income tax returns are often received as evidence of such agreements.

A deed by the husband to the wife raises a presumption that this was intended to convert the land into her separate property. But this presumption can be rebutted. 41 C.J.S. 1047.

In Arizona, California, and Nevada, a deed to husband and wife as joint tenants makes the property the separate property of each, which property they hold in ordinary joint tenancy. *Russo v. Russo*, 73 Ariz. 405, 242 P.2d 537; *Siberell v. Siberell*, 214 Cal. 767, 7 P.2d 1003. However, oral evidence can be admitted in court to show that the husband and wife really intended this to be community property, and such intention will prevail. *Gudely v. Gudely*, 41 Cal.2d 202, 259 P.2d 656. In New Mexico, the opposite is true. A deed to a husband and wife in joint tenancy gives them the land as community property, unless evidence can be found that the parties did not intend the land to become community property. *In re Trimble's Estate*, 57 N.M. 51, 253 P.2d 805.

In Idaho, Louisiana, and Texas, the rents of separate property are community property. In other states, rents of separate property are separate property.

A gift made to both spouses is community property.

§ 312. **Deeds and mortgages of community property.**   In Nevada and Texas, the husband may convey community property without the wife's signature, except that both must sign if the property constitutes their home. In other states, the wife must join in the deed.

Either spouse may convey or mortgage his or her separate property without the consent of the other, except in Texas, which requires the wife to obtain her husband's signature on deeds or mortgages of her separate property.

In any event, it is desirable and customary in most states for the husband and wife to join in any deed of land. And in most states, their joining is legally necessary where the land conveyed is occupied by the parties as their home.

In most community property states that require the wife's consent to a deed of community property, the wife's signature is also needed for a valid contract to convey community property. *Rundle v. Winters*, 38 Ariz. 239, 298 Pac. 929; *Chapman v. Will*, 77 Wash. 475, 137 Pac. 1041; *Elliott v. Craig*, 45 Ida. 15, 260 Pac. 443; *Adams v. Blumenshine*, 27 N.M. 643, 204 P.2d 66. The wife should also join in leases of community property, except short-term leases. *Bouman v. Hardgrove*, 200 Wash. 78, 93 P.2d 303.

§ 313. **Wills and descent of community property.**   The descent of community property when there is no will varies from state to state. It must be remembered in this connection that, regardless of the legal title, each spouse owns one half of the community property.

In California, Idaho, New Mexico, Washington, and Nevada the surviving spouse succeeds to the decedent's share of community property in the absence of a will. In Arizona, Louisiana, and Texas the decedent's share goes in whole or in part to his or her descendants. All community property states recognize the right to make a will by the first spouse to die except New Mexico where only the husband is given that right.

§ 314. **Dower and curtesy.**   Neither dower nor curtesy exists in community property states.

§ 315. **Divorce and separation.**   On entry of a divorce decree, the court usually divides up the community property between the spouses. And even without a divorce, the spouses may in most states enter into an agreement dissolving the community and dividing their property.

§ 316. **Homestead.**   When a family owns and occupies a tract of land as its home, that portion of the tract which does not exceed in area or value the limit fixed by law for homesteads is the family homestead, and certain rights, called homestead rights, are created therein. These homestead rights may, of course, extend to the entire tract if it is within the area and value limits fixed by law.

There are three principal motives behind the various state homestead laws. One is the protection of the family against being evicted from their home by enforcement of the claims of creditors. The homestead portion of the tract of land is protected against sheriff's sales on a judgment against the landowner.

The second object of the homestead laws is to protect the wife against the husband. The lawmakers thought it would be a good idea if the husband were not allowed to sell his own home if the wife was opposed to the idea. Evidently the theory was that the old home should not be disposed of until a new home suitable for the family had been provided. To accomplish this result, the lawmakers provided that the husband could not convey good title to his own home unless his wife signed the deed. It is therefore necessary that both husband and wife join in any deed or mortgage of homestead property, except, of course, a purchase money mortgage.

As a final protection of the wife against the husband and his creditors, the homestead laws provided some protection for the widow after the death of her husband. This was necessary because dower did not afford the widow adequate protection. Dower does not give the widow any right to the occupation of any real estate until a particular tract of land has been set apart or assigned to her as dower. (*See* Chapter 17.) Immediately upon the husband's death, the widow might be subject to eviction from the home. Protection was afforded by the laws providing for the widow's homestead. Even a husband who has quarreled bitterly with his wife cannot legally deprive her of this protection. A final development in this direction was the *probate homestead*, which created a home for the widow in land that the husband had never occupied as his home. In this regard, the widow's rights are superior to the rights of any creditor of the deceased husband. Land so occupied by the widow cannot be sold to pay the deceased husband's debts.

The homestead here discussed exists only under state laws and has nothing to do with the Federal Homestead Law.

For a valid deed or mortgage of the homestead, it is necessary that both husband and wife join in the same deed or mortgage. The wife is thus protected against the improvidence of the husband. In some states, it is necessary that the deed or mortgage of the homestead contain a clause expressly releasing or waiving all homestead rights, and in many states a deed or mortgage of the homestead land must be acknowledged in order to be valid.

Chapter 18

WILLS AND DESCENT

§ 317. In general. When a person dies without leaving a will, it is said that he dies *intestate*. Such a deceased person is spoken of as an *intestate*. Each state has a law, called the *statute of descent and distribution*, designating the persons who will take the land of an intestate landowner. These persons are known as *heirs*. Heirs who acquire title in this manner are said to take by descent, and the real estate is said to descend to the heirs. By virtue of the statute of descent, ownership of an intestate's land automatically passes to the heirs immediately upon the decedent's death.

The statutes of descent are based on principles of justice and equity and have for their purpose the making of such distribution of the property of the decedent as he would probably have made had he left a will.

§ 318. Course of descent where there are descendants. Statutes of descent vary from state to state. Children of the intestate and their descendants are usually preferred. Subject to the rights of the decedent's surviving spouse, which vary considerably from state to state, the property of an intestate usually goes first to his children and the descendants of deceased children. The property is divided into as many shares as there are children and as there are deceased children with surviving descendants. Each child of the deceased takes one share, and the descendants of a deceased child divide among them the share that their parent would have taken if living.

EXAMPLE: X, a widower, dies, leaving two children, A and B, each of whom has children of his own. There are also two other grandchildren, D and E, who are sons of C, a deceased child of X. A and B each take one third of X's estate, and D and E each take one sixth. The children of A and B take nothing.

§ 319. Course of descent in the absence of descendants. In the absence of children or descendants of children, the laws of descent of the various states make widely varying provisions for division of the estate among the spouse, parents, brothers and sisters, and other kindred of the deceased. Any attempt to outline the various statutory schemes of descent is beyond the scope of this text.

§ 320. Adoption. Taking another person's child into one's home and rearing him as one's own child does not constitute an adoption. For purposes of inheritance, the foster parent and foster child are complete strangers. As a rule, a court proceeding of some kind is necessary for an adoption. But when the necessary court order has been obtained, the adopted child becomes the legal heir of the adoptive parent as though he were a natural child.

§ 321. Illegitimates. Illegitimate children inherit from their mothers. In some states an illegitimate child also inherits from his father if the father acknowledges paternity in writing, some states requiring certain other formalities in this respect, such as signing of the document in the presence of witnesses. As a rule, subsequent marriage of the parents makes the child legitimate.

§ 322. Posthumous children. Children born after the death of the parent, *posthumous children*, inherit from such parent as though they had been born in his lifetime.

§ 323. Will defined. A *will* is a gift of property that is to take effect on the giver's death, unless the gift is revoked by the giver prior to that time. It is often referred to as a *last will and testament*. The party making the will is known as the *testator*, if male; *testatrix*, if female. A deceased person, spoken of as a *decedent*, is said to die *testate* if he leaves a will. A gift of land by will is called a *devise*, and a party receiving such a gift is called a *devisee*. A *bequest* is a gift of personal property— of a car, furniture, jewelry, or other objects. A *legacy* is a gift of money, and a party receiving a legacy is called a *legatee*.

§ 324. Codicil. A codicil is a supplement to a will, made subsequent to the making of the will and containing provisions whereby the testator adds to or otherwise alters his will. It must be signed and witnessed in the same manner in which a will is signed and witnessed.

As a rule, once a will is signed, the only changes that one can make in it are either by codicil or by a new will.

EXAMPLE: T makes a will by which, among other things, he gives A a legacy of $5,000. The will is duly signed and witnessed. Later, T takes the will from his vault and strikes out the $5000, substituting $100. The change is ineffective. The gift still stands at $5000.

§ 325.   **Deed and will distinguished.**   A deed must take effect in the grantor's lifetime. A will takes effect only upon the testator's death. Once a valid deed is made, even as a gift, the grantor cannot thereafter change his mind and divest the grantee of his ownership. The mere signing of a will, on the other hand, gives the devisees or legatees therein named no rights in the testator's property. Up to the time of his death, the testator may change his mind and give his property to someone else. If he dies without revoking his will and the will is admitted to probate, then the devisees and legatees acquire title to the things given them by the will.

§ 326.   **Disinheriting heirs.**   Subject to certain restrictions, a man may make a will giving his property to persons other than his heirs. His heirs are thereby said to be disinherited. Nevertheless, they are still his heirs, even though they receive nothing.

> **EXAMPLE:** A, a widower, dies leaving two children, B and C. He also leaves a will giving all his property to his housekeeper. The housekeeper receives everything. B and C receive nothing. Nevertheless, they are A's heirs.

This fact must always be borne in mind, since if a person leaves all his property to strangers, the heirs may decide to contest the will, perhaps on the ground that it is a forgery or that the decedent was insane when he made the will, and they may succeed in having the will declared void. If the heirs succeed in doing this, naturally they take the property, since a void will is no will at all, and the estate is treated as intestate.

§ 327.   **The testator.**   The age at which a person may make a will varies from state to state. Twenty-one is an age frequently fixed.

In order to be able to make a valid will, the testator must be of sound mind. Soundness of mind is difficult to define. A person need not be absolutely of sound mind and memory in every respect. A person may be quite eccentric and still be legally of sound mind. All that is required is that he have sufficient mental ability to know and remember who are the natural objects of his bounty (that is, he must know the persons to whom he would be naturally expected to leave his property, such as his wife and children), to comprehend the kind and character of his property, and to make disposition of that property according to some plan formed in his mind. The following do not render a person incapable of making a will: uncleanliness, offensive habits, old age, feeble health, defective memory, dissipation, belief in spiritualism, melancholy disposition, and so on. But if a person has become so feeble in mind that he cannot remember from hour to hour or day to day what he has said or done and cannot be trusted to transact the simple affairs of life, and if his memory has so far failed him that he cannot remember his relations to others, he is incapable of making a will.

Sometimes insane delusions will invalidate a will.

EXAMPLE: A delusion that the testator's mother and sister were no kin to him or that the testator's deceased wife appeared to him and told him to leave his property to her brother will invalidate a will.

§ 328. **Undue influence.** Voluntary action is an essential part of the legal conception of a will. A person may possess a sound mind and yet be so completely under the control and influence of others that he is incapable of making a will that reflects his wishes and desires. This power over the testator's mind is called undue influence. It is difficult to set aside a will on the ground of undue influence. Advice, persuasion, kindness, attention, or influence of affection do not constitute undue influence. However, the testator may be so feeble that a very little pressure will overcome his wish and substitute that of another. Merely talking to him may so fatigue him that he would do anything for the sake of peace and quiet. A will produced by such means may be set aside because of the undue influence.

§ 329. **Signature.** The will must be signed by the testator. If the testator cannot write, he may sign by mark. If he is too feeble to affix his mark, he may request some other person to sign for him in his presence. Some states require that the testator sign in the presence of witnesses. In order to prevent unauthorized additions to the will, many states require that the will be signed at the end.

§ 330. **Witnesses.** Every will, except a holographic will, must be witnessed. Two or three witnesses are usually required. The witnesses should be disinterested persons who are not receiving any gifts by the will. The witnesses should also sign the will to furnish written proof that they were present. As a rule, witnesses must sign the will in the presence of the testator, and in some states, it is also required that the witnesses sign in the presence of each other. The testator must sign the will before any witness signs.

§ 331. **Holographic wills.** In quite a number of states, Arizona, Arkansas, California, Idaho, Kentucky, Montana, Nevada, North Dakota, Oklahoma, Tennessee, Texas, for example, a will written entirely in the testator's own handwriting is valid even though it is not witnessed. Such a will is known as a *holograpic,* or *olograpic, will.*

§ 332. **Revocation.** A will may be revoked by burning, tearing, cancellation, or obliteration. For such destruction to constitute a revocation there must be both an act and an intention to revoke.

EXAMPLE: Testator ordered his son to throw the will into the fire, and the son instead threw another paper into the fire, with the intent to deceive his father. The will was not revoked. There was an intention to revoke, but no act of burning of the will.

A later will may revoke an earlier will.

EXAMPLE: *T* makes a will giving all his property to A. Thereafter, he makes a new will giving all his property to B. The new will automatically revokes the earlier will.

In some states, a will is revoked by the subsequent marriage of the testator. In other states, marriage alone will not revoke the will, but if a child is born of the marriage, this operates as a revocation of the will.

§ 333. **Death.** A will has no effect until the death of the testator.

§ 334. **Probate.** Before a will is operative, it must be filed in the proper court and admitted to probate. The court having the power to admit wills to probate is variously designated as a probate, surrogate, or orphan's court. Probate of a will simply involves establishing to the court's satisfaction that the will is genuine, that it has been signed and witnessed as required by law, and that the testator was of sound mind. When this proof has been made, the court enters an order finding that the will is, in fact, the testator's last will and testament. This constitutes admission of the will to probate.

§ 335. **Contest.** An opportunity is afforded the heirs of the testator, either before or after the will has been admitted to probate, to set aside the will on good cause being shown, such as the fact that undue influence was exercised, that the testator was not of sound mind, or that the will is a forgery. Such an attack on the will is known as a contest.

§ 336. **Rights of surviving spouse.** Laws exist in most states for the protection of the surviving spouse of a decedent. The decedent is not permitted to leave his widow penniless. These laws usually provide that if the surviving spouse is dissatisfied with the provision made for such spouse in the decedent's will, such spouse may, within a specified period of time, renounce or dissent from the will. Thereby such spouse loses all rights to any gift given by the will. In lieu thereof, such spouse usually receives dower, curtesy, or such other share of the decedent's estate as the spouse would have received had the decedent died intestate, depending on the local law.

Chapter 19

LIENS

§ 337. **Lien defined.**   A *lien* is a right conferred on certain classes of creditors to have their debts paid out of the debtor's property, usually by means of a sale thereof.

§ 338. **In general.**   If a creditor is an *unsecured creditor*, that is, if he has no lien on the debtor's land, the debtor may sell or mortgage the land, and his purchasers or mortgagees will be unaffected in any way by the creditor's rights.

> **EXAMPLE:** On January 5, 1968, A borrows $5,000 from B. A signs a promissory note for this amount, but he does not give B any mortgage on his land to secure repayment of the debt. B is therefore an unsecured creditor. On January 26, 1968 A borrows $500 from C and gives C a mortgage on his land. The giving of the mortgage creates a *lien*. The lien attaches to A's land at that time. C immediately records the mortgage. The recording of the mortgage perfects the lien. C is a secured creditor. If C forecloses his mortgage and becomes the owner of the mortgaged land by means of the foreclosure, B will have no rights whatever in the land so acquired by C. All persons acquiring any interest in the land after January 26 take subject to C's lien, i.e., enforcement of the lien will extinguish their interest. If B sues A on the note and gets a judgment for the debt prior to the completion of C's foreclosure, B will have a lien on A's land but the lien will be inferior to C's lien and will therefore be extinguished by C's foreclosure.

Often a lien creditor is required to take some steps to perfect his lien, that is, to make it effective as to any person but the debtor.

EXAMPLE: On January 30, 1968 the United States discovers that A, a taxpayer, has failed to pay $50,000 of his income tax and it therefore assesses a tax against him. On February 1, 1968 A sells and conveys his land in Chicago to B. On February 28, 1968 the United States files a notice of lien in the Recorder's office in Chicago. B is unaffected by this lien, since he purchased before the lien was *perfected* by filing.

A time limit is placed on the enforcement of virtually all liens. If the lien creditor fails to enforce his lien by appropriate action prior to the expiration of the specified period, his lien cannot thereafter be enforced.

EXAMPLE: A, a landowner, hires B to put a new roof on his house. A fails to pay for the roof, and B files a mechanic's lien against the land. In Illinois, where the land is located, such a lien has a duration of two years. B takes no action to foreclose his lien, and after two years have elapsed, A sells the land to C. C has good title to the land unencumbered by any lien of B's.

To determine a particular creditor's rights in the land in question, then, it is necessary to inquire: (1) Does he have a lien? (2) If he has a lien, when was it created, that is, when did it *attach* to the land? (3) Was the lien properly *perfected?* (4) What is the *duration* of the lien? (5) Has the lien been voluntarily released or waived by the lien creditor?

§ 339. **Types of liens.**   So far as real estate is concerned, the main classes of liens are *contractual liens, equitable liens,* and *statutory liens.*

EXAMPLE: A mortgages his land to B and B records the mortgage. B has a *contractual lien* on A's land.

EXAMPLE: X dies leaving certain vacant land to his sons, A and B. A fails to pay the real estate taxes, and B is therefore forced to pay all the real estate taxes. He has an *equitable lien* on A's share of the land as security for reimbursement for A's share of the taxes.

EXAMPLE: The principal statutory liens are *mechanics' liens, judgment liens, tax liens, attachment liens,* and *execution liens.*

§ 340. **Mechanics' liens.**   Mechanics and materialmen are persons who furnish labor or materials in the construction of improvements on land. A mechanic or materialman who has furnished such labor or material on the landowner's order can, by complying with certain formalities, acquire a lien on the land and improvements in question if the landowner fails to pay him. The lien is called a *mechanic's lien,* and the person furnishing the work or material is the *mechanic's lien claimant.* These liens resemble mortgages and in many states are foreclosed in the same manner as mortgages.

Certain kinds of labor and materials are not *lienable*. For example, if labor or materials are furnished to a tenant and the articles thereby produced are, in legal contemplation, *trade fixtures* and thus removable by him at the termination of his tenancy, a lien will not attach to the landlord's title.

EXAMPLE: A leases a store to B as a barber shop. C installs barber chairs at B's order. C has no lien on the land for any unpaid balance due on the chairs. The chairs are trade fixtures.

Generally, lienable work and materials must be such as become a permanent part of the building structure. Thus medical care furnished an employee of the contractor, even if the injury was suffered on the building site, is not lienable. Printing, stationery, and telephone service furnished the contractor are not lienable. Nor is the furnishing of tools, machinery, cranes, hoists, and so forth, lienable, for these do not become a permanent part of the building. 57 C.J.S. 536; 36 Am.Jur. 57. In a number of states the law has been amended recently to give a mechanic's lien for the rental of machinery needed in construction.

§ 341. **Contract or consent of owner.** Mechanics' liens laws differ from state to state in dealing with the problem of work ordered by one other than the landowner. In some states, a lien claimant must show that he was hired by the landowner *or his agent* to furnish the labor or materials for which a lien is claimed. Laws of this kind are known as *contract statutes*. In other states, it is sufficient if the lien claimant can show that the owner had knowledge of and consented to the doing of the work, even though the work was ordered by some person other than the owner, such as the tenant. These laws are known as *consent statutes*.

Consent usually involves more than a mere failure to object to the doing of the work. Often the landowner is powerless to prevent the third person, such as a tenant, from ordering the construction or improvements. Some *affirmative consent* by the landowner is required, as when a lease requires the tenant to erect a building. At times, however, the same result is reached regardless of which statute is applied.

EXAMPLE: A, a landowner, leases an obsolete movie theatre to B, the lease providing that B will use the premises only as a savings and loan association and that B will make the necessary alterations at his own expense. Here, if B fails to pay for the work and materials, those furnishing the same will have mechanics' liens on A's land. In a consent state, the lease is treated as giving consent for the doing of the work, and in a contract state the lease is regarded as making B the agent of A for the ordering of the work. Thus the result is at times the same whether the state is a contract or a consent state. 79 A.L.R. 962.

Knowledge and consent also figure in the situation where the landowner has entered into an installment contract to sell the land to a purchaser and the purchaser has ordered work done on the building. If the seller has no knowledge of the work and it is not provided for in the installment contract, the seller's title does not become subject to the mechanic's lien, and the lien attaches only to the buyer's equity. As in the case of leases, however, where the contract of sale expressly requires the doing of certain specific work, the resulting mechanic's lien claim is binding on the seller. 57 C.J.S. 573.

Whether work ordered by one spouse will ripen into a lien binding on the other spouse is a subject on which the laws differ from state to state. 57 C.J.S. 552, 592.

A number of states, including California, Colorado, Minnesota, Nevada, New Mexico, Oregon, South Dakota and Washington, have a special type of consent statute. In these states, the landowner is deemed to have authorized and consented to improvements ordered by others (tenants, contract purchasers, and so on) unless within a specified time of learning of the work (usually three to ten days) the landowner posts a notice of nonresponsibility in some conspicuous place on the premises. 123 A.L.R. 7, 85 A.L.R.2d 949. In Nevada, the notice of nonresponsibility must also be recorded.

As far as co-owners are concerned, no lien will attach to the interests of those co-owners who do not consent to the work.

> **EXAMPLE:** A father and his minor children owned the property as tenants in common. The father ordered certain labor and materials. The mechanic's lien attached only to the father's interest in the property. *Patrick v. Bonthius,* 13 Wash.2d 210, 124 P.2d 550. One co-owner cannot put a lien on the shares of his nonconsenting co-owners.

§ 342.   **Contractors and subcontractors.**   Mechanic's lien laws distinguish between *contractors* and *subcontractors*. A contractor is one who was hired by the landowner to construct the improvement. A subcontractor has not dealt directly with the landowner, but has a contract with, or was hired by, the contractor.

> **EXAMPLE:** A, a landowner, hires B, a general contractor, to build a house. B hires C to do the electrical work. C buys his electrical supplies from D. B is a contractor. C is a subcontractor. D is called a *sub-subcontractor,* though legally he is treated for all purposes as a subcontractor.

Since the legal rights of general contractors differ from those of subcontractors, and since the procedures that they must follow to establish their liens are also quite different, the distinction between general contractors and subcontractors is important. Laymen may sometimes mistake a general contractor for a subcontractor.

EXAMPLE: *A, a landowner, retains B as his architect to supervise construction and to let the various contracts for plumbing, electrical work, and so on. All the individual contractors are* general contractors, *for they are dealing with the landowner through his agent.*

In some states the law places on the landowner and on the construction lender the burden of seeing to it that the subcontractors are paid for their work and materials. This is something of an oddity. If I hire you to build a building for me, very likely the construction contract will call for me to pay the contract price to you. Nevertheless the law steps in and says that, despite the contract, my mortgage lender and I must hold back part of the contract price and pay it to the subcontractors. In order that the landowner may know those whom it is his duty to protect and also to enable him to hold back adequate funds to pay them, the law requires subcontractors to give the landowner personal notice of their liens within a set time, and failure to do so invalidates their liens. *Gray v. McKinley,* 34 Ala. App. 630, 43 So.2d 421. This notice must be given to all landowners.

EXAMPLE: *A and B own land in joint tenancy. They hire C to erect a building. C hires D to do the plumbing. D is a subcontractor. He serves notice of his subcontractor's lien only on A. D has a lien only on A's half interest in the land. He has no lien on B's share.* Liese v. Hentze, *326 Ill. 633, 158 N.E. 428.*

Service of such notice is not necessary if the general contractor has furnished the landowner a sworn list of subcontractors and all subcontractors are shown on this list. Where the notice is served on the landowner, the lien is limited to the work and materials set forth in the notice. *Roth v. Lehman,* 1 Ill. App.2d 94, 116 N.E.2d 413.

§ 343. **Performance by contractor.** In general, where the general contractor seeks to assert a lien, he must show that the contract was *substantially performed* by him. 57 C.J.S. 605. Likewise, any subcontractor seeking to assert a lien would have to show that his job was substantially performed by him. Where the contract specifies that no payment will be made without production of an architect's certificate, a general contractor claiming a lien must be able to produce the certificate. 57 C.J.S. 606.

§ 344. **Inception and priority of lien.** The law as to the particular time when a mechanic's lien attaches to the land varies from state to state. There are four definite groupings or classifications of states in this regard:

1. In Nebraska, and a few other states, the lien of any particular mechanic attaches when he commences *his* particular work. In such states, the mechanic's lien is not prior to any mortgage that was recorded prior to the commencement of the very work for which the lien is filed.

EXAMPLE: *A* and *B* commence work on a building and afterward the owner mortgages the land to *C*. Thereafter, *D* and *E* begin work on the same construction job. *A* and *B* have priority over *C*, and *C* has priority over *D* and *E*.

2. In many states (Arizona, Arkansas, California, Connecticut, Delaware, District of Columbia, Georgia, Idaho, Iowa, Kansas, Louisiana, Michigan, Minnesota, Montana, Nebraska, Nevada, New Hampshire, New Mexico, Ohio, Oklahoma, Rhode Island, Tennessee, Utah, Washington, West Virginia and Wisconsin) all mechanics' liens growing out of a particular construction job date back to the beginning of the job.

EXAMPLE: *A*, a landowner, hires *B* to erect a building, and *B* hires *C* to dig the foundation. *C* begins work in January, 1968. In February, 1968, *A* records a mortgage to *X*, which mortgage is intended to provide funds for construction. The carpenter, mason, electrician and so on come on the job in March, 1968. All mechanics' liens date back to January and all liens therefore have priority over *X*'s mortgage.

3. In a few states, Illinois and Maine, for example, a mechanic's lien attaches to the land as of the date of the contract for the improvement, that is, as of the date on which the owner ordered the work done.

EXAMPLE: *A*, a landowner, hires *B* on January 8, 1968 to build a building in Chicago. As is true of nearly all contracts for construction, the contract is not recorded. On January 10, 1968 *A* records a mortgage to *X*, which mortgage is intended to provide funds for construction. Work on the construction site begins on January 17, 1968. All mechanics' liens date back to January 8, 1968, and therefore all enjoy priority over *X*'s mortgage.

4. In a few states (New York and South Carolina, for example) a mechanic's lien does not arise as against mortgagees until notice thereof is filed in the proper public office.

EXAMPLE: *A*, a landowner, on January 8, 1968 hires *B* to erect a building. *B* commences work on January 12th. On January 19, 1968 *A* records a construction mortgage to *X*, and *X* disburses funds under this mortgage for such construction until February 28th, when a mechanic's lien claim is filed by a subcontractor. *X* discontinues disbursement and files a foreclosure suit. *X* has complete priority over the mechanics' liens, because all his disbursements were made prior to the filing of any mechanics' liens.

In some states (Alabama, Colorado, Illinois, Missouri, North Dakota, Oregon, South Dakota, Virginia, and Wyoming, for example) the law declares that a mechanic's lien for work or materials furnished after a mortgage lien has attached to the land shall have priority over the mortgage *as to the building but not as to the land*. In a number of these states the matter of priority of lien as between the construction mortgage and the mechanic's lien claimants is decided in a way that is quite disadvantageous to the mortgagee.

EXAMPLE: A, an owner of vacant land, procures a construction loan mortgage from X, which is recorded on January 10, 1968. On January 17th A hires B to build the building. Construction begins on January 24th. Mechanics' liens are filed. Both X and the mechanic's lien claimants file suits to foreclose. The court will hold that the mechanics' liens are a prior and superior lien as to the *buildings*, so that, in practical effect, the mechanics' liens will be a prior lien as to most of the value of the property and the mortgagee will have no choice but to pay off the mechanic's lien claimants. 107 A.L.R. 1012.

Of course, no great harm comes to the mortgagee if the landowner remains solvent and is able to pay off all mechanic's lien claimants. Unfortunately for mortgage lenders many construction projects end in bankruptcy for the landowner, so that the construction mortgagee and the mechanic's lien claimants are plunged into a contest as to their respective rights in the land and buildings.

§ 345. **Notice of lien.** In many states, laws require a mechanic's lien claimant to file a notice of his lien in some public office within some specified time, usually within some period after completion of the work. Usually it is required that this notice state the amount claimed to be due, the name and address of the claimant, the type of improvement, a description of the land, and the name of the landowner or landowners. 57 C.J.S. 693; 52 A.L.R.2d 12; 27 A.L.R. 2d 1169. The requirement that lien claims be filed within a specified time of the completion of the work often leads to controversies.

EXAMPLE: In Illinois, the law provides that lien claims must be filed within four months after completion of the work. X completes his work satisfactorily, but more than four months elapses before X realizes that he has failed to file his lien claim. X sends a workman back to perform some trifling task, like repairing a defective lock. This does no good. The job was really finished more than four months ago, and X cannot prolong this period by subterfuge. 57 C.J.S. 661.

§ 346. **Waiver and release of lien.** As construction or repair work goes forward, liens of the general contractor and subcontractors attach to the land. Both the homeowner and any mortgagee involved naturally want to get rid of these liens, which can be accomplished by procuring waivers of their liens from the parties furnishing labor or material. There are *partial waivers* and *final waivers*. Suppose that a subcontractor, such as a plumbing, electrical, or plastering subcontractor, has finished half his job and wants to be paid for that half. When the homebuilder pays him, he demands from the subcontractor a waiver of his lien for the work and materials furnished. This waiver recites that it waives all lien for *work and materials furnished*. This means, of course, for work and materials furnished *up to the date of the waiver*. No lien is waived as to the work still to be done. When final payment is made to that particular party, the homebuilder demands from him a final waiver, which waives all lien *for work and materials furnished or to be furnished* meaning that he has no lien at all on the land or buildings. Even if he must come back to repair or replace defective work or material, he can claim no lien on the property, which is important, because the objective is always to get the house built at the price and at the bids submitted by the various mechanics. There is trouble ahead if any of the mechanics is legally able to assert a lien for a sum greater than the amount he agreed to work for.

When a mechanic has filed a lien claim in some public office as required by law, it becomes necessary, when his claim has been paid or settled, to release his lien from the public records. As a rule, the waiver form is not appropriate for this purpose. Instead, a form called *release of mechanic's lien* is used. It is very similar to a release of mortgage and is filed in the same office where the lien claim has been filed.

§ 347. **Time limit on enforcement of lien.**   It is usually provided that a mechanic's lien ceases to exist unless steps are taken to enforce or foreclose it within a specified time, usually one or two years, after the filing of the lien claim.

§ 348. **Judgments.**   When *A* brings to a successful conclusion a lawsuit filed against *B* on some personal liability, such as that arising on *B*'s promissory note or because of personal injuries inflicted by *B*, the court enters an order directing that *B* pay *A* the amount found due. This order is a judgment. *A* is the judgment creditor; *B*, judgment debtor.

EXAMPLE: *A* obtains a judgment against *B*. The following year, *B* acquires title to a tract of land. The lien of *A*'s judgment immediately attaches to this land.

A judgment concludes with a direction that execution issue. An execution is an order, signed by the clerk of the court that rendered the judgment, directing the sheriff or some other public officer to sell the property of the judgment debtor in order to pay off, or satisfy, the judgment. The execution does not issue automatically. It is necessary for the judgment creditor to go to the court clerk and request its issuance.

The first step in the enforcement of the judgment lien is the issuance of the execution and its delivery to the sheriff. In some states, the sheriff then delivers a copy of this execution to the judgment debtor and demands payment of the judgment. The next step is a purely formal and technical one. It is known as a *levy* and consists of those acts by which a sheriff sets apart and appropriates a particular part of the judgment debtor's property for the purpose of satisfying the command of the execution. A levy on real estate often consists of nothing more than the sheriff's statement on the execution that he has levied on certain real estate, followed by a description of the real estate. Next, the sheriff publishes notice of the coming sale and posts copies thereof in certain public places. At the date fixed for sale, the sheriff auctions off the real estate to the highest bidder, who is usually the judgment creditor, since he can bid up to the amount of his judgment without producing any cash other than the sheriff's costs. In many states, there is a redemption period, just as in the case of mortgage foreclosure sales, one year being the period most frequently encountered. About one quarter of the states, however, have no redemption period whatever. Ultimately, if no reduction is made, a sheriff's deed issues to the purchaser.

A title acquired by such an execution sale, although not as precarious as a tax title, is nevertheless vulnerable to numerous objections and should be viewed with great suspicion.

The duration of a judgment lien varies from state to state. Ten years is the period most frequently encountered. This period is of great importance to prospective purchasers and mortgagees of real estate.

EXAMPLE: In Indiana, a judgment is a lien for ten years. A, who is about to purchase certain Indiana land from B, makes a check of the public records, which discloses that B has owned the land for fifteen years. A need only search for judgments against B, since all judgments against prior landowners will be more than ten years old. And A need not search for any judgments against B rendered prior to this ten-year period.

When a judgment is paid, the judgment creditor files a formal discharge of the judgment, known as satisfaction.

§ 349. **Attachments.** A judgment, obviously, cannot create any lien on the judgment debtor's land until judgment has been rendered. Nor can execution issue before there has been a judgment. In the meantime, the lawsuit may drag on and on, and an opportunity is afforded the defendant to dispose of his property and thus leave no real estate that can be sold to satisfy the judgment, when rendered. To prevent such a result, many states provide that on commencement of the suit, the plaintiff, that is, the person who has filed the suit, may, under conditions specified by the local law, have an attachment issued. As a rule, it is required that the plaintiff file a bond to indemnify the defendant for any injury that the latter may sustain by reason of a wrongful attachment. On filing of the bond and on compliance with the other conditions specified by the local law, a writ of attachment is issued, and the sheriff endorses on the writ a statement that he has levied on the defendant's real estate, which he thereupon describes. In addition, some states require that the sheriff issue and file in the register's or recorder's office a certificate describing the real estate attached and stating that the same has been levied on. A valid attachment creates a lien on the defendant's real estate, which can be enforced by issuance of execution after judgment has been rendered in favor of the plaintiff. It prevents the defendant from disposing of his real estate while the suit is pending.

§ 350. **Miscellaneous liens.**   Among the many other liens that may attach to land are federal estate tax liens; federal gift tax liens; federal internal revenue liens (usually for income tax); liens for state inheritance or estate tax, gift tax, income tax, corporation tax, sales tax, and so forth; and old-age assistance liens.

Chapter 20

MORTGAGES

§ 351. **Mortgage defined.** A mortgage may be defined as a conveyance of land given as security for the payment of a debt. On analysis, this definition discloses the existence of two elements: (1) Like a deed, a mortgage is a conveyance of land. (2) However, the object of the document is not, as in the case of a deed, to effect a sale of land, but to provide security for the payment of a debt.

§ 352. **History of mortgage law.** The history of mortgage law is the history of hundreds of years of ceaseless struggle for advantage between borrowers and lenders, and the lawbooks reflect the constantly shifting fortunes of this war. Occasionally the battle has gone in favor of the lenders. More recently, however, many laws favorable to the borrowers have been passed, and the battle has usually gone in their favor. To understand how the modern mortgage developed out of these centuries of struggle is to take a long step forward toward understanding modern mortgage law.

Much of our mortgage law comes to us from England. In that country, mortgage arrangements of various kinds existed even in the Anglo-Saxon times before the conquest of England by William the Conqueror in 1066. However, it will suffice for our purposes to begin with the mortgage of the fourteenth century. This document was a simple deed of the land, running from the borrower (mortgagor) to the lender (mortgagee). All the ceremonies needed for a full transfer of ownership took place when the mortgage was made. The mortgagee became the owner of the land just as if a sale had taken place. However, this ownership was subject to two qualifications:

1. The mortgagee, as owner, could oust the mortgagor, take immediate possession of the property, and collect the rents. However, the rents so collected had to be applied on the mortgage debt. For this reason, the mortgagee often permitted the mortgagor to remain in possession.
2. The mortgage described the debt it secured and stated a date of payment, known as the *law day*. The mortgage gave the mortgagor the right to pay the debt on the law day. If he did so, the mortgage provided that it was thereby to become void. This provision was known as the *defeasance clause,* for payment of the debt on the law day defeated the mortgage and put ownership back in the mortgagor.

In early times, the courts enforced the mortgage as it was written. Foreclosure proceedings did not exist. Failure to pay the mortgage debt when due, termed a *default,* automatically extinguished all the mortgagor's interest in the land.

§ 353. **The equity of redemption.** For many years no one dreamed of questioning this scheme of things. Then slowly at first, and later in greater numbers, borrowers who had lost their property through default began to seek the assistance of the king by presenting *petitions* to him. A typical petition by such a borrower would set forth the borrowing of the money, the making of the mortgage, the default in payment, and the resulting loss of the land. The petition would continue with the statement that the borrower now had funds and offered to pay the mortgage debt in full, with interest. The petition would then ask that the king order the mortgagee, who now owned the land, to accept the proffered money and to convey the land back to the borrower. The king had little time or inclination to tend to these petitions personally, and so he habitually referred them to a high official, the Lord Chancellor. Since the king was the fountain of all justice, it was the Chancellor's duty to dispose of these petitions justly and equitably, according to good conscience, and this he did. In cases of hardship or accident, for example, where the mortgagor had been robbed while on his way to pay the debt, the Chancellor would order the mortgagee to accept payment of the debt from the borrower and to convey the land back to the borrower. A mortgagee who refused to do as he was told was sent to jail. In time, by about the year 1625, what had begun as a matter of grace on the part of the king had developed into the purest routine. Borrowers filed their petitions directly with the Chancellor, who was now functioning as the judge of a court, and with routine regularity his order was issued commanding the mortgagee to reconvey. Thus a new and very important right was born, the right of the mortgagor to pay his debt even after default and in this manner to recover his property. This right came to be known as the *equitable right of redemption,* or the *equity of redemption.* Later the courts held that the mortgagor could sell this equitable right of redemption, that he could dispose of it by his will, and that if he died leaving no will, the right could be exercised by his heirs. You will perceive that as a result of these developments, the mortgagor, even after default, retained very important rights in the land. Technically the mortgagee became full owner of the land upon default, but practically the mortgagor could now be regarded as the owner even after default, since he could reacquire ownership by exercising his equitable right of redemption.

§ 354. **Waiver of right of redemption.**   The mortgagees reacted to the development of the equitable right of redemption by inserting in their mortgages clauses reciting that the mortgagor waived and surrendered all his equitable rights of redemption. The courts, however, nipped this idea in the bud by holding that all such clauses were void, since a needy borrower will sign anything and it is up to the courts to protect him. This rule flourished and exists in full vigor today. Any provision in the mortgage purporting to terminate the mortgagor's ownership in case of failure to make payments when due is against public policy and is void. *Once a mortgage, always a mortgage.* It cannot be converted into an outright deed by the mere default of the mortgagor. And no matter how the mortgage seeks to disguise an attempted waiver of the equitable right of redemption, the courts will strike it down.

EXAMPLE: At the time the mortgage was made the mortgagor signed a deed conveying the property to the mortgagee as grantee. He then delivered the deed to a third person in escrow with directions to deliver the deed to the mortgagee in case of default in the mortgage payments. This deed and escrow were held invalid as an attempted waiver of the equitable right of redemption. *Plummer v. Ilse,* 41 Wash. 5, 82 Pac. 1009; *Hamod v. Hawthorne,* 52 Cal.2d 78, 338 P.2d 387.

§ 355. **Development of foreclosure.**   The efforts of the courts to rescue the mortgagor in turn placed the mortgagee at a disadvantage. The mortgagee, it is true, became the owner of the land when the mortgagor defaulted, but he could not be certain he would remain the owner, for the mortgagor might choose to redeem. To remedy this situation a new practice sprang up. Immediately upon default in payment of the mortgage debt, the mortgagee would file a petition in court, and the judge would enter an order, called a decree, allowing the mortgagor additional time to pay the debt. If he failed to pay within this time, usually six months or a year, the decree provided that his equitable right of redemption was thereby barred and foreclosed. Thereafter he could not redeem his property. Thus developed the *foreclosure suit,* a suit to bar or terminate the equitable right of redemption.

The method of foreclosure just described is known today as *strict fore-*

closure. It is still used in Connecticut and Vermont and occasionally else-where.

The next development was foreclosure through public sale. The idea emerged that in mortgage foreclosures, justice would best be served by offering the land for sale at public auction, for if at such sale the property sold for more than the mortgage debt, the mortgagee would be paid his debt in full and the surplus proceeds of the sale would be salvaged for the mortgagor. This method of *foreclosure by sale* is the most common method of foreclosure in America today. This development constituted another major victory for the mortgagor. More important still, it led to another and even greater victory for the borrowers. As the practice of foreclosure by sale grew more common, the view began to emerge that *the mortgage, despite its superficial similarity to a deed, was really not a deed of conveyance but only a lien on the land—that is, merely a means of bringing about a public sale to raise money for the payment of the mortgage debt.*

§ 356. **Title and lien theories.**   The relatively recent view that the mortgage is not really a conveyance of land but only a lien, has reached its fullest development in the agricultural and western states. Certain states, called *title theory states,* still take the older view that a mortgage gives the mortgagee some sort of legal title to the land. In other states, called *lien theory states,* the view that the mortgagee has the legal title is entirely superseded by the view that he has merely a lien to secure his debt. Some states take a position midway between these two views. These are called *intermediate states.*

It is not possible, however, to draw any hard and fast line between these groups of states, since vestiges of title theory will be found in lien theory states, and many title theory states have adopted rules developed by lien theory courts. The differences in point of view are of importance in determining the mortgagee's rights with respect to possession and rents of the mortgaged property.

§ 357. **Statutory redemption.**   When a mortgage foreclosure sale is held, the equitable right of redemption ends. Indeed, the whole object of the foreclosure suit is to put an end to the mortgagor's equitable right of redemption. In the last hundred years, however, laws have been enacted giving the mortgagor an additional concession. Under these laws, the mortgagor is given one last chance to get his property back.

EXPLANATION: Suppose, for example, that a farmer whose farm is mortgaged has a bad crop year. He cannot meet his mortgage payments, and the mortgage is foreclosed. Perhaps next year the weather and crops will be good, and he will have enough to pay all of his debts. To afford farmers and other mortgagors one last opportunity to salvage their properties, many legislatures have passed laws allowing additional time, often one year, after the foreclosure sale during which the mortgagor can, by paying the amount of the foreclosure sale price, get his property back from the mortgagee. This right is called the *statutory right of redemption. Thus the equitable right of redemption ends and the statutory right of redemption begins with the holding of the foreclosure sale.*

§ **358. Types of mortgages.** There are several different types of mortgage instruments. Those commonly encountered are *regular mortgages, deeds of trust, equitable mortgages, and deeds absolute given as security for debts.*

§ **359. Regular mortgages.** The ordinary printed form of mortgage encountered in most states today is referred to herein as the regular mortgage. It is, in form, a deed or conveyance of the land by the borrower to the lender followed or preceded by a description of the debt and including a provision to the effect that such mortgage shall be void on full payment of such debt. The content of the additional paragraphs of "fine print" varies considerably.

§ **360. Deeds of trust.** The regular mortgage involves only two parties, the borrower and the lender. In the *trust deed,* also known as the *deed of trust,* the borrower conveys the land, not to the lender, but to a third party, in trust for the benefit of the holder of the note or notes that represent the mortgage debt.

The trust deed form of mortgage has certain advantages, the chief one being that in a number of states it can be foreclosed by trustee's sale under the *power of sale clause* without any court proceedings. The power of sale trust deed is used in Alabama, Alaska, California, Colorado, District of Columbia, Mississippi, Missouri, Montana, Nebraska, Nevada, New Mexico, North Carolina, Oregon, South Carolina, Tennessee, Texas, Virginia, Washington, and West Virginia.

§ **361. Equitable mortgages.** As a general rule, any instrument in writing by which the parties show their intention that real estate be held as security for the payment of a debt will constitute an equitable mortgage, which can be foreclosed in a court of equity.

EXAMPLE: R, a landowner, borrowed money from E and gave E a promissory note to evidence the debt. On this note R placed the following recital: "This note is secured by a real estate mortgage on" (here followed a description of the land). Actually no separate mortgage was executed. The court held that the note itself, with the quoted endorsement, constituted an equitable mortgage on the land, for it clearly expressed an intention that the land should stand as security for the debt. *Trustees of Zion Methodist Church v. Smith, 335 Ill. App. 233, 81 N.E.2d 233.*

EXAMPLE: R borrowed $500 for home improvements from E and signed an agreement not to sell or mortgage the property until the debt was paid. This is an equitable mortgage. *Coast Bank v. Minderhaut, 61 Cal. 2d 311, 392 P.2d 265.*

An instrument intended as a regular mortgage, but which contains some defect, may operate as an equitable mortgage.

EXAMPLE: When through inadvertence a trust deed securing a debt altogether omitted the name of a trustee, it was obviously ineffective to transfer title or create a power of sale in any one since it lacked a grantee. However, it was sustained as an equitable mortgage, which could be foreclosed by means of a foreclosure suit. *Dulany v. Willis*, 95 Va. 606, 29 S.E. 324.

§ 362.   Deeds absolute given as security.   Often when a landowner borrows money he gives as security an absolute deed to the land. By absolute deed is meant an ordinary quitclaim or warranty deed such as is used in sales of land. On its face the transaction looks like a sale and conveyance of the land. Nevertheless the courts treat such a deed as a mortgage, although they require convincing evidence that the deed was really intended only as security for a debt. But if such proof is available, the borrower is entitled to pay the debt and to demand a reconveyance from the lender, just as in the case of an ordinary mortgage; whereas if the debt is not paid, the grantee must foreclose just as if a regular mortgage had been made.

EXAMPLE: *R* owns his own home, which is already mortgaged to a bank. He needs money for medical expenses and goes to his brother, *E*, for a loan of $1000. *E* loans *R* the money but insists that *R* sign a simple promissory note due one year after date, also a quitclaim deed to his home. It is agreed orally that if the debt is paid when due, *E* will quitclaim the property back to *R*. *R* fails to pay the debt. *E* is not the owner of the land. He merely holds a mortgage on it, which he must foreclose. And remember that all the world has notice of the true nature of this deed, for undoubtedly *R* remained in possession, and possession imparts constructive notice.

In determining whether a transaction is a sale or a mortgage, the following circumstances are considered:

1. Adequacy of consideration. If *R* deeds to *E* land worth $10,000 and receives only $5,000, this tends to indicate that the transaction is a mortgage, for normally land will sell for its full value.
2. Prior negotiations between the parties. If *R* applies to *E* for a loan and the transaction is consummated by *R* giving *E* a deed to the land, this tends to show that the transaction is a mortgage. It is as if *E* had said: "I will loan you the money, but give me a deed as security." Of course if it appears that *E* rejected the application for a loan, this tends to show that the transaction is a sale. It is as if *E* had said: "I will not loan you any money, but I am willing to buy your land."
3. Subsequent conduct of the parties. If *R* receives money from *E* and gives *E* a deed to *R*'s land, but *R* thereafter remains in possession, paying taxes, insurance premiums, and so on, this tends to show that the transaction is a mortgage, for in a normal land sale the buyer takes possession.

§ 363. **Sale and leaseback—conditional sale.**   A deed absolute given to secure a debt, which the law treats as a mortgage, must be distinguished from a *conditional sale of land*. In the latter transaction, a landowner sells his land for its full value and the buyer contemporaneously grants the seller an option to repurchase the land, which the seller may or may not exercise, as he pleases. Often the buyer also leases the land back to the seller for a term of years. This type of transaction is valid. Its advantage to the landowner lies in the fact that he gets the full value of the property instead of the smaller amount that he could obtain on a mortgage, and he is under no obligation to repay this amount if he is willing to forego his repurchase of the land. In other words, he is not saddled with a debt, as he would be if he had made a mortgage on his land. The advantage to the buyer is that foreclosure is not necessary if default is made in the rent payments, since the transaction is a sale and lease, not a mortgage.

Use of this device in a modified form is common today. An industrial corporation wants money to use in its business. It sells its plant to an insurance company or other investor, receiving the full cash value. The investor then leases the land back to the industrial corporation. Hence the term *sale and leaseback*. The lease is usually for a term ranging between twenty and thirty years, and the tenant is given an option to renew the lease for an additional period. The rental on the original term pays back to the buyer an amount equal to the purchase price plus a return much higher than could be obtained on a conventional mortgage loan. The lease is a *net lease*, that is, the lessee is required to pay all real estate taxes, fire insurance, repairs, and so forth, so that all rental paid is "net" to the landlord.

Among the advantages to the lessee of such an arrangement are the following:

1. A tax advantage. In computing its income for income tax purposes, the lessee deducts its rent payments under the lease. Were the lessee merely a mortgagor, the only permitted deductions would be interest and depreciation. Also, if the building is not newly constructed, it may be that the current value and sale price are substantially less than the price paid when the seller-lessee bought the building, and the sale to the insurance company represents an income tax loss to the seller-lessee.

2. By selling the property for its full value to the lessor, the lessee obtains much more cash money than it could raise on a mortgage, for no mortgagee will loan up to 100 per cent of the value of the property.

3. Existing mortgages, corporate charters, debenture agreements, or other documents binding on the lessee may place restrictions on its right to borrow money. Since a lease is not a loan, the leaseback arrangement provides a method of getting around these restrictions.

4. A mortgage note would appear as a liability on the mortgagor's financial

statements. Liability for rent under a lease is a fixed and certain legal liability. Yet under accounting practice, it is not shown as a liability. It appears on the financial statement, if at all, only as a footnote. This facilitates borrowing, sale of stock, and so forth.

The chief disadvantages to the lessee are:

1. If the building goes up in value, the insurance company, not the lessee, will reap the benefit of this increase once the lease expires.

2. The lessee has all the burdens of ownership, for the lease requires the lessee to pay taxes, insurance, and so on. But the lessee lacks the freedom of action that an owner enjoys. Under the terms of the lease, the lessee cannot sell the leasehold without the consent of the insurance company. Even if the insurance company consents, there are many prospective purchasers who are reluctant to buy leaseholds. Moreover, the lessee cannot tear down or remodel buildings as business needs dictate unless the insurance company consents. Likewise, to erect new buildings would be foolish, for they would belong to the landlord at the end of the lease period.

§ 364. **Vendor's lien reserved by deed.**   In some states, a seller, in lieu of taking back a mortgage from the buyer, expressly reserves in his deed to the buyer a lien on the land to secure payment of the balance of the purchase price. Such a lien is called a vendor's lien. It is really a mortgage.

EXAMPLE: A, a landowner, conveyed to B by a warranty deed which warranted that title was free from all encumbrances excepting three certain notes executed by B, for which a vendor's lien was retained until said notes and the interest thereon should be fully paid. The court held that this clause created a lien on the land. Such a lien is regarded as partaking of the nature of an equitable mortgage. It is really a mortgage. It is governed by the same rules as a mortgage and must be foreclosed as such. Crabtree v. Davis, 237 Ala. 264, 186 So. 734.

Such a lien enjoys priority over subsequent liens and encumbrances and, like a purchase money mortgage, has priority over prior judgments against the purchaser. The grantee under such deed does not become personally liable for the purchase money unless he has signed a promissory note or otherwise obligated himself personally to pay the debt. And a purchaser from such grantee does not become personally liable to the holder of the vendor's lien unless by his deed he assumes and agrees to pay the unpaid balance of the debt. The debt may be assigned, and the assignee will have the right to foreclose the lien.

§ 365. **Application and commitment.**   A mortgage transaction usually begins with an application for a loan. The application serves a double purpose: (1) It is a source of information on which the lender will base his decision as to making the loan, and (2) it defines the terms of the loan contract. The application is usually a printed form prepared by the mortgagee and signed by the prospective borrower. After investigating the prospective borrower's financial circumstances and appraising the real estate, the prospective mortgagee may write the prospective borrower a letter stating that his application for a loan has been accepted. This letter is sometimes referred to as a *commitment*. The result is to create a contract for the making of the mortgage loan. 12 Univ. of Cincinnati L. Rev. 5.

From the discussion later in this chapter relating to the time when the mortgage becomes a lien of the land, it will become obvious to you that *it is desirable from the mortgagee's standpoint that he be obligated to make the loan*. If the application and commitment, taken together, are to constitute a binding contract for a loan, the application should state in detail all the terms of the mortgage loan, and the commitment should simply say, in effect, "Yes, we will make the loan on the terms stated in the application." Technically, the application is an *offer* by the mortgagor to accept a mortgage loan on the terms specified in the application. The commitment is an *acceptance* of the offer. *Burns v. Washington S. & L. Ass'n.*, 251 Miss. 789, 171 So.2d 322. Under basic contract law the acceptance of an offer creates a contract. If the letter of commitment makes any changes in the terms, it is technically a *counter-offer*, which legally is a rejection of the offer. There is no contract unless the landowner agrees to the new terms, which he may do by writing the word *accepted* and his signature on the mortgagee's letter of commitment. Since the application and commitment define the terms on which the loan is to be made and constitute a contract that neither party can change or add to without the other's consent, the application should state the terms in detail, including agreement of borrower to sign note and mortgage in a certain specified form; his agreement to furnish evidence of title and plat of survey at his expense; his agreement to sign chattel mortgage and assignment of leases and rents; provisions for deducting title charges and other charges from proceeds of loan; provisions that lender shall have possession of fire insurance policies and abstracts; the amount, premium, and character of insurance to be carried on the property; and so forth. (See § 345.)

§ 366. **The mortgage note.** After the mortgagee has given his commitment to make the loan, the mortgagor signs a promissory note and mortgage. The mortgage stands as security for payment of the note. *The chief function of the note is to make the mortgagor personally liable for payment of the mortgage debt.* If the mortgagor signs such a note and then decides that he does not want the building, he cannot simply abandon the property and move elsewhere. Wherever he goes he takes his personal liability with him, and if the mortgage is foreclosed, the mortgagee can obtain a personal judgment against him for any deficiency between the foreclosure sale price and the amount of the mortgage debt. Armed with such a judgment, the mortgagee can garnishee the mortgagor's wages or have his other property sold to pay the balance due.

§ 367. **Parties to the mortgage.**   The borrower, who corresponds to the grantor in a deed, is known as the *mortgagor*. The lender, who corresponds to the grantee in a deed, is known as the *mortgagee*. It is important that the names of the parties be given accurately and fully in the mortgage. The marital status of the mortgagor, as *bachelor, spinster,* or *widower,* should be recited. The same considerations that require the grantor's spouse to join in his deed require the mortgagor's spouse to join in his mortgage. A mortgage by a minor or an insane person is subject to the same objections that exist in the case of deeds. A mortgage by a corporation must be authorized by proper corporate resolutions, which should show that the money is being borrowed for proper corporate purposes. In general, the requirements relative to the grantor and grantee in a deed are applicable to the mortgagor and mortgagee in a mortgage.

§ 368. **Description of the mortgaged property.**   An accurate description of the mortgaged land is of great importance. Even greater care must be exercised in this regard than is necessary in the case of deeds, since a purchaser usually goes into possession of the land under his deed and thereby gives all the world notice of his rights, whereas a mortgagee rarely goes into possession and therefore depends entirely on the recording of his mortgage to give all subsequent purchasers and mortgagees notice of his rights.

When a mortgage is foreclosed, the mortgagee should be in a position to take over the mortgaged building as a functioning and operating unit. This is something that requires thought at the time the mortgage is made. For example, if the building contains personal property needed for its proper functioning, such as furniture in a furnished apartment building, some arrangement must be made to enable the mortgagee to take over these items in the event the mortgage is foreclosed. To accomplish this, it may be necessary to have the mortgagor sign a financing statement and security agreement under the Uniform Commercial Code on such personal property; for a real estate mortgage, although it covers fixtures, does not cover personal property.

Under the *package mortgage* method of financing, the loan that finances the purchase of a home also finances the purchase of equipment—stoves, refrigerators, dishwashers, or washing machines—essential to the livability of the property. Following the legal description in the mortgage is a clause containing a general, catch-all enumeration of the common items and a provision reciting that all such items are fixtures and thus part of the real estate. The package mortgage attempts to make certain articles fixtures by means of an agreement between the mortgagor and mortgagee, even though in the absence of such agreement the articles would be chattels. The practical advantages of this course are obvious. Installation of such equipment by the builder makes the house more saleable. Moreover, it enables the prospective home buyer to finance the initial purchase of such equipment at a lower interest rate and over a longer term than if the purchase were made separately from a department store. The legal objection to the use of the real estate mortgage to cover these articles has yet to be fully tested in the courts. When the article is actually removed from the mortgaged premises and then sold to a bona fide purchaser, it is then to all appearances a chattel, and in some states such a purchaser will acquire good title to the article. If this were not the law, any purchaser of chattels would incur the risk of losing them if it should later develop that they were wrongfully removed from mortgaged land. In other states, particularly title theory states, the real estate mortgagee is permitted to reclaim such articles, even when he finds them in the possession of an innocent purchaser. 97 *U. of Pa. L. Rev.* 180, 210. And generally a purchaser of such articles who buys them while they are still installed on the mortgaged land will not be protected. *First Mortgage Bond Co. v. London,* 259 Mich. 688, 244 N.W. 203; *Dorr v. Dudderar,* 88 Ill. 107. To prevent such articles from passing into the hands of a bona fide purchaser, mortgagees have initiated the practice of pasting a notice on the equipment itself stating that the article is covered by the real estate mortgage. Purchasers of articles so marked would not be protected if they saw the notice, since they would not be bona fide purchasers.

Since it is by no means certain that, even with elaborate fine-print clauses, the real estate mortgage alone will afford the mortgagee protection against the removal of readily removable articles, many mortgagees insist upon a separate security agreement and financing statement under the Uniform Commercial Code.

In other words, where chattels form a substantial part of the mortgage security, the mortgagor will give the mortgagee a security agreement, and both will sign a financing statement which will be filed with the appropriate chattel filings under the Uniform Commercial Code.

§ 369. **Debt.** In order for a mortgage to exist, there must be a debt for the mortgage to secure. A mortgage without any debt has no effect. Any contractual obligation reducible to a money value may be secured by a mortgage. The obligation secured is ordinarily one for the payment of money, such as a promissory note or bond. A bond is nothing more than a promise to pay money. The obligation secured may or may not be negotiable.

Although there must be a debt, it is not necessary that there be a *per-*

sonal liability for the payment of the debt. It is competent for the parties to make such bargain upon this subject as they please. They may agree that the mortgagee shall advance the loan and rely solely for his security on the real estate. *Bacon v. Brown*, 19 Conn. 29. In such case, the mortgagee cannot obtain a personal judgment or deficiency decree against the mortgagor should the mortgaged land prove insufficient to satisfy the mortgage debt.

The mortgage lien is measured by the amount of the mortgage debt. Thus if a mortgage recites a debt of $10,000, but actually only $5000 is loaned, the mortgage stands as security for only $5000. Likewise, the mortgage lien diminishes as the mortgage debt is reduced by payment. Thus if a mortgage of $10,000 is paid down to $5000, the mortgage lien is reduced accordingly, and if the mortgagee thereafter loans the mortgagor additional funds, these additional funds are not secured by the mortgage unless the mortgage contains a clause covering *future advances*.

§ 370. **Debt—priority of lien.**   Any discussion of mortgage debt inevitably involves questions of priority of lien. Often there will be two or more liens against the same property.

> **EXAMPLE:** *B* mortgages his property to *A* in 1951 and then mortgages the same property to *C* in 1952. If both mortgages are valid and both are properly recorded, *A's* mortgage is a *first lien,* and if he is compelled to enforce it by foreclosure, he will extinguish *C's* mortgage, which is a *subordinate* or *inferior lien.* Of course *C* has the right to pay *A's* mortgage to prevent this extinguishment and to foreclose for the amounts due on both mortgages. It is said, in such circumstances, that *A* enjoys *priority of lien.* *C's* lien is subject to *A's.*

The same situation exists when the liens are of different kinds.

> **EXAMPLE:** *A* acquires a mortgage lien on the property in 1948. *B* acquires a judgment lien on the same property in 1949. *C* acquires a mechanic's lien on the property in 1950. Normally, these liens have priority according to the time they attach to the land. *First in time is first in right.* There are, however, exceptions to the rule.

§ 371. **Debt—description of debt.**   A mortgage must in some way describe and identify the debt that it is intended to secure. 145 A.L.R. 369. The character and amount of the debt must be defined with reasonable certainty in order to preclude the parties from substituting debts other than those described. *Bowen v. Ratcliff*, 140 Ind. 393, 39 N.E. 860. Otherwise, in some states, subsequent mortgages, purchasers, or judgment creditors will acquire rights superior to those of the mortgagee.

> **EXAMPLE:** *A* borrows $10,000 from *B* and gives *B* his note therefor. To secure the loan, *A* gives *B* a mortgage, but the mortgage does not recite the amount of the loan. The mortgage is recorded. Thereafter, *X* obtains a judgment against *A.*

X's judgment is a prior lien, coming in ahead of B's mortgage. *Bullock v. Battenhousen,* 108 Ill. 28.

§ 372. Debt—future advances—in general—obligatory advances. A mortgage debt is rarely created at the same instant that the mortgage is signed. Normally the mortgagor will receive his money sometime after the recording of the mortgage. The question that arises is whether the mortgage has priority over junior mortgages, judgments, and other liens that may attach to the land before the money is paid out on the first mortgage. The problem usually arises in three situations:

EXAMPLE: An ordinary mortgage loan is applied for. The mortgage is executed and recorded. Payment of the mortgage money to the mortgagor is delayed pending the completion of a title search. A judgment or other lien attaches to the land after the recording of the mortgage. Thereafter the mortgagee's title search is completed, but since the search covers only the date of the recording of the mortgage, the mortgagee is unaware of the judgment. Thereafter the mortgagee pays out the mortgage money to the mortgagor. Discussion follows.

EXAMPLE: An ordinary mortgage loan is made and the mortgage money is properly paid out to the mortgagor. The mortgage contains a provision to the effect that it also secures future advances to the mortgagor not in excess of $2000, or some other sum. This is called an *open-end mortgage.* A year or so after the mortgage has been made, the mortgagor applies to the mortgagee for additional funds and receives an additional loan of $2000. Before he receives his money, a judgment or other lien attaches to the land. The mortgagee pays out the $2000 in ignorance of the existence of the judgment lien. Discussion follows.

EXAMPLE: A construction loan is involved. The mortgagee doles out the mortgage money as the building goes up, and before construction is completed other liens attach to the land. Discussion follows.

Where a mortgagee is obligated, by contract with the mortgagor, to advance funds to be secured by the mortgage, such mortgage will be a valid lien from the time of its recording, as against all subsequent encumbrances, even though the mortgage money is paid to the mortgagor after such subsequent encumbrances have attached to the mortgaged land. This holds true even though the mortgagee is actually aware of the existence of the subsequent encumbrances at the time he pays out the mortgage money. 80 A.L.R.2d 191, 196, 217, 219. Such advances are called *obligatory advances.* Because of the mortgagee's obligation to pay out the money, the mortgage debt is regarded as being in existence from the very beginning. The obligation is usually created in one of two ways: (1) Where the mortgagor has made written application for a mortgage loan and the mortgagee has given his commitment to make the loan, the mortgagee is contractually obligated to go through with the transaction. (2) Where a construction loan is involved, the obligation is usually created by a construction loan agreement, which is an agreement entered into between mortgagor and mortgagee when the purpose of the loan is to provide funds for the construction of a building. It obligates the mortgagee to make the loan but authorizes him to disburse the funds as the building goes up. It also binds the mortgagor to complete the erection of the building and to turn over to the mortgagee for disbursement such money as the mortgagor is furnishing from his own funds toward erection of the building. The agreement also authorizes the mortgagee to act as the mortgagor's agent in dealing with the contractor and subcontractors. This agreement should dovetail into the construction contract between the mortgagor and his builder, so that the builder will not be clamoring for money at a time when the mortgagee is not yet required to pay out funds.

Let us return to consideration of the application and commitment. It is not always easy for mortgage men to think of these documents as creating a contract for a loan so that the money subsequently advanced is an obligatory advance, and yet a simple illustration will prove that is the case.

EXAMPLE: A applies to ABC Corporation for a $1,000,000 mortgage loan at 5 per cent interest on his hotel building. The corporation gives a commitment to make this loan. Thereafter ABC Corporation refuses to honor its commitment. A goes to XYZ Corporation, which gives him a loan on the same property at 6 per cent interest. Without the slightest doubt, ABC Corporation is liable to A for the difference between 5 per cent and 6 per cent interest over the life of the loan.

Of course in all states, expenditures made by the mortgagee to preserve the lien of his mortgage, such as payments made by the mortgagee on delinquent real estate taxes that the mortgagor has failed to pay, are considered essentially obligatory expenses, and the mortgagee has the same lien for such advances as he has for his original debt.

§ 373. **Debt—future advances—optional advances.** Suppose that the mortgagee has not entered into a binding contract to make the mortgage loan. Advances under such a mortgage are called *optional advances*. Despite the fact that such mortgage is duly recorded, it is by no means certain that it will operate as a lien from the date of its recording as against all other liens attaching after that date. The argument that can be made against the mortgage is that a mortgage is a conveyance to secure a debt and that without a debt there is no mortgage. It must therefore follow that *until the money has actually been advanced to the mortgagor no legal mortgage exists, for until that time the mortgagor owes no money to the mortgagee and therefore no debt exists.* In the case of *obligatory advances,* the courts dispose of the argument by saying that since the mortgagee must at all events loan the money, as he has contracted to do, for all practical purposes the debt exists as soon as the obligation to make the loan is created. Since this obligation is normally created, either by application and commitment or by construction loan agreement, before the recording of the mortgage, an obligatory advance mortgage is good against the whole world, including subsequent lienors, from the date the mortgage is recorded. As to mortgages where the mortgagee has not entered into a binding contract to advance the funds, the problem is far more complex, as the ensuing discussion of the open-end mortgage reveals.

§ 374. **Debt—future advances—open-end mortgages.** The *open-end mortgage* provides that the mortgage secures not only the original note and debt, but also any additional advance that the mortgagee may choose to make to the mortgagor in the future. This means that if in the future the mortgagor wishes to borrow additional funds for the addition of a room or garage or for some other purpose, he can borrow this money from the mortgagee if the latter sees fit to lend it. The advantages are obvious. The expense of executing a new mortgage is obviated. The mortgagee's security is enhanced by the additions or repairs. Recourse to short-term, high-rate consumer financing is eliminated.

It is obvious that the open-end mortgage is an optional advance mortgage. That is, the mortgagee is under no legal obligation to loan the additional funds. The problem here is one of *intervening liens.*

EXAMPLE: A borrows $10,000 from B on January 31 and gives B a future, advance type (open-end) mortgage on A's land, which is duly recorded. On July 1, A borrows $1000 from C and gives him a junior mortgage on the land, which he records. On December 1, A comes to B and borrows an additional $1000 under the future advance clause of the mortgage. Will this new advance be part of the original first mortgage so that it will enjoy priority over the junior mortgage of July 1, or will the said junior mortgage enjoy priority over the new advance so that the new advance will be, in effect, a third mortgage on the property? In a majority of the states, the additional advance will enjoy priority over the intervening lien, the junior mortgage of July 1, unless B had *actual knowledge* of the second mortgage when he gave A the advance. In Illinois, Michigan, Ohio, and Pennsylvania, a mortgagee must, before making an optional future advance, search the records for intervening liens. *Record notice* of intervening liens is enough to give the intervening lien priority over the additional advance. 138 A.L.R. 566. In these states, title companies make special, inexpensive title searches to cover mortgagees who propose making additional advances.

A mortgage secures only the debt described therein. Hence a mortgage designed to secure optional future advances should draw attention to that fact. The older decisions are somewhat liberal in this regard. 5 *DePaul L. Rev.* 80; 81 A.L.R. 631. However, since the open-end mortgage has become popular, the notion that such mortgages should describe such future advances seems to be winning acceptance. At a minimum today, for safety's sake, the mortgage should specify the upper limit of the future advances to be made. Laws on the subject of open-end mortgages have been enacted (for example, in Connecticut, Florida, Kentucky, Maryland, Massachusetts, Montana, Nebraska, New Hampshire, North Dakota, South Dakota, and Rhode Island) and these should be consulted.

It is necessary, also, that the future advances fall within the description thereof given in the mortgage.

EXAMPLE: If the mortgage, by its terms, secures future advances made to the mortgagors, an advance made to one of the mortgagors probably is not secured by the mortgage. *Capocasa v. First Nat. Bank,* 154 N.W.2d 271 (Wis.). Likewise an advance made to a grantee of the mortgagors might not be secured by the mortgage. *Walker v. Whitmore,* 165 Ark. 276, 262 S.W. 678.

Finally, the documents evidencing the future advance should refer to the mortgage, so that it is evident that such advances were meant to be advances secured by the mortgage.

WARNING: If the mortgage makes no reference to future advances, any later document evidencing future advances must be executed and acknowledged like an original mortgage, recorded, and the title searches brought down to cover recording, for it is, in legal effect, a new mortgage on the property.

§ 375. **Debt—future advances—construction loans.** Complex questions involving future advances arise in connection with construction loans. (*See* Chapter 21.)

§ 376. **Debt—future advances—bond issues.** There is an exception to the rule that a mortgage securing optional future advances runs the risk of losing priority to intervening liens. A trust indenture securing an issue of bonds to be sold to the public enjoys priority as of the date it is recorded. All subsequent liens are junior to it, regardless of when the money is paid out. *Landers-Morrison-Christenson Co. v. Ambassador Holding Co.,* 171 Minn. 445, 214 N.W. 503. Since money will not be available to the borrower until the bonds are sold, any rule that would make bond sales vulnerable to intervening liens would make bond issue financing impossible.

§ 377. **Interest—usury.** The mortgage should state the rate and time of payment of interest, though failure to do so will not invalidate the mortgage.

Most states have laws limiting the rate of interest that may be charged. Charging a rate of interest in excess of that permitted is *usury*. The penalty for usury varies from state to state. Thus in some states, the entire mortgage is void if usury is present; in others, the lender forfeits all interest; in still other states, the lender only forfeits all interest in excess of the highest rate chargeable.

In a number of states a corporate borrower may validly agree to pay more than the normal permitted interest rate. 55 *Calif. L. Rev.* 207. The problem arises where an individual applies for a loan and the lender, it is later contended, forced him to incorporate for the purpose of agreeing to pay the higher interest rate.

> **EXAMPLE:** *A*, an individual, applies to *B* for a loan. *B* agrees to give *A* the loan, but later discovers that the interest rate is higher than the law allows. *B* directs *A* to form a corporation, and *B* makes the loan to the corporation. Except in New York, the corporation will be allowed to contend that the loan is usurious. *Felier v. Architect's Display Inc.*, 54 N.J. Super. 205, 148 A.2d 634.

> **EXAMPLE:** *A* applies to *B* for a loan, and *B* directs him to form a corporation, which has a capital of $1,000. *B* loans the corporation $100,000, and the loan is guaranteed by *A* individually. Again the loan is usurious, because it is clear that the loan is really being made to *A*, and the corporation is nothing but a sham. *Walnut Discount Co. v. Weiss*, 205 Pa. Super. 161, 208 A.2d 26.

Where a loan is truly a corporate loan, as where the corporation has ample assets and applies for a corporate loan, the fact that payment of the note is, for additional security, guaranteed by individual shareholders, does not invalidate the loan and the individuals have no right to raise the defense of usury. 63 A.L.R.2d 954.

It can be usurious to charge a borrower interest on the principal amount of the note, if the lender pays out only part of this amount.

> **EXAMPLE:** *A* signs a note for $100,000, but *B*, the lender, pays him only $90,000 retaining $10,000, as a "commission." *B* charges interest on $100,000. If the charges (interest plus commission) exceed the lawful rate on a loan of $90,000, the loan is usurious. *Smith v. Parsons*, 55 Minn. 520, 57 N.W. 311; *Garland v. Union Trust Co.*, 63 Okla. 253, 165 P. 197.

Brokers, in negotiating loans of other people's money, may charge the borrower a commission, even though the loan bears the highest rate of interest allowed by law. Such a commission is compensation to the broker for his services in obtaining the loan. But a commission charged *by the lender himself* in addition to the highest rate of interest renders the loan usurious. It is perfectly obvious that such a commission is merely a device employed to disguise a usurious transaction.

Lenders charge *points* because they want higher yields on their money than the stated interest rate in the mortgage.

> **EXAMPLE:** *A*, a builder, is selling a home to *B* and *XYZ* is giving *B* a mortgage of $10,000 for 20 years at 6%. *XYZ* demands five "points." This means he

will advance only $10,000 minus 5% thereof or $9,500 though he will expect to be repaid the full $10,000.00. That gives the lender a yield of 6.65%. If B absorbs the $500, the loan is usurious in states where 6% is the maximum interest that can be charged.

If interest is charged on the full amount from the beginning, but only part of the loan is disbursed initially, the balance being disbursed later, the loan can be usurious.

EXAMPLE: A signs a note for $100,000 on a construction mortgage. B, the lender, charges interest on $100,000 from the start, but the loan is paid out only as construction goes forward. If the interest charged on amounts actually loaned *from the time the money was loaned* exceeds the highest legal rate, the loan is usurious. *Williamson v. Clark* (Fla.), 120 So.2d 637.

A bona fide commitment fee, paid by the borrower to induce the lender to keep mortgage money available for a period of time if the borrower should need it, is not interest and has no effect on usury. *Poley v. Barton S. & L. Ass'n., 82 N.J.S. 75, 196 A.2d 682.*

Notwithstanding the fact that the mortgage bears the highest rate of interest permitted, the mortgagee may charge the mortgagor with the expenses involved in making the loan, such as cost of title examination or cost of survey.

The federal Truth in Lending Act requires the lender on a home or farm loan to disclose to the borrower the amount of any service charge, carrying charge or loan fee, the true interest rate, and other like information. Money penalties are provided if the law is not complied with.

§ 378. **Prepayment of mortgage debt.** In the absence of an agreement to the contrary, the mortgagee has a contractual right to have his money out earning the stipulated interest. Unless there is an agreement to that effect, the mortgagor has no right to insist upon making payment before maturity, even by offering to pay the principal and all interest to the maturity date. *Fuller v. Manchester Bank*, 102 N.H. 117, 152 A.2d 179. Accordingly, it is to the mortgagor's advantage to provide in the mortgage and mortgage note that the debt is payable *on or before* the due date, or that the debt is payable in monthly payments of a stated sum *or more*. Or a specific clause may be inserted conferring on the mortgagor the privilege of prepaying the mortgage debt. This is known as a *prepayment privilege*. In corporate trust deeds securing issues of bonds, the comparable provision is that providing for *redemption* of bonds prior to their stated maturity dates. Such provisions enable the mortgagor to refinance when money is cheaper or to retire the mortgage where he has entered into a contract of sale that requires him to deliver title free and clear of any mortgage.

Suppose that *A* is a mortgagor in a mortgage which allows him to make prepayments on any monthly payment date and that he then makes several payments of two or three times the amount specified in the mortgage. Suddenly a time arrives when he is pinched for money. He now contends that he has the right to skip several payments until the amount he has prepaid is exhausted. This contention will not prevail. In effect, the prepayments are applied on the last payments falling due. *Smith v. Renz,* 122 Cal. App.2d 535, 265 P.2d 160.

§ 379. **Subordination.**   When a first mortgage is canceled, a second mortgage on the property becomes the first lien unless provision is made against such an event. It is usually impossible to secure funds to pay off the first mortgage by substituting another mortgage on the property unless that later mortgage can be accorded the position of a first mortgage. For this reason, a mortgagor in a second mortgage should insist that a provision be included obligating the mortgagee thereafter to waive the priority of his mortgage in favor of any other mortgage executed to refinance the existing first mortgage.

When a mortgagee signs such a document waiving the priority of his mortgage, the legal effect is just as if the old mortgage had been executed and recorded after the recording of the new first mortgage. This is called a *subordination.* The old junior mortgage has been *subordinated* to the new mortgage. It has been placed in a junior position, so that foreclosure of the new mortgage will wipe out the old junior mortgage.

Other situations involve the idea of subordination. Suppose, for example, that *A* is leasing to *B* a floor of a building that he owns. *A* anticipates that in the future he may wish to place a mortgage on the building, either to refinance and pay off an existing mortgage or to accomplish some other purpose. The new mortgagee may insist that his mortgage be an absolute first mortgage, prior and superior to all other interests in the property. To go to all tenants in the building and beg subordination agreements from them at that time would be impractical. Therefore in *A*'s lease to *B*, *A* will provide that *B*'s lease will automatically be subject and subordinate to all future mortgages on the property. The signing of a subsequent subordination agreement is dispensed with.

The legality of these so-called *automatic subordinations* is a question that arises frequently.

EXAMPLE: *A* sells his orange grove to *B,* a land developer, for $500,000. *B* pays $200,000 cash and gives *A* a purchase money mortgage for $300,000. The mortgage recites that it is "subordinate to all construction loan mortgages hereafter to be placed on said premises or any part thereof." The subordination is void because it does not give the details of the construction loans. 13 *U.C.L.A.L. Rev.* 1298. At least the maximum principal, interest rate, and term, and mode of repayment of the construction loan should be stated.

Apparently, however, the court will view a blanket subordination *in a lease* "to all present and future mortgages" as valid. *Kirkeby Corp. v. Cross Bridge Towers, Inc.* 91 N.J.S. 126, 219 A.2d 343.

§ 380. **Acceleration.** The mortgage and mortgage note usually provide that in case of any default the entire principal sum shall become immediately due and payable. This clause is known as the *acceleration clause*. If this clause is not present, the mortgagee must file separate foreclosure suits as each installment of the mortgage debt falls due and is defaulted. Manifestly, the acceleration clause is one of the most important in the mortgage.

A question arising frequently relates to the validity of a clause in the mortgage permitting the mortgagee to declare an acceleration of the mortgage debt in case of a sale of the property by the mortgagor. Older mortgages sometimes call for lower interest rates than the current market calls for, and the mortgagee's legal right to declare an acceleration forces a purchaser of mortgaged land to reach an agreement with the mortgagee on a higher interest rate in consideration of the mortgagee's agreement not to accelerate. Such acceleration clauses, operative on the mortgagor's sale of the mortgaged land, are perfectly legal. *Baker v. Leight*, 91 Ariz. 112, 370 P.2d 268; *Jones v. Sacramento S. & L. Ass'n.*, 56 Cal. Rptr. 741; *Jacobson v. McCunaban*, 43 Wash.2d 751, 264 P.2d 253.

§ 381. **Foreclosure provisions and power of sale.** Provisions are usually included in the mortgage for the foreclosure thereof, and, in states permitting foreclosure by exercise of power of sale, the power of sale is fully set forth in the mortgage.

§ 382. **Partial release.** Where a mortgage conveys several distinct tracts of land, it is often provided in such a mortgage that on payment of a certain specified portion of the debt the mortgagor shall be entitled to a release of the mortgage as to a certain tract of land. Such a release is known as a partial release. In the absence of such a provision, the mortgagor is not entitled to any release of the mortgage except upon full payment of the mortgage debt. When a blanket mortgage is placed on an entire subdivision, such a provision is indispensable, since otherwise the subdivider could not furnish lot purchasers with clear title to their lots.

§ 383. **Waiver of homestead and dower.** In some states, a mortgage on homestead land must include a clause releasing and waiving homestead rights. Again, in some states, a mortgage signed by the spouse of the mortgagor should contain a clause stating that such spouse thereby waives all dower as against the mortgagee.

§ 384. **Execution.** The mortgagor and his spouse should sign the mortgage. Some states require that the word "SEAL" appear after their signatures. A corporation should always affix its corporate seal. In some states witnesses are required. The mortgage should also be acknowledged and delivered to the mortgagee.

§ 385. **Recording.** As a practical matter, a mortgage must be recorded, since an unrecorded mortgage is void as to subsequent purchasers, mortgagees, or judgment creditors who are ignorant of the existence of such mortgage. It is important that the mortgage be filed or recorded as soon after its execution as possible.

As a general rule, the priority of successive liens often is determined by priority of recording, the first mortgage recorded being a first lien on the land, the second mortgage recorded being a second lien, and so on. The importance of early recording thus becomes obvious, since foreclosure of a first mortgage will wipe out and extinguish all junior liens, such as second mortgages.

In states that have mortgage taxes, the recorder will want proof that the tax was paid.

§ 386. **Master mortgage.** To save recording expenses, mortgagees are turning to the *master mortgage*. A mortgage lender records his usual mortgage form with none of the blanks filled in. This is the *master mortgage*. Thereafter each mortgage recorded by the mortgage company simply refers to the book and page of the master mortgage for the fine print provisions, enabling the mortgagee to get all the necessary recordable data of each mortgage in a one-page document. Laws permitting this have been enacted in Arizona, California, Florida, Idaho, Maine, North Carolina and Pennsylvania, and many more states are certain to do likewise. Meanwhile in those states that do not have this law as yet, exactly the same result can be achieved by using some actual, existing, recorded mortgage as a master mortgage.

§ 387. **Possession and rents.** The difference in viewpoint between title theory and lien theory states is of greatest importance with respect to the mortgagee's right to the possession and rents of the mortgaged property. To illustrate the significance of this statement, let us list, in chronological order, some important dates in a mortgage situation: (1) the date when the mortgage is signed by the mortgagor, (2) the date when the mortgagor first defaults, (3) the date when the mortgagee files his foreclosure suit, (4) the date of the foreclosure sale, and (5) the date when the statutory redemption period expires and the mortgagee receives the deed under which he becomes the owner of the mortgaged property.

Let us first make our broad generalizations and thereafter list the particular points of difference that exist. In general, the title theory states regard the mortgage as retaining some of its early character, that is, they view it as a conveyance of the land, so that *immediately on the signing of the mortgage*, the mortgagee has the right to take possession of the property and collect the rents thereof. On the other hand, the lien theory states regard the mortgage as merely creating the right to acquire the land through foreclosure of the mortgage, so that the mortgagor remains the full owner of the land with the right to possession and rents *until the statutory redemption period has expired and the foreclosure deed has issued to the mortgagee.* In other words, at its most extreme, this difference in point of view represents to the mortgagee the difference between dates 1 and 5 in the list so far as the right to possession and rents is concerned. *In title states, therefore, rents are an important part of the mortgagee's security. In lien states, this is not so. Grether v. Nick,* 193 Wis. 503, 213 N.W. 304, 215 N.W. 571.

Now let us analyze the situation in somewhat greater detail, from the point of view just expressed:

1. In a number of *title theory states,* Alabama, Maine, Maryland, and Tennessee, for example, the mortgagee, immediately upon execution of the mortgage, has the right to take possession and collect the rents of the mortgaged property. *Darling Shop v. Nelson Realty Co.* 262 Ala. 495, 79 S.2d 793. The right exists even though the mortgage is silent on this point. There are two exceptions: (1) In recent times laws have been passed in some title states giving the mortgagor the right of possession until default occurs. In effect, these laws convert such states into intermediate states. (2) Many mortgage forms used in title states give the mortgagor the right of possession until default.

2. In *intermediate theory states,* Illinois, New Jersey, North Carolina, and Ohio, for example, the mortgagor has the right of possession until his first default, but after default the mortgagee has the right to take possession.

3. In *lien theory states,* in the absence of a contrary provision in the mortgage, the mortgagor is entitled to possession and rents at least until the foreclosure sale.

4. In some lien theory states, either by express provision in the mortgage or by a separate assignment of rents signed at the time that the mortgage is signed, the mortgagor may give the mortgagee the right to take possession and collect rents as soon as a default occurs, and such provisions are valid. *Penn Mutual Life Ins. Co. v. Katz,* 139 Neb. 501, 297 N.W. 899; *Kinnison v. Guaranty Corp.,* 18 Cal.2d 256, 115 P.2d 450; *Dick & Reuteman Co. v. Jem Realty Co.,* 225 Wis. 428, 274 N.W. 416. However, some of these lien theory states make special rules as to owner-occupied homes. In New York, for example, a home owner cannot be compelled to pay rent pending foreclosure. *Holmes v. Gravenhorst,* 263 N.Y. 148, 188 N.E. 285.

5. In other lien theory states, the provisions described in Number 4 are considered void as against public policy. *Rives v. Mincks Hotel,* 167 Okla. 500, 30 P.2d 911; *Mutual Ins. Co. v. Canby Inv. Co.,* 190 Minn. 144, 251 N.W. 129; *Hart v. Bingham,* 171 Okla. 429, 43 P.2d 447.

6. In all states, if the mortgagor, after defaulting in his mortgage payments, voluntarily turns over possession to the mortgagee, the mortgagee has the legal right to remain in possession. Notice that in Number 5 it is the clause in the mortgage binding the mortgagor to give up possession *at some future time* when default occurs that is held void. The same agreement made *after default* is valid. The mortgagee is then called a *mortgagee in possession.*

7. Whenever a mortgagee takes possession before he has acquired owner-

ship of the property by foreclosure, the rents he collects must be applied in reduction of the mortgage debt. A mortgagee does not become the owner of the property by taking possession. Foreclosure is still necessary.

　　8. Whenever a mortgagee has the right to possession and fails to exercise that right, allowing the mortgagor to remain in possession and to collect rents, the rents so collected belong to the mortgagor.

　　9. In many states, there is a statutory period of redemption. No general rule can be laid down as to the right of possession during this period, for each state has its own rule.

§ 388. **Practical aspects of the problem.** A mortgage lender seeks a regular return on a safe investment and does not wish to assume the responsibilities of management. A lender is most unlikely to make a loan that will require him to go into immediate possession of the land, and this right is therefore seldom exercised. On the mortgagor's default, however, it is imperative that prompt action be taken to seize the rents so that they will not be diverted to the mortgagor's own personal use. An eviction suit to enforce the mortgagee's right to possession is often a long, drawn-out affair, especially when the mortgagor is interposing all the legal obstacles available to him. However, if the mortgagee files a foreclosure suit, he can often have a receiver appointed in a matter of days, and this is the course usually preferred. Other technical reasons exist for preferring the remedy of receivership.

Courts differ as to the grounds for appointment of a receiver. Some say it is enough that the property be inadequate security for the mortgage debt. Other courts require a showing that the security is inadequate and that the mortgagor is insolvent. Still others appoint a receiver only when the property is in danger of destruction. 26 A.L.R. 33.

§ 389. **Leases antedating mortgage.** It is important to distinguish between the rights of a tenant under a lease made prior to the mortgage and those of a tenant under a lease made subsequent to the mortgage. When the lease is made subsequent to the mortgage, the mortgagee can, by foreclosing his mortgage, extinguish the rights of the tenant under his lease. When the lease antedates the mortgage, the mortgagee must respect the tenant's rights, and regardless of foreclosure, the tenant cannot be evicted prior to the expiration of the lease, unless, of course, he fails to pay his rent.

Again, *in title and intermediate theory states,* if the lease antedates the mortgage, then immediately upon the mortgagor's default, the mortgagor may serve a demand upon the tenant that he pay all rents to the mortgagee. Thereafter, the tenant must pay all rents to the mortgagee. *King v. Housatonic R. R. Co.,* 45 Conn. 226; L.R.A. (1915C) 200. Of course the tenant may continue to pay rents to the mortgagor until such demand has been served upon him.

In *lien theory states*, the mortgagee ordinarily is not entitled to make such a demand on the tenant. L.R.A. (1915C) 200.

§ 390. **Leases subsequent to mortgage.** Obviously, a mortgagor cannot make any leases that will give the tenant greater rights than he, the mortgagor, possesses. Most important, where the lease is subsequent to the mortgage it is inferior to the mortgage, and the mortgagee can extinguish the lease if and when he forecloses his mortgage. Likewise, in *title and intermediate states*, the mortgagor has no right to retain possession after default. Tenants who occupy by virtue of leases made after the making of the mortgage also have no right to retain possession of the premises after the mortgagor's default, and the mortgagee may evict such tenants. To avoid eviction, the tenant, upon the mortgagee's making demand for possession, may agree to pay rent to the mortgagee, and the mortgagor will have no right to collect further rent from such tenant. *West Side Trust & Savings Bank v. Lopoten,* 358 Ill. 631, 193 N.E. 462; *Del-New Co. v. James,* 111 N.J.L. 157, 167 Atl. 747; *Anderson v. Robbins,* 82 Me. 422, 19 Atl. 910. One disadvantage of this course is that such action automatically terminates the lease, and the tenant becomes a tenant either from month to month or from year to year. *N.Y. Life Ins. Co. v. Simplex Products Corp.,* 135 Ohio St. 501, 21 N.E.2d 585; *Gartside v. Outley,* 58 Ill. 210. (*See* Chapter 30.) If the lease is one favorable to the landlord, the mortgagee will prefer to have a receiver appointed, since in many states the receiver can hold the tenant to his lease.

In *lien theory states*, in the absence of some provision in the mortgage, the mortgagee is not entitled to collect rents even under leases made after the making of the mortgage.

When the lease is favorable to the landlord, a mortgagee will attempt to preserve the lease even though he wishes to consummate foreclosure of the mortgage. In some states, Florida, New Jersey, and New York, for example, a mortgagee may, if he so wishes, leave unaffected by his foreclosure a lease that was executed subsequent to the mortgage, and the mortgagee, on acquiring title by foreclosure, may hold the tenant on such lease. 109 A.L.R. 457. In other states, completion of the foreclosure automatically wipes out any lease made after the mortgage and thus relieves the tenant of further liability. 109 A.L.R. 455. In these states, there is nothing that the mortgagee can do to keep the lease alive after foreclosure.

Many lawyers feel that an express provision in the lease that it will survive foreclosure if the mortgagee desires will be valid, even as to a junior lease. Alternatively the tenant and mortgagee might enter into a separate agreement that they will sign a new lease on the old terms if the old lease is extinguished by foreclosure. Or as a further alternative the mortgagee and lessee may sign a subordination, under which the lease is made prior and superior to the mortgage. Bear in mind that many mortgage loans today are made in reliance on the financial strength and pulling power of the tenant, and loss of that tenant could be disastrous.

§ 391. **Assignment of rents.**   At the time the mortgage is signed, the mortgagee should require the mortgagor to sign a separate assignment of leases and rents. This document assigns to the mortgagee all the mortgagor's interest in all existing leases, all leases to be executed in the future, and all rents falling due after the date of the mortgage, all as additional security for payment of the mortgage debt. Lawyers have found that there is magic in the argument that the mortgage creates a lien on the land and that the assignment creates a lien on the rents. All existing tenants are notified of the making of the assignment. The assignment is recorded. 75 A.L.R. 268. The following rules are applicable:

1. In most lien theory states, an assignment of rents enables the mortgagee to reach the rents accruing prior to foreclosure sale and to treat them as part of the security for his debt. This gives the mortgagee in a lien theory state virtually as favorable a position with regard to rents as the mortgagee has in title and intermediate states. In one or two lien states, an assignment of rents, like the mortgage clause giving the right to take possession on default, is held invalid as being opposed to public policy. *Hart v. Bingham,* 171 Okla. 429, 43 P.2d 447. Also, in a few lien states, an assignment signed contemporaneously with the mortgage is given only limited recognition. In these states, after a default occurs and the assignment has been activated, rents collected by the mortgagee can be applied only to maintain the property or to pay taxes or insurance. They cannot be applied in reduction of the mortgage debt. *Mutual Benefit Life Ins. Co. v. Canby,* 190 Minn. 144, 251 N.W. 129; *Western Loan Co. v. Mifflin,* 162 Wash. 33, 297 Pac. 743.

2. Since the assignment does not contemplate that the mortgagee will begin collecting rents immediately upon the signing of the assignment, but only after a default occurs, the assignment is inoperative until it is activated by some action of the mortgagee. 59 C.J.S. 414, 422.

Rents collected by the mortgagor before the assignment is activated belong to the mortgagor. *Sullivan v. Rosson,* 223 N.Y. 217, 119 N.E. 405. Or they may become the property of a junior mortgagee who exercises greater diligence. If A holds a first mortgage and B a second mortgage on the same property, and if default occurs and B activates his assignment but A does not, B gets the rents. *Stevens v. Blue,* 388 Ill. 92, 57 N.E. 2d 451. Even specific language that the assignment will operate automatically on default has been held insufficient to activate the assignment. *Dime Savings Bank of Brooklyn v. Lubart,* 38 N.Y.S. 2d 252.

3. Everywhere the assignment is properly activated if, after default and pursuant to the assignment, the mortgagor consents to collection of the rents by, and the tenants begin paying rent to, the mortgagee.

4. In title and intermediate theory states, the assignment is activated on default by the mortgagee's serving notice on the tenants to pay rent to the mortgagee. The mortgagor's consent is unnecessary. *Grannis-Blair Audit Co. v. Maddux,* 167 Tenn. 297, 69 S.W. 2d 238.

5. In some lien theory states, the assignment can be activated in the same

manner as in title theory states. *Kinnison v. Guaranty Liquidating Corp.,* 18 Cal.2d 256, 115 P.2d 450.

6. In other lien theory states, the assignment can be activated only by the mortgagee's filing a foreclosure suit and applying for the appointment of a receiver. *Dick & Reuteman Co. v. Jem Realty Co.,* 225 Wis. 428, 274 N.W. 416; *Hall v. Goldsworthy,* 136 Kan. 247, 14 P.2d 659. Of course these same steps will serve to activate an assignment in a title or intermediate state.

7. In one or two lien theory states, an assignment can be activated only by the mortgagor's voluntarily turning over possession to the mortgagee or allowing the mortgagee to collect rents. *Hart v. Bingham,* 171 Okla. 429, 43 P.2d 447.

8. Rents collected by the mortgagee under an activated assignment must be applied to taxes, repairs, insurance, and, in most states, the mortgage debt.

9. Whenever a mortgagee acts under an activated assignment, he does not destroy existing leases, as sometimes occurs when a mortgagee takes possession under his mortgage. An assignment preserves valuable leases.

10. A mortgagee acting under an assignment is accountable to the mortgagor only for rents actually collected.

11. When a mortgagee who holds an assignment of rents sells and assigns his mortgage, he should also assign the assignment of rents to the assignee of the mortgage. *Koury v. Sood,* 74 R.I. 486, 62 A.2d 649.

With respect to the language of the assignment, some suggestions might be pertinent:

1. It should be a document separate from the mortgage and should be recorded. It should assign the mortgagor's interest in all existing leases and the interest of the mortgagor, or his assignee, in leases that may be executed in the future by the mortgagor, or his assignees. Leases of any importance should be specifically set forth in the assignment.

SUGGESTED CLAUSE: Notwithstanding that this instrument is present assignment of said rents, it is understood and agreed that the undersigned has permission to collect the same and manage said real estate and improvements the same as if this assignment had not been given, if and so long as only the undersigned shall not be in any default whatever with respect to the payments of principal and/or interest due on said loan, or in the performance of any other obligation on our part to be performed thereunder, but this permission terminates automatically on the occurrence of default or breach of covenant.

2. The mortgage should refer to the assignment of rents and the assignment of rents to the mortgage, so that the mortgagee can resort to one or the other as convenience dictates, and should permit entry under mortgage as to part of the premises and under assignment as to other parts of the premises.

EXAMPLE: As to one store in the building a lease junior to the mortgage is so unfavorable that it should be terminated and the tenant ousted. Enter under the mortgage.

EXAMPLE: As to another store a lease junior to the mortgage is very favorable. Enter under the assignment.

3. The right to cancel or alter leases should be included.

4. The assignment should include the right to use and possession of furniture, appliances, and so forth. While such a provision will be helpful, neither a rent assignment nor the appointment of a receiver is a substitute for a security agreement and financing statement under the Uniform Commercial Code. In other words, if there is valuable personal property on the mortgaged premises, for example, a hotel, the mortgagee may not have the legal right to the possession of such personal property unless he has legal chattel security. 44 Yale L. J. 701.

5. The assignment should include the right to operate the business and to take possession of books and records.

6. The assignment should confer the right to apply rents to the payments on furniture bought on credit, to insurance premiums on personal property, and so forth.

7. The assignee should be given the right to apply rents to the mortgage debt. Otherwise some states limit application of rents collected to taxes and maintenance. *Western Loan Co. v. Mifflin,* 162 Wash. 33, 297 Pac. 743.

8. The document should provide that the assignee shall not be accountable for more monies than he actually receives from the mortgaged premises, nor shall he be liable for failure to collect rents.

9. The document should forbid any cancellation or modification of leases and should also forbid any prepayment of rent except the normal prepayment of monthly rent on the first of the month.

10. Authority should be given the assignee to sign the name of the mortgagor on all papers and documents in connection with the operation and management of the premises.

11. The assignment should provide that any assignee of the assignment shall have all the powers of the original assignee.

12. It should contain a recital that (a) all rents due to date have been collected and no concessions granted and that (b) no rents have been collected in advance.

13. It should provide that the assignee may execute new leases, including leases that extend beyond the redemption period.

Of course neither an assignment of rents nor any other device can make a good lease out of a bad one.

EXAMPLE: A shopping center lease to a department store provides that if 5 per cent or more of the parking lot is condemned, the tenant may terminate the lease. This is a key lease, providing revenue for retirement of the mortgage. It must be amended, because if 5 per cent or more of the parking lot is condemned, for example, for a street widening, and the tenant terminates the lease, the mortgage will go into default.

If the lease provides for a security deposit by the tenant with the landlord, an assignment of leases and rents standing alone gives the mortgagee no right to the security deposit. *Anuzis v. Gotowtt,* 248 Ill. App. 536; *Keusch v. Morrison,* 240 App. Div. 112, 269 N.Y.S. 169; 52 C.J.S. 473. Specific language should be included in the assignment transferring all rights in the security deposit.

§ 392. **Active assignment of leases and rents.** In recent times mortgage lenders have turned to a device that has certain advantages where a building is to be constructed with mortgage funds for a high-credit tenant. As soon as the lease is made, the landlord assigns his interest in the lease and all rents thereunder to the mortgage lender. The assignment calls for the mortgage lender to begin collecting rents *immediately* on completion of the building. The lease refers to the assignment, and it also is recorded, thus making certain that the mortgagee's rights are treated as recorded rights, good against the whole world. The lease is a "net" lease under which all taxes, insurance premiums, and so forth are borne by the lessee, and no burdens or payments are borne by the lessor or the mortgagee. The rent payments exactly equal the mortgage payments. A mortgage accompanies the transaction, but the main security is the assignment. The loan is for the full cost of construction of the building. With a high-credit tenant like Sears or Woolworth, a lender can lend with complete security on a transaction of this sort. The assignment is good against a subsequent bankruptcy of the lessor. It also prevails over subsequent federal liens, subsequent creditors of the mortgagor, subsequent attempts of the mortgagor to cancel the lease or obtain prepayment of the rent. In short virtually nothing can occur that will prevent full collection by the lender. The typical assignment of rents is not considered quite as invulnerable as this *active assignment*.

§ 393. **Deed of mortgaged premises.**   Generally when mortgaged land is sold, the mortgage is paid and released during the process of sale, for the reason that the existing mortgage usually does not meet the financing requirements of the buyer. For example, if land is sold for $15,000 and there is an existing mortgage of $13,000; which has been paid down to $6,000, the buyer will want a new mortgage of more than $6,000 in order to swing the deal. Thus it becomes necessary to retire the old mortgage in the process of closing the sale. However, it is perfectly possible to sell mortgaged land without providing for retirement of the old mortgage. Thus, assume that A owns land worth $15,000 on which there is a mortgage securing a debt of $5,000. The arrangement between seller and buyer can be that there will be a payment to the seller of the sale price ($15,000) less the amount of the mortgage debt ($5,000), namely, in this case, $10,000. Obviously the understanding here is that the buyer will pay the balance of the mortgage debt. In this situation where the buyer is to pay the mortgage debt as and when it matures, the deed from the seller to buyer may take one of the following forms:

1. The deed provides that it is subject to the mortgage, *which the purchaser assumes and agrees to pay*. This is called an *assumption clause*.

2. The deed may merely recite that the property is *subject to the mortgage*.

3. The deed may be a quitclaim deed with no subject clause.

The following rules apply:

1. When the deed of the mortgaged premises recites that the grantee *assumes and agrees to pay* the mortgage or *assumes the mortgage,* it imposes on the grantee *personal liability* for the payment of the mortgage debt. *Schmucker v. Sibert,* 18 Kan. 104. The mortgagee, when he forecloses, obtains a deficiency judgment, or deficiency decree, against such grantee, this being a personal judgment against such grantee for the difference between the amount of the foreclosure sale and the amount of the mortgage debt when the sale price is less than the amount of the debt.

2. Where the deed merely recites that the land is taken subject to the mortgage, the grantee is usually not personally liable for the payment of the mortgage debt. *Pearce v. Desper,* 11 Ill. 2d 569, 144 N.E. 2d 617.

3. Where the mortgagor enters into a contract to sell merely his equity over and above the mortgage and thereafter gives the buyer a quitclaim deed, the buyer does not become personally liable to the mortgagee.

§ 394. **Deed by mortgagor to mortgagee.**   At times a mortgagor will find that he is unable to pay the mortgage debt. In this event, the mortgagee may, of course, foreclose the mortgage. Foreclosure, however, usually costs the mortgagee time and money, and he may wish to make some arrangement with the mortgagor for acquiring ownership of the land without the necessity of foreclosure. This is accomplished by means of an agreement between mortgagor and mortgagee whereby the mortgagor agrees to sell the land to the mortgagee for a small sum of money and the mortgagee, in return, agrees to cancel the mortgage debt. The mortgagor thereupon gives the mortgagee a deed, and the mortgagee cancels the notes and releases the mortgage. The courts are inclined to be suspicious of such transactions, since the mortgagee is in a position to exert pressure on the mortgagor. To give validity to such a sale by the mortgagor, it must appear that the conduct of the mortgagee was, in all things, fair and frank and that he paid for the property what it was worth, and that he did not coerce the mortgagor into signing the deed. In order to protect himself, a mortgagee entering into such a transaction should take the following precautions:

1. He should examine the title to the land to make sure that no other liens, such as judgments or junior mortgages, attached to the land after the date of the mortgage.

2. A written contract should be entered into between the mortgagor and mortgagee. This contract should show that it was the mortgagor, not the mortgagee, who proposed the transaction. This renders it difficult for any court to hold that the mortgagor was coerced, since the agreement itself shows that he took the initiative in the transaction. The contract should also provide that the deed is given in full satisfaction of the mortgage debt. *Rooker v. Fidelity Trust Co.,* 185 Ind. 172, 109 N.E. 766.

3. The mortgage should be released and the mortgage and mortgage note canceled. If the mortgage debt is not canceled, courts tend to regard the deed as

merely additional security for the debt rather than an outright sale of the mortgagor's equity. 129 A.L.R. 1495.

4. The mortgagee should not enter into any contract to resell or reconvey the land to the mortgagor, though he may safely give the mortgagor an option to repurchase the premises. 129 A.L.R. 1473.

§ 395. Assignment of mortgage.   Often a mortgagee wishes to sell his mortgage. The manner in which this may be accomplished depends upon whether the mortgage in question is a regular mortgage or a trust deed. A trust deed is usually given to secure a negotiable note. A negotiable note is one intended to pass from hand to hand, very much as money. Such a note may be payable to the bearer. In that case, merely handing the note to the purchaser will be sufficient to transfer title thereto. Endorsement is unnecessary. If the note is payable to the order of a named person, that person must endorse the note over to the purchaser thereof. In the case of a trust deed securing negotiable notes, a sale of the mortgage is effected by properly transferring the notes by delivery or endorsement, depending on the character of the notes.

In the case of a regular mortgage, it is necessary to execute an assignment, which is a brief form providing that the mortgagee, the assignor, transfers and assigns the mortgage and mortgage note to the purchaser thereof, the assignee. The mortgage is identified by a recital of the names of the parties thereto, its date, the recording date, the book and page of the record where the mortgage is recorded, and so on. The assignment should be signed by the mortgagee, acknowledged, delivered to the assignee, and recorded. The mortgage note, too, should be endorsed or delivered to the assignee. The assignee should also receive the original mortgage.

The mortgage cannot be assigned except in connection with a sale of the mortgage debt. The reason for this is that the mortgage exists only for the purpose of securing payment of the mortgage debt, and a person who does not own the mortgage debt can have no reason for obtaining the mortgage. Thus the assignee of the mortgage must insist on receiving the mortgage note, since if the mortgagee has already transferred the mortgage note to someone else, he can no longer make a valid assignment of the mortgage.

On the other hand, whatever is sufficient to transfer the mortgage debt will transfer a mortgage given to secure it. This is because the debt secured by the mortgage is the principal thing and the mortgage is a mere security for its payment. Thus if a regular mortgage secures a promissory note, a transfer of the note, without any assignment of the mortgage, will give the purchaser of the note a right to foreclose the mortgage. But as a practical matter, for the assignee's protection it is necessary, as above stated, to obtain an assignment of the mortgage. The reason for this is that in the case of a trust deed securing negotiable notes, everyone is supposed to know that it is likely that the notes will be sold. However, in the case of a regular mortgage securing a note payable to the mortgagee, unless an assignment of the mortgage is filed in the recorder's, or register's, office, subsequent purchasers or mortgagees of the mortgaged premises are entitled to assume that the mortgagee continues to hold the mortgage note.

EXAMPLE: A executed a regular mortgage to B to secure a note payable to B's order. B endorsed the note to C, but no assignment of the mortgage was recorded. Thereafter, A sold the mortgaged land to B, and B entered a satisfaction of the mortgage on the public records. B then mortgaged the land to D. It was held that D's mortgage was a first mortgage on the land, since when D took his mortgage on the land, the earlier mortgage appeared from the public records to have been released by the apparent owner thereof. *Bowling v. Cook,* 39 Ia. 200.

When the mortgage secures a nonnegotiable note, a purchaser of the mortgage takes it subject to all defenses to which it was liable in the hands of the original mortgagee. This means that if the original mortgagee has been guilty of fraud or some other conduct that would make it impossible for him to foreclose the mortgage, any person to whom he sells the mortgage will also be unable to foreclose.

EXAMPLE: A mortgages his land to B to secure a nonnegotiable note for $5000, but B never pays out the money to A. B sells the mortgage to C. C will be unable to foreclose the mortgage.

Shortly before the Civil War, in an effort to give the purchaser of a mortgage better protection than he had enjoyed in the past, American mortgage bankers began the experiment of having the mortgage secure a negotiable note. The experiment proved highly successful. In all states except Illinois, Minnesota, and Ohio, it is now the rule that *a holder in due course* of a negotiable note secured by a mortgage, that is, one who buys the note and mortgage in good faith before the debt is overdue and without knowledge of any infirmities, takes the mortgage as well as the note, free from defenses that would have been available to the mortgagor against the original mortgagee. The theory is that negotiable notes, like money, should pass freely from hand to hand, without the necessity of any inquiry by purchasers thereof as to the possible invalidity of the paper. And since the mortgage is a mere security for the note, it should enjoy the same protection that the law accords to the note.

EXAMPLE: A gave B a mortgage securing a negotiable note for $50,000, but never received any money from B. B sold the note and mortgage to C before the due date of the note. C can foreclose the mortgage even though A never received the mortgage money. As an innocent purchaser of a negotiable note, C is protected against any defenses that exist between A and B.

A purchaser of a mortgage can also be protected against infirmities existing as between the mortgagor and the original mortgagee by insisting that he be furnished a statement signed by the mortgagor stating that he has no defenses to the enforcement of the mortgage. This document is variously called a *waiver of defenses, estopped certificate, no set-off certificate,* or *declaration of no defenses.* Under standard mortgage practice, it is addressed to "all whom it may concern" and is signed by the mortgagor at the time the mortgage is signed.

The practical effect of a waiver of defenses is to give the assignee a legally enforceable mortgage even though the mortgage does not secure a negotiable note and the mortgagee could not have foreclosed. For example, if the mortgagee had paid out no money or had received payment in full, he could not foreclose. But an assignee who receives a waiver of defenses can foreclose, since he received the mortgagor's written assurance that the mortgage is valid and enforceable. 59 C.J.S. 531; 110 A.L.R. 457.

> **EXAMPLE:** A gave B a mortgage securing a note for $50,000, but never received any money from B. B sold the note and mortgage to C before the due date of the note. B also delivered to C a waiver of defenses signed by A. C can foreclose the mortgage even though A never received the mortgage money. As an innocent purchaser relying on a waiver of defenses, C is protected against any defenses that exist between A and B.

Before purchasing a mortgage, one should always check the public records for any prior recorded assignment of the mortgage, since in many states, where there are two or more assignments of the mortgage by the mortgagee, the first recorded assignment prevails.

The assignee should also obtain the mortgagee's evidence of title, assignment of chattel security agreements, if any, and other such papers.

§ 396. **Notice of assignment.** The purchaser of a note secured by either a regular mortgage or trust deed should always give personal notice to the mortgagor that he has purchased such note. If he fails to do so, and the mortgagor afterward in good faith makes a payment to the original mortgagee, this payment will reduce the mortgage debt accordingly. This rule is generally followed where the mortgage note or bond is nonnegotiable.

Except in Illinois and Minnesota, it is the rule that the purchaser of a *negotiable note* need not notify the mortgagor of his purchase, and if the mortgagor continues to make payments to the original mortgagee, he cannot claim that the mortgage debt has been reduced thereby. This places the burden on the mortgagor of demanding production of the mortgage note and endorsement of each payment thereon.

In Illinois and Minnesota, even where the mortgage secures a negotiable note, the mortgagor may continue to make payments to the original lender until he receives notice of the assignment. *Napieralski v. Simon,* 198 Ill. 384, 164 N.E. 1042. The Illinois-Minnesota rule is based on the inconvenience to the mortgagor of requiring production of the mortgage paper each time a payment is made on the mortgage debt.

Whenever notice of assignment is necessary, the notice should be given personally to the mortgagor. Merely recording an assignment of the mortgage ordinarily will not suffice. The mortgagor should not be subject to the burden of making constant searches of the records to see if the mortgage has been assigned, especially since it requires little effort for the assignee to serve a personal notice on the mortgagor. 89 A.L.R. 196. However, any purchaser of the property from the mortgagor is usually required to take notice of such a recorded assignment. *Erickson v. Kendall,* 112 Wash. 26, 191 Pac. 842.

§ 397. **Payment.** The mortgagor, to release himself from personal liability on his note, must see that he pays the money to the holder of the note. This is also true of any purchaser of the mortgaged premises. He is bound at his peril to pay the debt to the one entitled to receive payment. On paying the mortgage note, the party paying should demand that the canceled note be delivered to him. This prevents any further transfer or negotiation of the note and is of particular importance where payment is made prior to the maturity of the note. The mortgagee, of course, need not accept payment before maturity unless the mortgage grants the mortgagor the privilege of prepayment.

§ 398. **Payment to agent.** A mortgagor, before making payment to a pretended agent of the mortgagee, should ascertain the agent's authority by inquiring of the mortgagee or by requiring the agent to produce a power of attorney from the mortgagee. *Coxe v. Kriebel,* 323 Pa. 157, 185 Atl. 770.

§ 399. **Release, satisfaction, or discharge of mortgage.** Although the payment of the mortgage debt discharges the mortgage, it nevertheless remains on the public records as a cloud upon the title until it has been released. The common method of releasing a trust deed or deed of trust is by execution, acknowledgment, delivery, and recording of *a release deed (also called deed of reconveyance)* executed under seal by the trustee. Such release deed by its terms releases and reconveys to the mortgagor all the title and interest that was conveyed by the trust deed. In the case of a regular mortgage, a similar instrument executed by the mortgagee—or assignee, if the mortgage has been assigned—is often used. A mortgagee may execute a *satisfaction or discharge* of the mortgage, in which the mortgagee certifies that the mortgage debt has been paid and the mortgage is therefore discharged. In most states, provision is also made for the entry of a satisfaction upon the margin of the record of the mortgage itself.

§ 400. **Limitations and extension agreements.**   In all states, a promissory note ceases to be enforceable after a certain time if no payments are made thereon. Such a note is said to be barred by *limitations*. The period varies from state to state. In most states, the fact that the mortgage note is barred by limitations only prevents the obtaining of a personal judgment on the note and does not prevent foreclosure of the mortgage. But in other states, the mortgage is automatically barred whenever the mortgage note is barred.

In many states, if a period of twenty years elapses after the maturity date of the mortgage note, the mortgage is presumed to be paid. The mortgagee, however, may overthrow this presumption by proving that the mortgage has not been paid, but has been kept alive by partial payments of principal or interest thereon. Since this rule makes it dangerous to disregard even an old recorded mortgage, some states go further and provide by law that after a stated period of time, the mortgage becomes void. The period varies from state to state. In Michigan it is thirty years; in Kentucky, fifteen years.

Chapter 21

CONSTRUCTION LOANS

§ 401. **In general.** Construction lending encounters some rather technical rules of law and involves some rather complicated paper work. Nevertheless the need for it is great and growing. America's appetite for new construction is insatiable.

Building operations depend on mortgage credit. Before subcontractors (electrical contractors, plumbing contractors, and so forth) and building material suppliers put their labor and materials into a house, they want to know where their money is coming from. Since the builder lacks the capital to pay these people from his own funds, he must be able to show them that he has a dependable source of mortgage money. Even if a dependable source of mortgage money exists, subcontractors and materialmen want their money rather promptly. Materialmen may extend credit for thirty or forty days. Subcontractors often want payment when they complete their particular portion of the construction job, which means that some mortgage lender must be persuaded to advance the mortgage money as the building goes up. And the only assurance subcontractors and materialmen have faith in is a binding contract by the mortgage house to advance the mortgage money as construction goes forward. This contract arises when the builder, as prospective mortgagor, applies in writing to a mortgage lender for the required mortgage loan and the mortgage lender gives its written commitment to lend the money.

§ 402. **Interim and permanent loans—takeout commitments.**

A construction loan requires considerable supervision on the part of the lender. This is for the business reason that the mortgage lender wants assurance that construction of the house actually will be completed; that the construction will not be faulty, but be according to the construction plans and specifications approved by the lender; and that no mechanics' liens will arise in the process of construction. Not all mortgage lenders are willing to engage in construction lending. Some want long-term permanent mortgages on completed buildings. On the other hand, mortgage lenders who do engage in construction lending (*interim lenders*) do not want their funds tied up over the long period of time, often fifteen years or longer, that it takes to pay off a mortgage. They want to turn their capital over constantly. Their income is derived not from interest on mortgage loans, but from *commissions* which the builder pays in order to receive the mortgage loan and from *service charges*. This latter item requires a word of explanation. In order to keep its capital turning over, the interim lender expects to sell the mortgage loan, after completion of construction, to a bank, insurance company, or other investor that is willing to take the mortgage as a permanent investment. The sale is usually to a *permanent lender* with whom the construction lender has some permanent working arrangement, that is, the construction lender may be a *loan correspondent* for the permanent lender. After completion of the building, the mortgage is sold and assigned to the *permanent lender,* and, after sale of the mortgage to the permanent lender, the loan correspondent looks after the payment of taxes and insurance renewals, collects the mortgage payments, and remits the payments to the permanent lender, making a charge, the *service charge,* for this service. Before he agrees to finance construction of the house, the interim lender insists on the issuance of a *takeout commitment* by the permanent lender, that is, an agreement by the permanent lender to buy the construction mortgage after the house has been completed free from mechanics' liens and after all risks of construction are over.

SUGGESTION TO CONSTRUCTION LENDER: Make the construction loan commitment subject to the same conditions as those contained in the takeout commitment. That is, if the permanent lender is making requirements, for example, as to chain store and other key leases that he wants signed, the construction loan commitment should be subject to the same requirements, so that when these are met, all you need do is see that the building is finished properly and on time, and you can then demand that the permanent lender take over. It is even a good idea to have all the documents required by the permanent lender prepared and approved as to form by the permanent lender before the construction loan agreement is signed. This will avoid the pitfall of having the construction loan commitment signed and then running into an insoluble difference with the permanent lender, thus forcing you to look elsewhere for a permanent lender.

As an alternative to this type of takeout commitment, an alternative made necessary because construction loans to builders, both under FHA regulations and principles of mortgage lending, are smaller in amount than loans on completed houses, the construction lender may be willing to finance construction if the builder can procure from some permanent lender a commitment to make a new mortgage loan when the building has been completed, the proceeds of the new mortgage loan to be used to pay off the construction mortgage. This is also called a takeout commitment. In home construction these commitments to make a permanent mortgage when construction has been completed are of two kinds. There is the *conditional commitment*, which is given the builder by the permanent lender to make a permanent mortgage loan to the home buyer when the house has been completed and sold to a buyer whose credit meets with the permanent lender's approval and who will sign the permanent mortgage. Here the permanent lender is not taking any risk as to the builder's ability to sell the house, for he is not obligated to lend until an acceptable home buyer has been found. And then there is the *firm commitment*. Here the permanent lender agrees to make his mortgage loan to the builder as soon as the house has been completed. The risks incident to construction of the house are avoided by the permanent lender and left with the construction lender, but the permanent lender gambles that the builder will either be able to sell the house or, if not, that he, the builder, can pay off the mortgage. Firm commitments often contain an additional agreement by the mortgage house to make a larger, permanent mortgage loan when the house is sold to a home owner who will sign a new permanent mortgage.

When the loan arrangements contemplate that the construction mortgage will be released and a new mortgage given to a permanent lender, usually the first step is for the prospective mortgagor in the permanent mortgage (the home buyer, if one has been procured; if not, the builder) to apply to the permanent lender for the permanent mortgage loan. The permanent lender then gives its commitment to this mortgagor, who then gives an assignment of the commitment to the construction lender. After the assignment has been given, the construction lender notifies the permanent lender of the assignment, so that no modifications or cancellations between the mortgagor and the permanent lender will be binding upon the construction lender. In other words, the assignment of commitment and notice thereof give the construction lender the legal right to enforce the commitment against the permanent lender.

§ 403. FHA commitments. In many construction projects, permanent lenders will agree to furnish permanent financing only if they are assured that such permanent mortgage will be insured by the FHA.

As proof that the loan ultimately will be insured, the permanent mortgage lender wants a *commitment from the FHA obligating it to insure the loan.* In addition to commitments by mortgage lenders to *give* mortgage loans and by mortgage lenders to *buy* mortgage loans, there are commitments by the FHA to *insure* mortgage loans. Commitments given to approved mortgage lenders by the FHA are again of two types. There is the *conditional commitment to insure,* which is an agreement by the FHA with the builder to insure the mortgage when (1) the building has been satisfactorily completed according to FHA standards as verified by FHA inspections, and (2) the building has been sold to a home buyer whose credit standing is satisfactory to the FHA and who will sign the permanent mortgage. Then there is the *firm commitment to insure.* The FHA agrees to insure a mortgage executed by the builder after the building has been completed to the FHA's satisfaction. The commitment is not conditional on sale of the building to a satisfactory purchaser. However, the firm commitment usually provides that the FHA will insure a later mortgage for a larger amount if a satisfactory purchaser is found. For this reason, FHA firm commitments to a builder are often called *dual commitments.*

Notice that FHA insurance of a mortgage loan on a home does not become binding until the building has been completed. Except on certain large-scale projects, the FHA is unwilling to assume the risk that the building will not be completed.

§ **404. Construction loan agreement.** A construction loan is paid out in installments as construction goes forward. During the construction period, which may extend over a year on big jobs, other liens may come into being. It is important to preserve the priority of the construction mortgage over such liens.

EXAMPLE: A records a construction mortgage to B on February 1, 1968. On March 1, 1968, construction begins. On April 1, 1968, B makes his first disbursement of construction funds to the general contractor and subcontractors. On May 1, 1968, A records another mortgage to C to obtain funds for final completion of a building on another tract of land and receives this money on May 15, 1968. On June 1, 1968, B makes another disbursement on the construction mortgage. B will wish to be certain that this disbursement and all subsequent disbursements have priority over C's mortgage. C will argue that he comes ahead of all disbursements made after the recording of his mortgage. Hence it is important that B come under the protection of the *obligatory advances rule.* See § 372. This means that before disbursement begins on the construction loan A and B should sign a construction loan agreement which obligates B to pay out the money as construction goes forward. Two problems arise in this connection:

1. It may be contended that the advances are, in fact, optional (rather than obligatory) if the construction loan agreement authorizes the mortgagee to stop making loan advances under certain circumstances, for example, when the construction fails to go forward according to the agreement. 80 A.L.R.2d 201. The fact that the agreement

gives the lender the privilege of discontinuing disbursement does not render subsequent advances optional. *Landers-Morrison-Christenson Co. v. Ambassador Holding Co.* (Minn.) 214 N.W. 503; *Hyman v. Hauff,* 138 N.Y. 48, 33 N.E. 735. In all contracts if one party stops performing the other party may also do so, but he need not do so. Third parties, such as junior lienors (second mortgagees, etc.) cannot force the lender to decide the often extremely difficult question of whether the borrower is inexcusably in default. He may, if he wishes, continue to perform, and indeed the law encourages him to do so. Moreover, the construction lender has no real choice. A half-finished building, subject to vandalism and destruction by the elements, is no security at all, and all mortgagees have the right to protect their investment by advancing additional funds, such as taxes and construction funds, and such advances enjoy full priority over liens attaching after the recording of the mortgage.

    2. The provisions of the construction loan agreement tend to be rather general and vague, such as the requirement that insurance policies be "satisfactory to the lender." It is sometimes argued that the agreement is void for uncertainty. For example, what kind of insurance was meant? Fire? Builder's risk? Liability? If the contract is void for uncertainty, all advances by the lender would be optional, and the lender's various advances might be subordinate to other liens, such as judgment liens attaching during the course of construction. As a matter of law, it is not necessary that all details be settled with precision. Reasonable satisfaction and reasonable certainty are adequate guide lines for judges and businessmen. *Collins v. Vickter Manor,* 47 Cal.2d 875, 306 P.2d 783. Such contracts are not void.

A good part of the construction lender's requirements can be incorporated in the lender's *printed form* construction loan agreement. Any deviation from the form should be covered in advance in the loan commitment, for legally a lender cannot demand provisions in the construction loan agreement that are not in the loan commitment. The loan commitment should, of course, call for the borrower to sign the lender's standard form construction loan agreement as modified by the loan commitment. This enables the lender to omit from the commitment a mass of detail that might frighten away a timid borrower.

    § **405. Matters to be answered by construction lender before disbursement begins.**   In making a construction loan, the lender asks himself some questions an intending builder would ask, such as:

    1. Will the building violate zoning laws either as to type of building or set-back lines?
    2. Will it violate recorded building restrictions?
    3. Does the building have the legal right to connect to sewer and water?
    4. Will the building interfere with existing drainage or utility lines?
    5. What does the survey show as to the true boundaries and area of the property and encroachments by the building or by adjoining owners?

All mortgage houses also follow certain practical precautions in construction loans. Each subcontractor's bid is checked to see that there is no underbid or overbid. If he underbids, he may threaten to walk out on the job unless he gets more money. If he overbids, the value simply is not there for the work done. Mortgagees also check the financial rating of homeowner and builder to see that the job is within their financial capacity. They require the homeowner to put up his share of the construction cost with the mortgagee, and this money is the first money used as construction begins.

§ 406. **Construction loan disbursement.**   Before any disbursement is made on bigger jobs, the lender will obtain a certificate from his architect that work is in place (according to the building contract, plans, and specifications in the lender's files) warranting the disbursement requested; he will have the owner's signed direction to make the disbursement; he will procure lien waivers as construction proceeds; he will have the architect certify that the balance of loan proceeds will suffice to complete the building; the lender will stop disbursement if unauthorized extras appear or liens appear or if loan proceeds appear inadequate to complete construction; at each disbursement, a date-down survey will be furnished showing that new construction is within lot lines and does not violate building lines or other regulations established by zoning ordinances, building codes, or private building restrictions.

§ 407. **Mechanic's lien protection.**   A mortgagee paying out a construction loan must protect both itself and the mortgagor against mechanics' liens. This is not an easy task. To accomplish this purpose some mortgage lenders arrange with a title insurance company to examine mechanic's lien waivers as construction goes forward. Under one such arrangement (*interim certification*), the owner, having funds for the first progress payments, pays his contractor, subcontractors and materialmen when the first payment falls due. He then is given lien waivers by each of the parties so paid, which he delivers to the title insurance company. The title insurance company examines them for sufficiency, also checking each waiver against the general contractor's affidavit which lists the persons who furnished work and material. When it is satisfied, it issues an endorsement to its policy insuring that, to the extent of the money thus paid out, the property is free and clear of mechanics' liens. In reliance on this endorsement, the mortgage lender pays to the owner money equal to the first such progress payment, and the process is repeated until the building is completed.

Alternatively, the title company is given the mortgage money in escrow, as progress payments are due, and pays to the persons who have furnished labor and material, using checks that contain a lien waiver, so that each mechanic cashing a check automatically, by endorsing it, waives his lien to the extent of the money so paid.

§ 408. **Suggestions to the construction lender to protect against mechanics' liens.**   Whether the loan proceeds are paid out by a title company or the mortgagee itself, certain precautions are necessary:

1. In a majority of the states (called *priority states*), if a mortgage is recorded and becomes a lien on the property *before any construction begins*, the mortgage will enjoy priority over any mechanic's lien arising out of such construction.

It is obvious that if visible construction actually begins before the mortgage is recorded or becomes a lien, some or probably all of the mechanics' liens will be prior and superior to the mortgage. It is therefore necessary for any construction mortgagee to know exactly when construction begins.

SUGGESTION: Immediately after recording of the mortgage, let the lender take affidavits from the builder and homeowner that construction has not begun or material been delivered to the site, and let him verify this by an actual inspection of the premises. The inspector should make a written report, with a photograph of the property, which report should be signed and dated and held in the mortgage file against the possibility of litigation.

In this connection, it is to be observed that staking off lots, cutting trees, and removing brush do not constitute the commencement of construction. They are merely preparatory to the commencement of construction. *Clark v. General Electric Co.*, 243 Ark. 399, 420 S.W.2d 830; *Reuben E. Johnson Co. v. Phelps*, 156 N.W.2d 247 (Minn.). For work to constitute the commencement of construction, within the meaning of the rule, it must be of such a substantial and conspicuous character as to make it reasonably apparent that building has actually begun.

2. In any state where prior recording of the mortgage gives the mortgagee no protection, the mortgagee usually has no choice but to see that no mechanic's lien claims are filed. Keep in mind, also, that increasingly today courts require the construction lender to protect the mortgagor against mechanics' liens. The construction lender should therefore procure from the general contractor a sworn list of all the subcontractors he has hired, and as each disbursement is made, he procures a supplementary affidavit reflecting any changes. Each such affidavit shows how much work or materials each subcontractor has put in, and each subcontractor, on receiving payment of that amount, gives a *partial lien waiver* for all work and materials furnished *to the date of the affidavit*. The general contractor also gives such waivers. Dollar amounts recited in the affidavits are checked against dollar amounts recited in the lien waivers. Any discrepancy is questioned for it may reveal an unauthorized extra. As each subcontractor receives *final* payment for his work, he gives a *final waiver* for all work and materials *furnished or to be furnished* so that he can claim no lien for work needed to correct defective construction that shows up. Special state statutes should be followed. In Florida, the mortgagee should record the construction mortgage at least one day before notice of commencement of construction is recorded. In California, the mortgagee should record a notice of completion as soon as construction has been completed, for this starts the running of the period for the filing of mechanics' liens. (See § 345.)

The *landowner* also gives the mortgagee an affidavit listing all persons furnishing work or materials on *his order*, for some owners let work out to parties other than the main contractor.

The mortgagee makes payouts as the building goes up, according to a schedule included in the construction loan agreement. He makes payouts directly to the subcontractors. The general contractor often brings in waivers signed by subcontractors, states that he has paid them in full, and asks that he be paid the amount represented by these waivers. To comply is risky. A dishonest builder will forge lien waivers. Such waivers are void. And even if the lien waivers are genuine, the builder may have paid the subcontractors with "rubber" checks, and when the checks "bounce," the subcontractors may file foreclosure suits despite the lien waivers. Probably they will not prevail in such suits, for the homeowner or mortgagee relied on the lien waivers in paying out, and the courts would say that the subcontractors are therefore barred or *estopped* from repudiating their lien waivers. *P. A. Lord Lumber Co. v. Callahan,* 181 Ill. App. 323; *McClelland v. Hamernick,* 264 Minn., 345, 118 N.W.2d 791. Check each lien waiver carefully. Most of them come from corporations, and if the corporate seal is attached and a certificate of acknowledgment appears thereon, you can depend on its regularity. Trouble arises with respect to the thousands of unincorporated enterprises. You may get a lien waiver by "Triangle Plumbers," whoever they are, signed by "Joseph Doakes," whoever he is. He might be the office boy, of course, and wholly unauthorized to sign anything. Verify these the best way you can. Often a phone call will suffice.

Before making payment to any subcontractor, the lender should require him to sign a verified statement as to all material put into the job and any sub-subcontractors he has hired. Just as in many states the law requires you to see that all the general contractor's subcontractors are fully paid, so it is required in many states that you see that each subcontractor's sub-subcontractors are fully paid. If any material used was procured on credit, you must make payment to, and get a waiver from, the materialman for he is also entitled to a lien.

3. The lender should hold back part of the final payout until the time for filing or serving lien claims has been passed. (See §§ 342, 345.) Check the records for lien claims before making this last payout.

4. The mortgagee may insist that the building contract contain a waiver of all mechanics' liens and be recorded in the recorder's office. In some states (Illinois and Indiana, for example) this wipes out all mechanics' liens. 76 A.L.R.2d 1097. Its practical disadvantage is that subcontractors may refuse to work on such a job if they get wind of this blanket waiver.

Cross reference: § 444.

§ 409. Contractor's bonds.   On large construction projects surety company bonds are often employed to provide assurance that the building will be completed according to contract and free and clear of any mechanic's lien claims. Such bonds provide protection against events such as the following: (1) The general contractor goes bankrupt, and a new contractor demands a higher price to complete the building. (2) The general contractor finds that he has underbid the job and simply refuses to go forward with it. (3) The general contractor completes the job but fails to pay his subcontractors, who therefore file mechanic's lien claims against the property.

Since this area of law is extremely technical, some oversimplification becomes necessary. The owner gets his best protection when he receives two bonds from the surety company, both on forms approved by the American Institute of Architects (AIA). One bond, the *performance bond,* provides assurance that the building will be completed as per contract. If the general contractor fails to do so, the bonding company takes over and completes the job. The bonding company also gives the owner an AIA *payment bond* which assures the owner that material and labor furnished in construction of the building will be fully paid for, so that no mechanics' liens will be filed. These bonds contemplate that the owner will adhere to the construction contract. For example, contracts on big construction usually call for progress payments to be made at various phases of construction, and the general contractor is to be paid for a phase only when and if the owner's architect certifies that this phase has been properly completed and lien waivers have been produced by the general contractor showing that all subcontractors and materialmen have been paid for work and material on this phase. Such provisions protect the bonding company.

EXAMPLE: If the owner pays the general contractor in advance, before the phase is completed, or pays without requiring production of lien waivers as called for by the construction contract, the owner will lose all his bond protection.

The *payment bond* protects the subcontractors and materialmen. Thus, if a subcontractor is not paid, he can take his claim directly to the bonding company. And even if the owner loses all his bond protection on the performance bond because of his failure to abide by the construction contract, the subcontractors and materialmen retain their protection under the payment bond. 77 A.L.R. 62, 118 A.L.R. 66.

When an owner hires a reliable contractor and obtains surety bonds, he has good protection. The general contractor knows that if he falls down on the job and the bonding company is compelled to step in, the word will get around, and the contractor will be unable to get a surety bond on his next job. In other words, the contractor must keep his credit good with the bonding companies or he is out of business.

The mortgage lender who is advancing the construction funds also wishes to be protected by the surety bonds. Bonding companies are usually willing to add the name of the mortgagee as a party protected by the surety bonds. However, the bonding company will then add a clause to the bonds that is commonly called the *Los Angeles clause*. In practical effect, this clause makes the mortgage lender's protection contingent upon the owner's performing his part of the bargain under the construction contract. The philosophy here is that the bonding company carefully checks the general contractor and is willing to guarantee that *he* will do his job, but is unwilling to insure that *the owner* will do his job. Thus, for example, if a construction job will cost $10,000,000, of which $8,000,0000 will be supplied by the mortgage lender and $2,000,000 will be supplied by the owner, the mortgage lender is not protected if the owner fails to come up with his $2,000,000.

In certain situations the bonding company will be willing to give the construction lender a *completion bond*. This is a bond that assures the lender that the building will be completed according to contract and free and clear of mechanics' liens. Here the bonding company is assuring that both the contractor and the owner will perform properly. This would be in a situation, for example, where a bank is constructing a new bank building and is borrowing part of the construction money from an insurance company. The bonding company is willing to assure the insurance company that a top-notch contractor and a reliable bank working together will complete the building properly and free of all liens.

In some states, one wishing to free his land from filed mechanics' liens may procure and file in some public office a surety company bond protecting against such liens. *Jungbert v. Marrett*, 313 Ky. 338, 231 S.W.2d 84. Of course if such a bond is requested, the surety company will probably ask to have collateral put up, but the bond wipes out the liens and insures litigation at leisure with the mechanics' lien claimants if there is any contention that their work was done improperly. Almost everywhere, purchasers, mortgagees, and title companies will accept such surety bonds, even though there is no law that the bond wipes out the lien.

§ 410. **Negligence in disbursement.**   The mortgagee must exercise care in disbursing the loan proceeds for he may become personally liable to the mortgagor for any loss suffered by the mortgagor owing to the mortgagee's negligence.

EXAMPLE: (1) The mortgagee paid all construction funds to general contractor when the building was only one-third completed. *Robinson v. Keaton,* 239 Ark. 587, 393 S.W.2d 231. (2) The mortgagee disbursed construction funds without checking to see if construction work was in place to warrant such disbursement. *Equitable S. & L. Ass'n. v. Hewitt,* 67 Ore. 280, 135 P. 864. (3) The mortgagee paid out construction funds without demanding lien waivers or paid bills. In all such cases the mortgagee was held liable for loss resulting to the mortgagor. In other words, in recent times the courts have felt that the mortgagee paying out a construction loan has a duty to protect the mortgagor as well as his own interests. *Speights v. Arkansas S. & L. Assn.,* 239 Ark. 587, 393 S.W.2d 228; *Home Electric Corp. v. Russell,* 17 Utah 2d 276, 409 P.2d 388; *Hummell v. Wichita F. S. & L. Assn.,* 190 Kan. 43, 372 P.2d 67.

Chapter 22

CLOSING
MORTGAGE LOANS

§ **411. Closing defined.**   Just as a sale is *closed* by delivery of the deed to the buyer and delivery of the balance of the purchase price to the seller after examination of the title and disposition of other details, for the protection of buyer and seller, so a mortgage transaction is *closed* by delivery of the mortgage and note to the lender and disbursement of the mortgage funds to the mortgagor after attending to the details that insure the mortgagee that he has a good first lien on the property.

§ **412. Title defects.**   It is, of course, important to the mortgagee to be sure that his mortgage is a first lien on the land and that no title defects exist. Among the precautions he would take in this regard are the following:

1. Check mortgage for errors in filling blanks, signatures, witnesses, acknowledgment, etc. Have mortgage filed or recorded and bring abstract or other evidence of title down to cover the date of the recording of the mortgage before paying out. This will disclose any other liens that have appeared of record prior to the recording of the mortgage. Any such liens should be paid and released or subordinated to the mortgage. The prudent lender will weigh the true worth of the various means of evidencing title. Sophisticated lenders tend to insist on the ALTA mortgage title insurance policy. Among other advantages, it insures that the mortgage is valid and enforceable. It also insures against unfiled mechanics' liens, unrecorded leases, unrecorded easements, encroachments and other questions of survey, and lack of legal access to the mortgaged property. If the lender is forwarding funds to a title company's agent or its approved attorney, the lender should insist on receiving its *insured closing letter*, which

insures the mortgagee against embezzlement of loan funds or the agent's failure to follow the mortgagee's directions. This, incidentally, insures the lender that all prior liens shown on the title search will be paid off, for all mortgagee's directions require this, and the insured closing letter insures that this will be done. If the mortgage is being assigned to your company, require the title company to issue its endorsement to the mortgage title policy insuring the validity of the assignment and substituting the name of your company as the party assured.

2. Analyze all objections to the mortgagor's title disclosed by the examination of title. All defects in title should be cleared. If the title search reveals building restrictions or conditions, ascertain whether existing buildings violate such restrictions.

3. The mortgagee should inquire into the rights of parties in possession for the purpose of discovering unrecorded leases with options to purchase, unrecorded deeds and contracts, unrecorded easements, and so on. He must keep in mind the fact that the mortgagee, in nearly all states, takes his mortgage subject to the interests of all parties in possession of the premises.

4. The mortgagee should: (a) Inspect the building carefully for signs of recent work, and if any appears, demand to see paid bills and demand mechanic's lien waivers for any substantial work, as in construction loans. (b) Get affidavit from mortgagor that all work or materials furnished to premises have been paid in full, which, if false, will subject him to criminal prosecution. (c) If the building is occupied by persons other than the mortgagor (tenant, contract purchaser, and so on), see that notice of nonliability for mechanics' liens is posted on the property in the states where such notice is effective.

5. A survey should be obtained to determine whether any encroachments or other survey defects exist.

6. The mortgagee should obtain the usual mortgagor's affidavit to the effect that there are no judgments, divorces, bankruptcies, and so on against such mortgagor.

§ 413.   Zoning and building code violations.   A check should be made for violations of local zoning and building ordinances which the mortgagee might be compelled to remedy at his own expense were he to acquire title by foreclosure.

§ 414.   Insurance.   Existing fire insurance policies should be checked to determine that the amounts thereof are adequate and that the policies are properly written, and mortgagee clauses should be attached.

§ 415.   Suggestions as to the loan closing statement.

Seldom does the borrower receive the full amount of the mortgage loan. Various deductions are made for title searches, surveys, recording fees, and other items. Therefore, on disbursement of the loan, the mortgagee will prepare a loan settlement statement similar to that prepared in sales of land. This form should be used for three reasons: (1) it furnishes the borrower with a complete record of all disbursements made by the mortgagee from the proceeds of the loan; (2) it provides the mortgagee signed authorization by the borrower for all such disbursements and thus eliminates all possibility of any legal action that might be taken if the mortgagor claims improper charges were made against his loan; and (3) in those cases where there is no binding loan commitment, it fixes the date on which the mortgage becomes a lien on the land, since where there is no binding commitment, the mortgage does not become a lien on the land in some states until the date on which the loan is paid out to the mortgagor. In general, this settlement statement shows the full amount of the loan, and beneath that sum shows all deductions from it and their amount. It also shows the net amount available to the mortgagor and contains an acknowledgment by him that he has received that amount. The statement should be dated and signed by both mortgagor and mortgagee. The loan settlement statement is signed when the loan is closed.

§ 416. Documents of the loan file.

The mortgagee's loan file should include the following papers:

1. Application for loan, signed by borrower, and copy of mortgagee's letter of commitment.

2. Plat of survey

3. If loan is made to finance purchase of property, the mortgagee should have a copy of the contract of sale in his files. This will prove helpful in making appraisal of property.

4. Appraisal of property

5. Mortgage, mortgage note, chattel lien on personal property in building, and assignment of rents and leases

6. Assignment of mortgage and waiver of defenses if loan was purchased from original lender

7. Operating statement showing borrower's profit and loss figures for last fiscal year. Also audited financial statement. These help in determining borrower's financial responsibility on bigger loans.

8. Insurance policies, with mortgagee loss clauses attached

9. Abstract and opinion, mortgage title policy, Torrens certificate, or other evidence of title

10. Mortgagor's affidavit as to judgments, divorces, recent improvements, and other pertinent facts

11. Copy of escrow agreement, if loan was closed in escrow

12. Loan closing statement, including receipt for loan proceeds signed by borrowers

13. If loan was a refinancing loan, the canceled mortgage and note that was taken up by the new loan

14. Waiver of encroachments by FHA, and all other FHA documents, which, of course, applies only when loan is FHA-insured

15. Loan guaranty certificate and other documents needed in case of loans insured under the G.I. bill, or copies of such documents. If the loan is a G.I. loan, the form of application, loan closing statement, and appraisal report must be as specified by the regulations. The appraiser and credit agency should be required to submit two copies of their reports, so that mortgagee can retain copies for his files.

16. Subordination of reverter if one was obtained. If any other prior mortgage or other lien was subordinated to the current mortgage, the subordination agreement, of course, should also be in the loan files.

17. Certified copy of corporate resolutions if mortgage was made by corporation. If property mortgaged is all, or substantially all, of the assets of corporation, resolutions by both directors and stockholders may be necessary.

18. Will, trust indenture, or other trust instrument, or copy of these, if mortgagor is a trustee

19. Full copy of building restrictions affecting the mortgaged premises, particularly if loan is a construction loan

20. Leases to key tenants and assignments thereof to mortgagee

21. Where a franchised chain is involved, e.g., a Holiday Inn, the mortgage should give the lender the right to declare the mortgage debt due if the franchise is revoked. It should also provide that the mortgage can expend any sums needed to retain or revive the franchise and add these sums to the mortgage debt. Likewise, the mortgagee should have a side agreement with the chain that in case of foreclosure the chain will franchise the mortgagee as an operator and will render technical aid to bring the operation up to chain standards.

Chapter 23

FORECLOSURE
AND REDEMPTION

§ **417. Necessity of foreclosure.** When a mortgage goes into default after all efforts to salvage the property for the mortgagor by sale, refinancing, and so forth have failed, the mortgagee must foreclose his mortgage, for it is only by foreclosure that he can acquire ownership of the property.

§ **418. Types of foreclosures.** Methods of foreclosure vary from state to state. A common method involves a court proceeding filed by the mortgagee, called a foreclosure suit. In such suits the court orders a public auction sale of the property, and the sale is held by an officer of the court, called variously a sheriff, master in chancery, or commissioner. Up to the time of the foreclosure sale, the mortgagor, his wife, any junior mortgagee, or even the mortgagor's tenant may come in, pay off the mortgage, and stop the foreclosure. This, you will remember, is the equitable right of redemption. (See § 331.) In states that have statutory redemption, the highest bidder at the foreclosure sale usually receives a certificate of sale reciting that he will be entitled to a deed if no redemption is made. In states that do not have a statutory redemption period, the highest bidder receives a deed to the land, and this deed gives him ownership of the mortgaged land, free and clear of the rights of the mortgagor.

§ **419. Statutory redemption.** The equitable right of redemption is cut off by a sale under a foreclosure judgment, or decree, since that was the object of the foreclosure suit. After the foreclosure sale, in many states, an entirely different right arises, called the statutory right of redemption. Laws providing for statutory redemption give the mortgagor and other persons interested in the land, or certain classes of such persons, the right to redeem from the sale within a certain period, usually one year, but varying in different states from two months to two years after the sale.

Most statutory redemption laws were passed in a time when America was predominantly agricultural. Most mortgagors were farmers. When the weather was bad, crops failed, and foreclosures followed. It seemed logical to suppose that next year might bring better weather and good crops. Hence laws created the statutory redemption period, usually one year, and usually with the law so worded that the mortgagor had the right to possession during that year.

At the expiration of the redemption period, if redemption has not been made, the purchaser at the foreclosure sale receives a deed from the officer who made the sale.

Statutory redemption is usually accomplished by payment to the officer who made the sale, or to some other person designated by law, of the amount of the foreclosure sale and interest. After redemption the mortgagor holds the land free and clear of the mortgage and the foreclosure sale.

In a number of states there is no statutory redemption after sale. Immediately after the foreclosure sale a deed is given to the purchaser, and he thereupon acquires ownership of the land. In states that do not permit redemption after the foreclosure sale, provision is often made for postponing the sale in some way in order to permit the mortgagor to effect a redemption or discharge of the mortgage prior to the foreclosure sale.

§ 420. **Deficiency judgment.** A mortgage foreclosure sale is regarded as a payment of the mortgage debt in an amount equal to the sale price. If the foreclosure judgment, or decree, finds that there is $5000 due to the mortgagee on his mortgage, and the property is sold for $4500, the mortgage debt is thereby reduced by $4500, leaving a deficiency of $500 due the mortgagee. Since by virtue of the promissory note that usually accompanies a mortgage, the mortagor becomes personally liable to the mortgagee for the mortgage debt, the mortgagee is entitled to a personal judgment against the mortgagor for the amount of the deficiency.

In many states, laws have been passed limiting the mortgagee's right to a deficiency decree.

§ 421. **Foreclosure by exercise of power of sale.** In many states, mortgages may be foreclosed by exercise of a power of sale without resort to any court proceedings. If the mortgage is, in form, a trust deed, a provision will be found therein conferring on the trustee the power to sell the land in the event of a default in the mortgage payments. If the instrument is a regular mortgage, the power of sale is conferred on the mortgagee. However, in Colorado, the power of sale must be exercised by an official known as the public trustee, and in Minnesota, the sale is made by the sheriff or his deputy.

In states where this method of foreclosure is employed, the mortgage or trust deed spells out the events of default that will give the trustee or mortgagee power to sell the premises, and it also sets forth the notice of sale that must be given and the other formalities that must be complied with in making the sale. The state law may also specify the notice of sale that is to be given. In some states, personal notice to the mortgagor is necessary, but in others, advertisement is sufficient. Some state laws provide that a notice of default must be recorded and a stated period of time must elapse thereafter before the sale is held. This gives the mortgagor a final opportunity to pay his debt.

Unless the mortgage allows him to do so, the mortgagee cannot purchase the property at his own foreclosure sale, either in his own or his wife's name, or in the name of some third party, and if he does so, the sale may be set aside. *Mills v. Mutual B. & L. Assn.*, 216 N.C. 664, 6 S.E.2d 549. The trustee in a trust deed is likewise forbidden to purchase at his own foreclosure sale. However, the holder of the notes secured by a trust deed is permitted to purchase at the trustee's sale. Trust deed forms usually expressly permit the trustee to bid at the foreclosure sale, and such provisions are valid. Experience indicates that there will be fewer lawsuits attacking foreclosure sales if the sale is held by some impartial individual. A lender who uses some individual in his employment as trustee in his trust deeds often finds it expedient to appoint some disinterested third party as trustee if foreclosure becomes necessary.

The sale is usually at public auction, and a deed is executed to the highest bidder. Whether or not redemption is allowed depends on the local law.

§ 422. **Foreclosure by other methods.**   Other methods of foreclosure—strict foreclosure, foreclosure by entry and possession, and foreclosure by writ of entry—are allowed in a small number of states. These involve technical procedures that are only of local interest.

§ 423. **Mortgagee as purchaser at foreclosure sale.**   For several reasons, the mortgagee is often the only bidder at the foreclosure sale. For one, the mortgagee is allowed to bid up to the amount of the mortgage debt without producing any cash. The reason is obvious. If he were to pay cash, the officer holding the sale would have to hand the cash back to him in payment of the mortgage debt, for after all, the sale is held to raise money to pay the mortgagee. In practice, the handing back and forth of the cash is omitted. Again, in states that have redemption laws the highest bidder will not get ownership of or possession of the property until the redemption period is over, and then only if no redemption is made. Land speculators, who are the chief bidders at public land sales, are unwilling to have their money tied up for long periods with such uncertainty as to ultimate ownership of the property.

§ 424. **Soldiers' and Sailors' Civil Relief Act.**   The Soldiers' and Sailors' Civil Relief Act, passed by the Congress of the United States, affects mortgages in several ways.

1. The court in which proceedings to enforce the mortgage are brought is given power to stay or postpone the foreclosure proceedings.

2. If the landowner is in military service, the mortgage cannot be foreclosed by exercise of the power of sale contained in the mortgage unless the mortgagee first obtains a court order authorizing such foreclosure. If the mortgagee does not know whether or not the owner is in military service, he is gambling if he simply forecloses by exercise of the power of sale. If the owner is not in military service and has not been in military service within three months of the date of the sale, the sale is valid, while if the owner is in military service or was in military service at any time within three months of the date of the foreclosure sale, the foreclosure is void. For this reason, the mortgagee may prefer to foreclose his mortgage by foreclosure suit, even though the mortgage contains a power of sale, since he is thus assured of acquiring good title.

3. In states that have a redemption period following the foreclosure sale, it is now the law that the period of military service shall not be included in computing the redemption period. If a mortgage is foreclosed while the landowner is in military service, the redemption period may be indefinitely prolonged. *Bank of Springfield v. Gwinn*, 390 Ill. 345, 61 N.E.2d 249.

4. The holder of an obligation of a person in military service that bears interest at a rate in excess of 6 per cent is allowed to collect only 6 per cent interest during the period of military service, unless the mortgagor's ability to pay interest is not affected by his military service.

A career soldier is not entitled to the benefit of this statute.

Chapter 24

FHA LOAN INSURANCE

§ 425. **In general.** The Federal Housing Administration was established in 1934 to encourage improvement in housing standards and conditions, to provide an adequate home-financing system by insurance of housing mortgages and credit, and to exert a stabilizing influence on the mortgage market.

The FHA does not make loans or build houses, but it operates insurance programs under provisions of the National Housing Act. The FHA provides lenders with insurance against loss on home and housing project mortgages and property improvement loans made by them. The FHA charges a premium on every loan it insures, and this income—plus fees and interest received on its investments—is enough to pay its expenses and· to establish its insurance reserves.

The FHA mortgage program dealt with here is under Title II. Under Section 203 of Title II, Congress created an insurance fund to provide against possible losses due to the underwriting by the FHA of eligible mortgages on dwellings. The money is loaned by a private lender, not by the government. To be eligible for insurance under this section, the mortgage must meet the various conditions specified in the law and in the rules adopted by the FHA. The rules specify a maximum principal amount, maximum maturity, and maximum interest rate for all insurable loans. Each loan must be payable in monthly installments, which must include provisions for payments on real estate taxes, special assessments, ground rents, fire insurance, and the small mortgage insurance premium charged by the FHA for insuring the loan. The mortgage must be made on a form approved by the FHA and must be a first lien on land or on a lease that has not less than fifty years to run from the date of the mortgage.

If the lender wishes to have the loan insured, application by the borrower for the loan must be made on a form prepared by the FHA. After the loan has been approved by the lender, the application is forwarded to the FHA, together with a credit report on the mortgagors. If the loan is to finance new construction, plans, specifications, and other data must be furnished. If the loan is accepted for insurance by the FHA, a commitment for insurance is forwarded to the lender, which is then assured that if the loan is made, it will be insured under Section 203. When the FHA has ascertained that the terms of its commitment to insure have been complied with, it will endorse the mortgage note to show that it has been insured.

The cost of this insurance is covered by premiums that are collected by the lender from the mortgagor as an additional part of his regular mortgage payments.

Since the commitment is based upon the application, it is important that the application be filled out correctly. Correct information should be furnished as to street address, legal description, lot dimensions, and so on. Further, if the mortgage is later defaulted, the mortgagee must be able to deliver clear title to the FHA.

FHA considers the following title objections permissible:

1. Violations of a restriction based on race, color, or creed, even where such restriction provides for a penalty of reversion or forfeiture of title or a lien for liquidated damage;

2. a. Customary easements for public utilities, party walls, driveways, and other purposes.

   b. Easements for public utilities along one or more of the property lines and extending not more than 10 feet therefrom and for drainage or irrigation ditches along the rear 10 feet of the property, provided the exercise of the rights thereunder do not interfere with any of the buildings or improvements located on the subject property.

3. Easements for underground conduits which are in place and do not extend under any buildings on the subject property;

4. Mutual easements for joint driveways constructed partly on the subject property and partly on adjoining property, provided the agreements creating such easements are of record;

5. Encroachments on the subject property by improvements on adjoining property where such encroachments do not exceed 1 foot, provided such encroachments do not touch any buildings or interfere with the use of any improvements on the subject property;

6. Encroachments on adjoining property by eaves and overhanging projections attached to improvements on subject property where such encroachments do not exceed 1 foot;

7. Encroachments on adjoining property by hedges, wooden or wire fences belonging to the subject property;

8. Encroachments on adjoining property by driveways belonging to subject property where such encroachments do not exceed 1 foot, provided there exists a clearance of at least 8 feet between the buildings on the subject property and the property line affected by the encroachment;

9. Variations between the length of the subject property lines as shown on the application for insurance and as shown by the record or possession lines, provided such variations do not interfere with the use of any of the improvements on the subject property and do not involve a deficiency of more than 2 per cent with respect to the length of the front line or more than 5 per cent with respect to the length of any other line;

10. Encroachments by garages or improvements other than those which are attached to, or a portion of, the main dwelling structure over easements for public utilities, provided such encroachment does not interfere with the use of the easement or the exercise of the rights of repair and maintenance in connection therewith;

11. Violations of cost or set back restrictions which do not provide a penalty of reversion or forfeiture of title, or a lien for liquidated damages which may be superior to the lien of the insured mortgage. Violations of such restrictions which do provide for such penalties, provided such penalty rights have been duly released or subordinated to the lien of the insured mortgage, or provided a policy of title insurance is furnished expressly insuring the Commissioner against loss by reason of such penalties.

12. Customary building and use restrictions which:

a. Are coupled with a reversionary clause, provided there has been no violation prior to the date of the deed to the Commissioner; or

b. Are not coupled with a reversionary clause and have not been violated to a material extent.

13. Outstanding oil, water or mineral rights (or damage caused by the exercise of such rights) which are customarily waived by prudent leading institutions and leading attorneys in the community;

14. The voluntary or involuntary conveyance of a part of the subject property pursuant to condemnation proceedings or in lieu of condemnation proceedings, if;

a. The part conveyed does not exceed 10 percent by area of the property;

b. No damage to existing structures, improvements, or unrepaired damage to sewage, water, or paving has been suffered;

c. All of the payment received as compensation for the taking by condemnation or conveyance in lieu of condemnation has been applied to reduction of the mortgage indebtedness;

d. The conveyance occurred subsequent to insurance of the mortgage; and

e. There is included, with the documents and information furnished the Commissioner with the application for insurance benefits, a statement by the mortgagee that the requirements of this paragraph have been met.

Notice that FHA accepts certain "customary" easements and certain "customary" building and use restrictions. Formerly FHA made the decision as to what was acceptable. Today it is the mortgage lender and his lawyer who make this decision.

When the title evidence submitted in support of an insurance claim discloses the existence of these minor title exceptions, FHA will accept as satisfactory that which is acceptable to prudent lending institutions and leading attorneys in the community in which the property is located. Mortgage lenders may rely upon the advice of their attorneys as to what is common and customary in an area. It is unnecessary to ask the insuring office for a determination. The FHA will accept the determination of the mortgagee as to what is common and customary for the area.

If the mortgage lender's attorney concludes that a given title objection goes beyond what FHA allows, he submits the matter to the local insuring office, which may "waive" or accept the objection, or refuse to insure.

Despite the liberalization of the rules as above stated, it is still good practice for the lender, in his application for loan insurance, to describe fully all easements, restrictions and title objections, and, if, with full knowledge of these matters, FHA gives a commitment to insure, the lender is sure he has the insurance.

If, after acquiring ownership by foreclosure of the mortgage, the insured lender finds that the title is burdened with an objection he has not disclosed to FHA and which goes beyond the scope of the permitted objections, this will result in a reduction of the amount of debentures which FHA will pay for the property.

The Title II rules are different from the rules governing multifamily buildings. In the latter FHA attorneys pass on the title in each case before approving the loan for insurance.

The FHA will not insure property on which a racial restriction has been recorded subsequent to February 15, 1950, and prior to the recording of the insured mortgage. FHA rules forbid the placing of any racial restriction on the property until after the mortgage has been paid.

In the sale or lease of property that is subject to an FHA-insured mortgage loan, all racial discrimination is forbidden by law. Likewise, any lending institution must refrain from racial discrimination in making FHA loans. Executive Order 11063, November 14, 1962.

The FHA, of course, reserves the right to approve or disapprove the location or size of the land or the type of building thereon.

When the FHA is insuring a loan made to an operative builder, the builder must give the purchaser a warranty that the building was constructed in substantial conformity with the plans and specifications filed with the FHA.

The mortgagee should not release the mortgagor's personal liability or any property from the mortgage lien without FHA consent.

If the mortgagor defaults on an insured loan, the mortgagee must determine whether or not it will resort to the insurance provided by the FHA. The mortgagee, of course, may decide to keep the property after foreclosure and thus, in effect, disregard the insurance. If, however, the mortgagee decides to take advantage of its insurance, as will usually be the case, the mortgagee must notify the FHA of the default and promptly institute foreclosure proceedings. After acquiring title, the mortgagee must convey clear title to the Federal Housing Commissioner. In return, the mortgagee receives debentures guaranteed both as to principal and interest by the United States, which are, in effect, government bonds. These debentures bear interest. They are issued as of the date on which foreclosure proceedings were instituted or on which the property was otherwise acquired. They are issued in an amount equal to the unpaid amount of the principal of the mortgage plus all sums paid by the mortgagee for taxes, ground rents, water rates, and insurance on the property between the date of default and the date of conveyance. In certain cases, up to $75 will be added for foreclosure costs. In addition to the debentures, the mortgagee will receive a certificate of claim, which becomes payable upon disposition of the property by the FHA. This certificate is for an amount that is determined to be sufficient to cover all amounts due under the mortgage and not covered by the debentures, including reasonable attorney's fees, unpaid interest, cost of repairs made by the mortgagee after default, and foreclosure costs. The FHA will probably hold the property until a favorable opportunity for sale presents itself, whereupon it may realize enough to pay off the entire certificate of claim. If, however, the proceeds of sale are not sufficient to pay off the certificate of claim, the loss must be borne by the lending institution.

Other sections of the FHA law are beyond the scope of this discussion.

Chapter 25

SUBDIVISIONS,
LAND DEVELOPMENT,
AND DEDICATION

§ 426. **Dedication.**   Dedication involves the landowner's setting apart his land for some public use, followed by an acceptance of such donation by the public. Dedication is of two kinds—common law and statutory.

§ 427. **Common law dedication.**   No particular form is required for a common law dedication. It is not necessary that there be any written instrument. There must be an intention on the part of the landowner to dedicate his land to the public. He must, either by his words or acts, offer the land for some public use, and the public authorities must accept the offer. On acceptance of the offer, the city acquires an easement in the land dedicated.

EXAMPLE: A owned a tract of land. He fenced off the tract, locating the fence approximately thirty-three feet north of the south line of his land. This thirty-three-foot strip was used by the public as a road and was later paved by the city. A's acts showed an intention to offer the strip as a street, and the city's acts showed an acceptance of that offer. The city acquired an easement in the land for street purposes. Ownership of the street remained in A.

If the intention to dedicate is lacking, there is no dedication.

EXAMPLE: Suppose I own land abutting on a public street and have a store thereon located some five feet from the street line. To induce the public to look into my store windows, I pave the strip between the store and the street. This does not operate as a dedication of the strip as part of the street, for my intention here is simply to make a more profitable utilization of my private property, not to give it to the public. *Nickel v. City* (Mo. App.), 239 S.W.2d 519.

For the same reason, any sign placed on such a strip indicating that the same is private property will prevent the creation of a dedication, even though the public is permitted to use such strip. 18 C.J.S. 91. Some owners of private streets or alleys periodically place chains across the street or alley to show an absence of intention to dedicate.

§ 428. **Subdivision plats.**   Successful subdivision planning involves far more than the mere drawing of street and lot lines on paper; it includes the planning of neighborhoods. This planning begins with the selection of the raw land, the economical planning of streets, lots, and utilities, and the control of house design. After a plan has been arrived at, the lots, parks, and streets into which the land is to be divided are staked out by a land surveyor and permanent monuments are placed at the corners of the subdivision. After this has been done, the surveyor plots on paper the manner in which the land has been subdivided. This is called *platting the subdivision.*

The plat is signed and acknowledged by the owner. If the land is mortgaged, the mortgagee must join in the plat. 63 A.L.R.2d 1160. Then it is necessary to obtain the written approval of various city and other authorities. After all this has been done, the plat is recorded in the recorder's office. The filing of the plat constitutes an offer of statutory dedication and offer of ownership of the public places shown on the plat.

§ 429. **Dedicated areas.**   Plats often contain donations or dedications of areas for parks or schools. One common trouble with these dedications is their ambiguity.

SUGGESTIONS: 1. Do you want to create rights in the general public or only in the lot owners in the subdivision? For example, if you mark a tract of land on the plat as "beach" or "park," is it intended that the *general public* may use the area, or is it intended that only *lot owners* shall use the area? The decisions are conflicting. 11 A.L.R.2d 562. Make your intention clear. Place a legend on the plat as follows: "A perpetual easement appurtenant to each lot in this subdivision is hereby created for use of the area marked 'beach' as a private bathing beach only by owners of lots in this subdivision, members of their family, and guests. This must not be construed as a dedication to the general public. Ownership of the area is reserved to the subdivider and does not pass by any deed or mortgage of a lot."

2. To what *specific* use is the dedicated area to be put? For example, what is meant by such a general, ambiguous phrase as "public square"? Is it something like a park? Could a courthouse be built in it? a school? a church? a swimming pool? an athletic stadium? Spell out the specific use you want.

3. Who is to be the *legal* owner of the dedicated area? the city? the subdivider? the adjoining landowners? There is some advantage to putting ownership in the city. For example, it will usually rid the subdivider of the burden of paying taxes

on the area and will relieve him of personal liability for accidents that may occur on the area. Give the city a deed. Approval of a plat by a city is *not* an acceptance of ownership.

4. Is a *present gift* intended or merely some possible gift in the future? For example, what is meant by the phrase "reserved for park"? Does such a phrase create present rights in the lot owners or the city, so that the subdivider may not change his mind a year from now and build a house on the tract? Don't use ambiguous phrases.

5. Is the utility strip dedicated to the public? A plat often shows a strip across the rear of the lots marked *easement for public utilities*. Some courts feel that the use of the word *public* makes this a dedication to the public. *Padgett v. Oakbrook,* 231 N.E. 2d 466 (Ill.); but other courts disagree. *Island Homes* v. *City of Fairbanks,* 421 P. 2d 759 (Alaska). This should not be left in doubt, for if the strip is not dedicated to the public, there is some control over which companies come into that strip with their services.

Even where the public authorities never accept a particular street, public park, or other public area so designated on a plat, any lot owner in the subdivision has a private right to have the area used as platted and may obtain a court order forbidding any other use. *Newton v. Batson,* 223 S.C. 545, 77 S.E.2d 212; *McCorquodale v. Keyton* (Fla.), 63 So.2d 906.

Approval of the subdivision plat by the city or other public body is not an automatic acceptance of the streets, parks, and other public areas depicted on the plat. 26 C.J.S. 479. Acceptance is shown by the city's paving the streets, putting in sewers, and so on. Therefore, if you want the city to assume *immediate* responsibility for these areas, you had best get the city council to pass an ordinance accepting this dedication. And if you want the city to have complete ownership of a park, for example, it is best to give the city a deed to the area and have the city council pass an ordinance accepting it. Once an area has been dedicated, neither the subdivider nor the city can use the land for a purpose other than the dedicated purpose. *City of St. Louis v. Bedal,* 394 S.W.2d 391.

§ 430. **Subdivision regulation.** In many communities, the subdivision of land is subject to strict controls. The governing body of the city or village may retain in its own hands the power to approve or disapprove proposed subdivisions, or, where the state law permits, this power may be delegated to a planning commission. *Gore v. Hicks,* 115 N.Y.S.2d 187. Control over land subdivisions is exercised over the entire city and often a surrounding area of several miles. *Prudential Co-op Realty Co. v. City of Youngstown,* 118 Ohio St. 204, 160 N.E. 695; 11 A.L.R.2d 524. However, this power to *approve* plats of land outside the city limits does not confer power to *zone* the area outside the city. *City of Carlsbad v. Caviness,* 66 N.M. 230, 346 P.2d 310; *Village of Bensonville v. County of Du Page,* 30 Ill. App.2d 324, 174 N.E.2d 403. The city adopts regulations establishing standards of subdivision design, including regulations concerning utilities, streets, curbs, gutters, sidewalks, storm and sanitary sewers, fire hydrants, street lighting, street signs, and width, depth, and area of lots. No subdivision plat may be recorded unless it has been approved, and approval is withheld unless the plat complies with the regulations. In lieu of requiring installation of streets, utilities, and so on, before approval, the commission may accept a surety company bond guaranteeing that the installation will be made. It is impractical to install streets and then have them pounded to rubble as construction goes forward. 28 *Ind. L.J.* 514, 544.

If a subdivider records his plat without the required approval, he runs the risk that the planning board or the city may procure a court order stopping all sales. 29 *Ind. L.J.* 408. And in many states, selling land in an unapproved subdivision plat is subject to a fine. In some states, California, Michigan, and New Jersey, for example, the buyer of a lot in an unapproved subdivision may change his mind, abrogate the sale, and get his money back. 36 *N.Y.U. L. Rev.* 1214. In other states, Idaho, Iowa, Massachusetts, Michigan, Nebraska, Rhode Island, and Wyoming, for example, the buyer of a lot in an unapproved subdivision may sue the seller for damages. Building permits are refused where the lots front on an unapproved street. Sometimes the subdivider divides up his area into building sites, but instead of recording a plat showing these building sites as lots on the plat, he sells off the sites by metes and bounds descriptions. No plat is recorded. Any such attempted evasion of the law is ineffective. Such conduct can be fined, and a court order can issue forbidding such metes and bounds sales. In many states, the recorder of deeds will refuse to accept for recording a deed in a metes and bounds subdivision. Also, building permits will be refused the lot owners.

§ 431. **Forced dedication—unlawful restrictions on subdividers.** In recent times, as new subdivisions and homes have engulfed existing school, water, and sewer systems, subdividers have fought countless pitched battles against cities as to the validity of various regulatory provisions, mostly schemes for exacting land from subdividers for schools or parks (forced dedication) or for imposition of various charges on subdividers. Among the ordinances commonly sustained as valid by the courts are the following:

EXAMPLE: An ordinance requiring that the location, width, and alignment of platted streets conform to existing contiguous streets and to the city plan, and that abnormally steep grades, sharp curves, or dangerous intersections be avoided.

EXAMPLE: An ordinance requiring the subdivider to dedicate ample streets to the city. *Ayres v. City of Los Angeles,* 34 Cal.2d 31, 207 P.2d 1.

EXAMPLE: An ordinance requiring the subdivider to pave streets and install utilities, gutters, and storm sewers. *Brous v. Smith,* 304 N.Y. 164, 106 N.E.2d 503; *Petterson v. Naperville,* 9 Ill.2d 233, 137 N.E.2d 371.

Among regulations held invalid by some courts are the following:

1. EXAMPLE: Ordinance increasing price of building permit, listing various charges, vastly in excess of the cost of processing the permit. *Merrelli v. St. Clair Shores,* 355 Mich. 575, 96 N.W. 2d 144; *Daniels v. Point Pleasant,* 23 N.J. 357, 129 A.2d 265.

2. EXAMPLE: Ordinance charging the subdivider $400 per acre to connect to city sewer system. *City of Los Angeles v. Offner,* 55 Cal.2d 103, 358 P.2d 926.

3. EXAMPLE: Ordinances requiring subdivider to donate land for schools, parks, etc. *Pioneer Bank v. Mt. Prospect,* 22 Ill.2d 375, 176 N.E.2d 799; *Ridgemont Development Co. v. East Detroit,* 358 Mich. 387, 100 N.W.2d 301. Contrary decisions on this point are: *Jordan v. Menomonee Falls,* 28 Wis.2d 608, 137 N.W.2d 442; *Billings Properties Inc. v. Yellowstone County,* 144 Mont. 25, 394 P.2d 182; *Jenad Inc. v. Scarsdale,* 18 N.Y.2d 78, 218 N.E.2d 673.

4. EXAMPLE: Ordinance requiring subdivider to contribute money for school or park. *Kelber v. Upland,* 155 Cal. App.2d 631, 318 P.2d 561; *West Park Ave. Inc. v. Ocean Twp.,* N.J., 244 A.2d 1.

5. EXAMPLE: Ordinance limiting the number of permits a builder can receive at one time. *U.S. Home & Develop. Corp. v. LaMura,* N.J. 214 A.2d 538.

6. EXAMPLE: Ordinance requiring subdivider to pay city 10% of the value of the subdivision where the plat showed no open public spaces. *Coronado Develop. Co. v. McPherson,* 189 Kan. 174, 368 P.2d 51.

7. EXAMPLE: Refusal to approve plat because of the added burdens new housing would impose on public facilities. *Beach v. Planning Comm.,* 141 Conn. 79, 103 A.2d 814.

Examples 1, 2, 5 and 7 appear to lay down rules that most courts will follow. The decisions on requiring parks, schools and other open spaces are in hopeless conflict.

§ 432. **Tentative approval of plat.**   In recent times state laws generally require that before the subdivider submits a final plat for approval he must first submit a preliminary or tentative plat. The purpose of a preliminary plat is to give the approving authority an idea of the plan of the subdivision and to enable it to give the subdivider some assurance that he is proceeding in an acceptable manner. *Lake Shore Development Corp. v. Planning Commission,* 12 Wis.2d 560, 107 N.W.2d 590.

§ 433. **Resubdivisions.**   A platted area is sometimes *replatted* *or resubdivided.* For example, if an ill-conceived subdivision, using the old-fashioned gridiron pattern, were to be acquired by a modern developer, he would go to the city and request that all streets and alleys be vacated, that is, officially abandoned by the city. Thereupon he would resubdivide the area into larger, irregular lots on curvilinear streets with utility easements over the rear substituted for outmoded alleys.

§ 434.   **Sewer, water, and other utilities.**   When a land developer installs sewer, water, and other utilities in the streets or alleys of the development, the developer has no right to remove the utilities that he has installed. These utilities, as well as the street, are dedicated to the use of the lot owners. *Stegall v. Jackson,* 244 Miss. 169, 141 So.2d 236, 143 So.2d 298. *Selected Inv. Corp. v. Lawton* (Okla.), 304 P.2d 967; *City of Snyder v. Bass* (Tex.), 360 S.W.2d 426; *Oden v. Seattle* (Wash.), 432 P.2d 642. Suppose, however, that he buys ninety-five lots in an existing subdivision of one hundred lots. No utilities have been installed. Under the state law in this particular state, the city, not the lot owners, owns the street. He makes a contract in the city under which he is to install sewer and water pipes in the street but is to retain ownership thereof. This contract is duly recorded. Thereafter, the owners of the other five lots seek to connect to his sewer and water pipes. They have no right to do so. They did not buy their lots in reliance on any representation made by him and cannot connect with his pipes. *Atchison v. De Roo,* 332 Ill. App. 251, 75 N.E.2d 46. Of course the people who buy their lots from him and rely on his representations as to sewer and water are protected.

> **SUGGESTION:** A subdivider who wishes to retain ownership of his sewer and water mains, so that he can charge for their use, should make and record in the recorder's office a conveyance of such mains to his own water company before he makes any deed of lots to purchasers. Once a deed is made to a lot purchaser, it is arguable that the water main in the street in front of his lot belongs to the lot purchaser or is dedicated to his use, and therefore the subdivider cannot charge the lot purchaser for its use, where no deed to a water company has been recorded.

A city that operates a city water supply system must serve impartially and on like terms all who apply for service. *City of Danville v. Danville Water Co.,* 178 Ill. 299, 53 N.E. 118; 48 A.L.R.2d 1225. Hence, as a rule, the city should not deny the request of a land developer to service his development, as long as he is prepared to comply with its reasonable regulations. *Reid Development Corp. v. Parsippany-Troy Hills Township,* 10 N.J. 229, 89 A.2d 667. The city may, however, decline to extend its mains to an area not previously served where the cost of the extension would be grossly disproportionate to the individual needs presented. *Yardville Estates v. City of Trenton,* 66 N.J. Super. 51, 168 A.2d 429; 48 A.L.R.2d 1225. The demand for the extension of mains must be reasonable considering the need for it and the revenue obtainable. 94 C.J.S. 58. This does not mean that the particular extension must pay for itself. Lack of profit *on the extension* is important only insofar as it affects the over-all return *from the entire system. In re Board of Fire Commissioners,* 27 N.J. 192, 142 A.2d 85. Since real estate developers are a separate class of water users, the city may take the position that if the developer wants an extension, he must pay for it, on the theory that the city ought not to be asked to participate in the risk of failure of the developer's enterprise. *Woodside Homes v. City of Morristown,* 26 N.J. 529, 141 A.2d 8.

Generally, a city is under no obligation to furnish water outside the city limits. 48 A.L.R.2d 1230. This being true, if the city is requested to extend its pipes outside its limits, it may demand that the entire cost be borne by the party desiring the extension. *Yardville Estates v. City of Trenton,* 66 N.J. Super. 51, 168 A.2d 429.

In a few states, the city has the same duty to allow property owners to tie into its sewers as it has with respect to water pipes. *Knudson v. Neal,* 320 Ill. 136, 150 N.E. 626. But in most states, property owners are not allowed to tie into an adjoining sewer without the city's consent. 64 C.J.S. 266. Of course to protect the health of its inhabitants a city may *compel* a property owner to connect with its sewers at his own expense. 64 C.J.S. 267.

With respect to the services of a private utility company furnishing gas, electricity, and so on, a land developer can often reach an agreement by private negotiation for extension of service to his development. If, however, the company refuses to extend service, the question arises whether it can be compelled to make the extension.

In the first place, the company cannot be compelled to extend service into an area that it cannot legally serve. Usually the area in which the company can operate is defined by a certificate of public convenience and necessity issued by some utility commission. If the area is one in which the company can operate, the utility commission will nevertheless refuse to compel the company to extend its services into the area if the present demand is extremely low and the probability of an increased future demand is so low that the cost of extending service will be likely far to exceed any possible yield from the investment. 62 *Colo. L. Rev.* 317. However, if over the long run the extension can be expected to produce a profit, an extension will be ordered even though the cost of the newly extended service cannot be covered by reasonable charges for a considerable length of time. The company will be compelled to take a loss during the years of initial operation of the extension as long as it can continue to make a fair return on *all* of its property. 62 *Colo. L. Rev.* 317.

Subdividers often place dotted lines on their plats and mark the indicated areas *easement for public utilities.* This phrase is too brief and general. What type of facilities are included in the phrase *public utilities?*

SUGGESTION: Place a legend on the plat as follows: A perpetual easement is hereby created over, under, and across the area marked "easement for public utilities" as an easement appurtenant to each lot in this subdivision for the installation, use, maintenance, repair, and replacement of public utilities, including sewer, water, gas, electricity, telephone, and telegraph. Said areas are not dedicated to the public.

§ 435.   Suggested steps for subdividers, builders, and their mortgagees.

1. Check your local zoning and building ordinances to determine what type of structure the area is zoned for; what lot size and building area restrictions exist; what building ordinance setback lines exist on the front, rear, and side lines of the lots. Also check your building code for its requirements as to building construction, septic tanks, and such. In many areas, for example, septic tanks are wholly illegal, and the city can legally require you to put in sewer connections. 64 C.J.S. 267. If there is the slightest doubt as to your ability to get the area rezoned to permit the buildings you have in mind, plan to make your contract of purchase contingent on your ability to procure rezoning within a specified time. Keep in mind that even if existing zoning allows the type of *dwelling* you have in mind, it may forbid the shopping center, motel, cocktail lounge, swimming pool, or dining room you also have in mind. And if you have in mind installing your own sewage treatment plant, that may require rezoning a portion of the land.

2. Check the land itself carefully, considering: (a) Existing drainage; for example, do neighbor's ditches and ditch easements cut across your building sites? (b) Future drainage problems; for example, if you increase flow of drainage water into ditches or streams, you may face lawsuits from downstream owners. (c) Sewage problems; for example, consider possible legal objections by neighbors to location of your proposed sewage treatment plant. (d) Power lines, especially underground, and sewers that may cut across your building sites. It is usually impossible to compel a utility to remove its wires even though it occupies the land unlawfully, for it can remain, on paying for the land it occupies. (e) Streams, which you will not be permitted to obstruct or pollute. (f) Roads, streets, and alleys, both existing in fact and *paper streets,* existing only on recorded plats. These must be *vacated* (officially abandoned) by the city before you can build over them.

3. Submit your project informally to your local Planning Commission. The Commission will give you informal suggestions. Adopt them, for without subsequent formal Commission approval, your program is blocked. Find out what streets, parks, and other public places you will be required to dedicate to the public in your plat; what requirements exist as to location and width of streets; what you will be required to install in the way of street grading and paving, curbs, gutters, sidewalks, water and other utilities, fire hydrants, street lighting, and street signs. Many builders donate land requested by the village even where they consider this is illegal forced dedication, for they do not wish to engage in prolonged litigation or face harassment by village officials if the village loses the lawsuit.

4. Talk informally to your local FHA people, if FHA financing is contemplated.

They will want much the same information as the Planning Commission and will also give you many helpful suggestions as to lot and utility layout and protective covenants. Adopt their suggestions.

5. Consult with your Real Estate Commissioner if your state has such an official. Get his suggestions. Later submit the subdivision plat and your application and questionnaire formally to the commissioner. If he considers that fraud or misrepresentation is involved, he has the authority to stop your project. If your state has a law along these lines, it will probably require you to give each lot buyer a copy of the commissioner's report on your subdivision.

6. Check to see if you have the legal right to hook up with existing sewers. 64 C.J.S. 266. In this connection, remember that in some states property owners have the right to make contracts with the city under which sewers that they install in public streets are private, and no one may connect with them without permission from the owner. 64 C.J.S. 276. Check to see if you have the legal right to hook up with existing water supplies. Suppose, for example, that your subdivision lies just outside some city or town. In many, probably most, areas you have no legal right to connect with the town water supply. You may have to have your development annexed to the city. Alternatively, you may be able to make a contract with the city to service your development. Check the city's requirements in this regard. These may require incorporation of your development as a water and sanitary district. 94 C.J.S. 60. If you plan to form a profit-making corporation to provide water or sanitation, you will probably have to get a *certificate of convenience and necessity* from some local commission. Be sure you can get it. For example, a water system based on deep wells may not be acceptable to the commission. Existing companies offering such service may oppose you. Consider, also, that the rates you charge will be set by the commission. If you are in an arid state, check the law to see if existing water rights of the land can be converted to the new use that you have in mind, and remember that any increased use of water may bring objection from other users. If you are buying a water right, check it as carefully as you check title to the land you are buying. Plan to make your contract of purchase contingent on your ability to make satisfactory arrangements in all these regards within a specified time.

7. Check your local law to see if local regulations require you to have a contractor's license to build. If it does, and you lack a license, you probably will be unable to collect for work that you do, and mortgage lenders will refuse to extend you credit.

8. Get a good survey of the area that you intend to develop. If you plan to acquire for your subdivision various tracts of land from different owners be sure that they form one continuous, connected area, with no outstanding strips between the various parcels of land. (See § 58.)

9. Check every objection to title listed in the contract of sale as something you must take subject to. Easements, water rights, utility lines, or building restrictions must be set forth specifically, not generally. The document number and recorder's book and page of the easement or other instrument must be given, and your lawyer must read it and explain it to you before you sign the contract. *Consider whether any listed objection interferes with your plans.* If it will be necessary for the seller to join in the subdivision plat, the contract should require him to do this.

10. Within the time allowed by the contract, attend to the matters to which the contract was made contingent, such as procuring: (a) rezoning, if needed; (b) annexation to a city, if needed; (c) formal Planning Commission approval of a preliminary plat of subdivision; (d) formal FHA approval.

11. Make formal application to your mortgage man for a loan. With the application you will furnish plans and specifications of the houses that you plan to build, also a copy of the proposed subdivision plat (in the form required by the FHA

if FHA financing is contemplated), showing the lots and blocks, location of proposed buildings, walks, driveways. These documents should reveal that your project will comply with: (a) local ordinances; (b) building restrictions in deeds and plats; (c) FHA requirements; (d) Planning Commission requirements. Also submit detailed cost estimates, on the FHA form, and proposed selling prices and all other documents required for submission to the FHA, such as financial statement, description of materials, plot plans, and description of water supply and sewage disposal system.

12. Obtain FHA commitment to insure your mortgages if FHA financing is contemplated.

13. Having received FHA commitment to insure, the mortgagee now gives you its commitment to make the mortgage loans desired.

14. When all the contingencies provided for in your contract of sale have been taken care of, you are ready to close the deal, following usual closing procedures. (See Chapter 12.) Make sure that you are obtaining clear title to the entire subdivision tract. (See Chapter 14.) For complete protection in acquiring title, close the deal in escrow. (See Chapter 13.) See that the seller's deed and the title insurance policy contain no title objections that would hamper your construction, such as building restrictions, easements, drainage ditches, utility lines, roads, mineral rights, or oil leases. If you have been careful, these were not mentioned in the contract of sale and therefore do not belong in the deed. The deed should be recorded.

15. The subdivider now has his surveyor stake out the tract in accordance with the tentative plat. He also installs the required improvements, such as sewer, water, and paving, or gives a surety bond guaranteeing such installation. He then has his surveyor prepare the final plat and submits it to the Commission for final approval. In addition to the things already mentioned, this final plat will have a surveyor's certificate, certifying to the accuracy of the survey and plat; also the subdivider's certificate, certifying that he is the owner of the land, and his signature and notarial acknowledgment; a city engineer's certificate to the effect that all improvements—streets, sewers, and so on—have been properly installed or that a bond or certified check has been posted by the subdivider to insure their proper installation; building restrictions as required by the Commission, or an accompanying declaration of restrictions, which is referred to in the plat; certificate by the tax collector that all taxes are paid; and the approval of the Commission. The final plat is then recorded. Make no sales until your subdivision plat has been recorded. Any attempt to do so is a crime in many states; building permits will be refused the purchaser; and in any event a deed description that refers to an unrecorded plat is unacceptable to title companies.

16. Consult your local title insurance company and enter into a contract with it for the issuance of your title policies as houses are sold. Builders are given special, reduced rates by title companies.

17. Individual construction mortgages are recorded, and title is again examined to cover the recording of individual mortgages. A construction loan agreement is signed for each mortgage. Preconstruction affidavits are signed and a preconstruction inspection made. (See Chapter 21.) The mortgagee notifies the mortgagor to commence construction. Do not start construction until you receive this notice.

18. Get adequate insurance coverage before construction starts. Lawsuits for injuries to workmen or members of the public can ruin you. Get contractor's liability and workmen's compensation insurance. If you are building for a home buyer, he should be warned to procure his own liability insurance. Your insurance will not cover him. Fire and other insurance are indispensable. Get the builder's risk insurance policy.

19. As construction goes forward, the precautions suggested in Chapter 21 should be complied with.

20. The FHA requires that certain drawings and exhibits be kept available on the site for FHA inspectors. Each set of drawings has a number, and the same number must be placed on a board erected on the site, easily visible to FHA inspectors. As the building goes up, the mortgagee notifies the FHA at specified times to send out FHA inspectors.

21. Any change in plans—usually installation of additional items requested by home buyers who are now in the picture—must be cleared with the mortgagee and the FHA. Increasing the recorded mortgage to take care of extras is impracticable. Therefore the mortgagee should demand a deposit of 100 per cent of the extra cash needed.

22. If the house is sold during construction, the home buyer will usually want to apply for the larger mortgage loan that the FHA makes available to individual home buyers. A new application is sent to the FHA, together with a copy of the new contract of sale and a credit report on the home buyer. If satisfactory, the FHA issues a new commitment, and it will be the home buyer's new and larger mortgage that is ultimately insured.

23. When construction has been completed, get the home buyer to sign an acceptance of the completed house. Lenders insist on this.

24. After satisfactory completion of construction, the mortgagee sends the FHA commitment, a certified copy of the recorded mortgage, and the original mortgage note to the FHA. The FHA places its endorsement on the note so that it becomes an FHA-insured loan. The note is returned to the mortgage house.

25. If a sale to a home buyer takes place after the FHA has endorsed the note, it may follow one of two procedures: (a) If the home buyer has enough cash, so that the amount of the construction mortgage loan is all the credit he needs, he can buy "subject to" this mortgage. At this time the builder, as mortgagor, the mortgagee, and the home buyer should sign an agreement under which the mortgagor's personal liability on the mortgage note is released, and the home buyer becomes personally liable instead. This should be done only after procuring FHA consent to a substitution of the mortgagor, for otherwise the FHA commitment may be voided. This release of the builder's personal liability results in improving the builder's credit standing. (b) The construction mortgage can be released and a new mortgage in a larger amount signed by the home buyer, which, of course, requires a complete new application for FHA insurance. Most builders have, even in advance of construction, procured commitments from a mortgage house to make the permanent loan when a satisfactory home buyer has been found and they have FHA commitments to insure such loans.

Chapter 26

BUILDING CONSTRUCTION

§ 436.   Construction contracts.   There are different types of construction contracts:

> 1. I own a lot and hire you to build a house according to certain plans and specifications prepared by my architect. This is a construction contract only.
>
> 2. You are a subdivider and builder. I pick out a site in your subdivision, and you contract to build a house (like one of your model homes, perhaps) and deliver the house and lot at a specified price. This is a contract for the sale of land and for the construction of a house. Both the law of sale contracts and the law of construction contracts are applicable to this situation.
>
> 3. You are a subdivider and builder, and I decide to buy a house that I find in the process of construction in your subdivision. This is essentially the same as (2) above.

SUGGESTION TO HOME BUYER: When you buy from a professional subdivider and builder, you are often dealing with a man who does not yet own the land that he is selling you. He may have only an option or contract to buy the land. If the builder runs into financial difficulties, he may never be able to pay up his option or contract or be able to transfer ownership to you. Moreover, as financial troubles develop, mechanics' liens are filed and mortgage foreclosures instituted. In such case, you will find that the possibility of obtaining ownership or getting your money back is nil. Therefore it is best for you to get a deed to the property as early as possible, before you have put too much money in the house. And if you get your deed early in the game, a permanent lender may be willing to make a construction loan directly to you, thus saving the expense of a construction loan to the builder and permanent loan to you. In any event, before you trust a builder who is unwilling or unable to give you a deed at the beginning, get a credit report on the builder. Such a report can be procured at small cost from a credit rating firm and will give you a good line on the reliability of your builder. Look up "Credit Rating and Reporting Agencies" in your telephone book. The material houses with whom the contractor has been dealing are usually excellent sources not only of credit references, but also of information as to the contractor's ability to do the job. The home buyer should also request the contractor to give him the addresses of other buildings that he has built in the past. This will give the home buyer an opportunity to inspect the finished work of the contractor and to contact the owners for a recommendation. The finance houses with whom the contractor has done business in the past are also excellent sources of reference.

Obviously, any contract to build a house should contain a description of the house to be built. In this respect, most building contracts leave much to be desired. A few points are deserving of consideration. In the first place, many builders erect a model house that is shown to prospective purchasers. If the buyer likes the model, he may sign a contract to buy a lot and to have the builder construct a house like the model house, to which reference is made in the contract. This is an adequate description. A contract to build a house *like* another existing house is a contract to build an exact counterpart or copy of the existing house, in plan, kind, and quality of material. *Whaley v. Milton Const. Co.* (Mo. App.), 241 S.W.2d 23. Obviously, if the buyer wants certain variations from the model, these should be spelled out in writing in detail in the contract.

Other builders may have a number of different building plans to show prospects. Each of the plans has a supporting set of detailed specifications. Once the buyer has selected his particular plan, he signs a contract to have a house built *according to Ace Construction Company Plan No. 5 and specifications bearing the same number.* Again, such a description is adequate. *Hannan v. Handy,* 104 Conn. 653, 134 Atl. 71.

Then there is the home buyer who wants a house built according to his own particular ideas. Here detailed plans and specifications are of the utmost importance. In this area, experience reveals the pitiful ignorance of the average home buyer. Innumerable important items can be omitted from the specifications, and the home buyer will fail to detect the omission. Then as construction goes forward, various things come to light, and the home buyer finds that he must pay for "extras."

SUGGESTION TO HOME BUYER: When you contract to buy a house "like" a certain model house, you are contracting to accept all the shortcomings of the model. Many such homes are sold on the basis of "glamor" items, such as kitchens. You had better have an experienced person look the house over to see to the adequacy of the heating plant, drainage system, foundation and footings, and other important things about which you know little. It is best to procure the plans and specifications of the model house and have them checked by an architect or builder, for there is much in a house that can be wrong and yet not meet the eye.

§ 437.   **Extras.**   Extras are probably the largest factor creating disputes between owners and contractors. There is a propensity on the part of some contractors to bid low in order to get the job and then try to bail their way out of a losing job by claiming extras. Also, an owner is frequently "inspired" during the course of construction and orders changes or extra work and materials indiscriminately without a definite understanding as to the cost. A contractor who is providing extras does not have to make a competitive bid in order to obtain the work. There is therefore a tendency on the part of some contractors to charge more money for extras than the ordinary markup used in bidding for work. The contract should therefore specifically require that all extra charges must be reduced to a written instrument, signed by the owner, describing the work to be performed and the amount to be paid. Such a provision is valid. 2 A.L.R.3d 631. In the interest of both the contractor and the owner, this procedure should be religiously followed. The owner's architect has no power to waive this provision of the contract. He cannot order extras verbally. 2 A.L.R.3d 686. However, if the owner himself verbally orders the extra work, he is liable. 2 A.L.R.3d 658. By ordering the extras verbally, the owner has waived the provision requiring a change order to be in writing. Also, the contract should require the owner to deposit additional funds with the mortgage lender in order to assure the contractor and the mortgage lender that there will be adequate funds to complete the building when extra work or materials are ordered.

In addition to disputes with respect to the cost of extras, disputes often arise as to whether or not a given item is an extra or is included under the original contract. If the plans and specifications made a part of the contract are sufficiently detailed, the possibility of a dispute over whether a particular item is an extra can be minimized.

§ 438. **Progress payments.** If I hire you to erect a building on my land, the contract will almost certainly fix a total price for the entire job. However, your subcontractors will not wait for their money until the building is finished. Therefore the contract will call for *progress payments* to the general contractor and the subcontractors as the building goes up. A widely used formula provides for a payment of 35 per cent of the proceeds to the contractor when the house is under roof, 30 per cent of the contract price when the house is plastered, and the balance of 35 per cent when the building is completed and accepted by the owner. However, the contract often provides that only 85 per cent of the full amount of a progress payment due the *general contractor* is payable when the progress payment falls due. The owner holds back 15 per cent of each payment due the general contractor (often called a *retention*) until the building has been completed and accepted by the owner with all lien waivers produced. On big jobs, the contract will call for retentions on work done by the bigger subcontractors. After all, you cannot tell whether heating or air-conditioning will work till you try it, and if it doesn't, the retention is an effective inducement to get the necessary repairs done.

As a progress payment is demanded, the contract often calls for an inspection to be made by the owner's architect, who certifies that the work and material for which payment is claimed are in place and in accordance with the contract. If the owner has no architect, this inspection should be made by the mortgage lending institution. On FHA loans, an inspection will also be made by the FHA.

A question often arising is whether a contract that calls for progress payments is a total contract for a total job at a total price or can be broken up into as many parts as there are progress payments. In other words, is the contract divisible?

EXAMPLE: A contract to build a schoolhouse for a price of $2610 provided that $300 was to be paid when first floor joists were in, $300 when second floor joists were in, $1000 when the building was inclosed, $400 when the plastering was done, and the balance when the building was completed. After the plastering was completed and all payments made up to and including the payment due at that time, a windstorm destroyed the building. The court held: (1) A builder is not excused from completing the building by the fact that the building, while under construction, is destroyed or damaged by fire, storms, or sinking of the soil; he must rebuild and complete the job without a penny of additional compensation. (2) A building contract is entire; it is not divisible. A contractor who abandons the job, as this contractor did when the windstorm destroyed the building, has not earned a penny. Therefore he must refund to the owner all progress payments already made. *Superintendent of Schools v. Bennett,* 27 N.J.L. 513. On both points, the court was correct. 22 A.L.R.2d 1345.

However, if the contract is not to *build,* but to *repair* or remodel an existing building, the contractor is relieved of liability for further performance if the building is destroyed by fire or other casualty and the destruction is not due to the contractor's negligence. *Matthews Const. Co. v. Brady,* 104 N.J.L. 438, 140 A.2d 433. Moreover, the contractor can recover for the value of labor and materials furnished up to the time of the destruction.

§ 439. **Mortgage money.** Any builder who builds on contract for a landowner should insist that the landowner have a definite commitment for a satisfactory construction mortgage loan before construction begins, and the construction contract should be made subject to this condition.

SUGGESTION TO BUILDER: Require the landowner to furnish you a photostatic copy of the lender's commitment to make the mortgage loan.

§ 440. **Cash down payments from home buyers.** Builders usually insist that the home buyer make a cash down payment. What to do with it is the question. Home buyers are often reluctant to pay a builder a large sum of money before construction has begun. And builders are often reluctant to start construction when they have no assurance that the home buyer will be able to come up with the money. One solution is to have the home buyer deposit his money with the mortgage house that is financing construction. This is acceptable to the mortgage house, for under the typical construction loan agreement, this deposit is used for the initial stages of construction, and the mortgagee's loan money is not used until later stages of construction have been reached. Another idea is to deposit the buyer's money with some bank as escrowee, with directions to turn the money over to the builder as specified stages of construction are reached.

§ 441. **Architects.** A home buyer may hire an architect only to draw plans and specifications for his home or to draw plans and then to supervise the construction of the home. Since supervision requires time and attention, it entails greater cost. Usually it is best to pay the extra money and get the supervision. A house is built by a general contractor and numerous subcontractors. One or more of these may accidentally or intentionally try to use inferior work or materials. Only a supervising architect can prevent this. Some home buyers depend on the mortgage house or FHA inspectors to see that there is no cheating. Remember that inspections by mortgage men and the FHA cannot possibly be as thorough as those of your own architect.

Many building contracts provide that before the builder is entitled to receive any payment under the contract, the owner's architect must certify that the work has been properly done in accordance with the contract up to that point and that the builder is entitled to his payment. Usually the contract provides that the architect's certificate shall be conclusive on this question, which is a valid provision. If the architect disapproves the work, the builder will not receive the payment. 110 A.L.R. 137. However, the builder will collect without the architect's certificate if the architect is guilty of bad faith or gross error.

EXAMPLE: The owner persuaded the architect to refuse a certificate, although neither had any complaint about the work or materials furnished. This action is tantamount to fraud, and the builder will collect without the certificate. *Cerny Pickas & Co. v. Dallach,* 249 Ill. App. 424.

The builder will not be entitled to payment if the architect in bad faith issues a certificate when actually the certificate should have been refused.

EXAMPLE: The architect knowingly accepted badly defective building material and certified that the builder was entitled to payment. The owner, through his own inspection, discovered the fraud and refused to pay. He was within his legal rights.

There are other pertinent rules regarding architects:

1. An architect has only those powers and authorities that his employer sees fit to give him; in general, an architect has no power to order changes in a building contract signed by his employer or to order extra work unless the owner has specifically given him this authority, and all persons dealing with an architect are on notice of this limitation on his powers. If the architect, though having no authority to do so, repeatedly orders extra work and materials and the owner pays for them knowingly and without protest, as where the extra work shows as such in monthly payout orders signed by the owner, the architect by this course of conduct becomes authorized to order extras. 47 Cal. L. Rev. 665. Because controversies often arise as to the extent of the architect's authority, it is best that the contract between the landowner and the architect for the architect's services and the building contract between the landowner and the contractor both specify what authority the architect has to give orders to the builder, how such orders are to be given (whether verbally or in writing), and so forth.

2. A supervising architect has authority to order the contractor to correct work that has not been performed in a proper manner or according to the contract or the plans.

3. The architect is duty bound to use ordinary skill and reasonable care and is liable for loss caused by his *negligence*. For example, if the architect is negligent and produces faulty plans, as a result of which damage ensues (walls crack, foundation gives way, and so forth) the architect is liable to his employer. 25 A.L.R.2d 1085. Likewise if the architect negligently certifies that the builder is entitled to payments, whereas the work done is deficient in some respect and does not warrant payment, the architect is liable. 43 A.L.R.2d 1229. Moreover, he forfeits all compensation in such case.

4. Like other agents, the architect must be loyal to his employer. If he fraudulently and in collusion with the contractor certifies that work has been done properly, when, in fact, the contrary is true, the architect is liable and forfeits his compensation. The same is true if the architect has secret agreements with building suppliers under which the architect is given a rake-off or payment for supplies ordered from them.

5. Unless it has been otherwise agreed, all plans and specifications prepared by the architect become the property of his employer. However, the American Institute of Architects contract form specifies that these documents are the property of the architect.

6. Young and inexperienced architects often agree to produce plans to the owner's "satisfaction" or "approval." Here the architect will receive no payment whatever if the owner disapproves of the result.

7. As a rule, the architect cannot recover if his plans call for a building that will violate local building ordinances.

8. Assuming that the architect exercises ordinary skill and care, he is not liable if the contractor is guilty of negligence and damage ensues, as where the contractor fails to protect the building from the elements. The difficulty here is that in some cases (settling of foundations, for example) it is hard to determine whether the loss was due to faulty plans and specifications prepared by the architect, faulty supervision by the architect, or faulty performance by the contractor despite the architect's care. Here the courts are quite likely to say that such things cannot happen where the architect is alert.

9. Home builders often press an architect for some categorical or flat commitment as to the maximum cost of construction. Here there is danger that a statement by the architect will be interpreted as a guarantee that the building will not exceed such cost, and he will be liable if such cost is exceeded and will forfeit all compensation. 12 Vanderbilt L. Rev. 720.

Finally, you must remember that an architect may be hired only to draw plans and specifications, or he may also be hired to draw plans and supervise construction of the building. Obviously an architect hired only to draw plans has no liability for carelessness in the process of construction. He would be liable only if defective plans caused damage in the process of construction.

§ 442. **Substantial performance.** If a building contractor finishes the building in strict accordance with the plans and specifications and in a good and workmanlike manner, he is, of course, entitled to collect the full contract price. However, it is virtually impossible to complete a building contract in strict compliance with every tiny requirement of the plans and specifications. If the builder performs substantially according to the contract, he is entitled to collect the contract price, less a deduction that will compensate the owner for the builder's deviations from the contract. Substantial performance is hard to define. If the owner gets substantially the building that he contracted for, and the deviations are trifling and unintentional, there is substantial performance. For example, if I hire you to build a house according to my plans at a price of $12,000, and you fulfill your contract except that two rooms have the wrong wallpaper, which it would cost $100 to remedy, clearly there is substantial performance, and you are entitled to collect $11,900. The following are illustrations of cases where substantial performance was found lacking.

EXAMPLES: (1) The footings were inadequate for wet ground, so that the foundations sank and the floors sagged. *White v. Mitchell,* 123 Wash. 630, 213 Pac. 10. (2) The contract called for a six-room house, and the builder erected a five-room house. (3) The foundations and walls of the house cracked immediately after completion of construction due to a soil condition that the builder did not properly correct. *Newcomb v. Schaeffler,* 131 Colo. 56, 279 P.2d 409. (4) In New York, it is generally held that if the deviations amount to more than 10 per cent of the contract price, substantial performance is lacking. *Rochkind v. Jacobson,* 110 N.Y.S. 583.

If you contract to erect a building for me, and your performance is less than substantial, one of several consequences is possible:

1. If I am in a generous frame of mind, then even though the building is not the kind that you agreed to build, I may accept the building as a complete and satisfactory substitute for the building contracted for. Here I must pay the full contract price. No deductions are allowed because of the defects. *Zambakian v. Leson,* 77 Colo. 183, 234 Pac. 1065.

EXAMPLE: As the building went up, the owner inspected it and noticed the deviations from the contract. But he moved in, telling the builder that the building was satisfactory and that the contract price would be paid. This is full acceptance. All deviations were waived. *Hooper v. Cuneo*, 227 Mass. 37, 116 N.E. 237.

Often in these cases, you will find that the owner has with full knowledge of the defects paid the entire contract price. Since this is full acceptance, he cannot therefore sue the builder for damages because of defects he knew about when he paid his money. *Houlette & Miller v. Arntz*, 148 Ia. 407, 126 N.W. 796. And there are always words, acts, or both on the landowner's part indicating full acceptance of the building. *Aarnes v. Windham*, 137 Ala. 513, 34 So. 816. Often the builder has a printed form that he asks the landowner to sign. This form recites that the building has been constructed in complete conformity with the contract.

2. I may accept the building as substantial performance but reserve the right to deductions because of the deviations.

EXAMPLE: The owner discovers defects as the building goes up, protests the defects, but continues to proceed with the builder on the basis and assumption that their contract is still in force. *Otto Misch Co. v. E. E. Davis Co.*, 241 Mich. 285, 217 N.W. 38. The builder gets the contract price, less a deduction to compensate for the deviations. *Gray v. Wood*, 220 Ala. 587, 127 So. 148; 17 C.J.S. 1101, 1105.

3. I simply move into the building because it is on my land and I cannot avoid it. My attitude at all times after discovering the defects is that the builder has breached his contract and ought not be paid anything. Most courts will nevertheless award the builder the value of the building, on the theory that it must be worth something to the landowner and that to give the builder nothing would be unduly harsh. Other courts, however, are less merciful with the builder. They say that I have a right to use my own land and the buildings on it, and since the builder's performance fell short of substantial performance, he is entitled to nothing. 5 Corbin, *Contracts* 551; 107 A.L.R. 1411.

4. If I demolish the structure, or refuse to make any use of it, in most states you will be unable to collect a penny. 3 Corbin, *Contracts* 790.

§ 443. **Builder liability.** The obligations of the seller of a new house differ from those of the seller of an old house. And the obligations of the seller of a completed house differ from those of the seller of a house yet to be constructed. One who sells a house to be constructed has builder liability. One who sells a completed house does not. Suppose you, as a builder, have a house in the process of construction. X sees it and signs a contract to buy it. You have *builder liability* to X. As long as the seller has workmen on the job, the house is not fully completed, and therefore when the house is sold, the contract is treated as though it were a contract (1) to sell the land and (2) to finish the house. Builder liability means that the courts hold the builder on two counts: (1) He must build in a good and workmanlike manner. (2) The structure when completed, must be reasonably fit for its intended purpose. *Markman v. Hoefer*, 252 Ia. 118, 106 N.W.2d 59; *Jones v. Gatewood* (Okla.), 381 P.2d 158; *Fain v. Nelson*, 56 Wash.2d 217, 356 P.2d 302. These are called implied warranties.

EXAMPLE: Exterior stucco peeled off soon after the house was completed. The builder is liable. He has failed to build in a good and workmanlike manner. The same would be true if the concrete footings were faulty and the building settled, causing cracked plaster and ill-fitting doors. 4 *Western Reserve L. Rev.* 361.

EXAMPLE: X builds a barn for Y, but the hayloft collapses when filled with hay. X is liable. The structure is not fit for its intended purpose.

In addition to liability on the two implied warranties, a builder is liable for failure to use ordinary care and skill. For example, a builder must use ordinary care in the selecting of building materials, and if he should carelessly select beams of inadequate strength, he would be liable for injuries resulting from collapse of the house. However, if a builder uses ordinary care in the selection of building material, he is not liable for injuries caused by hidden defects in the materials.

EXAMPLE: You, as a builder, buy steel rods for roof trusses from a reputable dealer and, owing to hidden defects in the steel, the roof collapses. You are not liable, because you were not negligent.

There is an obvious defect in the law as above stated. The seller of a completed house has no builder liability.

EXAMPLE: A builder has fully completed a house at the time he sells it to you, and thereafter defects in construction come to light, such as inadequate waterproofing of basement walls, leaky roofs, faulty foundation, and so forth. The builder has no liability, because the implied warranties exist only where some construction remains to be done at the time the house is sold.

The buyer of a newly completed house is at a disadvantage, because in an older house time brings to light the defects in construction and the buyer can see the defects for himself. To cure this situation, efforts are being made to get builders to give express warranties. If I buy a newly completed house from you, I could insist that you sign a document requiring you to make good any defects in construction that come to light within a year of the date of your deed conveying the property to me. The FHA now requires such a warranty on loans that it insures.

There is a historical reason for the distinction between sales of completed houses and houses not yet completed. The old law, which is today undergoing much change, but which still holds true in many situations, tells us that, *when we buy a thing*, the rule is *caveat emptor*. We buy at our own risk unless we specifically demand and receive warranties of quality. This is the law applied to sales of completed houses. But the old law said that when you hire a man *to do a job*, he has a legal obligation

to do the work right, which is the law that we apply to sales of houses
to be constructed or completed.

> **NEW DIRECTIONS:** In a recent decision that has already attracted
> favorable comment (*Schipper v. Levitt & Sons, Inc.*, 44 N.J. 70, 207 A.2d 314, 26 U. of
> Pittsburgh L. Rev. 857; *Waggoner v. Midwestern Development, Inc.*, 154 N.W.2d 803), it
> was held that one who is in the building business has builder liability in the sale of a
> completed house, even to the extent of being liable for personal injuries suffered from
> defects in construction. This thinking is a departure from the traditional views expressed
> above, but is in line with many recent decisions holding manufacturers of products liable
> for injuries occasioned by defects in their merchandise. See also *Steinberg v. Coda
> Roberson Const. Co.* (N.J. April 1, 1968); *Humber v. Morton*, 426 S.W.2d 554 (Tex.
> 1968); *Totten v. Gruzen*, 52 N.J. 202, 245 A.2d 1; *Connolly v. Bull*, 65 Cal. Reptr. 689.

Liability for code violations. In every contract to build, it is implied
that the building will be constructed in conformity with all laws and
ordinances. It is rather universally required that a building permit be
issued by the city before construction is begun, and before such a permit
is issued, the plans and specifications will be examined by the city to see
if the building planned complies with all ordinances. However, after the
permit is issued, the builder may nevertheless (either willfully in order
to cut costs, or through ignorance or negligence) violate ordinances in
the process of erecting the building. If the building as constructed violates
laws or ordinances, the builder will be compelled to allow as an abatement or deduction from the contract price a sum adequate to remedy the
defects. *Schiro v. W.E. Gould & Co.*, 18 Ill.2d 538, 165 N.E.2d 286, 49 Ill.
B.J. 209. Or if the landowner discovers the ordinance violations after he
has paid the entire contract price, he may sue the builder for damages.
Gutowski v. Crystal Homes, Inc., 26 Ill. App.2d 269, 167 N.E.2d 422;
Brunke v. Pharo, 3 Wis.2d 628, 89 N.W.2d 221. Ordinance violations may
also render title unmarketable. (See § **173**.) Advertising for sale a building that contains ordinance violations may constitute a fraud upon the
buyer. (See § **210**.)

All of these legal remedies may be rather poor comfort to the landowner. If the building contains serious violations of ordinances, the city
may refuse to permit the owner to occupy his building. It may compel
demolition of the building. It may fine the landowner, and the fine may
be very substantial, for each day of violation is often considered a separate
criminal offense.

§ 444. Suggestions:

> 1. Before starting construction, the builder should give thought to the mechan-
> ic's lien problem. Before he can collect any money on his contract, he will be called
> upon to furnish a sworn statement showing all subcontractors and their contract prices.
> As he hires his subcontractors, he should make memoranda from which this affidavit
> can later be prepared.
> 2. The builder should also make arrangements to prove what work and ma-

terials are going into the building. If the builder is not paid and must establish a mechanic's lien claim against the premises, he must be able to prove in court (perhaps a year or so later) by truck drivers' tickets or other direct evidence of some witness present at the time, what materials were delivered to the building site and incorporated in the building. Often the owner's best defense to a mechanic's lien foreclosure is the builder's inability to prove by eyewitness testimony or original records made on the building site what materials went into the structure.

3. Before starting construction, the builder should provide himself with all necessary insurance as to fire, casualty, and liability.

4. Before starting, the builder should also take whatever steps are necessary to shore up his neighbor's building or to notify the neighbor to attend to this. My neighbor has the right to have my land support his *land* in its natural condition, so that if both tracts are vacant, I excavate near the line, and his soil falls into the excavation, I become liable to him for damages. However, if he erects buildings on his land, he has no right to have my soil support his *buildings*. But if I propose to excavate, I should notify my neighbor of my plans in good time, so that *he* may shore up and take other precautions to protect *his building*. Then if I proceed to excavate with due care, I will not be liable if his building tilts or collapses into my excavation if such fall is due to the weight and pressure of the building. Although I am not obligated, in the absence of a city ordinance, to support my neighbor's building, I may be liable to him for damage caused to his building by my excavation if the excavating is done without proper care. Failure to exercise proper care exists in the following situations: (a) where I fail to notify my neighbor of my intention to excavate, thus giving him no opportunity to protect his property; (b) where I notify my neighbor of my intention to excavate, but my excavation is deeper than, or different from, the excavation described in my notice; (c) where I leave my excavation open for a long period of time; (d) where I open the entire excavation at one time when it would have been possible and safer to dig in sections, as where the soil consists of sand, gravel, or loam; (e) where I allow water to collect in my excavation, and seepage of the water causes my neighbor's building to fall (*Horowitz v. Blay*, 193 Mich. 493, 160 N.W. 438); (f) where I allow water and silt from my neighbor's land to collect in my excavation, thereby withdrawing support from his buildings, which then fall (*New York Central v. Marinucci Bros.*, 337 Mass. 469, 149 N.E.2d 680; 50 A.L.R. 486). In many cities, ordinances have been passed that impose on an excavator a qualified duty to support adjoining buildings. A specified notice (ten days is common) of any intended excavation must be given the adjoining owner, and he is given a right of access to the excavation for the purpose of protecting his building. If the excavation is less than a specified depth (nine, ten, and twelve feet are common) and it becomes necessary for the adjoining owner to extend his foundations downward, he must do so at his own expense. But the cost of extending the foundation below the specified depth is borne by the excavator. Ordinances of this type are common throughout the South and on the Pacific Coast. All code requirements for the construction of protective coverings over sidewalks, for fences surrounding the excavation, for shoring up sidewalks and streets, and so on should be complied with.

5. Before starting on construction, the builder should procure a survey showing the exact boundaries of the premises with the corners plainly marked. He should thereupon recheck the applicable set-back ordinances and the provisions of all plat and deed restrictions. The building must comply with both public and private restrictions. He should especially watch for building line violations.

A building contract may contain the following provisions designed to protect the landowner against mechanics' liens:

1. A requirement that the building be completed free and clear of all mechanics' and materialmen's liens.

2. A clause waiving all mechanics' and materialmen's liens, both of the general contractor and all subcontractors and materialmen. If the state law requires a contract such as this to be recorded, the contract should be duly acknowledged (in order to qualify it for recording) and recorded.

3. A requirement that the contractor hold the landowner harmless against all mechanics' liens and mechanic's lien litigation.

4. A requirement that the landowner, his architect, and mortgage lender be furnished all contractors' statements, subcontractors' statements, partial waivers, and waivers of lien as construction goes forward according to the progress payments schedule.

5. A provision that subcontractors will be paid directly by the landowner or his mortgage lender, not by the general contractor.

6. A provision for a holdback of a percentage of all payments to the general contractor until a specified period of time has elapsed after completion of the building. This gives the landowner leverage to compel the general contractor to correct defective work without asserting any lien claim.

7. A provision that progress payments will be made only as a specified architect certifies that the work is in place and is satisfactory. The timing of the progress payments should coincide with the timing in the construction loan agreement.

With respect to the construction contract the following observations are pertinent:

1. Let the construction contract specifically provide at what stages payments are to be made, in what amounts, and how much is to be held back from each payment by the owner to insure correction of faulty work.

2. For the protection of all parties, let the construction contract provide what supervision the architect will provide, which should dovetail into the architect's contract with the owner; what drawings the architect will provide the builder; what authority the architect has to give orders to the builder; how such orders are to be given (whether verbally or in writing), and so on.

3. Where there is a supervising architect, be sure that the construction contract provides that no payments will be made except on the production of architect's certificates that the builder is entitled to receive payment and that the work done qualifies for payment both as to quality and quantity.

4. The contract should specify that the supervising architect has authority to order the contractor to correct work that was not performed in a proper manner according to the plans.

5. To prevent controversy, let the construction contract provide that final payment and acceptance by the owner will not bar any claims for latent defects.

6. Many construction contracts provide that the building is to be completed in a specified time and that the builder shall pay specified sums for delay beyond the specified completion time, except where such delays are caused by strikes, bad weather, and so forth.

7. Building contracts should provide that the builder be obligated to protect the landowner against liability to adjoining owners, members of the public, and employees and subcontractors, and also to take out insurance policies to protect against such liabilities.

Chapter 27

LAND USE CONTROLS:
BUILDING RESTRICTIONS

§ 445. **Private and public controls distinguished.** Use of land is controlled in two ways, namely, through *private* controls and through *public* controls.

> **EXAMPLE:** A buys 100 acres of farmland and divides it into 100 residential lots by means of a recorded plat of subdivision which specifies that all lots must be used only for the construction of single-family dwellings. This is *private* control of use of land by means of building restrictions.

> **EXAMPLE:** The City of X adopts a zoning ordinance by which part of the city is zoned for residential use, part for stores, and part for industry. This is *public* control of land use.

Private land use controls rest on the philosophy that where private ownership of land is recognized, as it is in America, ownership of land includes the right to sell it on such terms as please the landowner—including the right to restrict the future use of the land in some way that seems desirable *to the seller.*

There is a parallel, but quite different philosophy, namely, that use of land must be controlled, not in the interest of private individuals as such, but in the public interest. Both methods co-exist under our American law with some overlapping and some conflict.

Historically, private controls antedate public controls by many years.

Hundreds of years ago in England, a landowner might give away his land and include some whimsical or capricious requirement in his gift that, while legally enforceable, contributed nothing toward the practical control of land use.

EXAMPLE: Gifts on the following conditions were sustained by the courts: that the donor reside in the house on the land; that donee would lose the land if he were educated abroad; that donee must always write his name "T. Jackson Mason"; that the minister of donee's church always wear a black gown in the pulpit. 65 U. of Penna. L.R. 527.

If you bought a home in those early days, there was nothing to prevent your neighbor from constructing a slaughter house, tannery, or other offensive use adjoining your dwelling. Thus matters continued until 1848, when the courts first evolved the idea that if a land developer deeds out all the lots in the subdivision with identical restrictions providing, for example, that only single-family dwellings are permitted in the subdivision, *any lot owner can obtain a court order preventing any other lot owner from violating this restriction.* This was one of the great milestones in the history of law.

While this innovation was truly of immense importance, and remains so, certain problems arose.

EXAMPLE: A plat of subdivision provides that only single-family residences shall be erected in the subdivision and houses are built and sold in reliance on this restriction. X buys land across the street from the subdivision and erects a tannery thereon. There is nothing the homeowners can do.

For this reason, much later, and not really effectively until 1926 when the United States Supreme Court first sustained the validity of zoning ordinances, a new kind of land use control came into being, namely, a system of *public controls,* implemented by a *zoning ordinance* allocating permitted uses to the various areas of the city. This was and is a far more effective system of land use controls, one that controls the entire area of the city. In an area the city has zoned as residential only, which may and usually does embrace an area greatly exceeding in extent the area one private developer might acquire and restrict, all homeowners are protected against offensive uses.

This development, however, has not rendered private building restrictions obsolete.

EXAMPLE: A, a land developer, acquires 40 acres of land in an area zoned by the city for single-family residences. He records a plat of subdivision which contains restrictions that no residence shall be erected costing less than $75,000. This the city cannot do. Yet it definitely restricts the occupancy of the area in a way that seems desirable to the developer and his customers.

§ **446. Private restrictions in general.**   Private restrictions fall
into five main categories:

1. Whimsical or capricious restrictions imposed by the seller because of some
whim or prejudice, such as a restriction that neither tobacco nor liquor shall be used
on the premises sold or that there shall be no card-playing on the premises.
2. Covenants for the benefit of land sold or land retained. These last are
restrictions imposed by a landowner who owns two adjoining tracts of land and sells
one of them.

E X A M P L E :   A, owning lots 1 and 2, with a house on lot 1, sells vacant
lot 2 with a clause in the deed that no building shall be erected in the front thirty
feet of the lot. This protects the view from the front of A's house. Or A could have
sold the house lot, with a restriction that no buildings shall be erected on the front
thirty feet of the lot retained.

3. Restrictions imposed by a subdivider or land developer with a view to making the subdivision attractive, such as a restriction that only single-family dwellings shall
be erected in the subdivision. This is the most important category. These are the restrictions that create a *general plan.*
4. Affirmative covenants running with the land, discussed later herein. (See
§ 456.)
5. Conditions. These are restrictions providing for a reverter of title if they
are violated. They also are discussed later. (See § 453.)

§ **447. Creation of general plan restrictions.**   In order to at-
tract lot purchasers, a subdivider or land developer often evolves a building scheme or general plan for restricting the lots in the tract undergoing
development to obtain substantial uniformity in building and use. For
example, the plan often contemplates that only residences shall be erected,
thus excluding stores and industrial uses. The effect is to create a restriction that any lot owner may enforce against any other lot owner. Restrictions upon the use of property, imposed as a part of general plan for the
benefit of all lots, give to the purchaser of any lot a right to enforce such
restrictions against the purchaser of any other lot. Such restrictions are
enforced on the theory that each purchaser buying with knowledge or
notice of the general plan impliedly agrees to abide by the plan. *Wiegman
v. Kusel,* 270 Ill. 520, 110 N.E. 844.

E X A M P L E :   The map or plat of a certain subdivision provides that the
subdivision lots shall be used for residence purposes only. A, one of the lot owners,
seeks to open a store on his lot. Any lot owner can obtain an injunction preventing A
from using his lot for store purposes.

While general plan restrictions were originally created by incorporating
identical restrictions in all deeds by the subdivider, this is not the usual
practice today. The character that a particular development is to assume

is planned at the time that the acreage is first subdivided into building lots. The subdivider incorporates in the recorded plat or map of the subdivision itself uniform restrictions to which all lots are subject. Clearly the plan is general. And since every lot purchaser must take notice of the recorded plat, he has constructive notice of the restriction. Therefore any lot owner may enforce the restriction against any other lot owner. Recently these building schemes have become so elaborate that there is not enough room for them on the plat or map. Hence the restrictions are set up in a recorded *declaration of restrictions* recorded simultaneously with the plat and referred to in the plat. Legally this is as though the restrictions had been set forth in the plat. Subsequently, as sales of the lots are made, the deeds contain clauses stating that the land is subject to such recorded restrictions.

Of course the privilege of creating restrictions is by no means confined to subdividers. Any landowner is at liberty to insert restrictions in his deed when he sells and conveys the land. An enforceable restriction may be inserted in a contract for the sale of land. The landowners in a particular area may enter into an agreement subjecting their land to restrictions.

§ 448. **Enforcement of general plan restrictions.**   If a general plan restriction is violated, *the court will issue an order (injunction) forbidding the violation. Anyone who disobeys the order can be jailed. Structures erected in violation thereof can be ordered demolished. Stewart v. Finkelstone*, 206 Mass. 28, 92 N.E. 37. For a general plan restriction to be enforced, the one seeking enforcement need only show that the violator purchased his lot with notice of the restriction, either from a recorded document or from actual knowledge of the restriction. The question as to enforcement of a general plan type restriction, then, arises when one lot owner attempts to violate a restriction, and another lot owner seeks a court order prohibiting such attempted violation. The court will ask two questions: (1) Is there a general plan? (2) If there is, did the violator purchase his land with actual knowledge or with notice from the public records of the existence of the general plan? If the answer to these questions is in the affirmative, the restriction will be enforced, except in the situations hereafter discussed. (See § 452.)

§ 449. **Interpretation of general plan restrictions.**   The problem of framing restrictions that will carry out the intention of the subdivider is a difficult one. Much litigation has centered around this point.

Location restrictions.   When the plat or map of a subdivision shows a line designated as a building line extending across the front portion of the subdivision lots, this is sufficient to create a building line restriction. No substantial parts of buildings may then be erected beyond the building line. Building line restrictions may also be created by restrictions in the deed. The purpose of a building line is twofold: to insure a certain degree of uniformity in the appearance of the buildings and to create a right to unobstructed light, air, and vision. The fact that a small porch, awning, stoop, steps, or an overhanging bay window extends beyond the building line will not constitute a violation of the restriction. However, a so-called bay window that is really the front wall of the house is a violation of the restriction. 55 A.L.R. 332, 172 A.L.R. 1324.

CAUTION: When a restriction provides that no building shall be erected within a certain number of feet of the street line, it is the line where the lot meets the street that is meant. In other words, some plat of a subdivision shows this particular lot as fronting on some street. Where the lot ends, the street begins. Often enough, to be sure, the city paves only the middle part of the street strip, and laymen sometimes speak of this as the "street," which is erroneous. The street extends to the lot line and includes not only the roadway, but also the parkway or planted area, if any, sidewalks, if any, and so on. Building line restrictions are measured from the true street line, not from the curb line. *Trunck v. Hack's Point,* 204 Md. 193, 103 A.2d 343.

Residence purposes. Many restrictions provide that "the land shall be used for residence purposes" or that "only residences shall be erected on this real estate." Under this type of restriction, any kind of building devoted exclusively to residence purposes may be erected, including a duplex house or an apartment building. 14 A.L.R.2d 1376. If the restriction permits construction of only "private," "single," or "detached" residences, only single-family dwellings are permitted. *Flaks v. Wichman,* 128 Colo. 45, 260 P.2d 737.

If the owner occupies his residence, he may take in lodgers. However, if the building is completely converted into a boarding house, the restriction is violated, for this is a business rather than a residential use. Use of the premises as a tourist home also violates a residential restriction. *Deitrick v. Leadbetter,* 175 Va. 170, 8 S.E.2d 276. If the restriction provides that the premises shall be used only as a residence for one private family, this will prevent the letting of rooms to lodgers. *Sayles v. Hall,* 210 Mass. 281, 96 N.E. 712. It will also prevent the doubling up of two or more families.

Where the premises are restricted to residence purposes, the erection of a private garage for the use of the occupants of the main dwelling is permitted.

A restriction limiting the use to residence purposes is deemed to prohibit churches. *Housing Authority v. Church of God,* 401 Ill. 100, 81 N.E.2d 500; *Hall v. Church,* 4 Wis.2d 246, 89 N.W.2d 798; 13 A.L.R.2d 1239. Likewise, schools, parking lots, filling stations, and rest homes would be prohibited. 43 A.L.R. 1138, 124 A.L.R. 1012. As to incidental uses, such as doctor seeing patients, see 21 A.L.R.3rd 641.

Dwelling. Restrictions sometimes limit use of the land to dwelling purposes. In Illinois, New Jersey, North Carolina, Ohio, and Pennsylvania, such restrictions do not prohibit the erection of apartment buildings, since apartment buildings are "dwellings." *Leverich v. Roy,* 338 Ill.App. 248; 87 N.E.2d 226; 14 A.L.R.2d 1376. However, in Massachusetts, Michigan, and New Hampshire, apartments are not considered dwellings.

A good residential restriction might read as follows:

SUGGESTED FORM: Only one detached single-family dwelling and private garage appertaining thereto shall be erected on said premises. No use shall be made of said premises except such as is incidental to the occupation thereof for residence purposes by one private family residing in a detached, single-family dwelling.

This form has the following advantages: The phrase *single-family dwelling* keeps out apartments and other multiple dwellings. *Single dwelling* will not do the trick, because in some states, a restriction against single dwellings does not prohibit a duplex or apartment. 14 A.L.R.2d 1376. The use of the word *detached* keeps out duplexes or row houses. The stipulation as to occupation by one private family keeps out lodgers and prevents doubling up of families.

If a restriction merely specifies the *type of building* but is silent regarding the use of the building, an argument may be advanced that the building can be used for any purpose. As a rule, courts try to give effect to the obvious intention by holding that use of the structure must conform to the purpose for which it was erected. 155 A.L.R. 1000.

EXAMPLE: A restriction provided that "no structure shall be built except for dwelling purposes." A dwelling was erected. Later, the owner of the dwelling attempted to use it as a beauty parlor. The court held that the building could be used only for dwelling purposes. *Holderness v. Central States Finance Corp.,* 241 Mich. 604, 217 N.W. 764. Obviously, the restriction was badly drafted. If it had been properly drafted, litigation could not have arisen.

The restriction should restrict the use of the land as well as use of the building. If the restriction deals only with use of the *building,* the argument may be advanced that any use of the land is *permitted. Albrecht v. State Highway Commission* (Mo.), 363 S.W.2d 643. Again, courts will usually come to the rescue by holding that the intention was to restrict use of both building and land.

EXAMPLE: A restriction provided that no *building* erected on the land should be used for any purpose other than as a private dwelling place. The landowner attempted to use the *vacant land* as a parking lot. He contended that the restriction applied only to the use of buildings and therefore did not apply to vacant land. The court held that it was the intention to restrict use of both building and land.

Hoover v. Waggoman, 52 N.M. 371, 199 P.2d 991; 155 A.L.R. 528, 1007. Nevertheless, controversy could have been avoided if the restriction had been explicit. The word "premises" is broad enough to cover both land and building.

Often one will hear the argument made that a duplex is really two single-family dwellings connected by a party wall. To keep out duplexes, it is therefore advisable to have your restriction read that only *detached* single-family dwellings may be built.

Business purposes. When the restriction forbids use of the premises for business purposes, the following are among the uses not permitted: gasoline filling stations, billboards, and parking lots. Especially in older deeds, one is likely to find restrictions prohibiting use of the property for a "trade or business." Suppose a doctor uses a room of his home as an office for the practice of medicine. This would not violate such a restriction, because the practice of medicine is not a trade or business; it is a profession. *Auerbacher v. Smith,* 19 N.J. Super. 191, 88 A.2d 262.

Many restrictions are so poorly drafted that they fail to achieve their main purpose.

EXAMPLE: A restriction provided that "no flat roof dwelling house shall be erected." Since no other type of building was mentioned, a flat roof church could be erected. *Corbridge v. Westminster,* 18 Ill. App.2d 245, 151 N.E.2d 822.

You can see that many restrictions, particularly the older ones, are negative in form. They contain enumerations of prohibited uses, such as apartments and businesses. Such devices are doomed to failure. In the first place, nobody ever makes the list of excluded uses long enough, and nobody, of course, can cover the uses that do not even exist today but will crop up the future. This is why, particularly for residential property, modern restriction plans simply specify the one type of permitted use, that is, "Only detached single-family dwellings shall be constructed, and the premises shall be used only as a residence for one private family."

§ **450. Plans of buildings.** Often a scheme of restrictions provides that no building shall be erected until the plans and specifications therefor have been approved by the developer or subdivider. Such provisions are valid, but any refusal to approve plans will be set aside by the courts if such refusal is capricious, arbitrary, or unreasonable. *Hannula v. Hacienda Homes,* 34 Cal. App.2d 442, 211 P.2d 302, 19 A.L.R.2d 1268.

§ **451. Modification, extension, and release of general plan restrictions.** If the right to modify general plan restrictions is not reserved in the deeds, plat, or declaration, it takes a unanimous vote of all lot owners (probably also their mortgagees) to modify the restrictions

(*Steve Vogli & Co. v. Lane*, Mo. 405 S.W.2d 885), and this is rarely obtainable.

In recent restriction plans, subdividers have often included a clause giving themselves the right to waive or dispense with the restrictions as to some or all of the lots. This is dangerous. A number of courts have held that such a provision destroys the uniformity necessary to a general plan, and therefore the restrictions cannot be enforced by one lot owner against another. 19 A.L.R.2d 1282.

Where the right to modify the restrictions is reserved to the developer by the deeds, plat, or declaration, he may validly exercise this right. *McComb v. Harly*, 132 N.J.Eq. 182, 26 A.2d 891, 4 A.L.R.3rd 570.

In providing for periodical extensions and modifications of the restrictions in the declaration, thought must be given to the voting arrangements. (See § 581.)

Where the right to modify restrictions is reserved in the plat, declaration of restrictions or deeds, any modifications voted by the required majority must be general in their nature.

> **EXAMPLE:** A majority of the landowners voted to take one lot out of the restrictions so that a filling station could be erected on it. This was invalid. *Riley v. Boyle*, 434 P.2d 525.

And where the right to modify or release restrictions is reserved in the subdivider, only he can exercise the right, and when he conveys out all the lots, the right ends. *Pulver v. Mascolo*, 237 A.2d 97; *Richmond v. Pennscott Builders, Inc.*, 251 N.Y.S.2d 845.

§ 452. **Factors that render general plan restrictions unenforceable.** In considering what factors render restrictions unenforceable, it is necessary, first of all, to distinguish between restrictions that do not provide for a reverter of title and those that do, that is, conditions. We consider first the general plan type restrictions, which are traditionally enforced by means of an injunction, or court order, forbidding violation. Such orders are not granted lightly. Various circumstances are considered by the courts in determining whether such an order should be granted.

Change in neighborhood. A court will not, as a rule, enforce a restriction by injunction when the neighborhood has so changed in character and environment as to make it unfit to continue the original use. 4 A.L.R.2d 1111.

> **EXAMPLE:** A restriction provides that lots in the subdivision shall be used only for residence purposes. Gradually the neighborhood changes character, and stores and factories creep in. This often happens because no single homeowner wishes to incur the expense of hiring an attorney and litigating the right of his neighbors to violate the restriction. When it becomes impossible to characterize the area as residen-

tial, courts will refuse to enforce the restriction on the ground that it is no longer possible to carry the original plan into effect. However, if the change in neighborhood affects only a part of the subdivision while the remainder is unchanged, the restrictions may be enforced in the area that remains unchanged. *O'Neill v. Wolf,* 338 Ill. 508, 170 N.E. 669. Suppose A owns a house in a restricted subdivision, and in the same subdivision, but six blocks away, a number of violating structures are erected. A's acquiescence to these violations will not bar him from stopping a violation next door to him or in the same block. In other words, these previous violations are so remote from him that they do not constitute a change in his immediate neighborhood, nor could A be charged with undue neglect in enforcing his rights. *Meek v. Yarowsky,* 236 Mich. 251, 210 N.W. 226.

Numerous violations. Even when the restricted neighborhood has not changed its general character, the right to enforce a particular restriction may be lost by abandonment. When the property owners in the subdivision have violated the restrictions, and the violations have been so general as to indicate an abandonment of the original general plan, the restrictions will not be enforced. The reason for this is that the purpose of the restriction can no longer be carried out. It would be an injustice to a property owner to compel him to conform to a restriction that most of the other owners have violated when such enforcement would be of no benefit to the party seeking to enforce the restriction.

EXAMPLE: A building line was established across a block consisting of fifteen lots. On nine of the lots, buildings were erected that extended across the building line. The owner of a lot that had remained vacant began construction of a building that would also violate the building line. The owner of another vacant lot sought a court order to prevent this violation. The court order was refused. The value of the building line had been destroyed by the numerous violations. *Ewertsen v. Gerstenberg,* 186 Ill. 344, 57 N.E. 1051.

Violations by party who seeks to enforce restriction. One who violates a nonreverter type restriction in some substantial degree or manner cannot procure a court injunction restraining the violation of the restriction by others.

EXAMPLE: A plat restriction permits only single-family dwellings to be erected. A constructs a two-flat. His neighbor, B, now seeks to erect a three-flat. A cannot prevent this.

Delay in enforcing restrictions. Where a nonreverter type restriction, as distinguished from a condition, is involved, a person wishing to prevent a violation must act promptly.

EXAMPLE: A subdivision plat contains a nonreverter type building restriction forbidding the construction of anything but single-family dwellings. X, who owns a house in this subdivision, observes that Y, another lot owner, is erecting a filling station.

After construction of the station has been completed, X files a suit to have it demolished. The court will refuse to interfere. X has been guilty of undue delay. 12 A.L.R.2d 394.

Restrictions about to expire by lapse of time.   Many restrictions specifically state a time limit for their expiration. Suppose construction of a building that violates the restriction is begun a year or so before the restriction has expired by lapse of time. Here the courts may refuse to enforce the restriction for the simple, practical reason that to do so would be of little practical benefit. 32 *Tex. L. Rev.* 521.

State laws placing time limits on enforcement of restrictions.   A number of states, Arizona, Georgia, Massachusetts, Michigan, Minnesota, Rhode Island, and Wisconsin, for example, have enacted laws providing that after the lapse of a stated number of years restrictions become unenforceable. 15 *Kan. L. Rev.* 586. And in all states having marketability of title laws, restrictions will expire after the permitted time unless kept alive by new recording as provided in the law.

Other factors.   Courts are more merciful when the violation is not willful but is due to accident or mistake, as where my surveyor makes an error, and as a result my building extends over a building line. They are also more merciful toward minor violations than they are toward major violations. Of course if the party seeking to enforce the restriction has said or done something that would encourage me to go ahead with the violation, he will get no help from the courts.

§ 453. **Conditions.**   A condition is a restriction that is coupled with a *reverter* clause. This clause provides that if the restriction is violated, ownership reverts to the grantor in the deed.

EXAMPLE: A deeds a lot to B with a provision forbidding sale or use of intoxicating liquor on the lot and that in case of violation, ownership reverts to A. In time the premises are sold to X, who puts in a drugstore with a liquor department. A files a suit. The court will give the property back to A.

The outstanding characteristic of a condition is the fact that if it is violated, the grantor may get his land back by filing a suit to obtain possession. He need not pay any compensation for it. Any mortgages or other interests in the land created after the creation of the condition are extinguished if the condition is enforced, again without payment of compensation. This rule operates so harshly that courts are reluctant to construe a provision as a condition. In nearly all states, if the restrictive provision is followed by a clause providing that in the event of a violation of the restrictions the title to the land shall revert to the grantor in the deed, the restrictive provision is a condition. If the deed contains no reverter clause, that is, a clause providing for a reverter or forfeiture of title in the event of violation of the restrictions, the restrictive provision is usually a covenant. The nomenclature employed by the parties is by no means decisive as to the character of the restriction created.

EXAMPLE: A deed contained this clause: "These presents are upon the express condition that the said premises shall not be used or occupied as a tavern or public house." There was no reverter clause. It was held to be a covenant. *Koch v. Streuter,* 232 Ill. 594, 83 N.E. 1072. Violation would not cause a reverter.

Occasionally the condition is referred to herein as a *reverter type restriction.*

§ 454. **Enforcement of conditions.**   When a condition (that is, a reverter type of restriction) occurs in a deed but the condition forms no part of any general plan, enforcement is relatively simple. The condition can be enforced by the grantor in the deed, or, if he is dead, by his heirs. Other lot owners in the same subdivision cannot enforce the condition.

Suppose, however, that X subdivides a tract of land and in selling the lots includes in each deed an identical condition. Here the problem grows far more complex. One thing is clear. The same building restriction may be both a condition and a restriction. For example, if the restriction sets forth that it is a covenant and restriction on behalf of all lot owners in the subdivision and in addition, that the grantor may declare a reverter if the restriction is violated, then, of course, any lot owner can enforce the restriction by injunction, treating it as a nonreverter type general plan restriction, but the grantor may also enforce it by declaring a reverter of title. *O'Malley v. Central Church,* 67 Ariz. 254, 194 P.2d 444. Suppose, however, that one can deduce the existence of a general plan only from the fact that the conditions in all deeds happen to be identical. There is no language indicating that the provision is also to be treated as a covenant in favor of other lot owners. Here some courts are willing to allow other lot owners to enforce the condition on the theory that a covenant in their behalf must have been intended. *Sayles v. Hall,* 210 Mass. 281, 96 N.E. 712; *Simon v. Henrichson,* 394 S.W.2d 249; *Genske v. Jensen,* 188 Wis. 17, 205 N.W. 548. Other courts see only what is on the printed page. Since the provision reads like a simple condition, only the grantor or his heirs are permitted to enforce it. *Werner v. Graham,* 181 Cal. 174, 183 Pac. 945; *Whitton v. Clark,* 112 Conn. 28, 151 Atl. 305; *Finchum v. Vogel,* 194 So.2d 49 (Fla.); *Goodman v. Bingle* (Tex. Civ. App.), 48 S.W.2d 432.

A recorded condition can be enforced against any subsequent purchaser or mortgagee of the land. Enforcement of a condition by the grantor in the deed containing the condition, or by his heirs, if he is dead, extinguishes all subsequent titles and rights in the land.

EXAMPLE: A conveys a lot to B with a condition in the deed that the premises shall not be used for the sale of liquor. The deed provides that in the event of violation of this provision, title to the property shall revert to A. B sells and conveys the property to C, who places a mortgage thereon to D. Thereafter, C leases the building to E, and the latter uses the property for the sale of liquor. A brings suit to recover the land on the ground that the condition has been violated. A will be allowed to recover the land and all buildings erected on it without payment of any compensation, and he will have good title free and clear of the mortgage and lease.

For the above reason, mortgagees are often reluctant to loan money on land that is subject to a condition. In fact, many insurance companies, which are authorized by law to loan money on first mortgages only, cannot legally make a loan on land that is subject to a condition. The problem may be handled in a number of different ways.

1. The person who has the right to enforce a reverter (the grantor in the deed creating the condition, or his heirs) may always release the reverter outright to the landowner.
2. The person who has the right to enforce a reverter may *subordinate* this right to a mortgage by a document stating that the reverter right is *subject to* the mortgage. If the subordination is unequivocal, the mortgagee, when he forecloses, completely extinguishes the condition.
3. Many subdividers who place conditions in their deeds also include provisions in their deeds stating that the reverter right is subordinate to all mortgages. These provisions are broad in their terms and protect any mortgagee who may take a mortgage on the land.
4. In some instances title companies will insure against loss caused by a reverter of title.

§ 455. Factors that render conditions unenforceable.

In many states, especially where older court decisions are still followed, the factors discussed above that would prevent enforcement of a *nonreverter type* restriction have little application to conditions, that is, *reverter type* restrictions. For example, in nearly all states, the grantor in a deed containing a condition, or his heirs, if he is dead, has the right to enforce a condition even though the neighborhood has so changed that enforcement is of little practical utility. In one or two modern states, however, the change of neighborhood rule is now also applied to conditions, and conditions will not be enforced where the neighborhood has changed. *Letteau v. Ellis*, 122 Cal. App. 584, 10 P.2d 496; *Koehler v. Rowland*, 275 Mo. 573, 205 S.W. 217.

Again, in every state, laws exist allowing a certain time, often as long as twenty years, for the bringing of a suit to declare a reverter of title and to enforce a condition. This period of time runs not from the date of the deed containing the condition, but from the date the condition is violated. Often situations arise where, after the condition has been violated, no action has been taken to enforce the condition, and the landowner continues in possession, perhaps for several years. Mere delay in enforcing a condition, so long as the period allowed by law has not expired, does not, in most states, bar enforcement of a condition. But if the one who has a right to declare a reverter stands idly by, apparently acquiescing in the violation of the condition, sees valuable improvements being made by the landowner, and delays proceedings to enforce the condition until after the improvements have been completed, some modern courts feel that this conduct is so unfair to the landowner that they refuse to enforce the condition. 39 A.L.R.2d 1111.

In some states laws have been passed outlawing conditions after a certain specified period of time has elapsed from the date of their creation. *Trustees v. Batdorf*, 6 Ill.2d 486, 130 N.E.2d 111; 54 *Harv. L. Rev.* 248. But see *Bd. of Educ. v. Miles*, 15 N.Y.2d 364, 207 N.E.2d 181, criticized in 1965 Law Forum 941. Marketability of title laws also has this result.

Sometimes a general plan is revealed by the existence of identical conditions in deeds. In such case, if the owner of the reverter right follows a course of conduct that results in numerous violations of the conditions, he will, in some states, be denied the right to enforce any of the conditions. 39 A.L.R.2d 1133.

EXAMPLE: A, a subdivider, sold all the lots in the subdivision by deeds containing conditions against sale of intoxicating liquor. Later, he voluntarily released this clause as to a number of lots, and saloons were built on the released lots. He was refused the right to enforce any of the unreleased conditions. *Wedum-Aldahl Co. v. Miller*, 18 Cal. App.2d 745, 64 P.2d 762.

It can be seen that while the older and stricter court decisions freely allow the enforcement of conditions, the modern decisions are beginning to apply to conditions the same rules that they apply to nonreverter type restrictions.

§ 456. **Covenants running with the land.** The topic covered in this section is best explained by an illustration.

EXAMPLE: A owns two adjoining lots, Lots 1 and 2. A sells Lot 1 to B, and in the deed he inserts a clause stating that B covenants to keep in repair the fence between the two lots. Lot 2 enjoys the *benefit* of this covenant. Lot 1 bears the *burden* of the covenant. Any subsequent owner of Lot 1 must comply with this covenant and will be liable to pay damages to the owner of Lot 2 if he fails to do so. Any subsequent owner of Lot 2 will be able to enforce this covenant. *Such an affirmative covenant runs with the land,* much in the same fashion as an appurtenant easement runs with the land, the *burden* of the covenant running with Lot 1 and the *benefit* running with Lot 2.

Courts are somewhat reluctant to see land burdened with covenants that impose *personal liability* on subsequent owners, for such covenants tend somewhat to restrict saleability of such land. These requirements are of diminishing impōrtance today, for most covenants relating to land are *negative covenants,* that is, covenants *restricting the use of land, and these are enforced today by means of injunctions rather than damage suits.*

EXAMPLE: A, a subdivider, sells all lots in the subdivision by deeds providing that only single-family dwellings can be erected. B buys a lot and attempts to build a store. C, another lot owner, obtains a court order forbidding such construction.

In issuing such orders courts ignore all the technicalities that surround damage suits. As long as a property owner bought his land with notice, either actual or from the public records, that the land was bound by a covenant, he is subject to court injunctions compelling obedience. In modern times, in other words, the old-fashioned method of enforcing covenants by damage suits that may not be decided by a jury until years after the suit has been filed, and then may offer only a slim chance of persuading a jury or collecting the damages a jury may award, has given way to the new effective method of enforcing a restrictive covenant by a judge's injunction order that may issue within a few days after suit is filed. *Affirmative covenants,* such as those requiring payment of assessments for maintenance of common grounds in a planned unit development, still pose the problems relating to covenants running with the land. Owing to their somewhat technical nature these problems are not discussed further herein.

§ 457. **Racial restrictions.**   Racial restrictions, that is, restrictions prohibiting use or occupancy by, or sale of, the land to persons other than members of the Caucasian race are discussed in Chapter 35.

§ 458. **Suggestions:**

If you are about to buy real estate, you are concerned with several questions about restrictions: (1) Do any restrictions exist that will hamper or prevent the use you intend to make of this land or prevent construction of the building you have in mind? (2) What does the contract of sale say about restrictions? (3) Assuming that you are buying improved real estate and therefore have no building problem, are there reverter clauses in the restriction under which you may lose your title or that may hamper your financing of the real estate? (4) If there are restrictions, and the restrictions are desirable from your point of view, do you get the right to enforce them against other property owners?

In answering Question 3 above, keep in mind that if there is a condition containing a reverter clause, and some prior owner violated the clause by constructing the wrong type of building or by committing some other violation, the grantor in the deed containing the condition has the right to take the property away from you.

In answering Question 4 above, keep in mind the rules stated in the text. Lot owners get the best protection when the restrictions are incorporated in the map or plat of the subdivision, since this leaves no room for doubt that there is a general plan. The lot owners get the least protection in cases where the restrictions are imposed by the subdivider, who includes conditions in his deed to the lot owners. Except in a few states, only the subdivider or his heirs can, as a rule, enforce such conditions, and the subdivider is likely to lose interest once he has sold all lots in the subdivision. Also, when the sub-divider has created conditions, the lot owners must be prepared to go to him each time they mortgage their lands and buy from him a subordination of reverter. Mortgagees usually insist on this protection, and lot owners have no recourse but to pay for it.

If you are attempting to obtain the release of a restriction, you must keep in mind the rules regarding the persons who may enforce the restriction. For example, if you buy a lot in a subdivision, and the plat or map of the subdivision contains a restriction that only single-family dwellings shall be constructed, it is a waste of time to obtain the consent of the owners of the two neighboring lots to the construction of a two-flat building, because any lot owner in the subdivision can block construction of such a building.

Chapter 28

LAND USE CONTROLS:
ZONING AND BUILDING
ORDINANCES

§ 459. **Zoning—in general.** A comprehensive zoning ordinance is one that, by dividing the city into zones and allocating different uses to different zones, regulates the use that may be made of each parcel of land in the city.

Zoning ordinances are passed under the state's police power. Under this power, each state and its cities have the power to adopt such regulations as are necessary to protect the public health and safety. The segregation of industries, stores, and dwellings to particular zones in a city bears a rational relation to the health, safety, and general welfare of the community. The establishment of such zones prevents congestion of population, secures quiet residential districts, expedites local transportation, and facilitates the suppression of disorder, the extinguishment of fires, and the enforcement of traffic and sanitary regulations. The danger of fire is lessened by the exclusion of factories from residential areas. *City of Aurora v. Burns,* 319 Ill. 84, 149 N.E. 784.

Early zoning ordinances divided the city into three zones: residential, commercial and manufacturing. Only residences were permitted in residence districts. Both stores and residences were allowed in commercial zones. All types of uses were permitted in manufacturing zones. Modern zoning ordinances usually create a greater number of classifications. Residential districts may be divided into single-family districts and multiple-family districts. Multiple-family zones may be divided into *walk-ups* and *high-rise* (elevator building) zones. Commercial zones may be divided into retail and wholesale districts, industrial zones into heavy and light industry zones.

Although a zoning ordinance may be valid in its general aspects, it may be invalid insofar as particular parcels of property are concerned. *Nectow v. Cambridge*, 227 U.S. 183.

> **EXAMPLE:** A zoning ordinance zoned a small tract of land for residential purposes. This tract of land was cut off from other lots by railroad tracks and by the intersection of diagonal streets, was entirely surrounded by property zoned for industrial use, and was practically worthless as residence property. It was held that the zoning ordinance was not valid as to this particular tract of land. Insofar as the zoning ordinance limits property to a use that cannot reasonably be made of it, it is invalid. *Tews v. Woolhiser*, 352 Ill. 212, 185 N.E. 827.

§ 460. **Exclusive zones.**   Zoning ordinances nowadays are attempting to do more than keep industries and stores out of residential zones. They are attempting to exclude residences from commercial and industrial zones. Ordinances zoning certain areas exclusively for industrial purposes are fairly widespread and are valid. *Roney v. Board of Supervisors*, 138 Cal.App.2d 740, 292 P.2d 529; *People ex rel. v. Morton Grove*, 16 Ill.2d 183, 157 N.E.2d 33; *Lamb v. City of Monroe*, 358 Mich. 136, 99 N.W.2d 566. Obviously it is just as injurious to the welfare of the community to permit residential development of land needed for industrial expansion as it is to permit industrial expansion in residential neighborhoods. We must remember that in our growing country the supply of usable land is limited, and zoning is the chief tool that communities utilize to insure wise use of our limited land areas.

A city may validly adopt a zoning ordinance that excludes all industrial uses from the city. *Duffcon Concrete Products v. Borough of Cresskill*, 1 N.J. 509, 64 A.2d 347, 9 A.L.R.2d 678; *Valley View Village v. Proffett*, 221 F.2d 412. In other words, if the city area is well adapted for residence purposes and there are adjoining areas available for industry, the city may totally exclude industry from its borders. A city may legally exclude all apartment houses from its borders. *Fanale v. Hasbrouck Heights*, 26 N.J. 320, 139 A.2d 749. And the entire village may be zoned exclusively for residential purposes. 101 C.J.S. 823; *Connor v. Township*, 249 Minn. 205, 81 N.W.2d 789; *Village v. Foster*, 83 N.Y.S.2d 148.

§ 461. **Floating zones.**   In contrast to old fashioned zoning which allocates specific uses to clearly defined zones is the new concept of the *floating zone*. The ordinance permits certain designated uses, such as garden apartments or research laboratories, to locate in all, or nearly all, districts of the city by special permit issued by the zoning board if the project meets the requirements set forth in the ordinance. These requirements are basically designed to protect adjoining residential areas. A developer can select any area within the existing zones designated for that purpose, and if the zoning board approves his application, the land becomes reclassified for the uses designated in his application for permit. The new idea seems likely to be sustained by the courts. *Summ v. Zoning Comm.*, 150 Conn. 79, 186 A.2d 160; *Huff v. Board of Appeals*, 214 Md. 48, 133 A.2d 82; *Rodgers v. Village of Tarrytown*, 307 N.Y. 115, 96 N.E.2d 731; *Donahue v. Zoning Board* (Penna.) 184 A.2d 610; 23 *Md. L. Rev.* 105. This idea has been haled as a step away from the monotony of old-fashioned *cookie cutter zoning*, which produces lots as uniform as if cut out by a cookie cutter.

§ 462.   **Sinking zones—open space zoning.**   Somewhat akin to the problem of forced dedication (see § 431), is the problem of open-space zoning. Here the city enacts an ordinance permitting the zoning or planning board to approve a plat of subdivision calling for lots smaller than the minimum size set by the zoning ordinance (see § 468), provided the subdivider will deed to the city for public purposes the land he need not devote to building sites. The smaller sites mean smaller homes and less expense for streets, utilities, and so forth, and this provides an incentive to the developer to give the deed. These ordinances, with their provisions for sinking or shrinking lot size, are still largely untested in the courts. See *Chrinko v. So. Brunswick Tp. Planning Bd.*, 77 N.J.S. 594, 187 A.2d 221 and *Mountcrest Estates v. Mayor etc. of Rockaway Twp.*, 96 N.J.S. 149, 232 A.2d 674.

§ 463.   **Contract zoning.**   In *contract zoning* a landowner who applies for an amendment to the zoning ordinance rezoning his land is granted such amendment but is required to enter into a covenant or contract with the city, which covenant imposes some restriction that will protect the city or adjoining owners but which cannot be provided through zoning amendments.

EXAMPLE: A, a landowner, applied to the City of Omaha for an amendment rezoning his land from residential to shopping center use. The city did so, but required A to enter into a covenant with the city that he would maintain landscaped and unimproved a buffer zone 300 feet wide between the center and an adjoining residential area, the entire area to be rezoned back to residential if A failed to abide by his covenant. The whole scheme was held valid. *Buchholz v. City of Omaha*, 174 Neb. 862, 120 N.W.2d 270. New York and Massachusetts also follow this view. In Florida, Illinois, Maryland, and New Jersey this type of arrangement is held invalid because it is thought inconsistent with the philosophy of zoning, which requires allocation of uses by ordinance, not by covenants or agreements. *Treadway v. City of Rockford*, 24 Ill.2d 188, 182 N.E.2d 219.

§ 464.   **Urban renewal zones.**   In the cities where urban re-development projects exist, a form of zoning is found which is known as *urban renewal zoning.* When an urban renewal project is contemplated, professional planners are hired by the city. They evolve an urban renewal plan for the area to be redeveloped. This plan, when approved by the city, sets up a scheme of new uses for the area. Many cities will rezone an urban renewal area separately from the zoning for the rest of the city and will designate the redevelopment area as an urban renewal zone. This portion of the ordinance contains the regulations which require the area to conform to the provisions of the urban renewal plan. If a change in the urban renewal plan is later made, a corresponding change in the urban renewal zone can be made without affecting the zoning outside the redevelopment area.

§ 465. **Amendments and rezoning—spot zoning.**   Amendments to the zoning ordinance are constantly being sought by landowners whose land will thereby become more valuable. For example, land is more valuable for industrial or commercial purposes than it is for residential purposes; so rezoning of residential land for industrial purposes will greatly increase its value. Some of such rezoning is invalid. Particularly objectionable is *spot zoning,* where the city by amendment of its ordinances, singles out and reclassifies one piece of property in a particular zone without any apparent basis for such distinction. 51 A.L.R.2d 267.

> **EXAMPLE:** A zoning ordinance was amended to permit construction of a mortuary in a residential district. This was held invalid as spot zoning. *Mueller v. Hoffmeister Undertaking Co.,* 343 Mo. 430, 121 S.W.2d 775; 51 A.L.R.2d 263.

There is some tendency to permit stores to reappear in residential zones on the theory that an area totally residential is "socially dead." This is particularly true in urban development areas where stores were social gathering places in predevelopment days. 73 *Harv. L. Rev.* 246, 248. These "spots" are planned in for the benefit of the community, not for the store owners; hence they are not illegal spot zoning.

When a real change in circumstances has taken place since the original ordinance was passed, an amendment that conforms the ordinance to the new circumstances will be valid.

> **EXAMPLE:** At the time the original zoning ordinance was adopted, the only structure in an area zoned industrial was a factory. Thereafter, many single-family residences were built in the area, but no new factories. To protect the homeowners, the area was rezoned for residential purposes, the old factory remaining as a nonconforming use. This is valid rezoning. *Atlantic Coast Line R.R. Co. v. Jacksonville* (Fla.), 68 S.2d 570.

> **EXAMPLE:** Where an urban redevelopment displaced many families, creating a need for many units to house those displaced, a single-family dwelling zone

could be revised to permit apartments. *Malafronte v. Planning Board* (Conn.), 230 A.2d 606.

Suppose that an area is zoned for single-family dwellings, and a number of such dwellings are erected in the area. Later the city comes to the conclusion that the area is really better adapted for business. In some states, the city may validly do this, for it is simply correcting its original error and is acting in the public interest. Even though those who erected residences may suffer as a result, the general public good outweighs their suffering. *Eggebeen v. Sonnenburg*, 239 Wis. 213, 1 N.W.2d 84; 138 A.L.R. 495. But in other states, the view is taken that land is bought *in reliance on existing zoning* and the buyer has a right to insist that the zoning ordinance remain the same *unless some change in the area makes a change necessary. Phipps v. Chicago*, 339 Ill. 315, 171 N.E. 289.

An amendment to the zoning ordinance will not be valid if it zones an area for a purpose for which it is in no way adapted so that the area becomes useless.

EXAMPLE: In an area almost completely industrial, the city rezoned a portion for apartment purposes, hoping thereby to keep the area vacant until funds could be raised to buy it for a city playground. The rezoning is invalid. *Building Corp. v. City of Chicago*, 395 Ill. 118, 69 N.E.2d 491.

Where the amendment to the zoning ordinance is in the nature of a comprehensive revision of the earlier zoning ordinance, there is a strong presumption of its validity. The suspicion with which courts view amendments to a zoning ordinance is confined to individual piecemeal amendments. *City of Baltimore v. N.A.A.C.P.*, 221 Md. 329, 157 A.2d 433.

The courts have been liberal in sustaining rezoning of portions of residential areas to permit shopping centers. 51 A.L.R.2d 263; 76 A.L.R.2d 1172.

A city cannot validly contract with a landowner to rezone his property. *Gregory Manor v. Clifton*, 53 N.J.S. 482, 147 A.2d 595.

A city may legally rezone areas from residential to industrial in order to get additional tax revenues to support its schools. *Gruber v. Mayor*, 39 N.J.1, 186 A.2d 489.

§ 466. Churches. It is well established that a zoning ordinance must not exclude churches or synagogues from residential districts. 74 A.L.R.2d 377.

§ 467. Schools. *Public* schools, of course, are not subject to zoning ordinances. *Hall v. City of Taft*, 47 Cal.2d 177, 302 P.2d 574. The only controversy, then, relates to *private* schools. The courts are not in agreement on this question. The more general view is that private schools, like churches, cannot be excluded from residential areas. *Roman Catholic*

Welfare Corp. v. City of Piedmont, 45 Cal.2d 32, 289 P.2d 438; 11 *Miami L.Q.* 68.

§ 468. **Minimum lot size and building area.**   In many localities ordinances have been passed specifying the minimum lot size that may be built upon. The theoretical legal basis for these ordinances is the fact that by spacing buildings farther apart they prevent the spread of fire and provide for ample light, air, and privacy. Hence courts have held such ordinances valid. *De Mars v. Zoning Commission,* 142 Conn. 580, 115 A.2d 653. Obviously, however, no court will allow such regulations to run hogwild. For example, a regulation specifying a five-acre minimum lot size in New York City would be so completely out of touch with reality that the courts would strike it down. However, the farther out in the country, the larger the minimum lot size that the courts will sustain. In a rural area, a minimum lot size of five acres has been sustained. *Fischer v. Bedminster Township,* 11 N.J. 194, 93 A.2d 378; *Jones v. Town of Treadway* (Wash.) 425 P.2d 904. In a similar setting, a four-acre minimum has been sustained. *Senior v. Zoning Commission,* 146 Conn. 531, 153 A.2d 415. And even in a large city like Los Angeles where land values are high, a minimum frontage of fifty feet has been sustained. *Clemons v. City of Los Angeles,* 36 Cal.2d 95, 222 P.2d 439.

A recent development is the law that gives the purchaser of a lot containing less than the minimum area the right to declare the deed void on discovering such violation. Such laws are valid. *Clemons v. City of Los Angeles,* 36 Cal.2d 95, 222 P.2d 439. A purchaser who exercises this right is entitled to a refund of the purchase price he has paid, which provides a very effective method of enforcing the ordinance requirements.

Often such ordinances have been attacked on the ground that they are a form of economic segregation or *snob zoning.* And looking behind the scenes and reading between the lines, one can often discern that the old guard that runs a town has caused such an ordinance to be passed in order to keep out subdividers and new settlers. Courts are not permitted to probe into such hidden motives. As long as substantial reasons do, in fact, exist for the passage of such ordinances, and as long as the lot sizes specified are not clearly unreasonable, the ordinances will be held valid.

If I buy a lot of lawful size in a platted subdivision, and a zoning ordinance is later enacted that requires a greater minimum size, I may nevertheless build on this *substandard lot* if I own no adjoining land to which this lot can be attached. The city cannot legally prevent such use. 1954 Law Forum 196.

EXAMPLE: When a subdivision was laid out and the plat recorded, lots having a frontage of twenty-three feet were legal. A number of such lots were sold.

Thereafter, the city passed an ordinance making it illegal to build on a lot having less than sixty feet frontage. As to the lot in question the ordinance was invalid. *Milano v. Patterson,* 93 N.Y.S.2d 419.

The village is under an absolute duty to provide for these substandard lots. It cannot render them useless. *Long Island Research Bureau v. Young,* 159 N.Y.S.2d 414. Nor can the city compel the owner of a substandard lot to sell or to buy land from an adjoining owner in order to assemble a lot of the required size. *Brandau v. Grosse Pointe Parke,* 5 Mich. App. 297, 146 N.W.2d 695; *Krscnski v. Shenkin,* 53 N.J.S. 590, 148 A.2d 58; 16 *Syracuse L. Rev.* 612. A variance should be granted to the substandard lot. *Evans v. Augusta Board,* 113 Ga. App. 113, 147 S.E.2d 455. *Saravo Bros. v. Zoning Board,* 231 A.2d 9 (R.I.).

But if I own two adjoining thirty-foot lots and build a house on one and put my lawn on the other, and thereafter the village creates a fifty-foot minimum lot size, I will not be allowed to sell off the lot with the lawn on it. There is no hardship to me in leaving me where I planned to be when I built my house. *Galpin v. River Forest,* 26 Ill.2d 515.

Minimum lot size ordinances are apt to bear with excessive harshness on irregular shaped lots. As a rule, the owner of an irregular lot that was platted prior to the enactment of the zoning ordinance is entitled to put it to some use, and the city cannot prevent this by blind insistence on the minimum standards. *Jenckes v. Building Commissioner,* 341 Mass. 162, 167 N.E.2d 757.

A valid and buildable lot may become an illegal building site by conveyance of a portion thereof.

EXAMPLE: A owns a lot improved with a building. He sells a portion of the tract. As a result, the portion remaining is smaller than the minimum size allowed by law. Occupancy of the building is now unlawful. *Bronen v. Marmer,* 206 N.Y.S.2d 909.

EXAMPLE: A owned a number of contiguous platted lots. An ordinance was passed under which these lots were less than the minimum size. A could have divided the entire tract into legal size building sites. Instead he conveyed out alternate lots to his wife, so that neither he nor his wife held any legal size lot. These lots cannot be built upon. A himself created the situation of which he complains. *Corsino v. Groveer,* 148 Conn. 299, 170 A.2d 267. This is illegal checker boarding. 16 *Syracuse L. Rev.* 612.

Ordinances frequently forbid construction of buildings having less than a minimum floor area. If the requirements are reasonable, the ordinance is valid. 96 A.L.R.2d 1409.

EXAMPLE: A township zoning ordinance prohibited the erection of any building having a floor area of less than 768 square feet. It was held valid. *Lionshead Lake, Inc. v. Wayne Township,* 10 N.J. 165, 89 A.2d 693; *Dundee Realty Co. v. City of*

Omaha, 144 Neb. 448, 13 N.W.2d 634; *Thompson v. City of Carrolton* (Tex. Civ. App.), 211 S.W.2d 970. But in Michigan, such ordinances are not valid. 20 *Law & Contemporary Problems* 344.

Sometimes the city divides the residential area into zones and prescribes varying minimum building area requirements in the different zones. These ordinances are valid. *Cosmopolitan Bank v. City of Chicago,* 22 Ill.2d 367, 176 N.E.2d 795; *Bilbar Construction Co. v. Board of Adjustment,* 393 Pa. 62, 141 A.2d 851.

§ **469. Undeveloped areas.** A number of court decisions now appear to sustain the zoning of sparsely settled land as residential and agricultural, even if it is adapted for other uses. *Anderson v. Jester,* 206 Ia. 452, 221 N.W. 354; *DuPage County v. Henderson,* 402 Ill. 179, 83 N.E.2d 720; 101 C.J.S. 823. The problem here lies in the fact that zoning bodies, often counties, attempt to set aside undeveloped areas for residential purposes even though the land is not ripe for immediate residential development. Landowners may wish to use parts of the area now for business purposes. If zoning is postponed, and scattered businesses are allowed to spring up, the businesses will have to be given nonconforming use status, and that, of course, is not desirable. As long as the area is definitely in the path of residential development, as where it is on the outskirts of a rapidly growing city and the zoning is reasonable, taking into account the probable course of development of the area within a reasonable future time, the zoning is valid. 29 *Rocky Mt. L. Rev.* 202. But to zone as residential large areas of sparsely settled land where residential use lies somewhere in the dim future deprives the landowners of the possibility of enjoying for the indefinite future any income from nonresidential use. Such ordinances are held void. 3 *Syracuse L. Rev.* 292. Good planning of the location, extent, and boundaries of the zones will help to sustain the ordinance. The ordinance should be made flexible by the inclusion of numerous special exception categories for airports, sanitariums, and various industrial and commercial uses.

§ **470. Aesthetic considerations.** A number of court decisions now sustain zoning provisions that are based solely on aesthetic considerations. *Berman v. Parker,* 348 U.S. 26; 64 *Col. L. Rev.* 81; 14 *DePaul L. Rev.* 104.

EXAMPLE: An ordinance required new buildings to conform to the architecture of existing buildings. It was held valid. *State v. Saveland Co.,* 269 Wisc. 262, 69 N.W.2d 217.

§ **471. Accessory uses.** Every zoning ordinance recognizes that certain uses different from, but incidental to, the main use prescribed in the zone are normal. Such uses are legalized under the name *accessory uses.* Many accessory uses are found in residential zones.

> **EXAMPLES:** Coin-operated washing machines and dryers in apartment buildings, also pay telephones, postage vending machines, swimming pools and skating rinks for which a charge is made, milk vending machines, etc. are accessory uses. *Newark v. Daly,* 85 N.J.S. 555, 205 A.2d 459. Likewise, a food shop in a large apartment hotel is often permitted. A private garage on the rear of a residential lot is universally permitted. A doctor expects to see patients in his home even though he lives in a residential area.

§ 472. **Bulk zoning.** *Bulk zoning* is zoning that regulates the size and shape of the buildings to be erected and their location on the land. The purpose of this type of zoning is to control population density, open space, and access to daylight and air. The ordinance requires that any building erected must leave specified areas along the front, side, and rear of the lot which must not be built upon.

§ 473. **Variances.** Even the best ordinance may cause unintentional hardship to particular tracts of land. Some elasticity is needed if these hardship cases are to be dealt with. Most ordinances create a board, usually called the *board of adjustment* or *board of appeals,* which is given the power to authorize individual property owners to deviate from the terms of the ordinances where literal compliance would cause *undue hardship or practical difficulties.* This authorization is called a *variance.* The courts have worked out a number of requirements that must be met if a variance is to be granted.

1. The hardship must be special and peculiar to the particular property.

> **EXAMPLE:** A lot is so irregular in shape that if all the front, rear, and side line restrictions were observed, no building at all could be built on the lot.

If the hardship complained of is a condition which affects all property in the district, the hardship is not special and peculiar to any lot in the area and no individual lot owner will be granted a variance.

> **EXAMPLE:** Foul odors from a nearby industrial area exist in an area zoned as residential. No residential lot owner will be granted a variance to build a factory. A plea must be made to the authorities to amend the ordinance.

2. Hardship means that if the landowner complies with the provisions of the ordinance, he can secure no reasonable return from, or make no reasonable use of, his property. 29 *N.C.L. Rev.* 250. With respect to income property, a party seeking a variance must prove that the land in question, if devoted to its existing or any permitted use, will not yield a reasonable

return. This involves a detailed showing of the price paid for the property, the taxes assessed, expenses of operation, annual income, and so on. Then if the net income earned is not a reasonable return on the amount invested, hardship is shown. *Crossroads Recreation v. Broz*, 4 N.Y.2d 39, 149 N.E.2d 65. The landowner should also show that reasonable return cannot be anticipated from other permitted uses. *Forrest v. Evershed*, 7 N.Y.2d 256, 164 N.E.2d 841. The fact that a man could make more money by devoting his property to another purpose is not legal hardship. Everyone knows that land is worth more for commercial or industrial purposes than it is for residential, and yet most of our land must necessarily be zoned residential.

3. The hardship must not be self-created.

EXAMPLE: A departs from the plans attached to his application for a building permit and builds his home five feet closer to the side lines of his lot than the ordinance allows. When the building inspector stops him, A applies for a variance. He will not get it.

EXAMPLE: The city in question has an ordinance specifying a minimum lot area. A owns a building on a legal size lot. He then sells the building and enough of the land so that the building still occupies a legal building site. However, the portion of the lot left to A is now less than the legal size. He will not be given a variance to permit him to build. *Board of Zoning Appeals v. Waskelo*, 240 Ind. 594, 168 N.E.2d 72.

4. The proposed new use must not change the essential character of the neighborhood. It must be consistent with the general plan of the ordinance.

EXAMPLE: A variance will not be granted to permit introduction of a cemetery into an area zoned residential.

Some courts are so strict on this point that they will not allow a variance that changes the *use* permitted by the ordinance. In other words, they will allow deviations only from the area, height, and location regulations of the ordinance.

EXAMPLE: Some courts will not permit a variance for an apartment house in a single-family area because this would be a *use* variance. *Lee v. Board of Adjustment*, 226 N.C. 107, 37 S.E.2d 128, 168 A.L.R. 1.

However, most courts will permit a use variance where the hardship is great.

EXAMPLE: A owns a vacant lot in a single-family dwelling zone, and nonconforming apartment buildings are his neighbors on both sides, that is, these build-

ings were built before the ordinance was passed and are allowed to continue in operation. He will be given a variance for the erection of an apartment building. The sound
reason for this variance is that no one can be induced to build a single-family dwelling
on such a building site.

In granting a variance, the zoning board may impose conditions. *Vlahos
v. Little Boar's Head District*, 101 N.H. 460, 146 A.2d 257; Zweifel Mfg.
Co. v. Peoria, 11 Ill.2d 489, 144 N.E.2d 593.

EXAMPLE: The board may put in a condition that the architecture of
the permitted building conform to the architecture of neighboring structures, or that
certain areas be left open and landscaped.

A variance may be limited in time.

EXAMPLE: A variance given for five years is valid. *Bungle v. Board of
Supervisors,* 4 Cal. Reptr. 493, 351 P.2d 765.

A variance may, if so desired, be made personal to the applicant so
that a purchaser from the applicant would not be entitled to the benefit
thereof. *Maki v. Town of Yarmouth*, 340 Mass. 207 163 N.E.2d 633.

Questions may arise as to who may apply for a variance. Clearly the
landowner may do so. A contract purchaser is also qualified. However,
one who is merely negotiating for the purchase of the land cannot apply
for a variance.

§ 474. **Special exceptions.** A common provision in zoning
ordinances authorizes the board of appeals to issue special permits for
special purposes, such as public utility structures, churches, hospitals,
private schools, clubs, or cemeteries. Obviously, institutions of this character must be located somewhere, but some control must be exercised by
the zoning authorities over their location so that adverse effects on the
other property owners will be held to a minimum. Typically, the ordinance may list a number of different uses that may be licensed "where
public convenience and welfare will be substantially served." *Dunham v.
Zoning Board*, 68 R.I. 88, 26 A.2d 614. The distinction between special
exceptions and variances is a technical one. In the case of variances, the
board is given authority to authorize violations of the zoning ordinance
in hardship cases. In the case of special exceptions, the ordinance itself
lists certain cases in which certain special uses are to be permitted, and
the board only determines whether facts exist to bring the particular case
within the terms of the ordinance. *Stone v. Cray*, 89 N.H. 483, 200 Atl.
517. It is not necessary to show "practical difficulties or unnecessary hardship," as is true in variance cases. *Montgomery County v. Merlands Club*,
202 Md. 279, 96 A.2d 261.

NEW DIRECTIONS: Looking toward the future, one might hazard the guess that increasing resort will be made to the special exception technique. In other words, variances will be hard to get, because by and large they will represent unwelcome deviations from the zoning ordinance. But the things the city really wants, such as garden apartments, shopping centers, and research laboratories will be readily procurable by means of an elastic special exceptions provision in the ordinances. *Cameo Park Homes, Inc. v. Planning Commission,* 150 Conn. 672, 192 A.2d 886; *Ranney v. Istituto,* 20 N.J. 189, 119 A.2d 142.

In some states, the special exception is referred to as a *special use. Tullo v. Township of Millburn,* 4 N.J.S. 509, 149 A.2d 620. In others, it is called a *conditional use. Tustin Heights Assn. v. Board,* 170 Cal. App.2d 619, 339 P.2d 914.

§ 475.   **Nonconforming uses.**   It is customary for zoning ordinances to provide that a structure existing at the time the ordinance was enacted may continue to be employed for its purposes even though the remainder of the district is zoned for other purposes. Such exceptions are generally referred to as *nonconforming uses.* An exception is made as to nonconforming uses because it would be illegal to destroy property values by preventing the use of existing structures.

Zoning ordinances, in permitting nonconforming uses, permit ordinary repairs to be made, but they sometimes forbid *structural alterations* of a nonconforming building. A structural alteration is such as would change the physical structure of the building or would change an old building in such a way as to convert it into a new or substantially different structure.

EXAMPLE: A operated a milk plant which was a nonconforming use in a residential zone. His attempt to replace decayed wooden walls with brick walls was a prohibited structural alteration. *Selligman v. Von Allmen Bros. Inc.,* 297 Ky. 121, 179 S.W.2d 207; 87 A.L.R.2d 99.

Nonconforming uses, it is felt, should be gradually eliminated. *Cole v. City of Battle Creek,* 298 Mich. 98, 298 N.W. 466. The theory is that zoning seeks to safeguard the future in the expectation that time will repair the mistakes of the past. However, the treatment a particular nonconforming use will receive if it seeks to increase or change its use appears to vary considerably owing to differences in zoning ordinances. 87 A.L.R.2d 4.

Once a nonconforming owner abandons the use of his property for a nonconforming purpose, he loses his right to make a nonconforming use of the property and must thereafter use it only in conformity with the uses allowed to other properties in the neighborhood. 60 *Harv. L. Rev.* 807. Were the law otherwise, an owner could keep his property in a nonconforming class forever.

EXAMPLE: The owner of a nonconforming slaughterhouse took down the smokestack and definitely discontinued the slaughterhouse business. He thereby lost his right to make a nonconforming use. *Beyer v. Mayor of Baltimore,* 182 Md. 444, 34 A.2d 765. Also where an old nonconforming house trailer was sought to be replaced by a new one, the change was refused because the old use had been abandoned. *Town of Windham v. Sprague* (Me.) 219 A.2d 548.

But a mere temporary discontinuance of the nonconforming use, as when a landowner is temporarily unable to procure a tenant, will not constitute an abandonment of the right to resume such use. *Landay v. MacWilliams,* 173 Md. 460, 196 Atl. 293; 114 A.L.R. 993.

If a nonconforming building is either destroyed or partially destroyed by fire or other casualty, many ordinances forbid rebuilding. 60 *Harv. L. Rev.* 807.

Recently, ordinances have been passed that attempt to place a time limit on the right to continue a nonconforming use. To the extent that these *amortization ordinances* prohibit continuance of the nonconforming use after the useful economic life of the building has come to an end, most courts would consider them valid. 42 A.L.R.2d 1146. The question has come up often in connection with billboards and junkyards along highways, a subject on which interest has been focused because of the Highway Beautification Act of 1965. Title 23, U.S.C.A. § 131. This law, by controlling the flow of federal revenue into the highway construction program, offers inducements to the states to enact legislation for the removal of billboards, screening of junkyards, and acquisition of scenic easements along our highways. While the federal legislation contemplates use of the power of eminent domain to achieve its purposes, some states have attacked the problem by resort to the police power. One group of states sanctions removal of highway billboards by an amortization ordinance enacted under the police power. *Village of Gurnee v. Miller,* 69 Ill. App.2d 248, 215 N.E.2d 829; *Shifflett v. Baltimore County* (Md.) 230 A.2d 310; *McKinney v. Riley,* 105 N.H. 249, 197 A.2d 218; *Cromwell v. Ferrier,* 19 N.Y.2d 263, 225 N.E.2d 749. *Contra: State Highway Dept. v. Branch,* 222 Ga. 770, 152 S.E.2d 372; *City of Akron v. Chapman,* 160 Ohio St. 382, 116 N.E.2d 697; *City of Corpus Christi v. Allen,* 152 Tex. 137, 254 S.W.2d 759.

§ 476. **Effect of zoning ordinance on restrictions.**   Restrictions contained in a deed, plat, or property owner's agreement are neither nullified nor superseded by the adoption of a zoning ordinance. *Chuba v. Glasgow,* 61 N.M. 302, 299 P.2d 744. *Schwarzchild v. Wolborne,* 186 Va. 1052, 45 S.E.2d 152.

EXAMPLE: A deed provided that use of the land thereby conveyed was restricted to residence purposes. Thereafter, an ordinance was passed zoning this area for commercial purposes, and the owner attempted to construct a gasoline station thereon. It was held that the deed restriction would be enforced, and a court order was entered forbidding erection of the gasoline station. *Dolan v. Brown*, 338 Ill. 412, 170 N.E. 425.

However, a change of use in the zoning ordinance does help to show that a change in the neighborhood has taken place, and the court may well decline thereafter to enforce the building restrictions on the ground of change in neighborhood. *Goodwin Bros v. Combs Lumber Co.*, 275 Ky. 114, 120 S.W.2d 1024; *Austin v. Van Horn*, 225 Mich. 117, 237 N.W. 550; 26 C.J.S. Deeds § 171 (2); 1963 *Wis. L. Rev.* 323, 326.

NEW DIRECTIONS: The older zoning ordinances permitted residences to be erected in any other zone. The newer ordinances, by and large, forbid residential uses in commercial and industrial zones. Where the earlier building restriction calls for residential use and later zoning ordinance forbids residential use, the zoning ordinance supersedes the restriction. *1.77 Acres of Land v. State*, 241 A.2d 513; *Grubel v. MacLaughlin*, 286 Fed.Supp.24; 42 Calif. L. Rev. 596, 634.

§ 477. **Mortgages.**   Zoning laws are binding on mortgagees. When a mortgagee loaned money for construction of a building that violated a zoning ordinance, the court refused to protect him although he was ignorant of the fact that the ordinance was being violated, since in dealing with real estate, all who are interested are required to take notice of zoning laws. *Siegemund v. Building Commissioner*, 263 Mass. 212, 160 N.E. 795. Accordingly, a mortgagee making a construction loan should satisfy himself that the contemplated improvement complies with existing ordinances. Otherwise he may find construction of the building halted by a court order after part of his mortgage money has been paid out.

§ 478. **Enforcement of zoning ordinance.**   It is usually provided in the zoning ordinance that any property owner wishing to erect a building must first apply to the commissioner of buildings or other proper official for a building permit. Every such application must be accompanied by plans and specifications of the contemplated structure. The official inspects the plans and declines to issue the permit if a violation of the zoning ordinance is disclosed. If, despite the fact that the contemplated structure would violate the zoning ordinance, the building permit is nevertheless issued, any other property owner whose property would suffer special damage by erection of the proposed structure, for example, a neighbor, may, if he acts promptly, obtain a court order prohibiting the erection of the building. *Garner v. County of DuPage*, 8 Ill.2d 155, 133 N.E.2d 303. Although it is advisable to do so, the complaining property owner need not first request the public authorities to take action. *Fitzgerald v. Merard Holding Co.*, 106 Conn. 475, 138 Atl. 483. If the complaining owner acts promptly in asserting his rights, but construction of the building is nevertheless begun, the offending property owner may be ordered by the court to demolish the illegal portion of the structure.

EXAMPLE: Despite protests of an adjoining owner before the commissioner of buildings and the Zoning Board of Appeals, a permit was issued to a property owner to construct an apartment building that violated the zoning ordinance in that it did not have a one-foot setback for every nine feet of rise above a height of seventy-two feet. While litigation was pending to declare the permit invalid, the apartment building corporation proceeded with construction of the building. Eventually the courts declared the permit invalid, and the adjoining owner filed suit to compel the corporation to reconstruct the building to conform to the zoning ordinance. It developed that such reconstruction could be accomplished only at a cost of $343,837.07. Nevertheless, the court ordered the building corporation to reconstruct the building to comply with the ordinance. *Welton v. 40 East Oak St. Bldg. Corp.*, 70 F.2d 377.

It is quite generally held that if a permit is issued, and in reliance thereon erection of the building is begun, *the city* cannot thereafter enforce the zoning ordinance if it is discovered that the permit should not have been issued. Shellburne Inc. v. Roberts, 224 A.2d 250 (Del.).

§ 479. **Planning.** City and regional planning figures prominently in the life of many communities today. State laws authorize the adoption by planning commissions of master plans. Such a commission plans for the systematic and orderly development of the community, with particular regard for the location of future major street systems, transportation systems, parks, recreation areas, industrial and commercial undertakings, and residential areas; the creation and preservation of civic beauty; and other kindred matters, all looking not only to the present, but with a view to the orderly development of the unbuilt, as well as the built-up areas.

Generally the formulation of a master plan is not a precondition to the enactment of a zoning ordinance. True, the zoning ordinance must be rational and bear within itself some evidence of logical planning, but if that is present, it suffices. *Angermeier v. Sea Girt*, 27 N.J. 298, 142 A.2d 624; 13 *Ark. L. Rev.* 5.

§ 480. **Building codes.** Most cities have adopted building codes specifying in great detail various requirements as to the construction of buildings, including requirements as to fireproof construction, load and stress, size and location of rooms, means of exit, windows and ventilation, sanitary equipment, electrical installation, chimneys, heating plant, mechanical refrigeration, illumination of exits, and standpipes. Often these are divided into separate codes, such as the electrical code or plumbing code. Innumerable special provisions will be encountered relating to special types of structures, such as theaters, schools, hospitals, garages, amusement parks, billboards, canopies, marquees, illuminated roof signs, and grandstands. Hazardous use units, such as drycleaning establishments, grain elevators, or paint-spraying rooms, are also subject to special regulations.

The fact that a building was erected while an older, more lenient law was in effect does not insulate it from newer, more rigid requirements. As long as the new standards are reasonable, the old buildings must conform to them.

EXAMPLE: An ordinance required tenement houses to have a supply of water on each floor. All old buildings must comply with this ordinance. *Health Dept. v. Trinity Church,* 145 N.Y. 32, 39 N.E. 833.

EXAMPLE: An ordinance required all hotels for transients to provide automatic sprinklers. It was held valid. *City of Chicago v. National Management,* 22 Ill. App.2d 445, 161 N.E.2d 358.

A landowner who proposes to erect a building must establish not only that it will comply with the zoning ordinance, but that all requirements of the building code will be complied with. Hence an application for a building permit, with its accompanying plans and specifications, is examined not only for possible zoning ordinance violations, but also for possible violations of the building code. Thus the application may be handled by a number of different departments of the city, such as the fire department, board of health, or boiler inspection department, before the permit is finally issued.

Permits are required not only where new construction is contemplated, but also where enlargements, alterations, or substantial repairs of existing structures are to be made.

Many zoning and building ordinances provide that no newly constructed building may be occupied until inspected by a city official for violations of ordinances. If no violations exist, a *certificate of occupancy* is issued by the city. Obviously it is dangerous to buy and pay for a newly constructed building without determining that a certificate of occupancy has been issued.

Local ordinances often provide that the commissioner of buildings or other proper official shall make an annual inspection of certain types of buildings. If any violation of the building code is disclosed, the owner or occupant is required to make the necessary alterations to make the building comply with the code. It is customary in some localities for an intending purchaser to cause a search to be made in the various departments charged with enforcing the building ordinances, such as the tenement house department, the building department, the fire department, or the health department. If any record of an existing violation is thereby disclosed, the seller is required to cure the violation. In order to avoid delay in closing the deal, the seller may permit the buyer to retain a portion of the purchase price as security to insure the seller's subsequent removal of the violation.

§ 481.   **Historical sites legislation.**   Laws are springing up in the older sections of the country providing for preservations of historical sites.

EXAMPLE: The island of Nantucket was a famous seat of the whaling industry and, to a great extent, remains quaint and unspoiled. Massachusetts has enacted a law providing that no building there may be demolished or altered without a special permit, which will, of course, be refused if such action could detrimentally affect the quaint appearance of the island. Opinion of the Justices, 333 Mass. 773, 128 N.E.2d 557; 63 Columb. L. Rev. 708; 35 U. of Chicago L. Rev. 362.

§ 482.   **Demolition of buildings.**   A building that is dangerously unsafe is a public nuisance and may be demolished by the city authorities without payment of compensation to the owner. *City of Honolulu v. Cavness,* 45 Hawaii 232, 364 P.2d 646. Quite commonly laws and ordinances covering this situation go on to provide that the city has a lien, quite like a mortgage, on the vacant land for the expenses of demolition. This is called a *demolition lien.* In some states this lien is given priority over existing liens, such as mortgages.

Chapter 29

TAXES, SPECIAL
ASSESSMENTS, AND
FEDERAL INCOME TAX

§ 483. **In general.** General taxes are levied by various taxing bodies, such as states, cities, villages, counties, or school districts, to raise revenue needed for the performance of various public functions, such as maintaining roads, schools, parks, police departments, fire departments, county hospitals, and mental institutions. One of the most important sources of revenue is the tax on real estate. Although this tax is encountered in most, if not all, states, laws regarding levy, assessment, and collection of the tax vary considerably, so that few general statements can be made that will be universally true.

§ 484. **Steps in taxation.** The nine principal steps in real estate taxation are: budgeting, appropriation, levy, assessment, review of the assessment, equalization, computation, collection of the tax through voluntary payment by the taxpayer, and collection of the tax through compulsory methods, such as tax sale.

§ 485. **Budgeting.** Budgeting involves an annual determination of how much money is to be spent by each taxing body and for what purposes. Keep in mind that in each state there are numerous bodies—cities, villages, counties, school boards, and sanitary districts—that have the power to levy taxes, and each body must prepare its annual budget and make its annual appropriation and tax levy.

§ 486. **Appropriation.** Appropriation is the step whereby the taxing body formally enacts into law its decision to spend the money, with a specification of the particular purpose for which the money is to be spent, the amount to be spent for each purpose, and the source from which the funds are to be derived.

§ 487. **Levy.**   The appropriation usually provides that part of the money to be spent is to be raised by property taxation. It thereupon becomes necessary to levy a tax for this purpose. When the legislative body of some taxing unit, such as the village board of a village or the school board of a school district, votes to impose a tax of a specified amount on persons or property, this action is known as the levy of a tax. The levy is an indispensable step in arriving at a valid tax.

It is the levy that provides a field day for tax lawyers. Various technical defects will invalidate part or all of the tax levy, and attorneys for railroads and other big taxpayers are most astute in discovering these technical defects. As a rule, only those taxpayers who file proper objections may take advantage of these technical defects. Taxpayers who pay their money without formal objection cannot get their money back if the tax is later held invalid.

§ 488. **Tax rate limitations.**   In levying taxes, taxing bodies must see to it that they do not spend more than the law allows. Tax rate limitations will be found both in state constitutions and state laws.

§ 489. **Assessment.**   Assessment of real estate for taxation involves determining the value of each parcel of land to be taxed. In assessing real estate, a book or list is first prepared by the proper officer, containing a description of all the taxable real estate in his town, county, or district and the names of the owners thereof. This book is turned over to the tax assessor, who proceeds to place a valuation on each parcel of land and enters such valuation in the book. This book is called the *tax list* or *assessment roll*.

In assessing land, the assessor should consider various factors, such as market price of similar land, income, depreciation, obsolescence, and reproduction cost of buildings. Actual methods vary widely. Farmland is still usually taxed at its market value, but urban land is often assessed differently. In assessing urban land, assessors often place a value on the land as though it were vacant and then value the building at what it would cost to build today, deducting from this figure an allowance for depreciation. The two valuations are then added together to fix the total assessment. 35 *Mich. L. Rev.* 1229. Assessors may employ experts and use expert scientific procedures as a basis for their valuations. But any wholesale turning over of valuation to experts would be illegal, for it is the assessor's judgment, based perhaps on expert advice, but his own judgment nevertheless, that the law requires.

In some states, it is the practice to assess property at a certain percentage of its true value. This is not objectionable as long as the assessor assesses all property at the same proportion of its true value. Likewise, if all the property is uniformly overvalued, the courts will not intervene. The main thing is uniformity. If a taxpayer can show that his property was assessed at its full value, whereas the rest of the property in the district is uniformly assessed at less than its full value, the courts will lower the assessment complained of to the general level.

§ 490. **Uniformity.**   Under various constitutional provisions it is required that the taxation of property be equal and uniform, so that taxpayers owning tracts of substantially equal value will pay substantially the same amount of taxes. This is an ideal difficult, if not impossible, of attainment, and courts are aware of that fact. Hence if the assessor has made an honest mistake in assessing a particular tract of land, the courts as a rule will not intervene. Courts do not sit to correct mere errors in an assessment. The error can be corrected only by an appeal to the board of review or other body designated to review and correct the assessor's valuations.

§ 491. **Exemptions.**   Each state grants various exemptions from taxation. The nature and form of these exemptions vary from state to state. Common exemptions are those extended to public property, charitable organizations, schools, religious institutions, and cemeteries.

§ 492. **Review of assessment.**   All states provide some method by which the taxpayer can have the assessor's valuation reviewed and corrected by some higher authority. The procedures vary widely. In New England, the reviewing board is often a town tribunal, such as the selectmen. In other areas, the reviewing officials may be called a *board of equalization* or a *board of review.* In some states, a further appeal is provided to a higher board of review. In other states, the decision of the first board of review can be appealed directly to some court. 17 *N.C. L. Rev.* 118. As a rule, the taxpayer cannot appeal to the courts unless he has first tried his luck before the board of review or other initial reviewing body. *First Nat. Bank v. Weld County,* 264 U.S. 450.

§ 493. **Equalization.**   Equalization is the raising or lowering of assessed values in a particular county or taxing district in order to equalize them with the total assessments in other counties or taxing districts.

EXAMPLE: The board of equalization deducts a certain percentage from all assessments made in a certain township because the township assessor valued the property on a higher level than did the assessors of other townships.

This function is usually performed by a board known as the *board of equalization.* The board of equalization does not handle complaints of individual taxpayers, but raises or lowers the assessment of each county or taxing district as a whole in order to bring the assessment into line with assessments in other counties or taxing districts.

§ 494. **Computation of tax.**   The amount of the tax that a particular tract of land must pay is computed by multiplying the assessed value of the tract by the tax rate applicable to the land in that particular taxing district. The tax is then entered on the tax books.

§ 495. **Lien.**   Tax laws usually provide that real estate taxes are a lien on the land. Often it is provided that such a lien is prior and superior to all other liens, both those that antedate and those that come after the date on which the tax lien attaches to the land.

§ 496. **Payment.**   Payment to the proper official at the proper time discharges the lien of the tax.

When the *tax records* show a tax as paid, a purchaser or mortgagee who relies on such records is protected against enforcement of the tax should it later develop that the tax actually remains unpaid. *Jackson Park Hospital v. Courtney*, 364 Ill. 497, 4 N.E.2d 864. A number of states make provision for the issuance of a certificate by some tax official showing all unpaid taxes on the property, and purchasers who rely on such certificates are generally protected against errors in the certificate. *Burton v. City of Denver*, 99 Colo. 207, 61 P.2d 856; *Amerada Petroleum Corp. v. 1010.61 Acres of Land*, 146 F.2d 99; 21 A.L.R.2d 1273. When a landowner redeems from a tax sale and the certificate of redemption shows that all delinquent taxes have been thereby redeemed, a purchaser or mortgagee who relies on such a certificate will be protected if it later develops that some delinquent taxes in fact remain. *Jones v. Sturtzenberg*, 59 Cal. App. 350, 210 Pac. 835.

A purchaser or mortgagee is not ordinarily protected in relying on a *tax receipt* showing full payment of the taxes. Despite issuance of the receipt, the tax collector is allowed to show that a part of the tax remains unpaid. However, South Dakota has a law making a tax receipt conclusive evidence that all prior taxes have been paid.

§ 497. **Proceedings to enforce payment of taxes.**   Various special remedies are provided by local law for the collection of unpaid real estate taxes.

Tax sale is a common method. It is usually preceded by the giving of notice, often by publication, to the delinquent taxpayer. Unless the taxpayer appears and defends, which he may do if the tax is illegal or if he has some other defense, a judgment will be rendered for the amount of the tax and penalty due. This judgment orders the land to be sold. Thereafter, notice of the coming sale is published, and on the date fixed for sale the land is sold at public sale. Usually a certificate of sale is issued to the purchaser, stating that he will be entitled to a deed at the expiration of the redemption period if no redemption is made. In some states, the state, county, or city is permitted to bid at the tax sale.

The landowner or other persons interested, such as mortgagees, may redeem the land from the tax sale within the period specified by the local law. If redemption is not made, a tax deed is issued to the purchaser.

Although state laws vary as to the validity of tax titles, a tax title acquired through normal tax sale usually constitutes the flimsiest sort of title, since deviation from the technical requirements of the law will invalidate the title. In some states, however, a tax deed is regarded as a conveyance of good title to the land. *Thomas v. Kolker*, 195 Md. 470, 73 A.2d 886; *Shapiro v. Hruby*, 21 Ill.2d 353, 172 N.E.2d 775.

An alternative method of enforcement of the tax lien is by foreclosure, the procedure being similar to that employed in mortgage foreclosure. In some states, a good title can be acquired through tax foreclosure.

§ 498. **Soldiers' and Sailors' Civil Relief Act.**   The Soldiers' and Sailors' Civil Relief Act provides that when real estate is owned and occupied for dwelling, professional, business, or agricultural purposes by a person in military service or his dependents at the commencement of his period of military service and is still so occupied by his dependents or employees, such land cannot be sold for nonpayment of taxes or assessments except by permission of the court. The court will postpone the sale until after termination of the military service unless the ability of the person to pay such taxes or assessments has not been materially affected by reason of such military service. When the court does permit a sale or forfeiture of the property, the time allowed to redeem from such sale or forfeiture is extended so that redemption can be made at any time within six months after the termination of the military service. Also, the amount of interest or penalty that can be charged in case of any delinquent tax or assessment on such lands must not exceed 6 per cent per annum.

§ 499. **Special assessments.**   There is a distinction between public improvements, which benefit the entire community, and local improvements, which benefit particular real estate or limited areas of land. The latter improvements are usually financed by means of special, or local, assessments. These assessments are, in a certain sense, taxes. But an assessment differs from a general tax in that an assessment is levied only on property in the immediate vicinity of some local, municipal improvement and is valid only where the property assessed receives some special benefit differing from the benefit that the general public enjoys. In fact, if the primary purpose of an improvement is to benefit the public generally, as, for example, the erection of a county courthouse, it cannot be financed by special assessments even though it may incidentally benefit property in the particular locality.

Special assessments are often imposed for opening, paving, grading, and guttering streets, construction of sidewalks and sewers, installation of street lighting, and so on.

§ 500.   **Federal income tax.**   The subject of federal income tax is vast in scope. However, one can point out some common instances where this tax has an impact on real estate transactions in particular.

In selling your home, for example, the question arises whether a loss incurred (selling your house for less than your original purchase price) is an item that you can deduct in reporting your income. The answer is *no,* for this is considered a personal expense, like clothes and food.

Suppose, however, that you sell your home at a profit. If, as is usual, you owned this home for more than six months, you have a long-term capital gain. This is taxed at one-half of the ordinary income rates, but never more than 25 per cent of your full gain, whichever is lower. The manner of computing this gain is not difficult. First, determine your *unadjusted basis.* Generally this will be your cost, that is, what you paid for the property. Then you make all the adjustments necessary to determine your *adjusted basis.* Thus, to the basis you add commissions and legal fees, if any, that you paid in connection with the purchase of the property, along with the cost of any permanent improvements that you may have made. You are not required to reduce cost or other basis by depreciation while you held the property.

After reducing the sale price by any expense (such as commissions) incurred in connection with the sale, you subtract the adjusted basis from the net sale proceeds. The difference between the net sale proceeds and your adjusted basis is your gain.

The following example illustrates the computation:

Sale proceeds		$20,000
Less selling expenses:		
Commissions	$ 1,000	
Attorneys' fees	150	
Other expenses	20	1,170
Net proceeds from sale		$18,830
Cost of land and building:		
Purchase price	$10,000	
Expenses of acquisition (incl. attorneys' fees, surveys,		
title insurance, etc.)	300	
Improvement costs	1,000	11,300
Gain on sale		$ 7,530

You can reduce your taxable gain by being certain that *improvement costs* include all permitted improvement costs, such as cost of room extensions, air conditioning, modern heating system, new sidewalk, gardens, trees, shrubs, and even special assessments paid for street paving. Ordinary repairs are not permitted as improvement costs.

The example given shows the *buyer* as paying the cost of title insurance, which is the common practice along the Eastern seaboard. West of the Eastern seaboard, it is the common practice for the *seller* to bear the cost of title insurance.

If you sell your home and buy a new home within a year, and the purchase price of the new home equals or exceeds the sale price of the old home, instead of paying income tax on the profit you made in selling your old home, you simply apply this profit in reduction of the income tax cost or basis of the new home.

EXAMPLE: You sell your old home for $15,000, which gives you a profit of $4,000, and buy a new one within a year at a cost of $19,000. For income tax purposes, the profit of $4,000 is deducted from the $19,000, giving you a "basis" of $15,000 on the new home. Any sale of the new home for a price in excess of $15,000 is a taxable capital gain to you.

If you sell your house and buy a cooperative apartment, you can postpone taxes just as if you purchased another house. This is true whether you buy a condominium apartment, where you get a full title and deed, or the usual co-op proprietary lease.

Where you are buying another house or apartment, you can deduct from your sale price the cost of fixing up your old house to make it more readily salable. This can reduce the amount that you must reinvest in another home in order to avoid tax. Painting and repairs incurred for this specific purpose are generally legitimate improvement costs. But there are two limitations: The work must be done within ninety days before you sign the sales contract, and the bills must be paid within thirty days after the sale.

In preparing his income tax return, the homeowner should also keep in mind that he may deduct casualty losses from his income except that the first $100 of the loss is not deductible and must therefore be subtracted. These include damage from freezing and breaking of water pipes and radiators, and damage caused by sonic boom. Of course the homeowner deducts from his income real estate taxes and mortgage interest that he has paid during the year.

In buying and selling business property, several considerations should be kept in mind.

If possible, you should take gains and losses on sales of business property in separate years.

EXAMPLE: You sell Building A at a gain of $10,000 and Building B at a loss of $3,000. This loss of $3,000 reduces your capital gain to $7,000. But if you had waited until the following year to sell Building B, the loss of $3,000 could be used as a deduction from your ordinary income for that year. In the meantime, your capital gain of $10,000 in the previous year would still be taxable only at the low capital gains rate. In other words, you are better off using losses to reduce ordinary income, which pays a high tax, than to reduce capital gains, which pay a lower tax.

It is often advantageous to sell real estate on an installment basis rather than for cash. For example, if you sell Building A for cash, you must pay a tax on the entire profit thus made. But if you sell the building on an installment contract, with a down payment of 30 per cent or less you can spread this gain over the entire term of the contract. This installment sale method can also be used to reduce taxes on the sale of a residence.

Chapter 30

LANDLORD AND
TENANT

§ 501. **Leases and periodic tenancies.**   The relationship of
landlord and tenant may exist by virtue of a formal, written *lease* or of a
periodic tenancy, such as a *tenancy from month to month.*

> **EXAMPLE:** A sees an "apartment for rent" sign on a building, goes in,
> makes a verbal arrangement with the owner for the rental of an apartment, pays his
> first month's rent, and later moves in. He is a *tenant from month to month.*

> **EXAMPLE:** Facts as above, but the landlord and tenant, instead of
> agreeing verbally, sign a lease for one year. A is a tenant under a lease.

One important difference between leases and periodic tenancies relates
to the rights and liabilities of the parties during the existence of the land-
lord-tenant relation. When the relation of landlord and tenant exists without a written lease, the law implies certain rights and liabilities on the
part of both. In a *month-to-month tenancy,* for example, the tenant is
entitled to the exclusive possession of the rented premises, and the landlord has no right to enter thereon for the purpose of making repairs. But
in many leases, the parties expressly agree that the landlord shall have this
right. In other words, a lease is a contract, and most of the rights and
duties of the parties are governed by the provisions of the lease, whereas
in a periodic tenancy, the rights and duties of the parties are governed
by rules of law.

Another difference between a lease and a periodic tenancy relates to the termination of the tenant's right of occupancy. In the case of a lease, at the expiration date fixed in the lease, the tenant need not give notice to the landlord before moving out, nor is any notice needed by the landlord to the tenant. In the case of periodic tenancies, certain notices must be given in order to terminate the tenancy.

§ 502. **Tenancy from month to month.** A tenancy from month to month is generally created when no definite term of letting is specified by the parties and the rent is payable monthly. This kind of tenancy is very common. A tenant who pays rent monthly and has no lease is a tenant from month to month.

A tenancy from month to month cannot be terminated except by giving notice. That is, the landlord cannot evict the tenant unless he first gives the tenant the notice required by law, and the tenant continues liable for rent unless he gives the landlord the required notice. In many states, a month's or thirty days' notice is required, but the period varies from state to state.

The notice to terminate a month-to-month tenancy must state a proper termination date, and must give the tenant the full number of days notice to which he is entitled.

> **EXAMPLE:** A rents an apartment to B on a month-to-month tenancy beginning as of the first of the next month. In the state in question a landlord must serve a thirty days' notice to terminate such a tenancy. After some months, A serves a notice on November 1st terminating B's tenancy as of November 30th. The notice is void. It gives B less than thirty days' notice. A will lose the eviction suit and must serve a new and proper notice.

§ 503. **Tenancy from year to year.** A *tenancy from year to year* is one that continues for a year and then is automatically renewed for another year and from year to year thereafter unless due notice of termination of the tenancy is given at the time and in the manner required by law for the termination of the tenancy.

While a year to year tenancy can be created in other ways, it most commonly is created when a lease for a year or more has expired and the tenant continues in possession paying rent, which the landlord accepts, and the parties have made no other agreement as to the character of the tenant's occupancy.

When a tenant has a lease for a year or longer, and after the lease has expired the tenant remains in possession of the premises, it is said that the tenant *holds over*. The landlord may, if he wishes, hold the tenant as a tenant from year to year. Observe that it is the landlord who may hold the tenant. The tenant cannot, by holding over, compel the landlord to extend the tenancy. The landlord may evict the tenant if he wishes to do so. But if the tenant holds over, even for one day, he becomes liable for another year's rent should the landlord wish to hold him. *Clinton Wire Cloth Co. v. Gardner*, 99 Ill. 151. Once the landlord accepts the rent, he also is bound to the tenancy. And once the tenancy is established neither party can terminate it in the middle of the year. And if either party wishes to end the tenancy *at the end of a yearly period*, proper notice must be served for this purpose.

In certain situations, a tenant who holds over after his lease has expired will not become a tenant from year to year.

1. Before the lease expires, the landlord notifies the tenant that if he remains in possession he will do so as a tenant from month to month. Or the landlord and tenant may specifically agree that the tenant remains as a month-to-month tenant. In either case, the new tenancy is a month-to-month tenancy.

2. The lease contains a clause that if the tenant holds over without any new agreement being reached, he does so as a month-to-month tenant. The clause is valid.

3. Before the lease ends, the landlord and tenant negotiate for a new lease, and the negotiations are in progress when the lease ends. After the lease ends, the tenant remains in possession, paying a monthly rent. He is a month-to-month tenant. 32 Am. Jur. 781. Be careful, however, for if negotiations have ceased before the lease ends, a tenant holding over will be held as a tenant from year to year.

4. Suppose that when the lease ends the tenant is so ill that his doctor forbids him to move. In some states, this will nevertheless result in the creation of a year-to-year tenancy; in other states, a year-to-year will not be created. 32 Am. Jur. 780.

The rule that if a tenant holds over even one day after the expiration of his lease he becomes liable for another year's rent as a tenant from year to year is harsh, and some states have abolished or restricted it.

§ 504. **Tenancy at will.** A tenancy at will may be terminated by either party whenever he wishes to do so.

EXAMPLE: A tenancy at will arises under an agreement that the tenant may occupy until the premises are sold or rented to a third person, until the landlord is ready to construct new buildings, until the land is required by the landlord for his own use, or whenever the letting is for an indefinite term.

§ 505. **Lease defined.** A lease is both a contract and a conveyance. It is a conveyance by the landlord to the tenant of the right to occupy the land for the term specified in the lease. It contains a contract by the tenant to pay rent to the landlord and usually contains numerous other promises and undertakings by both landlord and tenant.

§ 506. **Necessity of writing.** In all but a few states, a lease for less than one year may be verbal, but a lease for a period longer than one year must be in writing.

§ 507. **Requirements of lease—in general.** Since in many

states, laws require a written lease to comply with requirements applicable to deeds, a lease in writing should comply with such requirements. In a written lease, the landlord is referred to as *lessor* and the tenant as *lessee*.

§ 508. **The lessor.** The landowner and his or her spouse should be designated as lessors. The same reasons that make it necessary for the wife or husband of a landowner to join in a deed requires the spouse to join in a lease. *Fargo v. Bennett,* 35 Ida. 359, 206 Pac. 692; *Benson v. Dritch* (Tex.), 244 S.W. 2d 339. (See § 162.) As a matter of business practice, short leases such as one-year apartment leases are often made by the owner without his wife's signature, for in such situations, trouble is extremely improbable. A lessor should be of age and of sound mind. When the lease is executed by an executor or trustee, the will or other trust instrument must be examined to determine if he has power to make the lease in question. If the lessor is a corporation, the lease must be authorized by the directors or stockholders, as required by the local law.

§ 509. **The lessee.** The lessee should be of age and of sound mind. If the lessee is a trustee or executor, the will or other trust instrument must authorize him to enter into leases such as the one in question.

§ 510. **Description of the premises.** The lease must describe the leased premises with certainty. There is a tendency in short-term leases to designate the leased premises inadequately. Of course if it is an entire building that is being rented, it is sufficient to describe it by street number, city, and state.

§ 511. **Duration or term of lease.** Leases are sometimes classified as *short-term* or *long-term* leases. This has no legal significance. With the exception of the rule that leases for more than one year must be in writing, the rules governing short-term and long-term leases are generally the same. Long-term leases often run for ninety-nine years. In some states laws have been passed limiting the duration of leases. The lease should fix the date on which the term of the lease begins and the duration of the lease. In fixing the term of the lease, it is better to avoid a description of the term as running *from* a particular day *to* another day, since a question may arise as to whether or not a lease from or to a particular day includes or excludes such day. It is better to describe the term as *commencing on* a certain day and *ending on* a certain other day.

§ 512. **Signature of lessor and lessee.** The signature of the lessor is necessary to give effect to a lease. It is the universal practice to obtain the lessee's signature also, though it is not essential that the lease be signed by the lessee if the lessee accepts the lease and takes possession of the leased premises. *Bakker v. Fellows,* 153 Mich. 428, 117 N.W. 52. It is customary to execute leases in duplicate. If the lessor signs one duplicate and hands this to the lessee, and the lessee signs the other duplicate and hands this to the lessor, the effect is the same as if both signatures had been placed on each duplicate. *Fields v. Brown,* 188 Ill. 111, 64 N.E. 1033.

§ 513. **Seal.**   In a number of states, written leases must be executed with the same formality as deeds. In these states, a lease should be under seal.

§ 514. **Witnesses.**   A few states require a lease that exceeds a certain specified duration to be witnessed.

§ 515. **Acknowledgment.**   Some states require leases that exceed a specified term to be acknowledged. In any case, if the lease is to be recorded, it should be acknowledged.

§ 516. **Recording.**   Even though a lease is not recorded, the tenant's possession will normally give the whole world constructive notice of his rights. However, this rule has been abolished in a number of states as to leases exceeding a specified duration, namely, one year in California, Florida, Georgia, Hawaii, Idaho, Mississippi, Montana, Oklahoma, Rhode Island and three years in Indiana, Minnesota, New Mexico, North Carolina, Ohio, Tennessee, Wisconsin, Wyoming. A few states specify longer durations. In all these states a lease exceeding the specified duration must be recorded.

In some states (New York and Ohio, for example) the law permits the recording of a brief *memorandum of lease* instead of the original lease.

§ 517. **Rent.**   Unless there is an agreement providing otherwise, rent is not due until the end of the rental period.

EXAMPLE: A agreed to rent certain premises to B as a tenant from month to month. Rent was fixed at $80 per month, but nothing was said as to time for payment of rent. The rent is not due until the end of each month.

Most leases, however, provide that rental is payable in advance on the first of each month.

Because of the embarrassment caused a landlord by his inability to put a new tenant in possession, and because of the difficulty attendant upon renting premises out of the normal season, a number of states require a tenant who remains in possession after the termination of his lease to pay double rent for the period intervening between the expiration of the lease and his eviction. And many leases provide that a holdover tenant shall pay double rent if he remains in possession after the lease has expired. The lease may provide for additional amounts other than double rent.

§ 518. **Percentage leases.**   Leases of retail locations often provide for a *percentage rent.* Such a lease usually provides a minimum fixed rent. Over and above this minimum, the rental is fixed at a percentage of the tenant's gross sales. The percentage of gross income that is to be charged usually presents no great problem, for commonly accepted percentages for each type of retail establishment are published periodically by the National Association of Real Estate Boards. However, it is obvious that if such a lease is prepared for a department store in a shopping center, it will be necessary to fix different percentages for different departments within the single store. Deductions from gross sales are usually allowed for sales and luxury taxes and merchandise returned by the shopper. Care should be exercised to include in gross sales all income from vending machines, telephone booths, pay toilets, lockers, weighing machines, stamp machines, and so on; and also services rendered on the premises, hairdressing and the like. Services rendered at cost, clothing alterations and employee's cafeteria, for example, are usually excluded. Income from subtenants and concessionaires is included. The lease should state whether *gross income* includes sales made by mail and sales to employees. The lease should require the tenant to conduct business throughout the year, for obviously, if the store is closed, the percentage rent stops or drops. Further, the lease should fix the hours and days on which the store is to be open. A provision should also be included forbidding the establishment of a competing store within a specified radius. Since the landlord is depending on the particular tenant's ability to run a profitable business, the lease should forbid any assignment or sublease or even the occupancy of the premises by anyone other than the tenant, unless the landlord consents. (See § 534.)

§ 519. **Ground leases and commercial leases distinguished— legal and financial aspects—mortgages of the leasehold.** There is no legal distinction between commercial leases and ground leases. Nevertheless, there are economic differences between them that have legal implications. A commercial lease is a lease of a building such as a store to a tenant. If the tenant agrees in his lease to make improvements, as a rule they are limited in scope. In a ground lease, the landowner leases the vacant ground to a tenant who covenants in the lease to erect a building on the premises. The true ground lease is a *net lease* under which the tenant pays all expenses including taxes, insurance, and repairs. The landlord in a commercial lease and his mortgagee are concerned with the tenant's credit standing, since this is their assurance that the rent will be paid. This is the reason, for example, why you will find a shopping center promoter looking for national chain stores as tenants. And because the landlord and his mortgagee depend on the cash flow from triple-A tenants, the lease will forbid any assignment or sublease without the landlord's consent. (See § 534.) In a ground lease, on the other hand, (1) the landlord looks for his security to the fact that the tenant will erect a valuable building on the property and will have to keep up his rent in order to prevent loss of his investment in the building by the landlord's forfeiting the lease for nonpayment of rent; and (2) the tenant expects to borrow money to erect the building. This makes it necessary to draft the lease in such a fashion that the lessee's rights under the lease (the "leasehold estate") can be mortgaged without the landlord's permission and the lease should so state. And since the mortgagee who forecloses will want the unhampered right to sell to anyone, the ground lease should not limit the lessee's right to assign without the landlord's consent. Also, the term of the lease should be long enough to make the mortgage on the leasehold a legal investment for banks, insurance companies, and other institutional investors. For example, a state law may provide that a mortgage on a leasehold is not a legal investment for banks or insurance companies unless the unexpired term of the lease exceeds twenty-one years. Some states have a fifty-year minimum.

To better enable the lessee to borrow money for the erection of the building, a ground lease may provide that the landlord will join in the mortgage, without, however incurring any personal liability by signing the mortgage note. Or the lease may provide that the landlord's title will become subordinate to the mortgage on the leasehold. The landlord who signs such a lease must understand that this weakens his legal position since foreclosure of the mortgage will extinguish his ownership. On the other hand, if the construction mortgage is only on the leasehold estate, foreclosure of the mortgage simply results in transfer of the leasehold to the mortgage lender who then becomes the tenant paying rent to the landlord.

When the construction mortgage mortgages only the leasehold, provision should be included in the lease for special notice to the mortgagee of the leasehold in case of default in payment of rent, so that the mortgage lender can step in and cure the defaults, thereby preventing a forfeiture of the lease which would cancel his mortgage. (See also § 535.)

§ 520. **Use of the premises.** Unless the terms of the lease prevent it, the tenant may use the premises in lawful ways that were not discussed during the lease negotiations. This use by the tenant is often a point of controversy. Many leases state that the premises are leased *for the business of selling cigars,* or *to be used as a real estate office.* Oddly enough, courts seem to feel that such language does not limit the tenant to the stated use. Unless the lease stated that the property is to be used *only* for a particular purpose, he may make any use of the property he wants to, so long as such use is not materially different from that to which the rented premises were customarily put. *Lyon v. Bethlehem Engineering Corp.,* 253 N.Y. 111, 170 N.E. 512; 51 C.J.S. 1017.

SUGGESTION TO LANDLORD: Include a clause under which the tenant covenants to use the property only for a specific purpose. Include at the end of the tenant's covenants a clause giving the landlord the right to terminate the lease if the tenant violates any of his covenants. Be sure you state clearly what the permitted use includes. For example, if you specify that the tenant is to operate a drugstore, does this permit a lunch counter?

When the lease definitely restricts the use that the tenant may make of the premises and the tenant branches out into some unauthorized business, the landlord need not terminate the lease, even if the lease gives him power to do so. He may, instead, procure a court order forbidding the tenant to engage in the unauthorized business. This is desirable when the tenant is a highly solvent one, such as a chain store, and the rent is favorable to the landlord. It also protects the landlord in those cases where he has agreed with other tenants not to allow competing businesses in the same building.

A lease of business property automatically gives the tenant the right to advertise his business on the leased property if the lease does not forbid this use.

> **EXAMPLE:** In the case of a lease of an entire building, it would include the exclusive right to place advertising signs on the walls and roofs of the building, for example, to maintain window signs and to have his name on a lobby directory board. In the case of a lease of a portion of a building, the lessee, not the landlord, would have the right to place advertising signs on the exterior walls of the portion leased to the tenant. 6 De Paul L. Rev. 63; 51 C.J.S. 1020; 20 A.L.R.2d 941.

Usually, however, where various floors are leased to different tenants, the landlord is considered as retaining exclusive possession of the roof. And obviously, if L leases the second floor to A and the third floor to B, A's signs must not not extend above the dividing line between the second and third floors.

A tenant of an apartment has no right to place a television antenna on the roof of the building. 6 *De Paul L. Rev.* 74. On the other hand, just as a tenant has the right to project outside of a window for the purpose of washing it, he would have the right to install an air conditioner that so projects, unless the lease forbids this. 6 *De Paul L. Rev.* 63.

§ 521.   **Incidental rights of lessee or tenant—services and easements.**   Among the incidental rights a tenant enjoys though not mentioned in his lease are:

> 1. The right of tenant, his guests, business visitors, deliverymen, etc. to use the means of access the building provides, namely, front and rear entrances, arcade entrances, lobbies, corridors, stairs, escalators, and elevators, suite entrances from reception rooms or private offices (though the landlord, through reasonable regulations, may require delivery to be made at a trademan's entrance, require freight to use freight elevators, etc.), also the right to use common toilets, common laundry facilities, etc., and the right to have electric wires and conduits, also water and steam and gas

pipes, cross the landlord's part of the property to service tenant's quarters. This is an aspect of the law of implied easements. 24 A.L.R. 2d 123.

    2. The right to have heat, hot water, etc. furnished where the only means of obtaining them consists of facilities controlled by the landlord for the benefit of all tenants.

§ 522. Premises in defective condition.

Unless the lease provides otherwise the landlord has no duty to the tenant to put the rented premises in a habitable condition or to make any repairs whatever. Even if the building at the time it is rented is in a dangerous or ruinous condition or even wholly unfit for occupancy or use, or if it becomes so after it has been rented, the tenant must pay the stipulated rent for the entire term of the lease. This rule places the burden on a prospective tenant of making a careful inspection of the premises before signing the lease.

Since the landlord has no duty as to the condition of the premises, he is not liable to the tenant or his family for injuries or property damage suffered because of obvious defects in the premises or because of the landlord's failure to repair. This would include such injuries as those sustained from the fall of an obviously defective ceiling or from falling on an obviously defective floor.

There are some exceptions to these rules:

    1. When the landlord lets for a short term of a few days, weeks or months a fully furnished house supposedly equipped for immediate occupancy as a dwelling, the landlord impliedly represents, in many states, that the premises are safe and habitable. If the premises are not habitable, as when they are infested with vermin, the tenant has the right to move out, and his liability for rent ceases. *Young v. Punich,* 121 Me. 141, 116 Atl. 26; 28 A.L.R. 48. Also, the landlord is liable to the tenant and his family for injuries sustained from defects in the rented premises or the furnishings thereof. *Hacker v. Netschke,* 310 Mass. 754, 39 N.E. 2d 644.

    2. Where there are concealed defects that would make the premises dangerous to a tenant and that the tenant could not discover on an inspection of the premises, but that are known to the landlord, the landlord must inform the tenant of the existence of such defects. If he fails to do so, and as a consequence an injury is suffered by the tenant, his family, or his customers or guests, the landlord is liable for such injuries.

    EXAMPLE: Premises were leased as a barber shop and residence. Sewer gas often escaped into the premises which fact was known to the landlord. He did not disclose this fact to the tenant, and the tenant and his family became seriously ill from sewer gas. The landlord was liable for the injuries.

    3. The landlord normally retains control over parts of the building used in common by the tenants, such as halls, stairs, elevators, and sidewalks leading from the building to the public street or sidewalk. With respect to such common facilities, the landlord must exercise due care to correct any dangerous conditions that develop. If he fails to do so, he is liable for injuries suffered by the tenant, his family, his customers and guests, or other persons lawfully on the premises, such as delivery men.

EXAMPLE: *L* leased a flat in his apartment building to *T*. The stairways were used in common by the tenants. A stair became defective, and this condition was brought to the attention of *L*, but he failed to correct it. *T* slipped on the stair and was injured. *L* was liable.

The duty of the landlord to use care to keep facilities used in common by the tenants in repair extends to appliances furnished by the landlord for the tenants' common use, such as laundry appliances, common toilets, playground equipment, and dumb-waiters. 25 A.L.R.2d 576. It also extends to the roof, chimneys, eaves, flues, and outside walls; also to the malls, walks, parking areas, etc. of a shopping center. 95 A.L.R.2d 1344.

4. Where the landlord, even though not legally obligated to do so, makes repairs, but is negligent in so doing, he is liable for any resulting injuries.

EXAMPLE: *L*, though not obligated to do so, repaired a floor in an apartment that he rented to *T*. The work was carelessly done, and *T* was injured. *L* is liable.

Under the rules relating to constructive eviction, if the landlord fails to keep the premises in repair this may give the tenant an opportunity to move out without liability for future rent under the lease. (See § 538.)

§ 523. **Lease obligating landlord to repair.** If the lease requires the landlord to make repairs, and the landlord violates this obligation, the tenant may pursue one of the following courses:

1. He may abandon the premises if they become untenantable.

2. He may make the repairs himself and deduct the reasonable expense or cost thereof from the rent.

3. He may occupy the premises without repair and deduct from the rent the decrease in rental value occasioned by the landlord's failure to repair. Here, however, the tenant runs the risk of having his lease forfeited for nonpayment of rent if he appraises the situation incorrectly.

4. He may pay full rent and sue the landlord for the decrease in rental value occasioned by the landlord's failure to repair.

When the lease obligates the landlord to repair, and he fails to do so, and the tenant suffers an injury as a result, some courts hold the landlord liable; others do not. The view that the landlord should be held liable is growing in favor. 163 A.L.R. 300, 310. In any event, the landlord has no duty to inspect the rented premises he has agreed to keep in repair, for normally the landlord has no right to enter on the rented premises without the tenant's consent. It is the tenant's duty to notify the landlord of any condition requiring repair, and no liability on the landlord's part arises until this has been done and the landlord has failed to make repairs as agreed. 163 A.L.R. 314.

§ 524. **Statutes imposing duty to repair.** The old rules relieving the landlord of the duty to keep rented premises in repair were evolved before the emergence of large cities, with the attendant problems of urban life. Obviously, workers of low income living in tenements in large urban centers can ill afford to keep their premises in repair. If the landlord fails to make needed repairs, they simply are not made. In many states, for example, Alabama, California, Connecticut, District of Columbia, Georgia, Iowa, Kentucky, Louisiana, Massachusetts, Michigan, Montana, New Jersey, New York, North Dakota, Oklahoma, South Dakota, and Wisconsin, laws have been passed imposing on landlords the duty to keep rented housing accommodations in repair. 45 *Ill. L. Rev.* 205; 93 A.L.R. 778, 17 A.L.R.2d 704. In California, Montana, North Dakota, and Oklahoma, the tenant is given the right to move out if needed repairs are not made, but if the tenant is injured because of the landlord's failure to make repairs, the landlord is not liable. In some states, Michigan, New Jersey, and New York, for example, the landlord is liable if the tenant suffers injuries as a result of the landlord's failure to make repairs. *Altz v. Lieberson,* 233 N.Y. 16, 134 N.E. 703; 17 A.L.R.2d 708.

EXAMPLES: In states following the New York rule, landlords were held liable for the following injuries: tenant injured by fall of ceiling, tenant injured as result of landlord's failure to repair hole in bathroom floor, and tenant's child injured when defective radiator valves blew off.

§ 525. Liability of landlord for injuries to third person.

As a rule, whenever a landlord would be liable to a tenant, as, for example, when the landlord is careless with respect to care of common stairways, he will be liable to others who stand in the tenant's shoes, such as members of his family, guests, employees, and business visitors and delivery boys.

There are other situations where a landlord is liable to a third person.

1. When the landlord rents the premises for a purpose that involves the admission of large groups of the public as patrons of the tenant (amusement park, theater, etc.) and at the time the lease, or any renewal lease, is signed, the premises are in a dangerous condition (dangerous doorways, steps, floors, etc.), the landlord is liable to the tenant's patrons for any injuries that they may suffer. *Webel v. Yale University,* 125 Conn. 515, 7 A.2d 215; 17 A.L.R.3rd 422, 873.

EXAMPLE: L leased premises to T as a tavern, dance hall, and restaurant and P, a patron, was injured while dancing when her heel caught in a floor register. L is liable. *Torwick V. Lisle,* 268 Minn. 197, 128 N.W.2d 330.

2. When the landlord reserves control over the rented premises, he may become liable for injuries.

EXAMPLE: L leased a pier to T, and in the lease reserved the right to inspect and repair the pier. He kept a crew on the job for this purpose. An employee of a concern using this pier was killed due to lack of care in maintaining a large iron door. L was held liable. *De Clara v. Barber Steamship Lines,* 309 N.Y. 620, 132 N.E. 2d 871.

3. With respect to pedestrians on public walks or streets adjoining the rented premises, there is an additional rule imposing liability on the landlord, namely: When the premises at the time of the renting are in a dangerous and defective condition, the landlord is liable to strangers for injuries resulting therefrom. 52 C.J.S. 105.

EXAMPLE: At the time the premises were leased to the tenant, a hole in the sidewalk leading to a coal bin was in a defective condition, and a pedestrian was thereafter injured as a result. The landlord was held liable. *Great Atlantic & Pacific Tea Co. v. Traylor,* 239 Ala. 497, 195 So. 724. The reason for this rule is that a dangerous condition of premises constitutes a nuisance, and the liability of the landlord results from his leasing premises on which a nuisance exists. *Morgan v. Sheppard,* 156 Ala. 403, 47 So. 147. The liability exists even though the defect is not concealed. And if the premises were safe when originally leased, but are defective when the lease is renewed, the landlord is liable for injuries sustained by strangers after the date of the renewal. Of course the tenant would also be liable for such injuries.

§ 526. Rent withholding—building code violations.

In Connecticut, Iowa, Michigan, and New York, laws have been enacted to the effect that where an apartment building has been constructed or an existing building has been remodeled into apartments, the landlord cannot collect rent for any period during which there is no certificate of occupancy. (See § 480.) Nor can the landlord evict the tenant for nonpayment of such rent. Such laws are valid. *Dreamy Hollow Apts. Corp. v. Lewis,* 4 Conn. Circ. App. 355, 232 A.2d 346. They are aimed against the practice of cutting up single-family dwellings into crowded and unsanitary living quarters through use of flimsy partitions. Other ordinances deny a slum landlord the right to collect rent as long as there are building code violations serious enough to be dangerous to life or health, and these ordinances also are valid. *Farrell v. Drew,* 19 N.Y.2d 486, 227 N.E.2d 824. It has also been held that a tenant cannot be evicted simply because he has complained to the city that building code violations exist. *Edwards v. Habib,* 36 L.W. 2731 (1968).

§ 527. Liability of tenant for injuries to third person.

When a stranger is injured by reason of a defective condition of the premises, it is often difficult to determine whether the landlord or tenant is liable. If the landlord has made no agreement to repair and the premises were in a safe condition when rented, and if the defective portion is in the exclusive possession of the tenant, the tenant is liable, but the landlord is not, since the landlord has no control over such premises and is in no position to prevent the dangerous condition.

EXAMPLE: A stranger slipped and fell into a coal hole that was defectively covered but was in a safe condition when the premises were rented. The basement into which the hole opened was used by the first-floor tenant. He alone had a key to this basement, and the landlord had no access thereto. The tenant alone was liable. *West Chicago Masonic Assn. v. Cohn,* 192 Ill. 210, 61 N.E. 439.

Or suppose the tenant of an upper floor goes out, leaving the water running, and the water runs over and drips through the ceiling and ruins rugs in the apartment beneath. The landlord is not liable since the tenant is in exclusive possession of his apartment, but the tenant is liable both to his landlord and to the tenant below, because the damage resulted from his carelessness.

§ 528. **Insurance.** The prudent property owner should protect himself against liability claims by taking out Owners', Landlords', and Tenants' Public Liability Insurance, commonly referred to as O.L. & T. insurance, which provides coverage against legal liability for accidents resulting in bodily injuries or death arising out of ownership, occupation, or use of the premises. Liability for injuries sustained by employees is not covered by this policy, but they should be covered by workmen's compensation or employer's liability insurance. Insurance should be obtained protecting the landlord against liability for property damage. If there is an elevator on the premises, insurance will be needed to protect against injuries arising through operation of the elevator.

§ 529. **Repairs and alterations by tenant—liability of tenant to landlord.** When the lease does not provide otherwise, the tenant has no duty to the landlord to make any substantial, extraordinary, or general repairs, such as the replacing of a worn-out furnace or water heater. But it is the tenant's duty to repair broken windows or leaking roofs and to take such other steps as are needed to prevent damage from the elements. If he fails to do so, he is liable to the landlord for any resulting damage. *Suydam v. Jackson,* 54 N.Y. 450.

The tenant must not make any material change in the nature and character of the building leased, as by removing walls, cutting new doorways, and the like, even though such alterations increase the value of the property. The theory is that when the tenant vacates the building, the landlord should find it in much the same condition as it was when the tenant took possession. *F. W. Woolworth Co. v. Nelson,* 204 Ala. 172, 85 So. 449.

When the lease obligates the tenant to *make repairs* or to *keep the premises in repair,* some courts say that the tenant must repair or rebuild if the building is damaged or destroyed by fire, flood, lightning, rain, accident, or other cause beyond the tenant's control. 45 A.L.R. 12, 106 A.L.R. 1358. Other courts today refuse to impose such a heavy burden on the tenant. *Seevers v. Gabel,* 94 Ia. 75, 62 N.W. 669. A lease provision for repairs may also require the tenant to replace rotten floors, a worn-out furnace, and the like. The tenant is liable to his landlord for damage occasioned by carelessness, as where damage results from the tenant's negligence in permitting a bathtub to overflow. 10 A.L.R.2d 1012.

§ 530. **Damage to or destruction of the leased premises.** Unless the lease provides otherwise, the rule is that when *land and building* are rented, the tenant is not excused from paying rent if *building* is destroyed by fire, flood, or wind.

EXAMPLE: A lease was made of the premises at 143 and 145 Lake Street, Chicago, Illinois. The buildings were destroyed by fire, but the liability for rent continued. A lease containing a description by street number leases the land as well as the building.

Quite a number of states, Alaska, Arizona, California, Connecticut, Kentucky, Maryland, Michigan, Minnesota, Mississippi, Montana, New Jersey, New York, North Carolina, North Dakota, Ohio, South Carolina, West Virginia, and Wisconsin, for example, have abolished this harsh rule. In these states, it is the rule that if the building is destroyed or rendered untenantable, the tenant is relieved of further liability for rent. 35 *N.Y.U. L. Rev.* 1284. Many lease forms provide that if the building is destroyed by fire, the lease ends automatically.

The rule that liability for rent continues when the building is destroyed does not apply to a lease of an apartment, flat, office, or floor of a building. Such a lease is not a lease of land.

EXAMPLE: The landlord leased the third floor of a building. The building was destroyed by fire. The landlord rebuilt. The tenant was not entitled to similar space in the new building, since destruction of the building ended the lease.

When the building is not destroyed, but the apartment is rendered untenantable by fire, leases usually provide that the landlord has a certain time in which to make the necessary repairs, and, in the meantime, the tenant is not liable for rent. Under this clause, if the landlord fails to make the repairs during the specified period, the lease ends automatically.

If the lease requires the landlord to *repair* the building, this may be interpreted as requiring him to *rebuild* it if it is destroyed by fire or other casualty. 38 A.L.R.2d 685.

§ 531. **Taxes.** In the absence of a provision in the lease to that effect, the tenant is not obliged to pay real estate taxes on the leased land.

§ 532. **Fixtures.** The respective rights of landlord and tenant in and to fixtures installed by the tenant are discussed in Chapter 3.

Trade fixtures not removed by the tenant before he moves out become the property of the landlord. The fact that such items are attached to the landlord's building seems to make this result natural and acceptable to the courts. However, as to the tenant's ordinary personal property that is not in any way attached to the building, for example, furniture or stock in trade, this does not become the landlord's property simply because the tenant has moved out or been evicted. The landlord must keep or store these articles for the tenant.

§ 533. **Cancellation clause.**   Leases may contain a clause conferring on the landlord the privilege of canceling the lease in the event of a sale of the property and upon giving a certain specified notice to the tenant. This clause is of value when the landlord sells the premises to a buyer who desires more or less immediate occupancy. Great care must be exercised in serving the notice of cancellation. For example, if the lease says that the *landlord* may cancel the lease in case of a sale, a notice served by his purchaser may be void. 163 A.L.R. 1019. Notice of cancellation should be served personally unless the lease specifically allows notice by mail. Each tenant is entitled to his own copy of the notice.

§ 534. **Assignments and subleases.**   Unless the lease provides otherwise, a lessee may assign his lease or sublet the premises. Whether a particular instrument is an assignment or sublease does not depend upon the name given the instrument by the parties. If the lessee transfers the *entire unexpired remainder* of the term created by the lease, the instrument is an assignment. If the lessee retains *part of the term, however small the part may be,* or transfers only part of the leased premises, the instrument is a sublease.

> **EXAMPLE:** *L* leases certain premises to *T* for a term beginning on May 1, 1950, and expiring on April 30, 1952, at a rent of $100 per month. On July 1, 1950, *T* executes to *X* a "sublease" for a term beginning on July 1, 1950, and expiring April 30, 1952, at a rent of $150 per month. The instrument is an assignment.

> **EXAMPLE:** *L* leases to *T* certain premises for a term beginning on May 1, 1950, and expiring on April 30, 1952. On July 1, 1950, *T* executes to *X* an "assignment" of said lease except the last day of the term. The instrument is a sublease.

The difference between assignment and sublease is important, since an assignee becomes liable to the original lessor for rent, whereas a sublessee is liable only to the sublessor, who, of course, is the lessee under the original lease. Of course the lessee in the original lease continues liable for rent to the original lessor, notwithstanding the assignment or sublease.

If the lease forbids an assignment without the lessor's consent, it does not necessarily prevent a sublease. If the lease forbids a sublease, it does not necessarily prohibit an assignment. As a rule, a commercial lease prohibits both assignments and subleases without the lessor's consent.

Suppose *L* makes a lease to *T Corporation,* and *X,* the holder of all the stock in *T Corporation,* sells all his stock to *Y.* This is not a violation of covenant not to make an assignment of sublease without the landlord's consent. The lease remains in *T Corporation.* Only the stock has been transferred. *Alabama Vermiculite Corp. v. Patterson,* 124 F.Sup. 441.

An assignment or sublease made without the lessor's consent, in defiance of the provisions of the lease, is not wholly void. If, after learning of the assignment or sublease, the lessor accepts rent from the assignee or sublessee, he waives his right to object to that particular assignment or sublease.

§ 535. **Mortgages of the leasehold.** If the lease contains no provision that would prohibit a mortgage of the leasehold, the tenant may place a mortgage on the leasehold estate created by the lease. In such a mortgage, the description of the mortgaged premises should read somewhat as follows:

Leasehold estate created by lease dated May 1, 19_____ and recorded in the Recorder's Office of _____ County, _____, on May 2, 19_____, as Document 1,000,000, from John Smith, as Lessor, to Henry Brown, as Lessee, demising for a term of years commencing on May 1, 19_____, and ending on April 30, 19_____, the premises described as follows, to wit: (here insert description of leased premises).

One difficulty with such a mortgage is the fact that the tenant may default in his rent payments, and if he does, the landlord may declare the lease forfeited. Of course if default and forfeiture occur, the mortgage is thereby extinguished. A side agreement between the landlord and mortgagee may provide that before forfeiting the lease the landlord will give notice of the default to the mortgagee and a stated time to cure to make good the defaults. It may also provide that if the lease is terminated, the mortgagee will be entitled to receive a new lease for the balance of the term on the same rent and terms as the old lease.

Another question that arises is with respect to the liability of the mortgagee for payment of rent. In title and intermediate states, which regard a leasehold mortgage as an assignment of the leasehold, the mortgagee becomes personally liable to the landlord for rent, under the rule stated in the preceding section that an assignee becomes liable to the original lessor for rent. *Williams v. Safe Deposit Co.,* 167 Md. 499, 175 Atl. 331. For this reason, it is a common practice in leasehold mortgages to omit the last day of the term, so that the mortgage mortgages the leasehold *except the last day thereof.* By excepting the last day of the term, the mortgage becomes a sublease rather than an assignment, and the mortgagee does not become personally liable to the landlord for rent due under the lease. Mortgages are treated as assignments or subleases depending on whether they cover all or less than all the unexpired term of the lease. In states that follow the lien theory of mortgages, a mere mortgage of the leasehold does not make the mortgagee liable for rent. 51 C.J.S. 586. (See also § 519.)

§ 536. **Deed of rented premises.**   A landlord may, of course, sell his real estate, and the buyer will take it subject to existing leases and periodic tenancies. The deed alone confers on the buyer the right to collect rent falling due after the sale and the right to declare leases forfeited for nonpayment of rent if that right is reserved in the lease. *Lipschultz v. Robertson*, 407 Ill. 470, 95 N.E.2d 357. So far as the collection of future rent is concerned, it is unnecessary that the lessor execute to his purchaser an assignment of his rights under existing leases, 52 C.J.S. 320.

A tenant has the right to continue making rent payments to his original landlord until he is notified of a sale of the property. Therefore, one who buys rented property should promptly notify all tenants that all future rent must be paid to him.

A serious question arises when the tenant prepays the rent called for by the lease and the property is thereafter sold. The buyer of the property no doubt assumes that he will be entitled to collect the future rents called for by the lease and is then confronted by a tenant armed with rent receipts for such rent. In some states, the tenant must pay such rent over again to his new landlord, whereas in other states, the rent payments are good as against the new landlord, 52 C.J.S. 348; 32 Am. Jur. 378.

§ 537. **Eviction.**   If the tenant is evicted from the premises by a stranger having a paramount or better title than his landlord, the tenant is not liable to his landlord for rent accruing after such eviction.

EXAMPLE: *R* mortgaged his land to *E*. Thereafter, *R* leased the mortgaged land to *T*. *R* defaulted in his payments on the mortgage, and *E* took possession of the premises, as he had the right to do under his mortgage, evicting *T*. *T* is not liable for rents accruing after the eviction, since *E* is coming in under a paramount title.

If the landlord wrongfully evicts the tenant, even from a part of the premises, the tenant's liability for rent ceases even though he continues to occupy the remainder of the premises.

EXAMPLE: The premises leased included a garage of which the landlord later took possession. The tenant continued to occupy the remainder of the premises. The tenant was not liable for rent. *Smith v. Wise Co.*, 58 Ill. 141.

The reason for this rule is that the tenant cannot be liable for full rent since he is enjoying only part of the premises, and he cannot be liable for a part of the rent because the landlord cannot, by his wrongful act, compel the tenant to accept and pay rent for a part of the premises when he, the landlord, has expressly agreed that the tenant will enjoy all of the premises.

§ 538. **Constructive eviction.** There may also be a *constructive eviction* by the landlord. If, as a result of the landlord's conduct, the premises become uninhabitable, this is tantamount to an eviction. The tenant may abandon the premises and thereupon cease to be liable for further rent. Although there is no actual eviction, there is the legal equivalent.

The landlord's failure to keep in repair the portions of the premises of which he retains control is a constructive eviction if the premises thereby become uninhabitable.

EXAMPLE: Certain plumbing under the landlord's control became defective, and sewer gas escaped into the tenant's apartment, making it uninhabitable. The tenant could abandon the premises. Other illustrations are walls of the building infested with rats or bedbugs and leaking roof under landlord's control. Even though the landlord is not at fault, as in the vermin cases, he is in a better position than the tenant to remedy the situation, and therefore the tenant is given the right to move out. 1 *De Paul L. Rev.* 80.

When the landlord is bound by the lease to keep the rented premises in repair or to furnish heat, water, and elevator service, and he fails to do so, the tenant may also abandon the premises if the rented premises are thereby made untenantable. Leases usually provide that if the failure to furnish heat is accidental and not due to the landlord's fault, it shall not constitute constructive eviction.

There cannot be a constructive eviction unless the tenant leaves the premises. Although the tenant may wait a reasonable time after notifying the landlord to furnish heat, he cannot remain in possession all winter and move out in the summer because of the landlord's failure in this respect.

§ 539. **Abandonment of the premises.** Leases now universally provide that if the lessee abandons the premises before the expiration of the lease, he shall nevertheless continue liable for rent until the expiration of the lease, and any reletting by the landlord shall not relieve the tenant of further liability. Unless the lease provides otherwise, upon abandonment of the premises by the lessee, it is the duty of the landlord in some states to *mitigate damages,* that is, to take charge of the property, and, if possible, relet or re-rent it and thus reduce the amount for which the lessee remains liable. 40 A.L.R. 190, 126 A.L.R. 1219. The lessor may deduct the expenses of such reletting, including commissions and decorating, from the rent collected on such reletting, and he may apply the balance on the original tenant's liability.

EXAMPLE: A leased premises to B for one year at $50 per month. After six months, B abandoned the premises. The premises were vacant one month and were then relet to C for $40 per month, the expenses of reletting, including commissions and decorating, being $50. The landlord thus realized on the reletting $200 minus $50, or $150. B's liability is $300 minus $150, or $150.

However, it is usual to insert a provision in the lease to the effect that the lessor shall not be under any obligation to relet. He may then permit the premises to remain vacant and sue the lessee for the full amount of the rent. This is the law in most states even in the absence of such a provision in the lease. 40 A.L.R. 190, 126 A.L.R. 1219. Ordinarily the landlord will relet the premises rather than permit them to remain vacant, for rent collections from an existing tenant are money in the landlord's hands, whereas the liability of the previous tenant is at best a doubtful asset.

If the landlord relets after abandonment of the premises by the tenant, there is danger that this may amount to a surrender or termination of the lease, thus releasing the tenant from further liability for rent. In some states, a reletting automatically releases the liability of the tenant who has abandoned the premises, whereas in other states, the tenant is released *unless* the landlord gives him notice of his intention to hold him liable despite the reletting. 110 A.L.R. 368. In the great majority of states, the question is regarded as one of intention. If the landlord's acts indicate an acceptance of the tenant's abandonment and an intention to regard the lease as terminated, the tenant's liability for future rent is terminated. 110 A.L.R. 368. In effect, there is a *surrender* (see § **540**). As above suggested, the notice given by the landlord is employed to show that he does not intend to treat the lease as terminated by the abandonment. Suppose, however, that the landlord relets to a new tenant for a new term longer than the term of the original lease. In some states, this is viewed as being inconsistent with the continued existence of the earlier lease, and the earlier lease is thereby terminated. *Ralph v. Deiley*, 293 Pa. 90, 141 Atl. 640; 61 A.L.R. 773. Therefore the lease provisions covering this point (*the abandonment clause*) should include clauses giving the landlord the right to relet for a term longer than the original lease without in any way releasing the tenant's liability.

§ **540. Surrender.** A *surrender* is an agreement by landlord and tenant to terminate the tenant's lease or tenancy, followed by a delivery of possession of the premises to the landlord. A surrender releases the tenant from liability for rent thereafter accruing.

EXAMPLE: Premises were leased by A to B for the term from April 1, 1903, to April 1, 1906. On March 31, 1904, B told A that he wished to give up his lease, and A accepted this offer, telling B to allow a new tenant, C, to move in and to turn the keys over to him, C. This procedure was a surrender, and B was not liable for rent accruing thereafter.

Observe that it is the agreement between landlord and tenant that distinguishes a surrender from an abandonment by the tenant.

If the landlord, with the tenant's consent, gives a new lease to a stranger during the existence of the tenant's lease, this is a surrender.

EXAMPLE: A leased a store to B, who sold the business to C. A then gave C a new lease. This is a surrender of the old lease.

The making of a new lease between landlord and tenant operates as a surrender of a prior inconsistent lease. If the tenant merely abandons the premises, the fact that the landlord accepts the keys does not constitute a surrender.

§ 541. Termination of tenancy for nonpayment of rent.   Virtually all leases provide that the lease may be forfeited and the tenant evicted for nonpayment of rent or for violation of the terms of the lease.

Although the lease contains a clause permitting the landlord to declare the lease forfeited for nonpayment of rent, the landlord must not suddenly declare a forfeiture if he has been in the habit of accepting tardy rent payments. He must first notify the tenant to pay his rent by a specified reasonable time, and if the tenant fails to pay within the time specified, then and only then may the landlord declare a forfeiture. *Cottrell v. Gerson,* 371 Ill. 174, 20 N.E.2d 74.

Year-to-year and month-to-month tenancies likewise may be terminated on the giving of a short notice specified by law if the tenant defaults in his rent payments.

When the landlord evicts the tenant because of the tenant's defaults, the tenant's liability for future rent is ended unless the lease contains a clause, called the *survival clause,* to the effect that the tenant's liability shall survive such eviction. Such lease clauses are now commonplace.

§ 542. Suggested clauses for leases:

Use of premises. In limiting the use to which the tenant may put the premises, avoid putting the tenant in a strait jacket. For example, a covenant that the premises will be used only as a high-class apartment building might raise questions as to use of space for restaurant, vending machines, medical departments of corporate tenants, and so on.

Description of leased premises.

1. If an entire building is leased, use a complete legal description.

2. If part of a building other than an entire floor is demised, a blueprint showing the space demised should be annexed to the lease as an exhibit. If part of a cellar or more than one floor is included, separate blueprints for each part or for each floor are recommended.

3. Rights in premises outside the leased property should be set forth, for example, the right to use subsurface space beneath adjoining streets. The effect on rental should be specified if the city sees fit to revoke the grant of subsurface space. If the tenant is to have the right to use adjoining parking space, an easement for this purpose should be included in the lease. In a commercial lease, at least brief mention should be made of the tenant's right to use elevators, hallways, stairways, lobbies, and so forth in common with others.

4. If the use of personal property is included in the lease, a schedule thereof should be annexed to the lease, identifying the property and describing its condition. Any obligation to maintain or replace personal property should be set forth along with whether or not title to the replacements is to vest in the landlord.

Repairs. The precise extent of the landlord's and tenant's duty to repair should be spelled out in as much detail as possible. If neither is to be required to replace a totally destroyed building, this should be specified. If the tenant is not to be required to replace worn-out heating plants and so on, spell this out.

Title to leased premises. The tenant should procure evidence of the landlord's good title to the leased premises. In addition, the landlord should warrant that his title to the leased premises is good and that the premises may lawfully be used under existing laws and ordinances for the purposes set forth in the lease.

Estoppel certificate when lease is assigned. Another clause that will more readily enable the owner of a leasehold to sell is a clause stating that when the lessee is about to make an assignment that the lease does not prohibit, the landlord will give an *estoppel certificate,* that is, a statement that all rents due and owing under the lease have been paid to date and that there are no breaches of covenant under the lease.

Mortgage protection. Where a lease contemplates that the leasehold will immediately be mortgaged, it is wise to include a clause to the effect that the lease must not be modified or terminated by the parties without consent of the mortgagee. It is also wise to remove from the lease the covenants over which the mortgagee has no control and which might hurt the mortgagee, for example, the clause terminating the lease in case the tenant becomes bankrupt.

Cross references: Most of the material in Chapter 31 relates to Landlord and Tenant problems.

SHOPPING CENTERS

§ 543.   **Types of shopping centers.**   There are three kinds of shopping centers. They are the small *neighborhood center,* the larger *community* or *suburban center,* and the mammoth *regional center.* Certain legal problems are common to all centers.

§ 544.   **Zoning problems.**   If the area in question falls outside the limits of any city or village, it may be subject to a county zoning ordinance. If it lies within a city or village, it will be subject to the local zoning ordinance. In either case, the zoning may prohibit business. The problem then becomes one of securing an amendment to the zoning ordinance or a special use permit.

After the local authority has been persuaded to amend the zoning ordinance or to grant a special use permit, the amendment must pass the test of the courts, for someone, possibly a businessman who will be adversely affected by the shopping center, may attack the rezoning. If the shopping center developer can demonstrate that the old zoning will work an unreasonable financial hardship on him without any benefit to the public, the amendments will be sustained. 51 A.L.R.2d 263; 76 A.L.R.2d 1172; 35 *Notre Dame Lawyer* 197. This is not considered illegal spot zoning. A shopping island in the middle of an area planned to be residential may be a benefit to the residential community. The shopping convenience of the adjoining residents is definitely a factor that the courts will consider in determining the validity of the rezoning. *Eicher v. Board of*

Zoning Appeals, 209 Md. 432, 121 A.2d 249. In this connection, the larger the area rezoned, the less likely it is that the action will be condemned as illegal spot zoning. *In re Lieb's Appeal,* 179 Pa. Super. 318, 116 A.2d 860. Again, there is a benefit to the public in these outlying shopping centers in that business decentralization diminishes traffic congestion within the city. *Bartram v. Zoning Commission,* 136 Conn. 89, 68 A.2d 308. This is especially true where downtown stores do not provide off-street parking. *Skinner v. Reed* (Tex. Civ. App.), 265 S.W.2d 850. Moreover, the shopping center increases the wealth of the city by attracting new business. *City of Waxahachie v. Watkins,* 154 Tex. 206, 275 S.W.2d 477. Thus it also creates additional tax revenues.

If, however, the authorities refuse to change the zoning to permit the center, it is difficult to persuade the courts to overthrow their decision.

§ **545. Vacation of streets.**   If the shopping center promoter finds that the land he proposes to acquire has been subdivided into lots, he faces the problem of *vacating* the streets and alleys depicted on the plat of the subdivision, for his buildings will no doubt stand in the path of such streets. This means, first of all, persuading the governing body of the city or village to pass an ordinance vacating such streets and alleys. By *vacation,* the city relinquishes all public rights in the streets and permits the streets to be closed. Downtown businessmen are often members of such governing bodies. They may view the prospect of a competing shopping area with hostility and vote against the vacation of streets.

All that part of the subdivision in which the vacated streets and alleys lie must be acquired by the promoter, because any lot owner whose land abuts on a street to be vacated can object to, and often block, a vacation. On the other hand, lot owners in the subdivision whose lots are remotely situated from the streets to be vacated have no standing to complain of the vacation.

In some states, when a street is vacated, title reverts to the original subdivider and it will therefore be necessary to procure a deed from him.

§ **546. Site planning.**   In the early development of the proposed shopping center layout, the location of the building area and parking facilities must be established. Tentative locations must be assigned to the key tenants and then adjacent parking allocated. In addition to preparing the initial shopping center layout to be used in connection with obtaining your first tenants, it is also necessary to have your architect prepare a front elevation of the project in order to establish the character of the architecture.

After leasing to the first two or three tenants of the project, the shopping center layout and the location of the buildings and parking lot may be stabilized.

§ **547. Leases—shopping center problems in general—lease**

clauses—mortgage financing.   Today, as never before, the mortgage lender looks to lease revenue to furnish the cash flow for debt service. The terms of the lease, in consequence, have become a matter of grave concern to the lender.

In general the lender wants some clauses in the lease that differ from the clauses the owner wants. The lender wants assured income to retire the mortgage, which means the unconditional liability of triple-A tenants. He wants protection against the landowner's acts or defaults that might destroy the lease.

Interim and permanent lender. As between lenders, the interim lender who finances the construction of the center, is concerned with construction and completion of improvements and compliance with tenant's requirements in this regard. But the takeout lender (see § 402) steps in after the tenants have accepted their leases and premises in writing, and has little interest in construction problems. On the other hand, the interim lender has no interest in rental income because he steps out of the picture as the tenants step in.

As for the landlord, he must satisfy the interim lender, the permanent lender, and the triple-A tenant if he is to get his financing, so he must defer to these parties to a great extent so far as lease clauses are concerned. Compared with the triple-A tenant, who has triple-A bargaining power, and the big insurance company that will be the permanent investor, the landlord-promoter is likely to be low man on the document totem pole. Parenthetically, to the extent that the permanent lender is looking for a good *landlord's lease* because he may one day be the landlord, he is also protecting the present landlord.

A young lawyer representing a landlord or his mortgagee should not feel that the standard, printed form of lease produced by a chain-store tenant is immutable. The chains are accustomed to negotiating changes in their printed forms. Hence the printed form must be read carefully and necessary changes required.

Clause specifying date of commencement of tenant's occupancy. The tenant will wish to defer his occupancy and commencement of rent payment until construction of the center has been completed and the other tenants are prepared to commence their occupancy. The landlord, however, will wish the tenant to begin his occupancy as soon as *his store* is completed. A compromise may require the tenant to occupy before the center is completed, but to pay only a percentage rent during that period. The lease may define the commencement of its term as the date construction of the shopping center is completed. *Wong v. D. Grazia,* Cal., 386 P.2d 817. This is dangerous because of the rule against perpetuities, for completion is technically an indefinite date in the future, and the rule against perpetuities makes such indefinite documents void. This threat is met by providing that the commencement of lease and completion of center shall be not more than five years from date of lease, otherwise the lease to be void.

Duration of leases. The key leases must continue in force as long as the mortgage debt remains unpaid so that the mortgage debt dwindles to nothing by the time the lease has run out. Small tenants can have shorter leases so that, if the key tenants wish to expand, space will be available for them to do so.

Amount of minimum guaranteed rent. Percentage leases all provide for a minimum rent to be paid. This minimum rent must be adequate to pay taxes, insurance, maintenance, and still leave enough to retire the mortgage debt.

Subordination clause. There are legal advantages to a lender in having the key leases prior and therefore superior to the mortgage. (See §§ 389, 390.) For one thing, in some states foreclosure of a senior mortgage automatically terminates a junior lease and the lender is powerless to prevent this. For a like reason the lender objects to a lease clause subordinating the lease "to all institutional mortgages now or hereafter on said premises." The lender is not consoled by the fact that the lease also provides (in the so-called *non-disturbance clause*) that despite foreclosure the possession of the tenant will not be *disturbed* as long as he pays his rent. This protects the tenant but not the landlord, for the tenant may seek to contend that this clause is one he may, but need not, take advantage of. The clause should provide that the subordination takes place only "if the mortgagee so elects." Also the lease should prohibit any subordination by the tenant to a junior mortgage, since foreclosure of the junior mortgage might then wipe out the lease.

Description of leased premises. Often a building is leased while the project is still on the drawing board. Here, preparing the description of the leased premises will pose problems. While the leased site may not be too definitely settled, the lease can nevertheless give an exact description of the *total area* of the center, taken from the title policy, abstract, or other evidence of the landlord's title. The leased site will then be described by reference to a sketch, preferably drawn to scale, attached to the lease. Usually this gives a complete layout of the center, with the location of the leased premises in the layout being indicated by crosshatching. The landlord will wish to reserve the right to make some changes in the layout of the center and the location of the store, at least until the center is substantially rented or the financing settled. But the tenant should demand covenants that: (1) parking area will not be reduced, (2) no change will be made that will reduce the visibility of tenant's store front, (3) no store will be allowed to project beyond tenant's store, and (4) tenant's space will not be reduced below certain minimum dimensions. Care must be exercised to be certain that the mortgaged property includes all facilities needed for successful operation.

EXAMPLE: A mortgage on a motel must include the swimming pool and the bar and restaurant as part of the mortgaged premises and if the bar and restaurant are leased to an outside operator the lease must be subordinate to the mortgage so that, on foreclosure, the whole operation can be acquired by the mortgagee.

Construction of center by developer. The lease will contain a covenant by the developer to build the center in accordance with the site plan, subject to such changes as the lease specifically permits. The lease naturally will require the landlord to construct any building that the tenant is to occupy.

Since the project may have only reached the stage of general overall design, final working drawings of the tenant's store will not be available at the time the lease is executed. A workable way to handle the situation is to attach to the lease a *synopsis* setting forth the construction to be performed. The tenant must covenant to furnish the landlord a store and fixture layout in sufficient detail so that the landlord can prepare drawings and specifications for the construction work. The landlord should covenant to furnish, when construction is completed, an architect's certificate that the premises have been completed according to the synopsis.

The lease should require the tenant to give the landlord an *acceptance letter* when the landlord has completed all required construction work on the leased premises. The permanent mortgage lender will insist on seeing such acceptances, for he counts on revenue from the tenants to pay off the mortgage and wants to know that the tenants have no excuse for seeking to be relieved of their leases. The landlord will find that if he allows the tenant to take possession before the acceptance is given, the tenant, knowing that the landlord must furnish the mortgage lender these acceptances, may demand additional work he is not entitled to under the lease.

Construction of interior by tenant. Some leases will simply require the developer to construct the exterior of the building and will require the tenant to construct all the interior work. Here the lease should: (1) Furnish at least some sort of *outline specifications* if final plans and specifications are unavailable, for the tenant cannot intelligently decide how much rent to pay unless he knows what the construction work will cost him. (2) Require the tenant to protect the landlord against mechanics' liens by furnishing a deposit, surety bond, etc., though a lease covenant by a triple-A tenant to pay all mechanics' liens may be sufficient. (3) Require the tenant to carry builder's risk, workmen's compensation, and other insurance during construction. (4) Require the tenant to hire labor that will not cause controversies with the developer's construction crew.

Percentage leases. For the landlord's convenience, it is desirable that all percentage leases be uniform with respect to the time of month when monthly statements of gross sales are to be furnished by the tenant.

Cancellation clauses. The lease should give either party the right to cancel if certain stages of the construction work have not been started by a specified date.

Key tenants. The smaller tenant will want the landlord to covenant: (1) that there are leases with stated key tenants, (2) that the leases are not cancelable, and (3) that the leases run for a specified period of time, and prohibit these tenants from discontinuing business. Such leases may further provide that if a named key tenant discontinues operations, the small tenant may cancel his lease. This is sometimes called the *follow-the-leader clause.* It is dangerous, for if a key tenant moves, the shopping center may collapse. Alternatively, it may provide that the small tenant pays a lower rent until operations are resumed by a major tenant of caliber equal to that of the tenant who moved out.

If a lease contains an assurance that "the following are tenants in the center under existing leases presently in force," it should contain some statement that the landlord does not warrant that they will remain in as tenants during the life of the lease.

Evidence of title. The lease should require the landlord to furnish the tenant evidence of good title to the leased premises, preferably a leasehold title insurance policy. (See § 251.) The tenant should check this policy to make sure there are no building restrictions forbidding the use he plans to make of the premises. In addition, the landlord should covenant that he has good title to the remainder of the center and should afford the tenant's lawyer an opportunity to check the landlord's title policy.

Radius clause. Objection can be raised to a clause which forbids the landlord to rent premises within a specified *radius* of the shopping center for a purpose that competes with the tenant's business. The shopping center promoter might sell the center, and set up a competing use outside the center, and the lender would be powerless to prevent a cancellation of the lease by the tenant for this breach of the landlord's covenant. Perhaps the lender can get the tenant to sign a side agreement that he will not cancel the lease for such cause as long as the mortgage remains unpaid.

Exclusives. Commonly, certain tenants are given the exclusive right to operate a certain type of business in the center. The fact that the tenant is given an exclusive imposes a restraint on the activities permitted other tenants. Hence it is important that the lease be recorded so that all other tenants are given notice of this restraint, and it is better for the exclusives clause to describe the center accurately, so that subsequent lessees are put on notice of the extent of the restricted area. 51(C) C.J.S. 625.

An exclusive should be carefully drafted or litigation will result. 97 A.L.R.2d 4.

EXAMPLE: A lease to a delicatessen forbids "other delicatessen shops" in the center. Would this bar a supermarket from handling delicatessen items? One court has said "Yes." *Parker v. Levin*, 285 Mass. 125, 188 N.E.2d 502. Another court has said "No." *Mook v. Weaver Bros.*, 59 F.2d 1028.

In general, where they are asked to enforce an exclusive, courts look for substantial overlapping of products and substantial competition. 97 A.L.R.2d 46.

EXAMPLE: A junior department store that operates a variety department violates, to that extent, an earlier exclusive given to a variety store. *Variety, Inc. v. Hustad Corp.*, 145 Mont. 358, 400 P.2d 408; 51(C) C.J.S. 635.

An exclusive should be broad enough to protect the tenant but not so broad as to hamper other and different enterprises that make only incidental sales of competing items.

EXAMPLE: A lease to a supermarket stipulates that no other store in the center should sell food for consumption off the premises. This would keep out a bakery that could well be a distinct asset to the center. An exclusive given a candy store obviously should permit a drug store to sell boxed candies.

Obviously, a lease given in 1967 cannot restrict the operations of a tenant who holds a lease given in 1966 or earlier.

A landlord's violation of an exclusive may entail drastic consequences.

EXAMPLE: The developer gave A an exclusive for a variety store and later leased another site in the center to B for a variety store. When A stopped B's operations, B successfully contended that there was a constructive eviction. (See § 538.) This released B of all liability on his lease. *Variety, Inc. v. Hustad Corp.*, 145 Mont. 358, 400 P.2d 408.

Where the lease gives the tenant an "exclusive," the lender will want the lease to provide that this can only be enforced by an injunction suit restraining another tenant from using the premises for the purpose in question. In other words, the lender will not want the tenant to have the right to terminate the lease for violation of the "exclusives" clause. It is not sufficient that the lease does not specifically give the tenant the right to terminate the lease for violation of the exclusives clause. Some courts have allowed the tenant to terminate his lease where the exclusives clause is violated on the ground that this was a "constructive eviction" of the tenant.

An exclusive may apply to additions to the shopping center as well as to the original center. 51(C) C.J.S. 623.

Covenant as to use of premises. The lease should state the use which the tenant is to make of the premises and contain a covenant not to use the premises for other purposes. Both provisions are necessary. (See § 520.) If this protection is lacking, a tenant who would like to "jump his lease" simply puts the premises to a use offensive to the other tenants and the landlord will be compelled to agree to a cancellation of the lease. Or, just as bad, the tenant may use the premises for a use for which another tenant has an "exclusive." Surprisingly, leases have been encountered which gave the tenant an "exclusive" but did not forbid him to use the premises for other purposes! Obviously the use must be one which is not forbidden by local zoning.

Parking area and malls—easements and covenants. The lease should contain a covenant by the landlord to furnish a parking area of prescribed size. The landlord should also covenant not to diminish the area of the parking lot or to materially increase the store area that uses it. The lease should grant the tenant an easement for customer and employee parking in common with customers and employees of the other tenants. Care must be exercised to make this an easement and not a license. (See § 25.) It is customary to include a provision barring a tenant's employees from certain choice areas of the lot. Employees arrive early in the day, before shoppers arrive, and are in a position to usurp preferred parking places unless the lease forbids this. The landlord customarily covenants to pave, light, and strip the parking area; to police it; to keep it lighted, in repair, and free of ice and snow. Parking is only one of many easements that are important to the high-credit tenant. Ingress and egress over the drives, walks, and malls, for example, is another. Indeed, the tenant's right to enjoyment of all the common areas should be set out in some detail. This prevents the landlord from curtailing improvidently the basic rights of the high-credit tenant so important to the successful operation of the tenant's business. Once an easement has been granted, it cannot be moved without the tenant's consent. To maintain a degree of flexibility, it is well to reserve to the landlord (and this right will accrue to the lender in the event of foreclosure, if the clause so states) the right to make reasonable changes in the location of the easements without curtailing their area or availability to the lease.

Restrictions on assignment of lease. The perfect commercial lease from the landlord's point of view contains an absolute prohibition against an assignment or sublease of the demised premises by the tenant, since this assures the landlord (and, incidentally, the mortgage lender) that the original triple-A tenant will remain in possession. But the tenant who wants to move will try to contrive subterfuges to get around the prohibition. Accordingly, assignment clauses are written to prevent subterfuges. The clause should forbid the tenant to assign, mortgage, encumber, or sublet without the lessor's consent. A prohibition should also be included against permitting the demised premises to be used by others through concessions or even through occupation by others. In the event the tenant is a corporation, it should be spelled out that any transfer, sale, pledge, or other disposition of the corporate stock or voting securities shall be deemed a prohibited assignment, though such a provision is obviously impossible in the case of corporations having numerous stockholders. A lease to a chain store may, at the chain's request, permit assignment to a subsidiary of the chain so long as the chain is willing to sign a guarantee of payment of rent and so long as the operation will continue in substantially the same fashion and without changes of signs or other physical features that "pull" shoppers to the area.

Before consenting to an assignment, the landlord and his mortgagee must determine that the assignee's operation will not violate an "exclusive." If the lease is a percentage lease, he should not consent to an assignment to a tenant whose gross volume of business is substantially smaller than that of the present tenant, for percentage rents are based on gross receipts, not net receipts.

Covenants in general. Every shopping center lease contains covenants on the part of the landlord and covenants on the part of the tenant. Among the provisions the lender hopes and expects to find are the following tenant's covenants: to operate his business continuously; to remain open a certain number of hours per day; to keep his quarters illuminated until some specified hour each night; to pay a proportionate share of maintaining, policing, lighting, and insuring the parking area and other common areas; to pay for central services such as air-conditioning, heat, water, janitorial service, and utilities, if landlord is to furnish same; to pay a share of any increase in real estate taxes over the amount levied when the center becomes operational; to repair and maintain the store *interior* including doors and windows and be responsible for glass breakage while the landlord covenants to maintain the exterior; to avoid trash accumulation; to submit proposed signs and awnings for landlord's approval (which chain stores will resist); and to maintain membership in a merchants' association.

Ordinarily the parties contemplate that any party who succeeds to the landlord's ownership or the tenant's leasehold will enjoy the benefit of and be bound by the covenants. It is best to spell this out in the lease. This insures the right of the lender to enforce these covenants against the tenant in the event he acquires ownership through foreclosure. By the same token, the tenant will have the right to enforce covenants on the part of the lessor. Hence the lender must analyze the lease covenants that place duties on the landlord to determine whether they are unduly burdensome, such as covenants to rebuild or repair, regardless of cost. It may be possible to negotiate a side-agreement with the tenant that specific burdensome covenants will not be enforceable against the lender.

The covenants on the landlord's part should be covenants that the lender is able to perform, if necessary, so that if the landlord defaults, the lender can step in and perform and thus prevent termination of the leases by the tenant.

EXAMPLE: A landlord who happens to own a nearby "Kiddieland" can covenant to furnish complimentary tickets to a tenant who sells children's shoes. A lender succeeding to ownership of the center could not perform this covenant, and so it must not be included in the "covenants that run with the land."

EXAMPLE: A mortgage covers *part* of a shopping center. A lease to a tenant in this part of the center requires the landlord to restore or replace *any building in the center* damaged by fire, etc. If the mortgagee forecloses he cannot restore any building in the other portion of the center and yet, as the new landlord, if he fails to do so he will be in default under the lease.

Cancellation clauses. Any clause giving the tenant a right to cancel out because of events other than the landlord's breach of covenant is disturbing to a lender. For example, the value of the lease is affected by any clause giving the right to cancel if *any* part of the parking lot is condemned, for example, for road widening or if the tenant's sales do not average a specified dollar amount (the *kickout clause*).

If the lease provides for cancellation in the event the landlord fails to pay "any" mortgage, this might include the lender's own mortgage and would pull the rug from under him when he needs protection most. If possible, the lease should provide that any lender will receive notice from the tenant of the landlord's breach of covenant and be given an opportunity to cure it before the tenant cancels the lease. There should be no objection to this if the notice is required only if the lender first informs the lessee in writing of his name and address. This is analogous to the situation in a leasehold mortgage where the landlord agrees to notify the lender of a tenant's default and to give the lender the right to cure it before the landlord declares a forfeiture of the lease. Alternatively, the lender may be able to procure a side-agreement with the tenant under which the tenant waives, as to the lender, the right to cancel the lease because of landlord's breaches of covenant, either altogether or until the lender has acquired ownership by foreclosure and can then control the situation. In one way or another, in other words, the lender should endeavor to insulate himself against the tenant's wriggling out of the lease because of the landlord's defaults, as the tenant will try to do if the lease proves economically disadvantageous.

Abatement of rent.   The lease, or the state law even in the absence of a lease provision, may give the lessee the right to an abatement of rent because of the landlord's breach of covenant. This is objectionable to the lender. The tenant conceivably could advance large sums of money to build an addition the landlord was obligated to build, and when the lender takes over the property by foreclosure he may be unable to collect rent until the tenant has recouped his expenditures. A good lender's lease would forbid withholding of rent by the tenant under any conditions, at least as to a lender.

Security deposits—prepayment of rent.   The lease should authorize the landlord to transfer to any institutional lender securities deposited by the tenant to insure payment of rent and should permit the lender to retain the securities until the tenant is entitled to their return. If a tenant has prepaid rent for the last part of the term, obviously this is rent the lender will not be able to collect if he becomes the owner by foreclosure, and this should be weighed in determining the value of the lease.

Option to purchase.   A lease clause giving a prior lessee an option to purchase the premises is a troublesome clause to the lender. In the first place, some fine lawyers believe such an option to be a prior "encumbrance" that makes the mortgage an illegal investment for an institutional lender. In the second place, no one can be certain of the consequences where there is an exercise of the option, with payment of the purchase price to the lessor. In many cases the courts have said that exercise of the option *relates back* to the date of the option. If exercise of the option *relates back,* it might wipe out the mortgage. At best exercise of the option results in prepayment of the mortgage with no prepayment premium. And if the option is in the form of a "pre-emption right" to purchase the property at a price the mortgagor is willing to accept from a third party, some court decisions hold that this gives the tenant the right to buy from the lender at a price equal to the foreclosure sale price if the mortgage is foreclosed. Finally, it certainly is objectionable to take subject to an option where the option price is or could be less than the mortgage debt. The option to purchase, therefore, should be subordinated to the mortgage. It is perfectly possible to subordinate the *option* without subordinating the *lease.* In the document subordinating the option to the mortgage it should also be provided that if the tenant exercises his option and thus becomes the owner of the property, the lease shall nevertheless remain in existence for the benefit of the lender, so that he can collect rent thereunder if default occurs under the mortgage.

Tenant's lien.   The tenant may have a lien on the land for some purpose, as for example, to insure return of a security deposit or because the tenant made some repairs or performed some other act that was legally the obligation of the landlord. This lien, in the case of a prior lease, may be prior and superior to the lien of the mortgage, and may possibly make the investment illegal in some states. This lien and, indeed, any other lien the tenant may have by virtue of his status as a tenant, should be subordinated to the lien of the mortgage, or the lease should contain a general clause making all the tenant's liens subordinate to any mortgage thereafter placed on the property to an institutional lender.

Assignment of rents.   The mortgage should be accompanied by a strong, detailed, recorded assignment of leases and rents, notice of which is sent to all existing tenants.

Chapter 32

THE CO-OP AND
THE CONDOMINIUM

§ 548. **Introduction.**   Today one can own an apartment in one of two ways, namely, either as a *cooperative apartment* (hereinafter, for brevity, referred to as a *co-op*) or as a *condominium*. To be sure, a condominium is a form of cooperative ownership, but since legal distinctions exist between the two types, a difference in nomenclature seems necessary.

§ 549. **Mechanics of traditional co-op ownership.**   Co-operative apartments can be organized on either a trust or corporate basis, but the latter is by far the more popular. Under the corporate arrangement, a corporation is formed, and ownership of the land and building is acquired by the corporation. The corporation places a mortgage on the land for the purpose of buying, or, if the land is vacant, for the purpose of building. Since no mortgagee will lend up to the full value of the building, the balance of the necessary funds is raised by sale of stock to the prospective tenants. When he has purchased a specified number of shares, the prospective tenant receives a long-term lease, called a *proprietary lease,* from the corporation. The word *proprietary* means that it *has the attributes of ownership,* that it gives rights equivalent *in economic benefit* to outright ownership. Legally, however, a proprietary lease is a lease and landlord and tenant law is applicable to it. This lease gives the tenant the right to possession of his apartment for the term specified in the lease, but requires the tenant to pay rent to the corporation, which rent payments consist of his pro rata share of the amounts needed to cover mortgage debt, taxes, and operating expenses. The annual cash requirements for the building are established by the board of directors of the corporation, and this sum is divided among the tenants in proportion to the number of shares allocated to each apartment, the bigger apartments having the larger shareholdings and assessments. Each tenant pays for his own stove, refrigerator, linoleum, decorating, and interior maintenance. Restrictions are placed on the right of the lessee to assign or sublet. The lease provides that it is subject to any future mortgage placed on the building by the landlord corporation. A mortgage usually requires a two-thirds vote of the tenants. This clause facilitates refinancing of the existing mortgage.

§ 550.   **Buying a traditional co-op apartment.**   If you are planning to buy a co-op apartment, the following suggestions will help you:

1. You cannot afford to have the title to the entire building brought down to date. What you can do is have your lawyer check the existing title insurance policy, abstract, and opinion to see that the building corporation has good title to the property (subject only to the mortgage and the proprietary leases). This title evidence may be several years old. Supplement this by getting an affidavit from the secretary of the corporation to the effect that the condition of title remains today as it was on the date of the title evidence which your lawyer examined and that no lawsuits are presently pending against the corporation.

2. If you are buying the lease and stock of a present tenant, get the secretary of the building corporation to sign an affidavit stating: (a) that the stock is in fact owned by your seller and is fully paid for; (b) that the lease is owned by your seller, free of any subleases; (c) that the stock and lease are free from any assessments other than the current ones shown on the financial statement submitted to you by the corporation; (d) that no defaults have occurred in the building's mortgage payments; (e) that none of the other tenants is currently behind in his payments; (f) that no proposal to remodel the building or increase assessments has come before the directors within the past year, for this may be why your seller is moving out; (g) how much space is rented to persons other than tenant-stockholders, for if this figure gets too high, you lose your income tax benefits; and (h) what insurance is carried presently. Get a certified copy of the directors' resolution authorizing your seller to sell you his lease and stock, for all co-ops restrict the right of the tenants to transfer their rights. Have your lawyer check the lease that you are about to buy and explain to you the restrictions (on remodeling of apartments, for example, or the right to sell, sublease, or operate a business in the apartment) and liabilities (special assessments, for example) that it creates. Have him explain what maintenance costs you must pay yourself, such as decorating. Be sure your contract for the purchase of the lease and stock specifies clearly what is included in the sale, for stoves, refrigerators, and so on are not supplied by management. If a husband and wife are buying, they probably will want to take title to the lease and stock in joint tenancy. Use the proper clause.

§ 551.   **Condominium—in general.**   In a condominium apartment, the purchaser of an apartment receives a deed that gives him *absolute ownership* of the apartment that he has purchased and ownership of an undivided interest or share in the common elements hereinafter described.

EXAMPLE: *ABC Corporation* acquires a tract of vacant land. It obtains a construction mortgage loan from *XYZ Bank* and erects a building containing fifty apartments. *E* wishes to buy one of these apartments, Apartment #1. *ABC Corporation* sells *E* a deed that conveys to him (1) Apartment #1, and (2) a 2 per cent interest in the ownership of the *common elements,* that is, everything but Apartments 1 to 50 inclusive. The common elements include the land itself including all the ground area and air space above it and around it except the apartments; the outside walls of the building; the foundation; the roof; the basement; the stairs; halls; foyers; elevators; swimming pool; janitor's apartment; water tanks; fire escapes; exits; heating plant; central air-conditioning; incinerator; pumps; ducts; machinery; and so on. Thus *E* winds up owning his own apartment just as if it were a separate house, and a 2 per cent interest in the common elements. As to the common elements *E* becomes a tenant in common with the other apartment owners, just as if a deed of the common elements had been made to *E* and his forty-nine neighbors *as tenants in common.* The construction mortgage, which covered all the land and the entire building, is released as to the two items conveyed to *E*, namely, his apartment and his share of the common elements. To finance his purchase, *E* borrows $15,000 which he obtains by giving to *DEF Corporation* a mortgage on Apartment #1 and his 2 per cent interest in the common elements. *E* now owns, as an absolute owner, his apartment and his 2 per cent interest in the common elements, subject only to his own mortgage to *DEF Corporation.* In becoming the owner of an apartment the condominium owner technically becomes the owner of the *space* bounded by the inner surfaces of the apartment walls. Under the condominium laws such ownership of *space* is perfectly legal. Indeed, that such space is part of the land and can be separately owned and conveyed has long been taken for granted. 4 *Powell, Real Property,* 721. (See also § 6.)

§ 552. Condominium—apartment ownership.

The ownership of the apartment may be in a single individual, in husband and wife as tenants by the entireties, in two or more persons as joint tenants or as tenants in common, in community property, or in a corporation or partnership, just as if the apartment were a separate tract of land.

§ 553. Condominium—the declaration.

Before any of the apartments are sold off, the owner-developer makes, signs, and records a *declaration* that contains certain basic items.

Suggestions as to items to include:

1. A description of the land and the building.
2. A description of each of the apartments, giving the number of each unit and all other data necessary for its identification.
3. A description of the common elements.
4. A statement of the share of each apartment owner in the common elements. This share should be expressed as a percentage rather than a fraction.
5. A provision that ownership of an apartment and of the owner's share of the common elements shall not be severed or separated and that any conveyance or mortgage of the one without the other is prohibited; also that any partition suit with respect to the common elements is forbidden.

6. A grant of easements to each apartment owner giving him rights of ingress and egress and other easement rights.

7. Building restrictions limiting use of the apartment to use by its owner for residential occupancy by his family.

8. Provisions relative to the administration of the property by an association of the condominium owners. This contemplates the creation of an association or nonprofit corporation consisting of all the co-owners and the drawing up of rules and regulations governing administration of the property. While details of operating rules may go into the *by-laws* of the corporation, the *declaration* should provide for creation of a basic central authority to manage the building, to adopt rules and by-laws, to see that all occupants obey the rules and pay their assessments, and to keep the common elements in repair.

9. A provision giving the condominium association the right to levy assessments on the apartment owners for maintenance, etc., and creating a forecloseable lien on each apartment for any delinquency in paying the assessments applicable to each apartment unit, and stating the maximum assessment permitted.

10. A provision that in case an apartment owner chooses to sell his apartment, the condominium association shall have the *right of first refusal,* that is, the right to buy the apartment at the same price the apartment owner's buyer is willing to pay. This device must not be used as a means of racial discrimination. 50 Calif. L. Rev. 317. (See Chapter 35.) The declaration should provide that the right of a first refusal does not apply to a sale made by a mortgagee who has acquired an apartment by foreclosure.

11. Provision that in the event of total or substantial destruction of the building by fire or other hazard, or where the property reaches obsolescence, a stated percentage of co-owners' votes shall determine whether to rebuild or sell the property. A number of states have laws on this point.

12. A provision that each condominium owner is to keep his apartment in repair at his own expense but is not to interfere with the exterior of the building or any of the common elements.

13. A provision is needed stating that all easements, covenants, and agreements in the declaration run with the land. Some statement is also needed that the benefit and burden of these covenants run with each family unit. A provision should be included that when any apartment owner sells, his personal liability for future breaches of these covenants ends with the sale.

14. A provision should be included giving a majority of the apartment owners the right to amend the declaration and by-laws and providing that such amendment shall be binding on all present and future landowners. (See Chapter 34.)

§ 554. **Land descriptions in the declaration.** The declaration should be executed by the landowner, acknowledged and witnessed in accordance with the local requirements for recording, and should be recorded in the recorder's office.

It should describe the following elements: (1) the land comprising the entire project area, for which a traditional legal description can be used, but which should be given a distinctive designation, for example, *the project parcel;* (2) each apartment, by whatever method is employed, giving it in addition a distinctive number, as *Apartment Parcel 1;* (3) the land and space that are to be owned in common by the apartment owners, for which one shortcut would be a description such as *the project parcel excepting Apartment Parcels 1 to 100, both inclusive, all hereinabove described,* and which can also be given a designation, for example, *the co-ownership parcel.*

§ 555. **Provisions of the deed.**   The individual deed of a family unit need not necessarily be a complex document insofar as its legal description is concerned. The basis for such description will already have been provided by: (1) recording of the subdivision plat, (2) recording of the declaration to which were appended the land and apartment surveys containing legal descriptions of the various apartments, or (3) recording of the declaration to which were appended the land survey and building floor plans, in which case the legal descriptions of the apartments will have been set forth in the declaration. (See also § 556.)

Thus in the deed, the legal description of the individual apartment could be as follows:

PARCEL I

The absolute and indefeasible fee simple title to the parcel of land, property, and space designated as Apartment Parcel 100 in the plat of subdivision recorded in the Recorder's Office of _____ County, _____ on November 1, 19____ as Document No. 123456 (or: "in the Declaration recorded, etc." as the case may be).

The description of the common elements could be as follows:

PARCEL II

The absolute and indefeasible fee simple title to an undivided 2 per cent interest in the land, property, and space known as Lot 1 in Block 1 in Jones Subdivision, in Section___, Township___, North, Range___ East of the _____ Principal Meridian, excepting from said Lot 1 all the land, property, and space designated as Apartment Parcels 1 to 100, both inclusive, in the plat of subdivision recorded in the Recorder's Office of _____ County, _____ on November 1, 19____ as Document No. 123456 (or: "in the Declaration recorded, etc." as the case may be).

The apartments excepted in Parcel II should, of course, consist of all the family units in the building. Should there be any units that are intended to be rented for commercial facilities, they should not be included among the apartments excepted, since they would be classed as part of the common elements.

An additional paragraph could be included in the developer's deed to the first purchaser of an apartment, conveying all the rights, benefits, easements, privileges, options, and covenants created by the declaration. It will do no harm to repeat in this clause the statement that these run with the land, for it is this document that gives life to the covenants.

Because of a dearth of modern cases touching on the specific question of whether ownership of the space occupied by an apartment or upper floor in a building would survive destruction of the building, it would be advisable to include in the deed a provision that it is the intention of the parties thereto that the ownership rights thereby conveyed shall so survive.

§ 556. **Description of apartments.** There are three methods by which a unit of air space can be described:

1. *The subdivision plat method.* You record a plat of subdivision of air space and the air lots representing the individual units by means of a drawing. This will permit conveyance of a particular unit by its number, as shown on the plat.

2. *The land and apartment survey.* A survey is first made of the land, showing the location of the building. Space surveys of each unit on each floor are then made showing the elevation of the floor and ceiling surfaces, the dimensions of the inside surfaces of the walls of each unit, and their location with reference to the boundaries of the land projected vertically upward.

3. *Floor plan method.* In lieu of individual apartment surveys, make a survey of the land showing the location of the building and attach to it floor plans showing each unit's location, dimensions, and elevation from the ground floor surface, with a certification by the architect that the building was built substantially in accordance with the plans.

The fear has been expressed in some localities that the building may settle and thus cause an apartment to shift into, and encroach upon, the air space allocated to another apartment. One way of dealing with this problem is to recognize it in the declaration and to create easements in the declaration to maintain such encroachments, should they occur. 50 *Cal. L. Rev.* 303.

§ 557. **Suggestions in purchasing a new condominium:**

1. It is necessary to determine that the condominium documents conform to the state law. If not, dangerous consequences ensue. For example, the tax assessor may refuse to give your apartment a separate tax assessment.

2. Be sure that the structure conforms to local zoning ordinances and does not violate private restrictions such as those in a recorded plat or deed restrictions.

3. Determine whether the contract provisions giving the developer the right to cancel out if a stated percentage of apartments are not sold are likely to be invoked, considering, in this case, the percentage already sold.

4. Check whether the burden of assessments for maintenance, etc., falls entirely on the apartments sold or is shared by the developer in proportion to the apartments remaining unsold and still owned by the developer.

5. Check whether the voting rights of the sold apartments give the apartment purchasers at least a minority representation in the home owners' association. For example, if a majority vote of the apartments in the building can elect a home association board of directors, the developer will have absolute control until a majority of the apartments are sold.

6. Check whether the documents require all purchasers to get their financing from a specified mortgage lender and, if so, what the lender's terms are likely to be.

7. Consider whether the prospective occupancy is such that the membership is likely to vote future assessments for maintenance and renovation in excess of your financial abilities as a purchaser.

8. The first contract of sale for a condominium apartment will permit the developer to amend or modify the declaration, but should not permit him to increase the buyer's assessments, or to increase the apartment cost, or to reduce the seller's obligation to pay the expenses on unsold apartments.

§ 558. Title requirements—purchase of old or new condominium covering the apartment and its share of the common elements.   A prudent purchaser of an apartment will demand a title insurance policy. Preferably it will contain specific coverage against mechanics' liens. It should also contain assurance that there are no delinquent condominium assessments, for such condominium assessments are, by law, a foreclosable lien on the apartment. In this connection, the management group furnishes the title company a certificate that all assessments have been paid, and the title company takes the risk of any inaccuracy in this certificate. The title company, in addition to making its usual search of the public records, also searches for assessment liens filed by the management group, for in some states these must be recorded. The title company also satisfies itself that the right of first refusal has been properly eliminated, and its policy insures the purchaser on this score. To supplement this coverage, the purchaser should demand a letter from the secretary of the condominium's board of directors that no unusual special assessments are in contemplation, for an apartment may go on the market because its owner wishes to avoid payment of a large assessment, for example, for automatic elevators.

§ 559. Condominium—mortgage provisions.   A mortgage of a condominium should state that the mortgagor's breach of the covenants in the declaration or a failure to pay condominium assessments gives the mortgagee the right to declare the entire mortgage debt due. Likewise the mortgagee should have the right to pay delinquent condominium assessments and add these sums to his mortgage debt. The insurance requirements of the mortgage will differ from the usual insurance requirements because of the master policy. The mortgage also provides that the apartment owner will not vote to amend the condominium declaration without the mortgagee's written consent.

§ 560. Condominium—state regulation.   In some states the condominium declaration may constitute a *subdivision*, requiring approval of public authorities, as in the case of plat of subdivision. Likewise in some states (Arizona, California, Hawaii, Michigan, and Virginia, for example), the offering of condominium apartments for sale requires some official approval under the local *Blue Sky Law*, which is the law protecting purchasers of unlisted stocks.

§ 561.   **Condominium—insurance.**   Insurance of the condominium is a problem that, to some extent, has not been solved as yet.

Each condominium owner, to be sure, can obtain fire and other hazard insurance on his apartment and his undivided interest in the common elements. However, should a loss occur, the damage to the common elements (stairs, halls, outer walls, etc.) must be repaired as a single enterprise for the benefit of all condominium owners. Moreover, the cost of repairing the common elements will greatly exceed the value of any condominium owner's share in those elements. Even if the condominium owner is willing to run the risk of under-insuring, his mortgagee will not be willing to do so. This means that in addition to the condominium owner's hazard policy, some sort of *master policy* must be taken out by the condominium association of apartment owners provided for in the declaration and by-laws. The master policy must be so written that recovery thereunder is not diminished by the presence of *double insurance,* that is, by the existence of policies in the individual apartments as well as the master policy. The apartment policy also should provide that it is not *contributory,* that is, recovery on the master policy is not reduced by recovery on the individual policy. Since the master policy, in effect, protects the interests of all apartment owners as parties assured, it should contain a provision that acts of any apartment owner (arson, increasing hazard, etc.) do not invalidate the master policy.

Most lawyers feel that any loss over a stated amount should be paid to a trustee named in the condominium declaration. This trustee must be authorized in the declaration to *adjust the loss,* that is, to agree with the insurance companies as to the amount of the loss. The declaration should also provide that no apartment owner shall have the right to hire contractors for rebuilding of the common elements. This exclusive right should be given the trustee. It might be well for the declaration to require each individual apartment policy to be filed with the building manager, so that potential conflicts with the master policy could be eliminated.

At the present time the modes of handling the condominium insurance problem vary considerably and no one method seems to be completely satisfactory.

§ 562.   **Condominium — termination — destruction of building.** The situation where the building is destroyed by fire or other casualty varies from state to state. Where rebuilding takes place with adequate insurance funds, the problems are not excessively complex. Where, however, a percentage of the owners have the right to vote to sell the property and divide the proceeds, problems exist unless the state law spells out a program, which has been done in some states (e.g., New York, Hawaii, Mississippi, Nevada, Illinois and Missouri).

§ 562a.   **Advantages and disadvantages of condominium ownership.**   The advantages the condominium enjoys as compared with the co-op method are these:

1. The condominium owner has his own mortgage covering only his apartment and his share of the common elements. The advantage to him, as against co-op ownership, is very great. Under the co-op form, if any substantial number of tenants get into financial difficulty, as happens during an economic depression, the blanket mortgage covering the entire building could go into default, and the resulting foreclosure would wipe out all the tenants. Similarly, each condominium owner receives his own real estate tax bill covering his apartment and his share of the common elements.

2. The advantages the condominium enjoys with respect to mortgage financing should make the condominium easier to sell or re-sell than a co-op, since it enlarges the number of potential buyers.

EXAMPLE: A owns a condominium apartment which he can sell to B for $30,000.00. B can obtain a mortgage loan of approximately $24,000.00, so that he needs only $6,000.00. A's existing mortgage, whatever its amount, would be paid off in the process, just as if A were selling a house. If A were selling a co-op in a comparable building on which the building mortgage had been paid down to 50 per cent of the property value, A would be selling his apartment equity for $15,000.00, subject to the building mortgage, and he would have to find a buyer who has $15,000.00 in cash, for lenders do not lend on co-ops.

3. Again, if a person desires a debt-free shelter, as many senior citizens do, a condominium purchaser can pay cash for his apartment, as many purchasers do. A co-op purchaser has no choice but to accept his apartment subject to the mortgage on the building.

4. Co-op leases provide that the lease may be terminated for failure to meet a monthly assessment or because the apartment owner has become bankrupt or been guilty of objectionable conduct. The condominium owner is more secure in this regard.

The advantages a co-op enjoys over a condominium are these:

1. In a co-op, the apartment owner has the right to leave. If he has bad luck and cannot keep up his monthly payments, he can sublease his apartment, sell it, or at the worst, give it back to the landlord corporation. The modern co-op lease gives the lessee the right to cancel the lease after a specified number of years by surrendering his stock and his lease to the landlord corporation. In the condominium, the owner, having signed a note and mortgage, has no right simply to "walk away." In case of default and foreclosure, there is always the possibility of a deficiency judgment.

2. Another advantage that the co-op possesses is the ease with which one can control the type of neighbors one will have in the building. In the co-op, the lease provides that it cannot be assigned or subleased except with the written consent of the landlord corporation. The stock certificate provides that it can be transferred only in connection with an authorized transfer of the lease. This method has the advantage of simplicity and unquestioned legality. *68 Beacon St. v. Sohier,* 289 Mass. 354, 194

N.E.303; *Weisner v. 791 Park Ave. Corp.,* 6 N.Y.2d 426, 160 N.E.2d 720. Probably these restrictions must be exercised "reasonably." *Mowatt v. Lake Shore Drive Corp.,* 385 F.2d 135. For example, a refusal of consent based solely on racial grounds would not stand up in court. In the condominium method, the situation is more complicated. Typically, each owner of a condominium apartment holds his apartment subject to a right of *first refusal* should he desire to sell. Such a right of first refusal is probably valid. *Gale v. York Center Community Co-operative, Inc.,* 21 Ill.2d 86, 171 N.E.2d 30. However, the method is clumsy. Also, since it calls for the apartment owners to buy the apartment at the price the selling apartment owner can obtain from an outsider, it requires a special assessment on the apartment owners.

3. Getting rid of a co-op owner who defaults in his monthly payments or fails to abide by the by-laws is easier in the co-op than in the condominium. Just as an ordinary lease can be terminated for default in rent or breach of covenant, so also a co-op lease can be terminated for like grounds and the co-op lessee evicted by quick and inexpensive forcible detainer proceedings. *Green v. Greenbelt Homes, Inc.,* 232 Md. 496, 194 A.2d 273. In a condominium, if a particular apartment owner fails to pay his monthly assessments a lien on his apartment can be foreclosed, just as a mortgage is foreclosed, but the proceeding is costly and time-consuming. Making the condominium owner behave, when his conduct becomes objectionable, is difficult.

4. The condominium, since it is owned by many people, not by a single corporation as in the case of the co-op, has no feasible way of putting a mortgage on the building in its later years when remodeling or repairs are needed. A few states have laws covering this point.

5. Where for one reason or another it becomes advisable to sell the building and the tenants wish to do so, this can be accomplished in co-ops by a vote of a percentage of the shareholders (who, of course, are the tenants). A two-thirds vote usually suffices. In the case of a condominium, sale of the building is apt to require a unanimous vote, except in certain special situations, as where the building is destroyed by fire.

In both co-ops and condominiums the apartment owner enjoys the benefits of ownership. As the value of the building goes up and the mortgage is reduced by payment, his equity increases.

Both the condominium owner and the co-op owner have the right to defer payment of income tax on a capital gain where the apartment is sold at a profit. Both have the same right to deduct from income for income tax purposes all payments made on mortgage interest and real estate taxes.

Chapter 33

PLANNED UNIT
DEVELOPMENTS

§ 563.   **The planned-unit idea.**   The *planned unit development* (hereafter referred to as PUD) is one of the newer ideas in housing. Such developments consist of townhouses, homes, apartments (both garden and high-rise), or combinations of such buildings, all with common open areas and some with private recreation facilities. The advantages offered are:

> 1. Lower priced homes achieved by cost savings through more efficient land use and planning.
> 2. Small, private yards with a minimum of maintenance chores and a maximum of time and energy for recreational activities in the common areas.
> 3. Common areas of green open space providing an attractive setting.
> 4. In some cases, shared facilities for swimming, golf, fishing, etc. and a recreation center for crafts, meetings, and other group activities.
> 5. Maintenance furnished by homeowners' association.

§ 564.   **Cluster housing.**   The phrase *cluster housing* means that the individual homes, row houses, or apartment buildings are grouped together on relatively small plots of land with large surrounding areas of land left open for common recreational and park developments. The cluster form of development is economical because the clustering of houses reduces the cost of supplying utilities and roads.

§ 565.   **Home association described.**   An important feature of most planned-unit developments is the home association which is vested with control of the common areas.

A home association is a nonprofit corporation operating under documents through which (1) each homeowner is automatically a member, with voting rights usually allocated at one vote per family unit, and (2) each homesite is automatically subject to a charge for a proportionate share of the expenses for the home association's activities, such as common property maintenance. Outdoor lighting, street maintenance, furnishing water, tree pruning, garbage and trash collection, private policing, and exterior maintenance of individual home properties are among the services a home association may undertake.

§ 566. Outline of legal steps to take in creating a PUD.   The PUD documents should:

1. Legally create an automatic-membership, nonprofit corporation with voting rights in each family unit;

2. Include a contract by the developer to convey ownership of the common areas to the home association within a reasonable, definite time;

3. Appropriately restrict the uses of the home lots and common areas;

4. Grant each lot owner easements for the use and enjoyment of the common property;

5. Create a lien on each home lot for assessments which will (a) assure sufficient funds for maintenance of the common areas but (b) provide adequate safeguards for the lot owners against undesirably high charges;

6. Include covenants by the home association to operate and maintain the common areas.

Before the first lot is sold, the land developer incorporates the nonprofit home association, and records the land subdivision plat and declaration of covenants and easements for all of the land in the planned unit. His plat identifies (1) property to be transferred to public agencies, such as any proposed public streets, (2) the individual homesites, (3) the common areas to be transferred by the developer to the home association, and (4) any other parcels, such as a church site or shopping center, to be kept by the developer or transferred to others.

Recorded contemporaneously with the plat is a *declaration of easements, covenants, restrictions, and liens.* It is hereafter referred to as the *declaration.*

§ 567. Common areas—plat provisions.   Since it is imperative that the common areas be kept in the ownership of the home association and not dedicated to the public, the recorded plat must bear on its face a legend relative to all the common areas indicating that the area is *not* dedicated to the public and that its ownership is reserved to the developer (who later will deed it to the association). If such a legend is lacking, courts may hold that any area having the appearance of common ground, is, by implication, dedicated to the public. However, since the home buyers will want the developer to deed the land to the home association, an agreement to do so should be contained in the plat or in the accompanying declaration. Also appropriate language must be incorporated in the text of the plat to indicate that the homeowners take easements in the common properties but no ownership therein. This means that the legend on the plat should be quite comprehensive, as:

> Full ownership of the tracts marked *park, playground, private lake, golf course* (describe all other such areas) is retained in ABC (the developer) for ultimate conveyance to XYZ, a non-profit corporation whose membership will be composed of homeowners in this development, all according to the provisions of the declaration of restrictions, easements, liens, and covenants filed contemporaneously herewith, and hereby made a part of this plat. Conveyances of lots in this subdivision shall not be deemed to convey title to any part of the retained areas. Said areas are not dedicated to the public. With respect to the total area embraced in this plat, and all parts thereof, easements, covenants, liens, and restrictions are created in and by the declaration aforesaid.

§ 568. **Common areas—agreement of developer to convey to home association.** The declaration will contain an agreement that not later than a set date the developer will convey the common areas to the home association. The declaration should be signed as *accepted* by the home association so that it can enforce this agreement.

§ 569. **Common areas—easements—paramount rights of home association.** The declaration should create easements in favor of all of the homeowners in the development for access over the private walks and streets, for utilities, water, sewers and other services, and for use of the common areas, etc., but it should make such easement grant expressly subject and inferior to certain rights of the home association. These rights should include the right of the association to exercise, free and clear of all private rights created in the homeowners, the following rights: (1) the right to borrow money for community improvements and to secure the loan by a mortgage on the common properties; (2) the right of the association to suspend the enjoyment of the common areas by any homeowner and the furnishing of services by home association (garbage removal, furnishing water, etc.) to the delinquent homeowner while his maintenance assessments remain unpaid; (3) the right to manage, maintain, and control the common areas for the benefit of the homeowners, and to promulgate reasonable rules toward this end; (4) the right to dedicate part or all of the common properties to the public for public use; (5) the right of the home association to charge reasonable admission and other fees for the use of the common areas.

§ 570. **Common areas—public or private ownership—right to dedicate.** The right to dedicate part or all of the common properties to the public is also important. Since many planned unit developments seek out less expensive land beyond the boundaries of existing villages or cities, the home association, on occasion, is set up initially to furnish urban services to the community. As soon as a village is formed and is prepared to furnish urban services (streets, sewer, water and the like), the home association may choose to transfer these systems to the village. Provision for such ultimate transfer must be made in the declaration. It is true that public ownership of the other common areas (swimming pools, etc.) would eliminate the burden of paying real estate taxes thereon and the cost of maintaining the common areas, but such public ownership, especially of recreational common areas, would encourage public use, which would adversely affect the residents of the subdivision; hence it is to be avoided. An alternative is the creation of a public district with the same boundaries as the development. This public body can levy assessments for maintenance but is responsive to the wishes of the voters who are homeowners in the development.

§ 571. Common areas—artificial lakes. In some planned developments, an artificially created lake is one of the attractive common facilities. It is quite clear that neither the public nor any public body has any rights whatever in lakes so created. The developer has the legal right to reserve to himself the right to dictate who may use the lake or he may grant this right to the homeowners. *Mayer v. Grueber*, 29 Wis. 2d 168, 138 N.W.2d 197; *Thompson v. Enz*, 154 N.W.2d 473.

§ 572. The declaration—building restrictions. The declaration will establish a comprehensive general plan of restrictions governing minutely the structures and uses permitted in the development both on the homesites and on the common areas. The plat or declaration should also vest in the home association the right to pass upon the plans of any structure to be erected by any home buyer. 19 A.L.R.2d 1274.

§ 573. The declaration—covenants. The declaration will contain covenants binding on each homeowner to pay the assessments levied on his lot for maintenance charges, which covenants create a *personal liability* on which a personal judgment can be obtained by the association against a defaulting homeowner. It will also contain covenants by the home association to (1) maintain and operate the common property, (2) administer architectural controls, (3) enforce other covenants, and in some cases (4) maintain all or part of the exterior of individual homes. The covenants provide for amendments, but any amendment requires a vote of the homeowners.

§ 574. The declaration—lien for maintenance. The declaration provides for the imposition of a maintenance assessment, usually annually, on each lot in the development. Home associations tend to operate somewhat informally. The danger here is that if procedures grow too lax (meetings held on days other than those set in by-laws, notice of meeting lacking or defective, etc.), the assessments made by the association may be declared invalid. *Noremac, Inc. v. Centre Hill Court,* 164 Va. 151, 178 S.E. 877.

§ 575. **The declaration—restraints on sales.**   Any provision in the declaration or deeds that a homeowner cannot sell his lot except by consent of a majority vote of the association is invalid. Such a clause is an illegal *restraint on alienation. Mountain Springs Ass'n. v. Wilson,* 81 N.J.Super. 564, 196 A.2d 270. Likewise invalid is any clause that only a member of the home association can purchase a homesite. *Ibid.* Nor can the declaration or by-laws of the association provide that sales by a homeowner to a future purchaser can only be made to a purchaser approved by the association. *Tuckerton Beach Club v. Bender,* 91 N.J.Super. 167, 219 A.2d 529; *Connor v. Rockwood,* 320 Mass. 473, 69 N.E.2d 454. But it is safe to provide that any homesite purchaser automatically acquires membership in the home association as a normal incident of home ownership.

§ 576. **Mortgage provisions.**   A mortgage on a PUD homesite should contain a covenant of the mortgagor to pay all assessments and a covenant not to vote to amend the declaration without the mortgagee's written consent.

§ 577. **Condominium compared.**   Although there is nothing in the concept of the condominium which would prevent its use for a PUD, basically there is no need to create a condominium. A PUD home has its own mortgage as does a condominium apartment. Furthermore, it is not necessary to distribute the ownership of the common properties among the lot owners as in condominiums. The PUD makes a different but satisfactory provision for the common areas.

§ 578. **Zoning.**   The old-fashioned zoning ordinance, with its rigid allocation of specific uses to specific zones, its building lines, and its minimum area requirements, does not lend itself to the PUD type of development. Cluster development calls for smaller homesites, the land subtracted from homesites being added to common areas. However, the PUD can, it seems, be listed as a special exception in the zoning ordinance. 73 Harvard L. Rev. 251. Alternatively, the zoning ordinance may include a special section devoted to the PUD, calling it variously a *Community Unit Plan, Dwelling Groups, Group Housing, Planned Residential Development,* or *Planned Building Groups.* 73 Harvard L. Rev. 253. Because approving a development of this character involves a considerable exercise of discretion, it seems wise to provide that final approval of a developer's proposal to create a PUD zone should rest with the city council, just as if an amendment to the zoning ordinance were being considered, and some ordinances so provide. *Rodgers v. Village of Tarry-*

town, 302 N.Y. 115, 96 N.E.2d 731; *LaRue v. East Brunswick,* 68 N.J. Super. 435, 172 A.2d 691; *DeMeo v. Zoning Comm.,* 148 Conn. 68, 167 A.2d 454; 73 Harvard L. Rev. 255. The applicant for such zoning may, under many ordinances, be a government agency, for urban redevelopment plans sometimes call for a PUD.

The village cannot thrust PUD zoning on the landowner if the land is not suited to that purpose.

EXAMPLE: The land was located in an exclusively business area. Zoning change to PUD was held illegal. *Gable* v. *Village of Hinsdale,* 230 N.E.2d 706.

Chapter 34

THE DECLARATION OF RESTRICTIONS, EASEMENTS, LIENS, AND COVENANTS

§ 579. **In general.** In today's land transactions property rights of considerable complexity are generated. This is true particularly of the condominium, the planned unit development (PUD), and the town house. Supplementing the local zoning ordinance in such developments there will be found a scheme of private building covenants, easements, liens and restrictions. The landowner in a condominium or PUD will covenant to do a number of things, for example, to pay maintenance assessments, which are foreclosable liens on the homesites or apartments. Each landowner in a condominium, PUD, or town house will enjoy a number of valuable easements over his neighbor's property, and his own property will be subject to easements in favor of his neighbors. There is general agreement among property lawyers that these detailed rights should be set forth in a *declaration of restrictions, easements, liens, and covenants,* and that only relatively brief reference should be made to them in the deeds of conveyance.

The legality of this device rests upon the rule that if a recorded document, such as a deed, makes reference to another document recorded in the same office, the two are read together. Thus the provisions of the declaration are treated legally as "set out" in the deed. 82 A.L.R. 412, 416.

§ 580. **Restrictions.** Since all that is needed to create enforceable building restrictions is a recorded document that gives public notice of such easements, a recorded declaration will again suffice for this purpose, when followed by deeds referring thereto. *Davis v. Huguenor,* 408 Ill. 468, 97 N.E.2d 295; *Kosel v. Stone,* 146 Mont. 218, 404 P.2d 894; *Lawrence v. Brockelman,* 155 N.Y.S.2d 604.

There will be restrictions as to the homesites or apartments and restrictions as to the common areas. For obvious reasons, the developer must not retain the right to modify the restrictions. This may destroy the general plan and render the restrictions unenforceable. 19 A.L.R.2d 1282. Also the declaration must be recorded before any deed or mortgage is recorded, for any deed recorded before the declaration will not be subject to the restrictions, easements, or other rights created by the declaration. All deeds are expressly made subject to the declaration.

For the protection of the developer in a PUD, a provision should be included making it clear that restrictions covering the present development do not "pour over" into his subsequent neighboring developments. *Craven County v. First-Citizens Bank and Trust Co.,* 237 N.C. 502, 75 S.E.2d 620.

It is usual to provide that the restrictions will run till a stated date, and then continue for successive ten-year periods unless altered or abrogated by a vote of the lot or apartment owners. Care must be exercised in expressing the percentage vote. A *majority of the lot owners* is not the same as a vote of *the owners of a majority of the lots.* For example, a lot owner may die leaving fifteen heirs, and a question will arise whether they are entitled to one vote or fifteen votes. Probably one vote per homesite or per apartment is a workable rule, such vote to be cast only if a majority of the owners of that lot or apartment agree on their vote. The same observations are applicable to an amendment of the declaration in any other respect.

§ 581. **Easements.** Since the law does not specify any particular form an easement must take, the creation of easements by means of a recorded declaration followed by a deed containing grants and reservations of the easements is universally recognized as a proper means of creating easements. The right to use the common areas must be accomplished by the creation of easements and covenants. It should not be done by *dedication.* A dedication is a giving of rights to the *public.* Hence, use of the word *dedication* is to be avoided for this word has no place in the creation of private, as distinguished from public, rights. *Drye v. Eagle Rock Ranch, Inc.,* 364 S.W.2d 196 (Tex. Civ. App.).

§ 582. **Party walls.** Where party walls are involved, as in the town house, the declaration will contain a detailed provision regarding same, including a provision that the cost of reasonable repair and maintenance shall be shared by the owners who make use of the wall in proportion to such use.

§ 583. **Lien of assessments.** Both in the condominium and

the PUD, the home association will want a provision in the declaration giving it the right to levy assessments on the homeowner for maintenance of the common areas. Again, this can be done in the declaration, since the law requires no great formality for the creation of equitable or contractual liens. *Prudential Ins. Co. v. Wetzel*, 212 Wis. 100, 248 N.W. 791. Such assessment liens are enforceable by foreclosure, like a mortgage. *Rodruck v. Sand Point*, 48 Wash.2d 565, 295 P.2d 714. The lien serves an important purpose. As the section on covenants shows, the declaration also gives the association the right to *sue* the homeowner for assessments, and to get a judgment against him. The covenants, in other words, create *personal liability*. But where the homeowner is financially irresponsible, or simply disappears, so that summons cannot be served upon him, the lien for his delinquent assessments can be foreclosed. Both methods of enforcement should be provided for. The declaration should state that any delinquent assessment bears interest at the highest legal rate and that attorney's fees are collectible as part of the assessment.

§ 584.   **Lien and assessments—priority thereof with respect to mortgages.**   In both the condominium and the PUD there will usually be two liens, the lien of the mortgage on the home or apartment, and the lien of the assessments. Obviously a question will arise as to whether foreclosure of a mortgage will wipe out delinquent assessment liens or *vice versa*. A mortgage recorded subsequent to the recording of the deed and declaration creating the lien is subject and subordinate to such lien, even as to assessments accruing subsequent to the recording of the mortgage. *Prudential Ins. Co. v. Wetzel*, 212 Wis. 100, 248 N.W. 791. Foreclosure of the assessment lien wipes out the mortgage. Mortgages that antedate the effective date of the declaration or deeds will be prior and superior to the assessment liens (*Kennilwood Owners' Ass'n. v. Kennilwood*, 28 N.Y.S.2d 239), so that foreclosure of the mortgage will cut out all unpaid assessments and the future liability of the lot to pay assessments. This creates a potential conflict. Mortgagees, especially those who are required by law to loan only on first mortgages, will insist that the lien of all assessments, even those created by an earlier declaration, be subordinated to the lien of their mortgages. The wishes of the mortgagee must prevail, since otherwise financing cannot be obtained. However, once the mortgage is foreclosed and the mortgagee has become the owner of the lot, the lien of future assessments should be binding on the mortgagee, as they would be on any other homeowner. This can be accomplished by a clause in the declaration as follows:

SUGGESTED   FORM: The lien of the assessments provided for herein shall be subordinate to the lien of any mortgage or mortgages now or hereafter placed upon the properties subject to assessments and running to a bank, savings and loan association, insurance company or other institutional lender; provided, however, such subordination shall apply only to the assessments which have become due and payable prior to a sale or transfer of such property pursuant to a decree of foreclosure, or any other proceeding in lieu of foreclosure. Such sale or transfer shall not relieve such property from liability for any assessments thereafter becoming due nor from the lien of any such subsequent assessment.

§ 585.   Covenants.

The creation of covenants that will impose *personal liability* on future landowners, for example, to pay maintenance assessments, is a technical matter. Hence in this instance it seems desirable to refer to the declaration for the text of the covenants, but to spell out *in the deed* the language by which the grantor and grantee, and their successors in ownership, agree to perform their covenants. Likewise, a covenant binding on the association to maintain the common areas, collect assessments impartially, and the like seems desirable. Of course, where the plan is that the association will provide, at its expense, maintenance of the homesite and of the exterior of the home, that must be spelled out in detail in the declaration.

§ 586.   Association as a vehicle for enforcing restrictions, liens, and covenants.

The enforcement of *restrictions, liens,* and *covenants* can legally be transferred through the declaration to an association or corporation formed by the home or apartment owners. *Merrionette Manor Homes v. Heda,* 11 Ill.App.2d 186, 136 N.E.2d 556; *Nesponsit Property Owners' Ass'n. v. Emigrant Industrial Savings Bank,* 278 N.Y. 248, 15 N.E.2d 793; *Rodruck v. Sand Point Maintenance Comm.,* 40 Wash.2d 565, 295 P.2d 714.

§ 587.   Deed clauses to implement the declaration.

To fully implement the declaration it is necessary to insert a clause in the deed to the home buyer or apartment buyer. Such a clause might be as follows:

SUGGESTED FORM: Subject to Declaration of Easements, Restrictions, Liens, and Covenants dated _____ and recorded in the Office of the Recorder of Deeds of _____ County, as Document No. _____ which is incorporated herein by reference thereto. Grantor grants to the Grantee, his heirs and assigns, as easements appurtenant to the premises hereby conveyed, the easements created by said Declaration for the benefit of the owners of the parcel of realty herein described. Grantor reserves to himself, his heirs and assigns, as easements appurtenant to the remaining parcels described in said Declaration, the easements thereby created for the benefit of said remaining parcels described in said Declaration, and this conveyance is subject to said easements and the right of the Grantor to grant said easements in the conveyances of said remaining parcels or any of them, and the parties hereto, for themselves, their heirs, personal representatives, and assigns, covenant to be bound by the covenants, restrictions and agreements in said document set forth. Said covenants and restrictions are covenants running with the land both as to burden and benefit, and this conveyance is subject to all said covenants and restrictions as though set forth in full herein. The land hereby conveyed is also subject to the liens created by said Declaration, and same are binding on the grantees, their heirs, personal representatives, and assigns. All of the provisions of said Declaration are hereby incorporated herein as though set forth in full herein.

§ 588. Sale by homeowner.   The declaration should provide that upon sale of a home or apartment, the seller shall not be liable for assessments levied or covenants or restrictions breached thereafter. Unless this clause is included there is a legal possibility of continuing liability. It may also be desirable to give the home association the first option of buying the home. *Gale v. York Center Community Co-op,* 21 Ill.2d 86, 171 N.E.2d 30. This provides some control over the character of new occupants.

§ 589. Membership corporation.   The declaration will set forth who the members are to be in the home association created for a PUD or for a condominium.

§ 590. Marketable Title Acts.   Under the Marketable Title Acts, rights in land, including covenants, restrictions, private assessment liens, and, in some instances, easements also, terminate after a stated period of time unless fresh recordings are made to keep these interests alive.

Chapter 35

RACIAL INTEGRATION
IN HOUSING

§ 591.   **Federal legislation—the 1968 law.**   A federal "open occupancy" law was enacted in 1968. It goes into effect in stages, the last
stage taking effect on January 1, 1970. This text deals with the law as of
that date.

The law covers dwellings, including homes and multi-family residences
(two-flats, duplexes, apartments), also vacant land acquired for construction for such purposes. No doubt acquisition of vacant land zoned for
residential purposes will be regarded as subject to the law. Probably condominiums and co-ops will be regarded also as coming under the law.
The law applies to sales, leases, and all types of rental arrangements. It
does not include properties used *exclusively* for commercial or industrial
purposes. But if *part* of the building is used for residential purposes, the
building is subject to the law.

The law creates new and important rights. Some are spelled out fairly
clearly. Others will come into sharper focus only after the Supreme Court
has interpreted the law. Some observations can be made. Where bias
against a person is based on race, color, religion, or national origin, it is
unlawful:

1. To refuse to sell or lease or negotiate for sale or lease because of
such bias, or to discriminate in the furnishing of services or facilities.

   EXAMPLE: A landlord cannot furnish maid service to white tenants and
refuse this service to Negroes.

2. To discriminate in exacting terms of the sale or lease, for example, by asking a higher price because of the race of the buyer.

3. To advertise in the newspapers or post notices on the building that particular races will not be welcomed as buyers or tenants.

4. To state that a dwelling is not available, where such statement is made because of the race of the party seeking to buy or rent.

5. For a lender to refuse a party a loan or to insist on higher interest rates or harsher loan terms because of racial reasons.

6. For real estate brokers to refuse membership in their organizations or multiple-listing services because of racial reasons.

7. To induce a person to sell by creating fears of racial change in the neighborhood.

Sale or rental of a single-family house is exempted if the house is sold or rented without the use in any manner of the facilities of a real estate broker or salesman and without the publication or posting of an advertisement indicating bias toward non-Caucasians. The purpose here is to avoid (a) any inference that state-licensed machinery (brokers) can be employed to achieve discrimination and (b) the public humiliation to prospective purchasers or tenants occasioned in publication or posting of a notice that they are unacceptable as tenants or buyers.

But even if sold through the owner's efforts, the sale is not exempt if the seller owns more than three houses at any one time. Probably this exclusion for an owner of three houses is intended to benefit the person who owns a home and a summer or winter home.

As to this special exempt category (the seller who owns three houses or less), the exemption is limited in a highly technical way. The exemption applies only to a house in which the owner *resides* at the time of the sale or to an unoccupied house of which he was the most recent resident. Where this residence requirement is not complied with, the exemption applies only to one sale every two years. In other words, if I own three houses, live in one, and rent out the others, I am exempt from the law as to each of the rented houses only as to sales two or more years apart. One gathers the impression that Congress was willing to exempt from the law a bona fide owner of three homes who seeks to sell them, as his circumstances dictate, without the aid of a broker. But Congress wanted no subterfuges which would permit a professional builder of residences to escape from provisions of the law. The law also exempts sale or rental of a dwelling meant for occupancy by no more than four families living independently of each other if the owner lives in one apartment.

As of the date this book went to press, the validity of this law had not been passed on by the Supreme Court, but in view of the *Jones* decision, hereinafter discussed (see § 592), it is generally assumed that the law is valid.

Enforcement of the law is complex. In general, the Secretary of the Department of Housing and Urban Development (HUD) is entrusted with the machinery of enforcement. The following procedures are available, namely:

1. If there is a substantially equivalent remedy under a state law or ordinance, HUD notifies the appropriate state officials.

2. If within 30 days no action is taken by state officials, the party discriminated against may file suit in a federal court or in a state court.

3. The court may award damages, issue injunctions restraining violations of the law, and set aside deeds or leases, except that no deed or lease shall be set aside if entered into before a court order has issued and the grantee or lessee had no actual knowledge of the proceedings. One is left with the inference that a court that sets aside a deed to a white person can order a sale thereof to a Negro who made an earlier comparable offer and was rejected because of racial bias. The court may also award damages to a party who proves he has been unlawfully discriminated against.

4. The United States Attorney General may obtain injunctions restraining violations of the law.

5. In certain instances the law provides for fines against, or imprisonment of, persons using force or threat of force to bring about racial discrimination in housing.

§ 592. Federal legislation—the 1866 law.   In a law passed by Congress in 1866 it is provided, in part, that American citizens of every race and color shall have *the same right* throughout the country to purchase, lease, sell, hold, and convey real and personal property as is enjoyed by white persons. Laying stress on the phrase "the same right," the Supreme Court has held that this law prohibits all racial discrimination, private and public, in the sale and rental of property. Thus, every "racially motivated refusal to sell or rent" is prohibited. *Jones v. Alfred H. Mayer Co.*, 392 U.S. 409 (1968). This law to some extent overlaps the Civil Rights Act of 1968, to some extent goes beyond it, and to some extent omits protection afforded by the 1968 law.

EXAMPLE: A owns his home which he occupies with his family. This is the only land he owns. He offers it for sale without employing a broker, but declines to sell to B, a Negro. His refusal is motivated by B's race. This refusal is wrongful. Observe that such a situation is expressly omitted from the coverage of the 1968 law under which a person owning only one home and selling it without a broker is not forbidden to discriminate.

EXAMPLE: In the example given above, B seeks the aid of the Attorney General of the United States. He will not succeed. The 1866 law makes no provision for furnishing such aid.

EXAMPLE: A refuses to sell his *store* to B, a Negro, his refusal being racially motivated. This refusal is prohibited by the 1866 law, but does not come under the 1968 law.

EXAMPLE: A owns a large apartment building. For racial reasons he refuses to rent an apartment to B, a Negro. Both laws forbid this type of discrimination.

As the Supreme Court has pointed out, the law of 1866 does NOT do the following:

1. It does not forbid discrimination on grounds of *religion or national origin:*

EXAMPLE: A, a member of *XYZ Church,* owns only one home. He offers his home for sale without the aid of a real estate broker. As purchasers appear, he states verbally that he will sell only to members of *XYZ Church.* The 1866 law does not forbid such action.

2. It does not deal specifically with discrimination in the provision of services or facilities in connection with the sale or rental of a dwelling, for example, furnishing maid service to apartment tenants.
3. It does not prohibit advertising or other representations that indicate discriminatory preferences.
4. It does not refer explicitly to discrimination in financing arrangements or in the provision of real estate brokerage services.
5. It does not enable a rejected purchaser or tenant to call upon the Attorney General or any other federal officer for aid.
6. It makes no *express* provision for the bringing of damage suits by rejected purchasers or tenants, but the court has indicated it has kept an open mind on the question of whether a right to damages could be implied or inferred from the language and purpose of the law.

To the extent that such omissions are covered by the 1968 law, probably they lack practical significance so far as dwellings are concerned. For example, as to dwellings, the 1968 law forbids *all* advertising and all FOR SALE or FOR RENT signs that indicate racial bias and it forbids *all* discrimination in the furnishing of services or facilities in connection with rental or sale of a dwelling.

And, to repeat, while the 1968 law does not apply to stores, factories, or structures other than dwellings, these are covered by the 1866 law; though, again, while the 1866 law covers all buildings it is less comprehensive in the details of enforcement.

Problems arise here because Congress in enacting the 1968 law had assumed the 1866 law was more or less a dead letter as earlier court decisions had indicated, but after the 1968 law was enacted the Supreme Court breathed life into the 1866 law, and we are now faced with two somewhat inconsistent laws relating to the same subject.

The Supreme Court has indicated that some rather effective remedies are available for enforcement of the 1866 law.

EXAMPLE: In 1965 A, a Negro, seeks to purchase a home from B, a professional builder, in a subdivision owned by B. B rejects A, his rejection being racially motivated. A files an injunction suit against B to prohibit B from so discriminating. In 1968 the court enters a judgment ordering B to sell to A at the price prevailing at the time of the wrongful refusal in 1965 which is substantially less than the current market of such a home. B must absorb this loss. This example is the precise fact situation in *Jones v. Alfred H. Mayor Co.*

§ 593. **Court decisions.** The first significant decision in the area of racial discrimination in housing was *Shelley v. Kraemer*, 334 U.S. 1, 3 A.L.R.2d 441 (1948). This decision struck down as contrary to the Constitution of the United States a state court decision enforcing *by injunction* an agreement by property owners not to sell or lease to a Negro. Our Constitution, the court stated, forbids any *state action* including *state court action* that tends to create discrimination. Later the Supreme Court held that no party to such an agreement could sue *for damages* any other party who violated it by selling or leasing to a Negro. *Barrows v. Jackson*, 346 U.S. 249 (1953). The thing forbidden by these decisions is *state action* such as the issuance of court orders attempting to enforce racial covenants. These decisions did not state that racial covenants are *void*. They simply prohibited court action to enforce them.

As a result of the federal legislation heretofore discussed, these decisions probably are no longer significant. Racial covenants are probably totally invalid now.

§ 594. **State laws, court decisions, commission rulings and orders.** An increasing number of states and cities have enacted laws and ordinances forbidding racial discrimination in housing. Such laws set up commissions to hear complaints of racial discrimination. The following are illustrations of state commission orders and court decisions enforcing local open-housing laws:

EXAMPLE: An apartment owner discriminated against a Negro by refusing to rent him an apartment. The Negro filed a complaint with the state commission. An order was entered requiring the owner to rent an apartment to the Negro at the regular prevailing rental and to desist from acts of discrimination in rental practices against the Negro or any other persons because of race, religion or national origin. *In re Ruth*, 12 Race Relations Rep. 1703 (Calif.).

EXAMPLE: A home owner stated before witnesses that he would not sell to Jews. He therefore refused to sell to the complaining party, a Jewish person, and later entered into a contract to sell to a Gentile. The commission ordered the owner to sell to the Jew at the same price the Gentile offered. Observe the quandary of the seller here, who may find he has a legal liability to the Gentile. *Tisman v. Burda*, 12 Race Relations Rep. 1966 (N.Y.).

EXAMPLE: A commission ordered a landlord to rent an apartment to a Negro who was refused the apartment because of racial bias. *Huber v. Penna. Comm.,* 12 Race Rel. Rep. 1482 (Penna.).

EXAMPLE: A commission ordered the landlord to rent to a Negro who had been refused occupancy for racial reasons. White tenants who later moved in with knowledge of the problem were required to vacate. *City of N.Y. v. Camp Const. Co.,* 11 Race Relations Rep. 1949 (N.Y.).

EXAMPLE: A white subdivision was subject to a recorded Declaration giving the home owners' association a pre-emption option, that is, the right to buy any homesite at the same price another party would offer. A homeowner entered into a contract to sell to a Negro. The contract was specifically made subject to the recorded Declaration. The association then gave notice of exercise of its pre-emption privilege. The court held that exercise of such a privilege would be illegal under the state fair housing law if done solely because of racial bias. *Vaught v. Village Creek,* 7 Race Relations Rep. 849.

EXAMPLE: The court sustained a commission order ousting a white tenant because he was not a bona fide tenant ignorant of the landlord's earlier attempt to discriminate against a Negro seeking to rent the same apartment. *Feigenblum v. Comm.,* 278 N.Y.S.2d 652.

EXAMPLE: The commission found the landlord guilty of discrimination in rejecting a Negro tenant but refused to oust a white tenant to whom the landlord later rented the apartment. The white tenant was an innocent party unaware of the discrimination. The court sustained this ruling. *Comm. v. City Builders, Inc.,* 277 N.Y.S.2d 434.

EXAMPLE: A Negro bought a vacant lot adjoining the seller's home, using a white nominee to accomplish the purchase. When the seller discovered the identity of the real purchaser he brought suit. The court refused to set aside the transaction. *Hirsch v. Silberstein* (Pa.), 227 A.2d 638.

EXAMPLE: A landlord had no right to evict a tenant because the tenant married a Negro. *Prendergast v. Snyder,* 50 Cal. Rptr. 903 413 P.2d 847.

EXAMPLE: Land developers have been ordered to sell houses to and build houses for Negroes. *Stanton Land Co. v. Pittsburgh,* 32 Law Week 2314; *Don Wilson Builders v. Superior Ct.,* 33 Cal. Rptr. 621; *Marano Const. Co. v. State Comm.,* 259 N.Y.S.2d 4.

EXAMPLE: The mere fact that public housing is located in a Negro neighborhood is not discrimination. *Gautreaux v. Chicago Housing Authority,* 265 Fed. Supp. 582.

EXAMPLE: The location of public housing (with multi-racial occupancy) in a white neighborhood is not discriminatory or capricious for that reason. *Philbrook v. Chapel Hill* (N.C.), 153 S.E.2d 153.

EXAMPLE: An ordinance was held invalid where it created a "buffer zone" between Negro and white residential areas and required deeper wells and larger septic fields in this area. *Anderson v. Forest Park,* 239 Fed.Supp. 576.

§ 595. **Ordinances.**   Quite a number of city ordinances forbidding discrimination, for example, by real estate brokers, have been upheld as valid. *Chicago Real Estate Board v. Chicago,* 36 Ill. 2d 530, 224 N.E.2d 793.

§ 596. **Terms of sale or lease where the court orders sale or lease to a Negro.**   In analyzing the commission orders and court decisions sustaining them, one is struck by the fact that the courts have evolved something quite novel in real estate law. They have ordered the creation of contractual arrangements against the wishes of one party to the contract. They have ordered a landowner to lease to, to sell to, or to build for a Negro who has been discriminated against because of racial bias. 16 Stanford L. Rev. 849. What remains unanswered is what the courts will do with the innumerable technical details of real estate transactions; namely, the permitted objections to title, the type of title evidence to be furnished the buyer, what prorations are to be made, what surveys and chattel searches are to be required of the seller, and so on. It is one thing to require a seller to sell to a particular buyer. It is quite another thing to spell out the terms of the transaction on the basis of which the deal is to be closed. No doubt, regulations, court decisions, and commission orders will clarify this situation in due time.

§ 597. **Proof of discrimination.**   Basically what current legislation forbids is *discrimination. Discrimination* is not merely a state of mind. *Prejudice* is a state of mind, but *discrimination* is prejudice coupled with action or inaction motivated by that prejudice.

Discrimination can be shown by *express* proof of intention.

EXAMPLE: A builder stated that "no one is going to force me to sell a house in this development to a Negro." This proves discrimination if followed by sales only to white persons. *Jones v. The Haridor Realty Corp.,* 37 N.J. 384, 181 A.2d 481.

Or it may be established by circumstantial evidence.

EXAMPLE: A offered a house for sale for $35,000.00 on terms set forth in a broker's listing. Promptly B, a Negro, tendered an offer at the price and terms stated. A refusal of B's offer is evidence of discrimination, especially if A sells later to a white person at the same price, thereby showing that his refusal of B was not motivated by a desire to withdraw the house from sale.

INDEX

REFERENCES ARE TO SECTIONS

A

Abstracts (*see* Evidence of title)
Acknowledgments:
 certificate of acknowledgment, 103
 date, 110
 defined, 102
 expiration of officer's commission, 113
 false acknowledgment, 114
 foreign acknowledgments, 109
 invalidity, 108
 liability of notary, 114
 necessity, 105, 108
 seal of officer, 112
 signature of officer, 111
 venue, 107
 waiver of dower and homestead, 104
 who may take acknowledgment, 106
Adjoining owners, lateral support, 444
Adoption (*see* Descent)
Adverse possession, 65
Agency, 83
Air rights, 6, 7
Architects, 441
Assignment of rents (*see* Mortgages, rents)
Attachments, 349
Attorney in fact, 83

B

Bona fide purchaser (*see* Recording)
Bonds (*see* Building construction)

Brokers:

 amount of compensation, 145
 authority of broker, 156
 care and skill, 153
 commission, when earned, 139
 conflict of interest, 150
 contract of employment, 132–137
 contract of sale, 153
 co-owners, listing by one co-owner, 132
 defined, 129
 deposit, 148
 disclosure and nondisclosure, 151
 double agency, 149
 duration and termination of employment, 143
 duties, 149–154
 employment, 132–137, 143
 exclusive agency, 136
 exclusive right to sell, 137
 license, 130
 lien, 147
 loyalty, 149, 150
 misappropriation by, 148
 misrepresentation by, 152
 multiple listing, 138
 net listings, 146
 no deal, no commission, 140
 notices, 143
 open listing, 135
 performance required, 139
 procuring cause, 141, 142
 purchase price paid to broker, 148
 revocation of employment, 140

Brokers (*Cont.*)
  sale for less than price fixed, 144
  salesman distinguished, 131
  termination of employment, 143
  unauthorized practice of law, 155
Building codes, 480
Building construction (*see* Chapter 21):
  architects, 441
  builder liability, 443
  cash down payments from home
    buyers, 440
  code violations, 443
  construction contracts, 436, 444
  construction loans (*see* Construction
    loans)
  contractors' bonds, 409
  contracts, 436
  destruction during construction, 438
  extras, 437
  mortgages, 439 (*see* Mortgages, Con-
    struction loans, Closing mortgage
    loans)
  performance, 443
  progress payment, 438
  substantial performance, 442
  suggestions, 444
  violations of zoning and building ordi-
    nances, 443
Building erected on wrong lot, 16
Building ordinances (*see* Zoning and
  building ordinances)

C

Cemetery lots, 62
Chattel, *defined,* 8
Closing a cash real estate deal:
  affidavit of title, 229
  apportionment or prorating, 225–227
  bulk sales affidavit, 222
  closing date, 223
  closing statement, 225–227
  documents to be obtained by buyer,
    229
  documents to be obtained by seller,
    230
  leases, 218, 219, 225, 227
  matters to attend to after closing, 231
  matters to attend to at closing, 224
  matters to be considered before clos-
    ing, 221
  prorating, 225–227
  questions the parties should ask, 220
Closing deals (*see* Closing a cash real
  estate deal)
Closing mortgage loans:
  closing statement, 415

Closing mortgage loans (*Cont.*)
  defined, 411
  documents of the loan file, 416
  evidence of title, 412
  insurance, 414
  insured closing letter, 411
  loan closing statement, 415
  precautions, 412
  title defects, 412
  zoning and building code violations,
    413
Community property, 73, 309–315
Condemnation (*see* Eminent domain)
Conditions (*see* Restrictions)
Condominium:
  advantages, 562a
  apartment ownership, 552
  assessments, 553, 563, 584
  association of owners, 553, 583, 586,
    589
  buying a traditional co-op, 550
  common elements, 551
  condominium described, 551
  covenants, 553
  declaration, 553 (*see also* Declaration
    of restrictions, easements, liens,
    and covenants)
  deed provisions, 555
  defined, 551
  descriptions, 554, 555, 556
  destruction of building, 562
  disadvantages, 562a
  easements, 553
  expenses and repairs, 553
  in general, 548, 551
  insurance, 561
  land descriptions, 554, 555
  lien for expenses, 553
  mechanics of co-op ownership, 549
  mortgage problems, 559
  ownership of condominium, 552
  partition of common elements, 553
  plats, 556
  right of first refusal, 551, 563
  state regulation, 560
  suggestions in purchasing a new con-
    dominium, 552
  taxes, 563
  termination, 562
  title requirements, 558
Construction loans:
  commitments, 402
  construction loan agreement, 404
  contractor's bonds, 409
  disbursement, 406
  FHA commitments, 402, 403
  in general, 401

Construction loans (*Cont.*)
  interim lenders, 402, 547
  loan correspondents, 402
  matters to be considered before dis-
    bursement begins, 405
  mechanic's lien protection, 407, 410
  negligence in disbursement, 410
  permanent lenders, 393, 402, 538, 547
  procedure in making and paying out
    construction loans, 404–410
  service charges, 402
  takeout commitments, 393, 402
Contracts of sale:
  abandonment, 204
  acknowledgment, 193
  adjustment or prorating, 187
  agents, 190
  assignment, 197
  building code violations, 173, 219
  building restrictions, 172
  buyer, 163
  certainty, 167
  chattels, 219
  completeness, 166
  contingent contracts, 182, 183
  damage suits, 200
  date, 188
  deed by seller, 168, 198
  delivery, 192
  deposit, 181
  description of land sold, 165
  dower of seller's spouse, 162, 303
  drafting a contract, 219
  earnest money, 181
  easements, 171
  effect of, 195
  effect of deed, 196
  encroachments, 175
  evidence of title, 179 (*see* Chapter 14)
  fairness, 206
  forfeiture, 200, 201, 203, 219
  form of contract, 158, 160
  fraud and misrepresentation, 208–217
  installment contract, 158, 178, 183,
    200, 219
  insurance, 186
  leases and tenancies, 174
  liens, 170
  marketable title, 169–177
  merchantable title, 169–177
  minimum requirements of contract,
    160
  misrepresentation (*see* Contracts of
    sale, fraud and misrepresentation)
  mistake, 207
  mortgages, 170, 183, 219

Contracts of sale (*Cont.*)
  necessity of written contract, 158, 159
  nondisclosure (*see* Contracts of sale,
    fraud and misrepresentation)
  offer to purchase, 160
  options, 218
  oral contract, 159
  payment provisions, 164
  performance, 199
  permitted objections, 169
  possession, 184
  prorating, 187
  purchase price, 164
  remedies, 200–203
  rents, 184
  requirements, 160
  rescission, 201
  restrictions and conditions, 172 (*see
    also* Restrictions)
  risk of loss, 186
  sale price, 164
  satisfaction, of party to contract, 182
  seal, 191
  seller, 161
  signature, 189
  specific performance, 201–203
  spouse of seller, 162
  subject clause, 169
  suggestions as to drafting, 219
  survey, 219
  taxes, 185
  terms of sale, 160
  time for performance, 178, 199
  time of essence, 178, 180, 200
  title, 169–180
  type of deed, 168
  types, 158
  vendee's lien, 202
  vendor, 161
  warranties of building, 205, 219
  witnesses, 194
  zoning and building ordinances, 173,
    219
Co-operatives, 548, 549, 550, 563
Co-ownership:
  contracts of sale, 292
  dower, 300
  in general, 277
  joint tenancy, 278–283, 291–293
  mortgages, 296
  obligations of co-owners, 296
  partition, 295
  rents and possession, 296
  survivorship deeds, 280
  tenancy by the entireties, 284–293
  tenancy in common, 278, 294
Corporations (*see* Deeds)

Covenants (*see* Restrictions, Declaration of restrictions, easements, liens, and covenants)
Crops (*see* Trees and crops)
Curtesy, 73, 307, 308

D

Declaration of restrictions, easements, liens, and covenants:
assessment liens, 583, 584
building restrictions, 580
covenants, 585
deed clauses, 584, 587
easements, 581
homeowners' association, 586, 589
in general, 579
lien of assessments, 583
marketable title acts, 590
mortgages, 584, 585
party walls, 582
restrictions, 580
sale by homeowner, 588
Dedication (*see also* Subdivisions):
common law dedication, 427
defined, 426
forced dedication, 431
Deed of trust (*see* Mortgages)
Deeds:
acceptance, 92
acknowledgment (*see* Acknowledgments)
after-acquired title, 80, 97
by agent or attorney, 83
bargain and sale deed, 70
blank deeds, 75
consideration, 76
corporations, 72, 74
date, 82
defined, 66
delivery, 87–92
description, 79
exceptions and reservations, 100
fee or easement conveyed, 99
form, 101
fraud, coercion, and mistake, 96
grantee, 74
grantor, 72
insane persons, 73, 74
joint tenancy (*see* Co-ownership)
minors, 73, 74
mortgaged land, 101
official conveyances, 95
power of attorney, 83
purpose of deed, 101
quitclaim deed, 68
recording (*see* Recording)

Deeds (*Cont.*)
requirements, 71
restrictions, 101
seal, 84
signature, 83
special warranty deed, 80
spouse of grantor, 73
state tax, 86
subject clause, 101
suggestions on the preparation of deeds, 101
support deeds, 77
title conveyed, 97–99
types, 67
unincorporated association, 74
waiver of dower and homestead, 81
warranties of title, 80
warranty deed, 69, 80
witnesses, 85
words of conveyance, 78
Deficiency judgment or decree (*see* Foreclosure and redemption)
Descent:
adoptions, 320
course of descent, 318, 319
in general, 317
illegitimates, 321
intestacy defined, 317
posthumous children, 322
share of surviving spouse, 305, 306, 336 (*see also* Dower)
Descriptions (*see* Land descriptions)
Dower:
abolition of, 488
assignment of, 299
consummate dower, 298
contracts for purchase of land, 303
deed requirements, 73
defined, 297
divorce, 308
election, 305, 306
election between will and dower, 305, 306, 336
in general, 297
inchoate dower, 298
joint tenancy and tenancy in common, 300
leaseholds, 302
mortgages and other liens, 301
purchase money, 301
release of, 304

E

Easements:
appurtenant, 18
closing a deal, easement problems, 262

Easements (*Cont.*)
  creation of:
    agreement, 24
    condemnation, 32
    declaration of easements, 42
    deed, 29, 30, 121, 122, 125
    express grant, 22
    express reservation, 23
    in general, 21
    implied grant or reservation, 27, 28
    mortgage, 26
    necessity, 29
    plat, 33
    prescription, 30, 31
    will, 28
  defined, 17
  dominant tenement, 18
  drafting, 22, 23, 26, 39
  exceptions and reservations, 23
  in gross, 20
  license distinguished, 19
  maintenance and repair, 37
  mortgages, 26
  parking on easement, 36
  party driveway, 19, 28, 30
  party walls, 25
  plat easements, 429
  private alley and private driveway, 30,
    37
  public streets and highways, 31, 33
  railroad, 32, 99
  recording, 22
  repairs, 37
  right to profits of soil, 35
  row housing, 34
  running with land, 18
  sale of, 18
  scenic easements, 32
  servient tenement, 18
  suggestions in preparation, 39
  tenant's easements, 28, 521
  termination, 38
  title insurance, 252
  town houses, 34
  use of, 36
Embezzlement, 145, 237
Eminent domain, 64
Encroachments, 65, 175
Encumbrances (*see* Contracts of sale,
    Deeds, warranties of title)
Equity of redemption (*see* Mortgages)
Escrows:
  clearing title, 233
  conflict between contract of sale and
    escrow agreement, 237
  contents of escrow agreement, 235
  defalcation, 239

Escrows (*Cont.*)
  defined, 232
  embezzlement, 239
  escrow agreement, 235
  instructions, 235
  irrevocability, 236
  long-term escrows, 241
  mortgages, 240
  operation and purpose, 233
  relation back, 239
  requirements, 234
  when title passes, 238
Estates in land, 60
Evidence of title:
  abstract, 243–245
  abstracter, 244–245
  abstracter's liability, 245
  certificate of title, 247
  commitments, 254
  defined, 242
  examination of title, 246
  risks involved in relying on record title,
    248
  title insurance, 249–254
  Torrens system, 255
Exceptions and reservations, 100
Executions, 348

F

Fee simple (*see* Estates in land)
FHA, 402, 403, 425, 435
Fire insurance (*see* Insurance)
Fixtures:
  agreement as to removal, 13
  agricultural fixtures, 12
  air conditioners, 11
  barber chairs, 12
  beds, 11
  bowling alleys, 12
  building erected on wrong lot, 16
  buyer of land, rights of, 11, 16, 17
    landlord and tenant, 11, 12
  defined, 10
  domestic fixtures, 12
  gasoline pumps and tanks, 12
  gas stoves, 11
  landlord and tenant, rights of, 11, 12
  machinery, 11
  mortgagee, rights of, 13, 14, 368
  package mortgage, 368
  refrigerators, 11
  removal of, 4, 5, 11, 12
  restaurant equipment, 12
  screens, 11
  seller and buyer of land, 11, 16, 17
  severance, 15

Fixtures (*Cont.*)
soda fountains, 12
storm windows, 11
tests to determine whether article is fixture, 11
tenant's rights, 12
trade fixtures, 12
Uniform Commercial Code, 14
venetian blinds, 12
Foreclosure and redemption:
deficiency judgment, 420
development of foreclosure, 355
necessity for foreclosure, 417
power of sale, 421
purchase by mortgagee at foreclosure sale, 423
redemption, 353, 354, 419, 420
Soldiers' and Sailors' Civil Relief Act, 424
statutory redemption, 357, 419
strict foreclosure, 355
types of foreclosures, 418

G

Gas, 5
Gas stove, as fixture, 11
Government survey (*see* Land descriptions)

H

Heirs, 317
Homestead, 316

I

Income tax, 500
Insane persons (*see* Deeds, insane persons)
Inspection of premises, 127
Insurance:
acts of assured, 268
amount recoverable, 267
assignment of policy, 276
business interruption insurance, 262
co-insurance, 272
comprehensive coverage, 260
contract of sale, 275
co-owners, 266, 307
defined, 256
description of property, 264
development of standard policy, 257
double insurance, 271
extended coverage endorsement, 259
hazards covered, 258–262
homeowners' policies, 260

Insurance (*Cont.*)
hostile and friendly fires, 261
increase of hazard, 270
insurable interest, 265
interest covered by policy, 266
mortgages, 273, 274
policy, 257
rent insurance, 262
unoccupancy clause, 269
when protection attaches, 263

J

Joint tenancy (*see* Co-ownership)
Judgments, 348

L

Land:
defined, 3
land titles (*see* Estates in land)
Land descriptions:
adjoining owners, 49
area or quantity, 48
bounded on streets or highways, 54
buildings, 57
correction, 53
defined, 41
erroneous, 53
foreign grants, 50
general descriptions, 46
government survey, 43
indefinite descriptions, 51
land assemblies, 58, 219
metes and bounds, 42
omissions, 52
parts of lots, 56
plat, 44
popular names, 45
street address, 47, 165
streets and highways, 54, 219
tax bills, 59
waters, 55
Landlord and tenant (*see also* Leases):
abandonment of premises, 539
advertising signs, 520
alterations, 529
constructive eviction, 538
conveyance of rented premises, 536
deed of rented premises, 536
defects in building, 522–529
easements of tenant, 521
eviction, 537, 538
fixtures (*see* Fixtures)
heat, hot water, and other services, 521

Landlord and tenant (*Cont.*)
  insurance, 528
  leases (*see* Leases)
  leases and periodic tenancies distinguished, 501
  liability for injuries, 522–529
  month to month tenancy, 502
  notice to terminate tenancy, 541
  periodic tenancies, 502, 503
  personal property of tenant, 532
  rent, 517
  rent withholding, 526
  repairs, 522–529
  services, 521
  surrender, 540
  taxes, 531
  tenancy at will, 504
  tenancy from month to month, 502
  tenancy from year to year, 494, 503
  termination of tenancy, 541
  use of premises, 520
  year to year tenancy, 503
Land titles and interests in land:
  adverse possession, 65
  cemetery lots, 62
  condemnation, 64
  estates in land, 60
  life estates, 61
  modes of acquiring title, 63
Land use controls (*see* Restrictions, Zoning)
Lateral support, 444
Leases (*see also* Landlord and tenant):
  abandonment of premises, 539
  acceptance by lessee, 547
  acknowledgment, 515
  assignment, 518, 519, 534, 547
  cancellation clause, 533
  commercial lease, 519
  construction of buildings, 547
  constructive eviction, 538
  conveyance of rented premises, 536
  covenants, 547
  damage to or destruction of leased premises, 530
  deed of rented premises, 536
  defined, 505
  description of premises, 510, 547
  duration of term of lease, 511
  eviction, 537
  exclusive, 547
  fixtures, 532
  follow-the-leader clause, 547
  ground lease, 519
  holding over, 503
  lessee, 509
  lessor, 508

Leases (*Cont.*)
  liability of landlord and tenant, 522–529
  long-term lease, 511
  mortgages, 535, 547 (*see also* Mortgages)
  necessity of writing, 506
  non-disturbance clause, 547
  option to purchase, 547
  percentage leases, 518
  periodic tenancy distinguished, 511
  radius clause, 547
  recording, 516
  rent, 517
  rent withholding, 526
  repairs, 522–529
  requirements, 507–516
  sale and leaseback, 363
  seal, 513
  services, 521
  shopping center leases (*see* Shopping centers)
  signature, 512
  sublease, 518, 519, 534
  subordination clause, 547
  suggested clauses, 542
  surrender, 540
  taxes, 531
  termination for nonpayment of rent, 541
  use of premises, 520, 547
  witnesses, 514
License, 25
Liens:
  attachments, 349
  defined, 337
  executions (*see* Executions)
  in general, 337
  judgment liens (*see* Judgments)
  mechanics' liens (*see* Mechanics' liens)
  miscellaneous liens, 350
  types, 339
Life estates, 76
Loan insurance, 425

M

Managers, 157
Marketable title (*see* Contracts of sale)
Mechanics' liens (*see also* Construction loans, Closing mortgage loans):
  building contracts, 444
  closing mortgage loans (*see* Chapter 22)
  construction loans (*see* Chapter 21)
  contract or consent of owner, 341
  contract purchaser, 341

Mechanics' liens (*Cont.*)
  contractors and subcontractors, 342
  co-owners, 341
  defined, 340
  in general, 338
  inception and priority of lien, 344
  knowledge and consent of owner, 341
  landlord and tenant, 341
  leases, 341
  lienable work and material, 340
  mortgages, 344
  notice and filing of liens, 345
  performance by contractor necessary, 343
  release, 346
  subcontractors, 342
  time limit on enforcement, 347
  trade fixtures, 340
  waiver, 346
Merchantable title (*see* Contracts of sale)
Minerals:
  conveyance of, 4
  as part of land, 4
Minors (*see* Deeds)
Mortgages:
  acceleration clause, 380
  acknowledgment, 384
  application for loan, 365
  assignment of, 395, 396
  assignment of rents, 387, 391, 392
  assumption, 393
  bond issues, 376
  chattel liens (*see* Chattel liens)
  chattels, 368
  closing mortgage loans (*see* Closing mortgage loans)
  commission, 377
  commitment, 365, 393
  commitment fee, 377
  conditional sale, 363
  construction loans, 375, 401–410
  contract of sale (*see* Contracts of sale, mortgages)
  conveyance by mortgagor to mortgagee, 394
  conveyance of mortgaged premises, 393
  correspondents, 402
  debt, 369–376
  deed absolute given as security, 362
  deed by mortgagor to mortgagee, 394
  deed of mortgaged premises, 393
  deed of trust, 360
  defined, 351
  delivery, 384
  description of mortgaged property, 368
  discharge, 399

Mortgages (*Cont.*)
  easements (*see* Easements)
  equitable mortgage, 361
  equity of redemption, 353
  escrow (*see* Escrows)
  estoppel certificate, 395
  execution, 384
  extension agreement, 400
  fire insurance (*see* Insurance)
  fixtures (*see* Fixtures)
  foreclosure, 355 (*see also* Foreclosure and redemption)
  foreclosure provisions, 381
  future advances, 369–376, 404
  history of, 352
  insurance (*see* Insurance, Loan insurance)
  interest, 377
  interim financing, 402, 547
  intermediate states, 356, 387, 389, 399
  leases, 389, 390
  lien theory, 356, 387, 389, 390
  lieu of foreclosure transactions, 394
  limitations, 400
  loan insurance (*see* Loan insurance)
  master mortgage, 386
  mechanics' liens (*see* Mechanics' liens)
  mortgagee, 367
  mortgagor, 367
  negligence in disbursement, 410
  nominee's liability on mortgage, 183
  note, 366
  open-end, 374
  packaged mortgage, 368
  partial release, 382
  parties to mortgage, 367
  payment, 397, 398
  payout of loan proceeds (*see* Chapters 21 and 22)
  permanent lenders, 402, 547
  points, 377
  possession, 387–392
  prepayment of mortgage debt, 378
  priority of liens, 370–376 (*see also* Recording, constructive notice)
  property mortgaged, 368
  purchaser's liability for mortgage debt, 393
  receiver, 388
  recording, 385
  redemption, 353–355, 357 (*see also* Foreclosure and redemption)
  regular mortgages, 359
  release, 382, 399
  rents, 387–392
  sale and leaseback, 363
  satisfaction, 390

Mortgages (*Cont.*)
 seal, 384
 signature, 384
 subordination of mortgage, 379
 takeout commitment, 402
 title theory, 356, 387, 389, 399
 trees and crops (*see* Trees and crops)
 Truth in Lending Act, 377
 trust deed, 360
 types of mortgages, 358
 usury, 377
 vendor's lien, 364
 waiver of defenses, 395
 waiver of dower and homestead, 383
 waiver of right of redemption, 354
 witnesses, 384

N

Notice (*see also* Recording):
 actual knowledge, 126
 possession as notice, 127

O

Oil and gas, 5
Options, 218
Ordinances (*see* Zoning and building ordinances)

P

Parks, 429, 431
Partition, 295
Partnerships (*see* Deeds)
Party driveways, 19, 28, 30
Party walls, 25
Personal property, 8
Planned unit developments:
 artificial lakes, 571
 assessment liens, 575, 583
 building restrictions, 572, 587
 cluster housing, 564
 common areas, 559–563, 567–571
 condominium compared, 577
 covenants, 573, 583, 585
 declaration, 573 (*see also* Declaration of restrictions, easements, liens, and covenants)
 deed clauses, 584, 587
 described, 563
 easements, 569, 581
 in general, 563
 home association, 565, 586, 589
 legal steps, 566
 liens for maintenance, 574, 583
 Marketable Title Acts, 590

Planned unit developments (*Cont.*)
 mortgage provisions, 576, 583
 restraints on sales, 575
 restrictions, 580
 zoning, 578
Planning commissions, 479
Plats, 428–435 (*see also* Subdivisions)
Possession as notice, 127
Power of attorney, 83
Property, real and personal, distinguished, 8
Prorating, 225–227

R

Racial integration in housing (*see* Chapter 35)
Real property, 8
Recording:
 acknowledgment, 148
 actual knowledge, 127
 chain of title, 123
 constructive notice, 116
 defective instruments, 122
 error in description, 122
 foreign language, 121
 instruments entitled to recording, 120
 liens that need not be recorded, 128
 mortgages, 119, 122, 123, 125
 necessity, 115
 notice from recording, 116
 office, 117
 personal property records, 14
 persons protected, 119
 prerequisites to valid recording, 122, 123
 record as notice of contents of deed or mortgage, 125
 tract indexes, 124
 Uniform Commercial Code filings, 14
 what constitutes recording, 118
Redemption (*see* Foreclosure and redemption, Mortgages)
Refrigerator, as fixture, 11
Restrictions:
 abandonment of restrictions, 452
 apartments, 449
 bay windows, 449
 building line, 455
 business purposes, 449
 change in neighborhood, 452
 churches, 449
 conditions, 446, 453–455
 covenant for benefit of land sold or land retained, 446
 covenant running with the land, 456
 covenants, 446, 455

Restrictions (*Cont.*)
   creation, 447
   declaration of restrictions, 447
   delay in enforcing restrictions, 452
   dwelling, 449
   enforcement of general plan restric-
      tions, 448, 452
   in general, 446
   general plan, 442–452
   interpretation, 449
   location restrictions, 449
   modification, extension, and release of
      general plan restrictions, 451, 580
   plans of buildings, 450
   practical considerations, 458
   private and public restrictions, 445, 446
   racial restrictions (*see* Chapter 35)
   release or modification, 451
   residence purposes, 449
   reverter clause, 453
   suggestions, 458
   time limits on restrictions, 452
   violations by party seeking enforce-
      ment, 452
   zoning, 476
Reverters, 453

S

Sale and leaseback, 363
Salesman, 131
Screens, as fixtures, 11
Security agreement, 14
Sewers, 434, 435
Shopping centers, 543–547
   leases, 547
   mortgage financing, 547
   site planning, 546
   types of shopping centers, 543
   vacation of streets, 545
   zoning problems, 544
Soldiers' and Sailors' Civil Relief Act,
   424
Sources of real estate law, 1, 2
Special assessments, 499
Storm windows, as fixtures, 11
Streets:
   condemnation, 32
   dedication, 427, 429
   defined and described, 54
   descriptions of land, 54
   easement for, 31, 32, 64
   vacation, 545
Subdivisions:
   approval, 429, 430, 432
   common law dedications, 426
   dedicated areas, 429

Subdivisions (*Cont.*)
   dedication, 426, 427 429
   FHA, 435
   forced dedication, 431
   planning commission, 435
   plats, 33, 428
   regulation, 430, 431
   resubdivisions, 433
   sewer, water, and other utilities, 429,
      434, 435
   suggested steps for subdividers, build-
      ers, and their mortgagees, 435
   utilities, 429, 434
Survey, 221

T

Taxes:
   appropriation, 486
   assessment, 489–493
   budgeting, 485
   computation, 494
   enforcement, 497
   equalization, 493
   exemptions, 491
   in general, 483
   income tax, 500
   levy, 485
   lien of, 495
   payment, 496
   proceedings to enforce payment, 497
   review of assessments, 492
   Soldiers' and Sailors' Civil Relief Act,
      498
   steps in taxation, 484
   tax rate limitations, 488
   tax titles, 497
Tenancy by the entireties (*see* Co-ownership)
Tenancy in common (*see* Co-ownership)
Title insurance, 249–254
Torrens system, 255
Trees and crops, 9
Trespass, 7
Trust deed (*see* Mortgages)

U

Uniform Commercial Code, 14
Usury (*see* Mortgages, interest)
Utilities (*see* Subdivisions)

V

Vendor's lien, 364

W

Wills:
  after-born children, 332
  codicil, 324
  contest, 335
  deed and will distinguished, 325
  defined, 317, 323
  disinheriting heirs, 326
  holographic will, 331
  marriage as revocation, 332
  probate, 334
  revocation, 332
  rights of surviving spouse, 305, 306, 336
  signature, 329
  testator, 327
  undue influence, 328
  witnesses, 330

Z

Zoning and building ordinances:
  accessory uses, 471
  aesthetic considerations, 470
  amendments, 465
  building codes, 480
  building permits, 480
  bulk zoning, 472
  certificate of occupancy, 471
  churches, 466

Zoning and building ordinances (*Cont.*)
  conformity to master plan, 479
  contract zoning, 463
  defined, 459
  demolition of buildings, 482
  effect on restrictions, 476
  enforcement of, 478
  exclusive zones, 460
  floating zones, 461
  historical sites, 481
  in general, 450
  inspection of existing structures, 480
  master plan, 479
  minimum lot size and building area,
    468
  mortgages, 477
  nonconforming uses, 475
  planning, 479
  restrictions, 476
  rezoning, 465
  schools, 467
  sinking zones, 462
  special exceptions, 474
  special uses, 474
  spot zoning, 465
  substandard lots, 468
  territorial limits, 568
  undeveloped areas, 478
  urban renewal zones, 464
  validity, 459, 465, 468, 470, 476
  variances, 473